TCP/IP Addressing

TCP/IP Addressing

Designing and Optimizing Your IP Addressing Scheme

Second Edition

Buck Graham

Morgan Kaufmann

AN IMPRINT OF ACADEMIC PRESS

A Harcourt Science and Technology Company

San Diego San Francisco New York Boston
London Sydney Tokyo

This book is printed on acid-free paper. ♾

ACADEMIC PRESS
A Harcourt Science and Technology Company
525 B Street, Suite 1900, San Diego, CA 92101-4495 USA
http://www.academicpress.com

Academic Press
Harcourt Place, 32 Jamestown Road, London NW1 7BY, UK

Morgan Kaufmann
A Harcourt Science and Technology Company
340 Pine Street, Sixth Floor, San Francisco, CA 94104-3205 USA
http://www.mkp.com

Library of Congress Catalog Number: 00-107414

International Standard Book Number: 0-12-295021-6

Printed in the United States of America

00 01 02 03 04 IP 6 5 4 3 2 1

This book is dedicated to my wonderful wife Julie.

Thank you for giving me
the time and opportunity to write this book.

Contents

Section II IP Address Layout 125

Preface

Over the last seven or eight years, I have been designing data networks for large corporate clients. In my current job, I work more with wireless operators who are building data backbones in preparation for the oncoming Wireless Internet. No matter whether the network is being used by a carrier or by a large enterprise, networks the sizes of these demand special address architecture considerations. In order to achieve any level of efficiency, it is necessary to develop an optimal addressing scheme as the cornerstone that you can build the large network upon.

There are more than a handful of technical books available at this time that deal with the TCP/IP protocol stack and intricacies of a TCP/IP network. Some are no more than recapitulations of the published Request for Comments (RFC) that serve as the standards; others focus their discussion on points of interest such as routing protocols. When I first wrote this book there was no book on the market that specifically discussed TCP/IP addressing. Among all of the general TCP/IP books, I could not find a good reference that gave concise examples of how to apply IP addressing to the types of networks that were being built. I must not have been the only one. The first edition of this book sold over 25,000 copies. I have received many compliments on the book, and; I must admit, one or two distasteful comments. You can't please everyone.

This second edition is, in my opinion, much improved over the first edition. It remains an excellent source of information for folks wanting to learn about IP addressing for the first time as well as a concise reference for seasoned network professionals. Specifically, this second edition covers:

- hosts versus network addressing
- The rules of IP addressing
- special-case addresses
- IP address subnetting
- routing considerations when designing an addressing scheme
- addressing for optimal route aggregation
- addressing for LAN, frame relay, ATM and point-to-point networks
- remote access concentration and RADIUS
- calculating the efficiency of an addressing scheme
- classless interdomain routing (CIDR)
- multicast addressing
- mobility in IPv4 and IPv6
- IP version 6 (up to date!)
- Tons and tons of examples!

I want to thank a few people who helped to make this and the previous book happen. I regretted not doing this in the first edition so bear with me (or skip this section). First and foremost, I can never say thanks enough to my wife, Julie. That out of the way, thanks to all the folks that I worked with at Wal-Mart in Bentonville (Tom Newell, Brenda Crumpler [or whatever your name is now], Mike Nicholson, Mike Fitzgerel, Darin Cooper, Robert Clark, Shon Samples, and others). Everybody else in no particular order: Bill Rolfe, Mike McKee, Carl Norden, Steve Johnson, Vibeke Staal-Weiland, Charles Carvalho, Bill Matthey, Bob Buckley, Jon Hooper, Tom Goodwin, George Biles (who painted my porch for me so that I could keep working on this book), Bert Whyte, Pete Loshin, Ken Morton, Art Bergreen, Rick Mentel, and Chuck Nuffer. Of course we all owe tremendous gratitude to the folks who work on the IETF and other standards bodies for doing such a great job writing the Request For Comments and the Internet Drafts. Without them, this Internet stuff would not have been possible. If I missed anybody, *lo siento mucho*.

There is one other thing that I would like to add about this book and the way I present the topic. For those of you who are already familiar with classful versus classless addressing, the book starts with classful addressing and gets into classless addressing in the coverage of CIDR. Perhaps the next edition of the book will dispense with classful addressing altogether (except for a small section on historical IP addressing issues). For now, with classful addressing still in wide use, I will continue to introduce classful IP addressing first. If you don't know the difference between classful and classless addressing, don't worry. This book will explain all about it.

section

I

Addressing Prerequisite Topics

The first section of this book provides a coverage of the topics that I consider to be essential to the understanding of the IP addressing discussions in Sections II and III. The chapters within this section could be skipped, based on your level of competence. However, I would suggest that, at a minimum, you scan the chapters and read the summaries. In particular, Chapters 3 and 4 introduce key concepts that should not be missed.

Chapter 1 provides an introduction to the TCP/IP protocol stack and builds a communications model from the physical layer to the application layer. Chapter 2 discusses the IP address found in an IP datagram. Class A, B, and C networks, the unicast networks, are discussed along with the subnetting of networks to achieve greater utilization. Chapter 3 presents a comparison of the TCP/IP protocol to the OSI reference model. Network devices are then presented according to the layer in which they operate. Repeaters, bridges, routers, and gateways are discussed along with some of their inherent limitations with respect to IP addressing. Chapter 4 discusses the impact of addressing upon routing and vice versa. RIP, OSPF, and static routing mechanisms are discussed, with special attention to addressing considerations.

chapter 1

TCP/IP Overview

This chapter provides a general introduction to the TCP/IP communications protocols. It will cover the link, network, transport, and application layers and the network functions that each provide. Illustration 1-1 depicts the TCP/IP protocols and how they relate to one another.

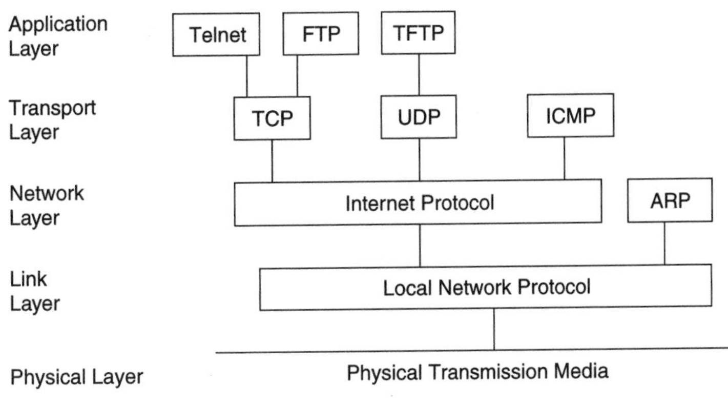

Illustration 1-1 Protocol Relationships

A note before I begin: Throughout this book, I make reference to the Assigned Numbers RFC, RFC 1700. When I wrote this book, RFC 1700 had been published for three years. In my naïveté, I expected that when it got time to create the second edition, a new Assigned Numbers RFC would obsolete RFC 1700. This has not happened. RFC 1700 stands as a snapshot of number assignments by the IANA in October of 1994. I have since found a Web site that has all the current information:

ftp://ftp.isi.edu/in-notes/iana/assignments/

Since RFC 1700 remains the most current Assigned Numbers RFC (and to save a boatload of edits), I have elected to leave all the references to RFC 1700 in the book. To get more current information about number assignments, check the above Web site.

The Physical Layer

The best place to start a discussion of any engineered system is at the bottom. For networks, the bottom is the physical medium used to carry the signal from point A to point B. Examples include

- Unshielded twisted pair (UTP)
- Coaxial cable
- Radio frequency

To support the data services provided on the network, standards for the transmission media had to be created. The physical layer embodies those standards.

The Link Layer

Next up the protocol hierarchy is the local network protocol. In TCP/IP this layer is referred to as the link layer and includes Ethernet, Token Ring, FDDI, Frame Relay, ATM, PPP, or other media. It really does not matter what the lower layer is as far as the user processes are concerned. At least that was the design goal — to be independent of the underlying topology. In reality the farther you move upward, away from the local network protocol layer, the less evident it becomes what the physical network is or what it looks like. Take a look at Ethernet (Illustration 1-2), one of the most common link layer protocols. Ethernet is defined by RFC 894.

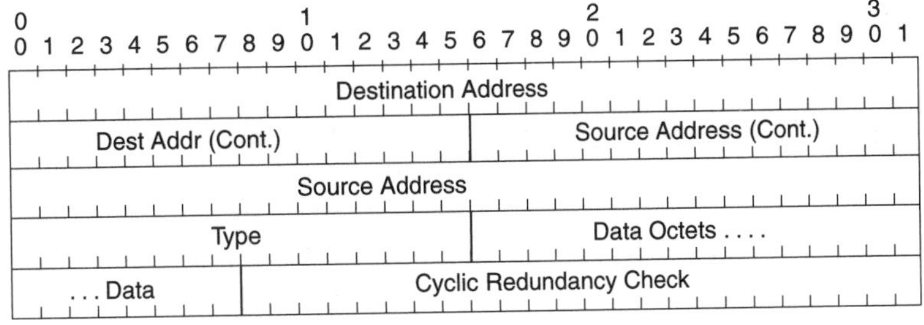

Illustration 1-2 Ethernet Encapsulation (RFC 894)

Note that the Ethernet header has a destination address and a source address. The addresses at the link layer are called *hardware addresses.* These six octet addresses have become commonly known as *MAC addresses.* MAC is the abbreviation for media access control. This is somewhat of a misnomer, since MAC is concerned with specific aspects of link management on a LAN and does not directly deal with or define hardware addressing on the LAN. It got the nickname "MAC address" by being the address used at the MAC layer, a sublayer of the link layer. This being said, I will admit that I am one of those network folks who use "MAC address" and "LAN address" interchangeably to refer to the hardware address. So scold me.

The bottom line is that Ethernet, Token Ring, FDDI, Frame Relay, ATM, and most other network media interfaces have a hardware address associated with them. The exceptions to this are most point-to-point protocols, such as SLIP (Serial Line Internet Protocol) or PPP (Point to Point Protocol). There really isn't much need for hardware addresses on point-to-point protocols, since the hosts on both ends know the other's identity with absolute certainty.

Hardware addresses can be locally or globally administered. A locally administered address is one for which an administrator defines what the address is that is assigned to a hardware interface. Hardware addresses, especially LAN addresses, are rarely locally administered. Ethernet network interface cards (NICs) come preprogrammed with a hardware address that indicates the manufacturer. Ethernet hardware addresses are constructed with the leftmost three octets reflecting the manufacturer and the rightmost three octets reflecting a serial number assigned to the interface by the manufacturer. Ethernet hardware addresses are most often displayed as a series of 12 hexadecimal numbers, in pairs separated by hyphens, as in 08-00-03-78-9A-BC. You may occasionally see them unhyphenated. Additionally, some network analyzers, such as Network Associates Sniffer, give the option of displaying the addresses with the manufacturer's name substituted in place of the first six hexadecimal digits, such as ACC-78-9A-BC. Table 1-1, an excerpt from the Assigned Numbers RFC, RFC 1700, shows a partial list of the Ethernet vendor address components.

Vendor Address	Vendor
00000C	Cisco
00000E	Fujitsu

00000F	NeXT
000010	Sytek
00001D	Cabletron
008037	Ericsson Business Comm.
00DD00	Ungermann-Bass
00DD01	Ungermann-Bass
020701	Racal InterLan
026086	Satelcom MegaPac (UK)
02608C	3Com: IBM PC, Imagen, Valid, Cisco
02CF1F	CMC: Masscomp, Silicon Graphics, Prime EXL
080002	3Com (Formerly Bridge)
080003	ACC (Advanced Computer Communications)
080005	Symbolics: Symbolics LISP machines
080008	BBN
080009	Hewlett-Packard

Table 1-1 Excerpt of Ethernet Vendor Address Components from Assigned Numbers RFC, RFC 1700

Looking again to the Ethernet header in Illustration 1-1, note the field denoted as Type. That field indicates what protocol the Data field will next be interpreted as. Although Ethernet types are administered by Xerox Systems Institute, Palo Alto, CA, the Assigned Numbers RFC also indicates the legal values that the Type field may have encoded in it (with the caveat that the list is contributed, unverified information from various sources). Table 1-2 is an excerpt of Ethernet types from the Assigned Numbers RFC.

Ethernet		Exp. Ethernet		Description
Decimal	Hex	Decimal	Octal	
000	0000–05DC	—	—	IEEE802.3 Length Field
257	0101–01FF	—	—	Experimental
512	0200	512	1000	XEROX PUP (see 0A00)
513	0201	—	—	PUP Addr Trans
1536	0600	1536	3000	XEROX NS IDP
2048	0800	513	1001	Internet IP (IPv4)
2049	0801	—	—	X.75 Internet
2050	0802	—	—	NBS Internet
2051	0803	—	—	ECMA Internet
2053	0805	—	—	X.25 Level 3
2054	0806	—	—	ARP
32821	8035	—	—	Reverse ARP
32923	809B	—	—	Appletalk
33079	8137–8138	—	—	Novell, Inc.

Table 1-2 Excerpt of EtherTypes from Assigned Numbers RFC, RFC 1700

Again, this list is not complete, and the disclaimer would indicate that the Assigned Numbers RFC should not be expected to be complete. The point I wanted to make here is that the value 0x0800 (the 0x prefix indicates that the value is in hexadecimal notation) indicates that the Ethernet frame is encapsulating an IP datagram. A value of 0x0806 indicates that the Ethernet frame is encapsulating an Address Resolution Protocol (ARP) packet. Also note that the EtherType 0x809B is used for AppleTalk and that EtherTypes 0x8137 and 0x8138 are used by Novell (0x8137 indicates a Netware Ethernet_II frame). This table illustrates that TCP/IP is only one of many protocols that can run over Ethernet. Lastly note that the values in the range 0x0000 through 0x05DC have the description "IEEE802.3 Length Field." If the value in the EtherType field falls within this range, the frame is interpreted to be an IEEE 802.3 frame, not an Ethernet frame, and the indicator of the protocol found in the frame's payload is the Type field in the IEEE 802.2 SNAP header. Please note that the term *Ethernet* is often used to refer to a CSMA/CD (carrier sense multiple access with collision detection) network running 10 Mbps over Thinnet, Thicknet, or UTP and a variety of other media. Ethernet has a specific frame type, but most people use the term in a general sense and don't differentiate between IEEE 802.3 and Ethernet frames.

I have focused mainly on Ethernet as the link layer protocol, with a few references to other protocols such as Token Ring, SLIP, ATM, and Frame Relay. Don't get too caught up in the link layer, at least not in this book. If you want to examine the nuts and bolts of other media, there are plenty of good books to assist you with them. The point of this discussion is to sketch out a header that you might expect to see at the link layer. For now just accept that each link layer protocol might or might not have a hardware address associated with it. Further, if it is a general-purpose link layer protocol — that is, it does not serve only one master (protocol) — it will have some mechanism, such as the EtherType field, to define what the next higher-layer protocol is that is being carried in its payload.

The communications model that we have developed to this point is fairly limited and looks something like Illustration 1-3. A local network interface card (LNI-1a) sends a packet of data to the other local network interface card (LNI-1b), using a link layer protocol to wrap the data and deliver it with some level of certainty. This system works fine if you have a single physical network and all of your devices are attached to that same physical network. Assuming that you had some sort of a directory service so you could cross-reference a user or a service on the network to the hardware address of the network interface card, you could function quite effectively. The addition of TCP/IP as the upper-layer protocol extends this communications model to look like Illustration 1-4, which shows an application program (don't read more than that into it for now) communicating with another application program.

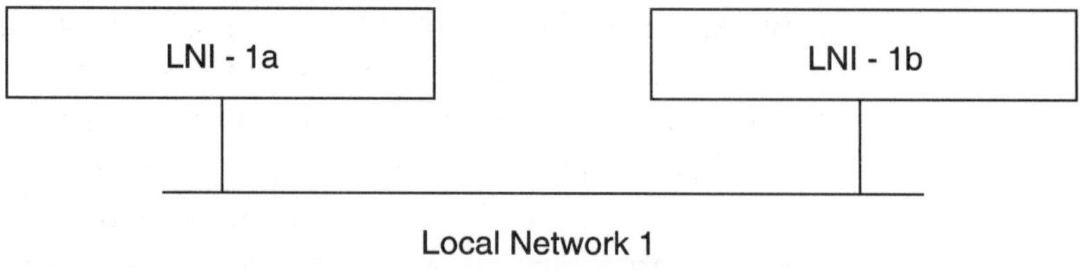

Illustration 1-3 Simple Communications Model

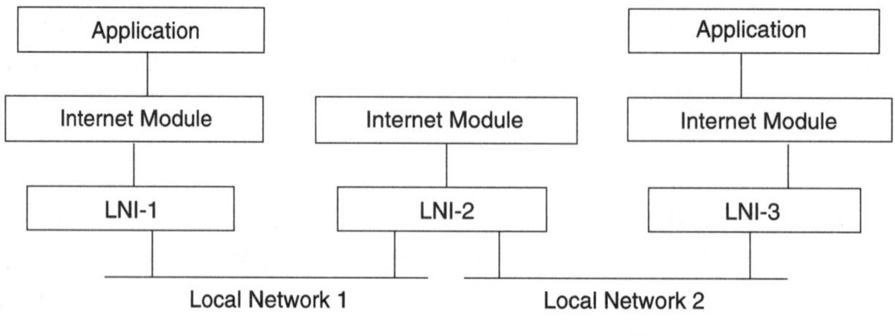

Illustration 1-4 Three-Level Communications Model

For the sake of the following walkthrough, consider that the application on the left is sending data to the application on the right. The data for the application program goes through an Internet module that encapsulates it with an Internet header. This data and its encapsulating Internet header passes through the local network interface (LNI-1), where it is encapsulated into a header specific to the type of network for the local network. It is then transmitted on the local network to the hardware address of the other local network interface on Local Network 1. The receiving Local Network 2 interface verifies the integrity of the local network header and removes it to reveal the Internet header that is encapsulating the original application data. An examination of the Internet header reveals that the destination of the packet can be found on the other local network to which it is attached. The packet is forwarded through the local network interface (LNI-2), where it is encapsulated for transmission with a header unique to the type of Local Network 2 and sent to the local network interface denoted by the hardware address. The receiving local network interface checks the integrity of the local network header and removes the local network header to reveal an Internet header. The frame is passed up to the Internet module, where the packet is determined to have arrived at its destination. The Internet header is removed, and the data is passed up to the application program. Transfer complete.

That was a gross simplification of the Internet Protocol. I apologize for the pain, but I wanted to make sure that you understood a few points:

- First, in the example what the local networks were was not relevant. They could both have been Ethernets, or one could have been a Token Ring and the other a Frame Relay; it just does not matter.
- Second, the Internet module was receiving data from an application program and passing it across multiple physical networks to another application program via a relay of Internet modules.
- Third, somehow the Internet modules knew how to pass the Internet frame so that it would reach the destination of the second application program.

Hold on to those three things. The first one deals with the issue of transparency of the underlying physical networks. I have discussed this before. I used an Ethernet frame as an example but asked that you trust me when I told you that somehow, some way, the frame would be transmitted across a network to its correct destination and there would be an indication, if necessary, of how to interpret the frame encapsulated within the link layer header. In the case of Ethernet, there would be a 0x0800 in the EtherType field, which would indicate that the contents of the Ethernet frame's data field should be passed to a process that we previously identified as the Internet module. The Internet module implements the Internet Protocol (IP) and interprets and constructs IP headers.

Keep holding on to the other two concepts from my diatribe on the gross simplification of the communications model. I will get there eventually. In the meantime, this should be starting to take shape for you.

The Network Layer

The local network interface verifies the integrity of the link layer header and strips it off. The bits that are left are supposed to be an IP frame, at least that is what the Type field in the link layer header indicated it was supposed to be. What is it that is left? Illustration 1-5 shows an IP header. I will briefly detail each of the fields in the header, as in Table 1-3. However, all fields that are not relevant to this book are left to you, should you feel compelled to know more than I present.

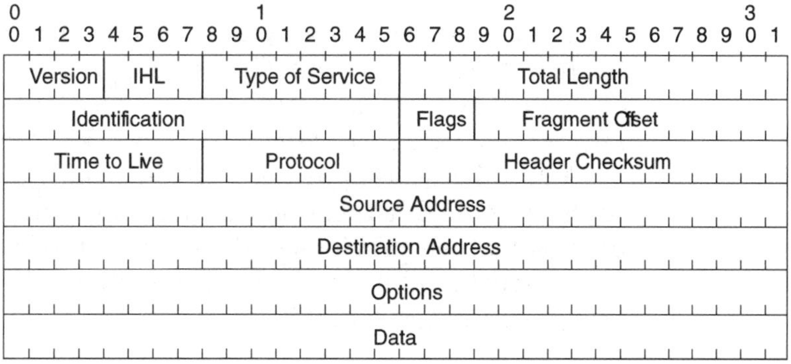

```
 0                   1                   2                   3
 0 1 2 3 4 5 6 7 8 9 0 1 2 3 4 5 6 7 8 9 0 1 2 3 4 5 6 7 8 9 0 1
+-+-+-+-+-+-+-+-+-+-+-+-+-+-+-+-+-+-+-+-+-+-+-+-+-+-+-+-+-+-+-+-+
|Version|  IHL  |Type of Service|          Total Length         |
+-+-+-+-+-+-+-+-+-+-+-+-+-+-+-+-+-+-+-+-+-+-+-+-+-+-+-+-+-+-+-+-+
|         Identification        |Flags|      Fragment Offset    |
+-+-+-+-+-+-+-+-+-+-+-+-+-+-+-+-+-+-+-+-+-+-+-+-+-+-+-+-+-+-+-+-+
|  Time to Live |    Protocol   |         Header Checksum       |
+-+-+-+-+-+-+-+-+-+-+-+-+-+-+-+-+-+-+-+-+-+-+-+-+-+-+-+-+-+-+-+-+
|                       Source Address                          |
+-+-+-+-+-+-+-+-+-+-+-+-+-+-+-+-+-+-+-+-+-+-+-+-+-+-+-+-+-+-+-+-+
|                    Destination Address                        |
+-+-+-+-+-+-+-+-+-+-+-+-+-+-+-+-+-+-+-+-+-+-+-+-+-+-+-+-+-+-+-+-+
|                          Options                              |
+-+-+-+-+-+-+-+-+-+-+-+-+-+-+-+-+-+-+-+-+-+-+-+-+-+-+-+-+-+-+-+-+
|                            Data                               |
+-+-+-+-+-+-+-+-+-+-+-+-+-+-+-+-+-+-+-+-+-+-+-+-+-+-+-+-+-+-+-+-+
```

Illustration 1-5 Example of Internet Datagram Header

- *Version:* Had I written this book a few years ago, I would have told you that the value in this field will always be 4. Well, maybe not, but I certainly would not have been likely to go into much more depth than that. These first four bits of the IP header are used to dictate how the Internet module should parse the header. Once again referring to my copy of the Assigned Numbers RFC, I find the valid version IDs that can be found in the Version field of the IP header are those listed in Table 1-3. The version that you will find in use almost exclusively throughout the Internet and TCP/IP is version 4. RFC 791 defines version 4 of IP (IPv4).

Decimal	Keyword	Version
0	—	Reserved
1–3	—	Unassigned
4	IP	Internet Protocol
5	ST	ST Datagram Mode
6	SIP	Simple Internet Protocol
7	TP/IX	TP/IX: The Next Internet

Decimal	Keyword	Version
8	PIP	The P Internet Protocol
9	TUBA	TUBA
10–14	—	Unassigned
15	—	Reserved

Table 1-3 Assigned Internet Version Numbers (RFC1700)

Now I am going to ask that you trust me. The Assigned Numbers RFC that I used to get the information was published in October 1994. Although this is the most current publication as of this writing, it is still out of date. Versions 6 (SIP), 7 (TP/IX), 8 (PIP), and 9 (TUBA) were all subsumed or made obsolete by a new Internet Protocol, IP version 6 (IPv6 is the subject of Chapter 13). You will soon be seeing much more of the Internet Protocol that has a 6 in the version field.

- *Header Length:* Four bits used to identify where the header ends and where the data begins. The IP header is not a constant length. This is a result of the Options field, which follows the Destination Address field and precedes the Data field.
- *Type of Service or Differentiated Services:* This field has changed usage in the last couple of years with the conception and introduction of Differentiated Services (DiffServ or DS) into IPv4. Prior to DiffServ, this field was known as the Type of Service or TOS field. Both the DS and the TOS fields are presented below, starting with the older Type of Service field.

  Type of Service field. The TOS field is actually two fields in one, as shown here.

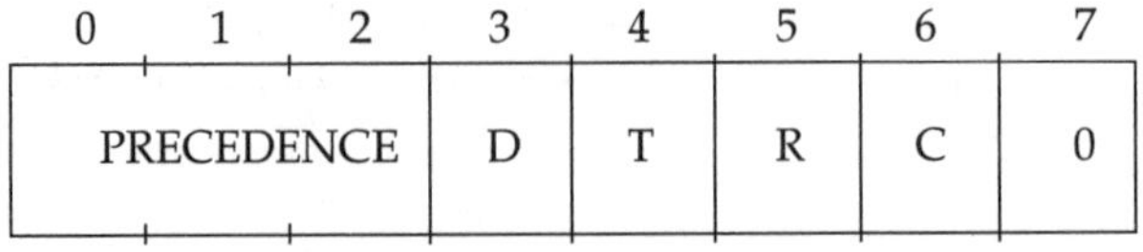

0 1 2	3	4	5	6	7
PRECEDENCE	D	T	R	C	0

The high-order three bits are the Precedence field and the next four bits are the Type of Service flags. These TOS flags can influence how routing decisions are made for the packet being examined. The flags are

D	Delay
T	Throughput
R	Reliability
C	Cost

They are set to bias a potential routing decision in favor of their respective factor.

The three bits that represent the Precedence field influence the treatment of the packet while it is in queue in a router. Congestion in routers results in a growth of queues and delays associated with traversing the queues. The Precedence field permits the router to select certain packets for earlier transmission over other, less time-sensitive packets. The possible values are

111	Network control
110	Internetwork control
101	CRITIC/ECP
100	Flash override
011	Flash
010	Immediate
001	Priority
000	Routine

The low-order bit (bit 7) of the Type of Service field has been reserved. That field is rarely used or implemented.

Differentiated Services field. This is an 8-bit field that is used to permit administration of classes and priorities of IPv4 and IPv6 packets in traffic passing through routers. RFC 2474, "Definition of the Differentiated Services Field (DS Field) in the IPv4 and IPv6 Headers," defines its intended usage. The DS field is allocated as follows.

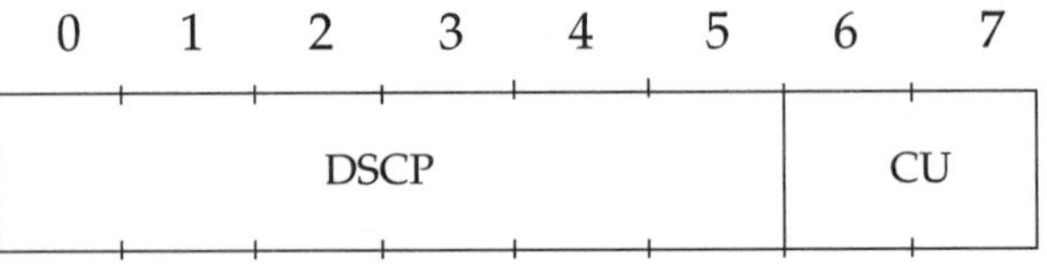

DSCP: differentiated services codepoint
CU: currently unused

Bits 0 through 5 comprise the differentiated services codepoint (DSCP). Each router along the forwarding path of the packet may examine the value of the DSCP to determine what kind of special treatments it needs to provide to the packet as it is being forwarded. The router may even alter the DSCP as necessary to provide a specific treatment. In that way, the router can provide differentiated service to all packets with the same DSCP value.

Several DSCP values are defined in advance and have global significance. One of these is a DSCP of binary 000000. This maps to the default per-hop behavior, which is basically best-effort routing without any preference. There are also some predefined DSCPs that permit compatibility with the older IP precedence bits of the TOS field in the IPv4 header. These are DSCP values of xxx000. RFC 2474 says that a DSCP with a value of 111000 should get the highest preferential per-hop behavior and a value of 001000 should get higher preference than the default per-hop behavior but lower preference than the per-hop behavior mapped to DSCP 111000.

Bits 6 and 7 of the DS field are not used currently.

- *Total Length:* Sixteen bits. The total length of the IP datagram. This includes the header and the data.
- *Identification:* Sixteen bits. A unique number used to identify the IP datagram.
- *Flags:* Three bits. The two low-order bits control fragmentation of an IP datagram. Bit 1 is the "don't fragment" bit. Bit 2 is the "more fragments" bit.

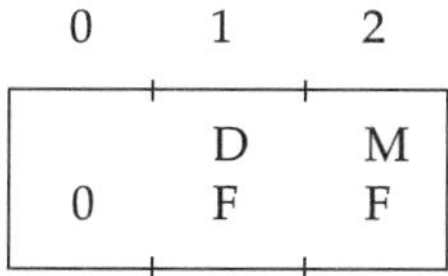

- *Fragment Offset:* Thirteen bits. Controls the reassembly of the IP datagram.
- *Time to Live:* Eight bits. Controls the number of hops that an IP datagram is permitted to traverse before it is purged. A datagram with a TTL of 0 must be discarded.
- *Protocol:* Eight bits. Defines the next-higher protocol found in the data portion of the IP datagram. Table 1-4 is an excerpt from the Assigned Numbers RFC as an example of the values that might be found in the Protocol field of an IP header. Make sure that you take a moment to locate ICMP, IGMP, TCP, and UDP in this partial list.

Decimal	Keyword	Protocol
0	—	Reserved
1	ICMP	Internet Control Message
2	IGMP	Internet Group Management
3	GGP	Gateway-to-Gateway
4	IP	IP in IP (encapsulation)
5	ST	Stream
6	TCP	Transmission Control
7	UCL	UCL
8	EGP	Exterior Gateway
9	IGP	Any private interior gateway
10	BBN-RCC-MON	BBN RCC Monitoring
17	UDP	User Datagram
18	MUX	Multiplexing
27	RDP	Reliable Data
29	ISO-TP4	ISO Transport Class 4
46	RSVP	Reservation
88	IGRP	IGRP
89	OSPFIGP	OSPFIGP
101-254	—	Unassigned
255	—	Reserved

Table 1-4 Sample IP Protocol Values

- *Header Checksum:* Sixteen bits. This is computed only on the IP header and is used as an indicator of the integrity of the IP datagram's header.

- *Source Address:* Thirty-two bits. The IP address of the originator of the IP datagram. This will be discussed in much greater detail in Chapter 3.
- *Destination Address:* Thirty-two bits. The IP address of the intended recipient of the IP datagram.
- *Options:* Variable length. Options are seldom used these days but some options that might be found include:

  Security

  Stream identifier (obsolete)

  Source route

  Record route

  Timestamp
- *Data:* Variable length. The payload of the IP datagram.

The addresses in the IP header are the subject of the next chapter. For now, consider a directed transfer of data from one computer to another. In this case the source address and the destination address are referred to as unicast addresses. More specifically, the addresses refer to one and only one interface. The latest iteration of the communications model is redrawn in Illustration 1-6.

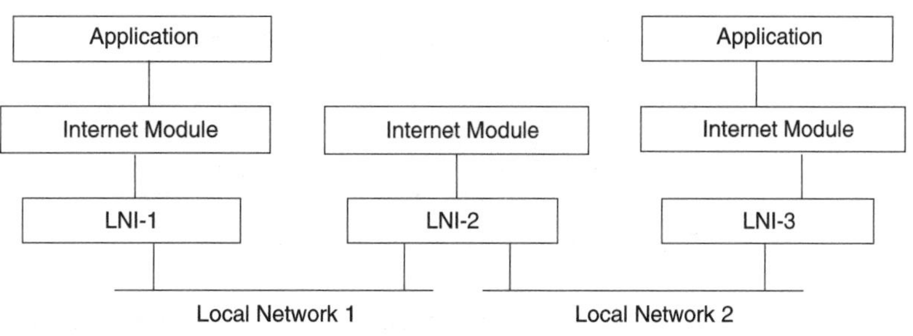

Illustration 1-6 Three-Level Communications Model

The leftmost and rightmost Internet modules interface to application programs. When this was last discussed, it was vague as to what the applications programs were or what they did. Now that the fields of the IP header have been discussed, it is possible to revise the communications model to show a bit more detail (see Illustration 1-7).

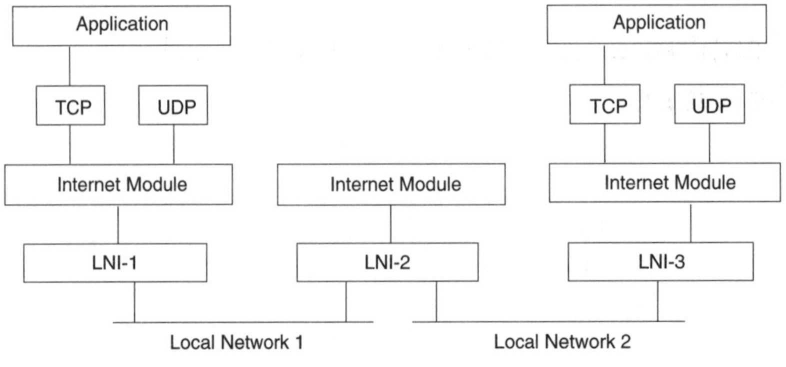

Illustration 1-7 Communications Model with Transport Layer

This revision was based on the presence of the protocol field in the IP header. I asked that you take note of the values 1, 2, 6, and 17, which indicate that the IP datagram's data field has information in it that should be interpreted as ICMP, IGMP, TCP, or UDP frames, respectively. In the prior model, the IP module was getting "application data" from a source and passing it to another vague source in another part of the network. The Protocol field allows us to put names on those vague application programs of the prior model. The current communications model still has an application program, but it is one layer higher than it was previously.

Note that only the leftmost and rightmost Internet modules have TCP and UDP modules connected to them. Both TCP and UDP will be discussed further, but suffice it to say now that TCP and UDP provide transport services to user applications.

The Internet module, IP, provides transport services across an internetwork for specific protocol services but does not guarantee the integrity or delivery of the data. It does provide a pretty good indication that the IP header has not been corrupted. This is a function of the IP header checksum.

Reliable and Unreliable Transport Services

A transport service can be classified as reliable or unreliable. Several characteristics can be used to classify a transport service into one or the other category.

Reliable transport services typically:

- *Establish connections:* In the same manner that you would place a voice call through the "plain-old telephone service" (POTS) and establish that the person that you intended to call was on the other end before you began your conversation, a reliable transport service will establish a data connection context that the data transfer "conversation" will use for the duration of the "call." Because of this connection establishment, there can be only two end points in a reliable transport service.
- *Acknowledge packets:* In a reliable transport conversation each packet that is sent must be acknowledged by the remote side. Timers are implemented that provide the sending side with an indication that an inordinate amount of time has elapsed since a packet was sent and there is a "good chance" that the packet was lost. The expiration of such a timer would trigger a retransmission of the suspected lost packet. In actuality, the

original packet might have been received and the acknowledgment packet lost.

- *Implement validation sequences:* This includes checksums, cyclic redundancy checks (CRC), and forward error correction (FEC) codes. These validation sequences have various capabilities to detect single or multiple errors or even to correct errors at the receiving end. The number of bits required, how they are implemented, where the codes are placed in the data, and the complexity of the calculation all depend on the amount of noise expected in the channel on which the data is being transmitted and the merits of not having to ask for a retransmission. The simplest to implement is the checksum.
- *Implement flow control:* This is a mechanism by which a remote system can dictate the amount of data it is capable of receiving. This pacing keeps an optimal amount of data in buffers so that applications can keep a steady flow into their processes without having to wait for more data to be transmitted as a result of packet loss due to buffer overflows.

Unreliable transport services typically:

- *Do not establish connections:* Whenever a communications system uses an unreliable transport, it typically does not check to see whether the other site is available before it sends the data. The analogy of placing a phone call was used to illustrate a reliable connection-oriented service. A non-connection-oriented service can be illustrated with the postal system (nonregistered mail). A person who wishes to communicate via mail writes the letter (constructs the message), places it in an envelope, addresses it (encapsulates it in a header), affixes a stamp on it (pays the tariff), and posts it (transmits it). Then the postal system takes responsibility for the letter and makes its best effort to deliver it. The sender has no idea how long it will take for the letter to be delivered other than what past experience indicates. The sender does not know whether the addressee receives the letter or reads it. In the data communications industry, a packet of data that is sent via an unreliable service is called a datagram. This is not the first time that the term has been used in this chapter. This would suggest that IP is an unreliable service, and it is. One further note: Since there is not an established connection, it is possible to send the same datagram to more than one location, as in multicasts and broadcasts.

- *Do not acknowledge packets:* A datagram "stands alone." It is sent with the understanding that the services that are charged with its delivery will attempt to deliver it — using "best effort." The datagram may be discarded, or the destination application may not be capable of accepting it. No message will be sent to the sending application to indicate that it was received. Similarly, the sending application will not start a timer whose expiration would indicate that the packet might be lost.
- *Implement validation sequences:* Checksums can be implemented in as little as one bit to indicate that the sum of all the bits in a packet is an odd value or an even value. The more bits that a checksum is implemented with, the smaller the chance that multiple errors would result in a valid checksum. With as few as 16 bits, a protocol can implement a pretty robust error detection mechanism. This is to say that for a small penalty, it is prudent to implement some sort of integrity verification mechanism. Naturally, it would follow that unreliable protocols are not likely to implement extremely complex algorithms for the forward correction of multiple errors.

- *Do not implement flow control:* Unreliable transport protocols typically do not have any pacing inherent in their design. If a packet is lost due to an overrun of buffers, too bad.

TCP/IP has two transport protocols. They are at extreme ends of the reliable–unreliable spectrum. The reasoning behind this is that if you want reliable communications, you can use TCP and pay the price of the overhead. All the services provided by TCP are well engineered and debugged. If you want to take your chances with an unreliable datagram service and understand the limitations, use UDP. UDP is a bare-bones transport service with little overhead. There is no "gray area" transport service that implements some feature set in between UDP and TCP. If the application requires a limited reliability feature, it must be implemented in the application itself, and UDP must be used.

Transmission Control Protocol

The Transmission Control Protocol (TCP) is the transport protocol in the TCP/IP suite that handles reliable data transmission. The previous section discussed each of the features found in a reliable transport service, so it should be no surprise to find an implementation of some of them here. Illustration 1-8 shows the format of the TCP header.

0 1 2 3
0 1 2 3 4 5 6 7 8 9 0 1 2 3 4 5 6 7 8 9 0 1 2 3 4 5 6 7 8 9 0 1

Source Port | Destination Port
Sequence Number
Acknowledgement Number
Data Offset | Reserved | URG | ACK | PSH | RST | SYN | FIN | Window
Checksum | Urgent Pointer
Options | Padding
data

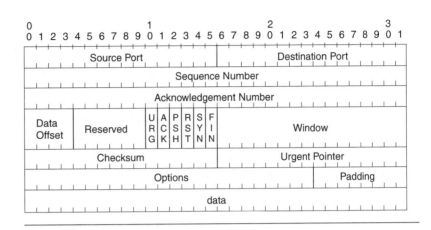

Illustration 1-8 TCP Header Format (Note that one tick mark represents one bit position.)

The header contains, in addition to other fields, an acknowledgment, a sequence number, and a checksum that account for the acknowledged communications and validation sequence service commonly found in a reliable protocol. Not so obviously, because it is more of a procedural aspect of the protocol than a function of the header, TCP also implements connection-oriented communications and flow control. Evidence of this is the sequence number and acknowledgment number fields. Certain fields in the header are used in the procedure, such as the SYN flag, which synchronizes the communications session during connection establishment. For additional information, please refer to a specialized TCP/IP protocol text.

The point I want to make with regard to TCP is that all the fields in the header are there for the purposes of establishing the identification of the applications that are using the TCP transport services and providing reliable, connection-oriented services to those applications. Note the Source Port and Destination Port fields, which identify the applications using the TCP service. The port fields are 16 bits in length and thus can handle a value from 0 to 65,535. The values of 0, 1023, and 1024 are reserved. The values in the range 1 to 1023 are called *well-known ports.*

These ports are administered by the Internet Assigned Numbers Authority (IANA), and the values of these ports, along with their use, can be found in the Assigned Numbers RFC. Table 1-5 is an excerpt of the well-known ports for TCP from the Assigned Numbers RFC.

Service	Port #	Description
tcpmux	1/tcp	TCP port service multiplexer
echo	7/tcp	Echo
systat	11/tcp	Active users
daytime	13/tcp	Daytime
qotd	17/tcp	Quote of the day
chargen	19/tcp	Character generator
ftp-data	20/tcp	File transfer [default data]
ftp	21/tcp	File transfer [control]
telnet	23/tcp	Telnet
smtp	25/tcp	Simple mail transfer
time	37/tcp	Time
nameserver	42/tcp	Host name server
nicname	43/tcp	Who is

Table 1-5 Selected TCP Well-Known Ports

Telnetd is a daemon (a process) that acts as a server (in a client-server model) providing a simple remote terminal connection to the TCP/IP host that it is running on. Telnetd typically listens on the well-known port (23) for a connection request, although it is possible to configure it to listen on another port. If it is configured to listen on a port other than port 23, the user would have to know in advance what port the client should attempt a connection on. The standard port is 23; hence it is the well-known port. If the client is not instructed to attempt a connection on a specific port, it will attempt the connection on port 23, the default.

Ports in the range 1024 through 5000 are special-purpose ports known as *ephemeral ports*. They are known as such because of their typically short usage. Ephemeral ports are the ones that the client uses when it initiates a connection with a server. Their "lives" span only the time during which the connection is made with the server. When the conversation ends and the service is no longer needed, the ports are released to an available pool.

Ports above 5000 are available for any use. Typically a user would make a specialized TCP/IP service available through one of these ports. For instance, if I had a piece of software that I wanted to make available for download but did not want to do it through the normal "anonymous" FTP site at my company, I could set up an FTPD daemon to listen to port 17000, and I would make the portion of the file system where the software resided accessible to that daemon. I would instruct the users of FTP to port 17000 to get my software. It does not have to be a common service that I make available through one of these ports; it could be a home-grown service that does not warrant petitioning the IANA for a port allocation.

User Datagram Protocol

The User Datagram Protocol is the transport service that TCP/IP provides for connectionless, unreliable service. Illustration 1-9 shows the UDP header format. No doubt you will note the significant lack of complexity in the UDP header as compared to the TCP header. Source Port and Destination Port serve the same functions as in TCP, although they are unique from those of TCP. True, some functions are provided in both

TCP and UDP, and they have the same number. An example of this is the chargen service, which is available through both UDP and TCP on port 19. Table 1-6 is an excerpt from the Assigned Numbers RFC for the UDP well-known ports.

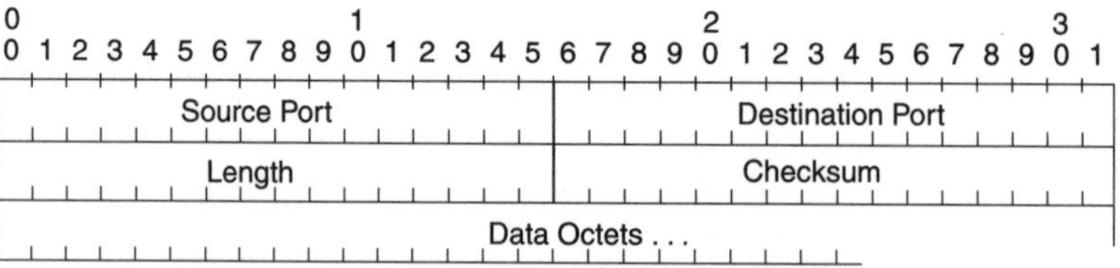

Illustration 1-9 User Datagram Header Format

Service	Port #	Description
tcpmux	1/udp	TCP port service multiplexer
echo	7/udp	Echo
systat	11/udp	Active USERS
daytime	13/udp	Daytime
qotd	17/udp	Quote of the day
chargen	19/udp	Character generator
smtp	25/udp	Simple mail transfer
bootps	67/udp	Bootstrap protocol server
bootpc	68/udp	Bootstrap protocol client
tftp	69/udp	Trivial file transfer
finger	79/udp	Finger
www-http	80/udp	World Wide Web HTTP
nntp	119/udp	Network News Transfer Protocol
snmp	161/udp	SNMP

snmptrap	162/udp	SNMPTRAP
bgp	179/udp	Border Gateway Protocol
ipx	213/udp	IPX
biff	512/udp	Used by mail system to notify users
who	513/udp	Maintains databases showing who's who
uucp	540/udp	UUCPD

Table 1-6 Selected UDP Well-Known Ports (RFC 1700)

TCP/IP Connections

The communications model can now be revised one last time (Illustration 1-10). This model again replaces the vague application program with a specific example illustrating the source and destination of data. Now, just as an exercise, let's look at what it took to get to this point. Let's start with a user on the left side who wants to get a file off the host system on the right side. The user reviews the choices for getting the file and narrows the options down to two file transfer programs, FTP and TFTP. The File Transfer Protocol (FTP) is implemented to use TCP services that provide for a reliable, connection-oriented transfer. Trivial File Transfer Protocol (TFTP) uses services from UDP — the connectionless, unreliable service. Sounds scary to rely on UDP for a file transfer, but it really is not that bad since some reliability features have been included in the TFTP application that were absent from its underlying transport mechanism. Our user chooses the reliable FTP. The user specifies the remote host's IP address to the FTP client application, which, through TCP and IP, crosses the Internet to the IP module on the rightmost side of the diagram. This IP module examines the IP header's protocol field and determines that the data contained in the datagram's data fields is a TCP segment. After a few checks, the header is stripped away and the data passed to the TCP process. The TCP process looks at the destination port (along with a few other things) and sees that the data in the TCP segment should be passed in entirety to port 21. There is a process listening to port 21. In this case the process is FTPD, the File Transfer Protocol Daemon (server). Fortunately, even though the headers were stripped off along the way, the source port and source IP address were passed along with the data to the FTP Daemon. Now the FTP Daemon knows how to return any data that the client on the far end of the connection requires.

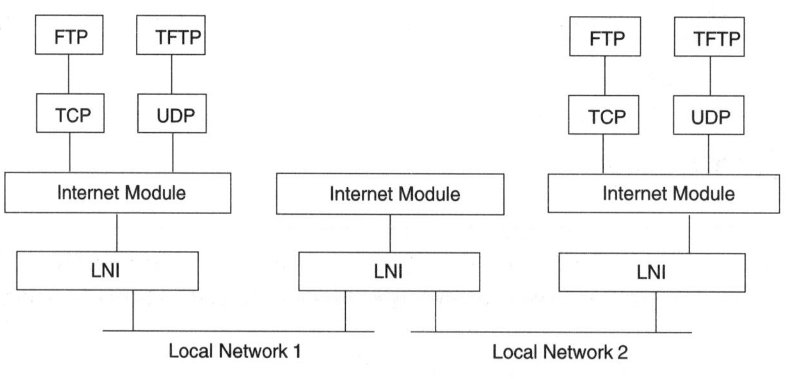

Illustration 1-10 Complete TCP/IP Communications Model

I intentionally glossed over some processes that are essential to the entire communications session. Throughout this chapter the discussion has moved from the physical network and the associated link layer protocols all the way up to the TCP/IP applications such as FTP, TFTP, and Telnet. These applications do not require the knowledge of the lower-layer details. All that is required for an application to communicate with another application across a TCP/IP internetwork is what is referred to as an *association.* Associations are an abstract of the form

> {protocol, source IP address, source port, destination IP address, destination port}

This association uniquely identifies a connection throughout an entire internetwork. Half of the association, the IP address and port combination, is often referred to as a socket. A socket reference without an indication of protocol is not useful, because it is not unique. It is useful to be able to refer to the UDP socket of

> {destination IP address, destination port}

to uniquely identify half of a TCP/IP conversation.

Summary

TCP/IP is a protocol suite that is implemented in layers. The following layers are found in the protocol architecture:

- Application
- Transport
- Network
- Link
- Physical

In a TCP/IP environment the application needs to know very little about the physical or logical architecture of the network.

The architecture is transparent to the user processes. In many cases the user is required to know only the IP address of the remote system where the desired service is resident.

The link layer is used to transport data between interfaces on the same network medium. Link layer protocols implement device driver functions and typically have knowledge only of devices that are physically attached to the medium and refer to them by their respective hardware addresses. Examples of link layer protocols include Ethernet, Token Ring, Frame Relay, and PPP.

The network layer is responsible for the routing and relaying of datagrams in the internetwork. Examples of protocols at the network layer include the Internet Protocol (IP), ICMP, and IGMP. ICMP and IGMP rely on transport services provided by IP, but they cannot be logically removed from the network layer because of the functions they provide.

The transport layer protocols provide end-to-end data delivery services to user applications. TCP, the Transmission Control Protocol, provides a reliable, connection-oriented transport service. UDP, the User Datagram Protocol, provides a bare-bones connectionless, unreliable transport service.

The application layer protocols provide functions for remote terminal login, file transfers, network management, mail transfer, file system sharing, and information retrieval. In general, the applications provide the general utility to the network.

Two points are important to understand after reading this chapter. First, starting at the link layer protocols, it is possible to look at a certain field in each layer's encapsulating header to determine how to interpret the data portion of that layer. The reverse encapsulation process is often described by the analogy of "peeling away an onion." Second, a TCP/IP connection requires five pieces of information to be fully described. These pieces are the protocol, the source IP address, the source port, the destination IP address, and the destination port. Together these are known as an *association.*

Practice Questions

The four questions cannot be answered using only this book. You will have to find a source for IANA number assignments such as RFC 1700 or the IANA Web pages:

ftp://ftp.isi.edu/in-notes/iana/assignments/

1. What is the Ethernet Vendor Address for Synoptics?
2. What EtherType has been allocated to Apollo Computer?
3. What is the IP Protocol value for "Chaos"?
4. What service is available on well-known port 179?
5. What range of ports are known as "ephemeral ports"?

chapter

2

IP Address Fundamentals

In Chapter 1 I presented an overview of the TCP/IP communication protocols to show how the protocols work together to provide a transport service to the user processes, or application layer. In this chapter, I will cover the details of the IP address that I postponed in the discussion of the network layer.

The Internet protocols have become widely known as TCP/IP. TCP/IP has become the moniker for the entire suite of protocols including, but not limited to, the Transmission Control Protocol, User Datagram Protocol, Internet Control Message Protocol, Address Resolution Protocol, and Internet Protocol. The addresses associated with these protocols have become commonly known as TCP/IP addresses. This, however, is not altogether accurate. These addresses apply only to the Internet Protocol, or IP, as it is most commonly referred to. When I say "IP address" throughout this text, I am referring to an address of the format defined and used in the Internet Protocol version 4.

On Names, Addresses, and Routes

I have not yet seen a coverage of IP addressing that does not lead with a summary of a paper published in the *Proceedings of COMPCON*, Fall 1978, by John Shoch. Far be it for me to break with tradition. This paper was titled "Internetwork Naming, Addressing, and Routing" and delineated the difference among a name, an address, and a route. Although it might seem intuitive to many of us at the present, the distinction, as Shoch pointed out, is that a *name* is an identifier for an object, an *address* is where the object can be found, and a *route* is the path taken to get to the address. In those days of dealing with PUP (PARC Universal Protocol), it was not altogether clear what the distinctions were until Shoch clarified the terms.

In her book *Interconnections,* Radia Perlman provides a more in-depth perspective on the terms:

- *Name:* A name is location independent, with respect to both the source and the destination. If something is the name of a destination, it will remain unchanged even if the destination moves, and it is valid regardless of which source is attempting to reach the destination. An example of a name is a Social Security number, which remains unchanged even if the number's owner moves. Sometimes fields that are names are referred to as *identifiers* or *IDs*.
- *Address:* An address is valid regardless of the location of the source station, but the addresses may change if the destination moves. An example of an address is a postal address. The same destination postal address works regardless of the location from which a letter is mailed. However, if the destination moves, it is assigned a new address.
- *Route:* A route is dependent on the location of both the source and the destination. In other words, if two

> sources specify a route to a given destination, the routes are likely to differ. And if the destination moves, all routes to it are likely to change. An example of a route is, "To get to my house, go west 3 miles and take a right turn at the first light. It's the last house on the left."

Given that she says a "route is dependent on the location of both the source and the destination," it would seem that the example she provides would be more technically accurate to start with "To get to my house *from your house,* go west 3 miles. . . ." A route is not valid without a starting point of reference, even if it is implied by or relative to your current position.

With regard to these terms, there is very little confusion over what a route is. However, there are numerous examples in the industry of places where the term *address* is used when the term *name* should have been. It will be seen, by the end of the chapter, that an IP address is really both a name and an address at the same time.

The IP Address

Recall from the previous chapter that the IP header has a format as shown in Illustration 2-1. We categorically call IP addresses the two fields named Source Address and Destination Address. The IP address is 32 bits in length. Although there are some special-case uses for this address, it is most generally used to simultaneously identify both the network to which a host is attached and the interface that connects the network and the host together.

The address is able to identify the network and the interface through a division of the 32 available bits into two logical fields called the *network portion* and the *host portion.* The host portion is also commonly referred to as the local address part of the address. The network portion can have as few as 8 bits and as many as 30 bits allocated to it. The host portion has whatever bits the network portion is not utilizing; therefore it can have as many as 24 bits and as few as 2 bits allocated to it. This will be explained later. The allocation of bits between these two portions is facilitated by the use of two devices. The first is a *prefix code* that enables a host or a user to look only at the first few bits of an IP address to determine the classification of the IP address. The class of an IP address dictates the minimum number of bits allocated to the network portion. The second device, used to determine a further split, is called a *network mask.*

0 1 2 3

0 1 2 3 4 5 6 7 8 9 0 1 2 3 4 5 6 7 8 9 0 1 2 3 4 5 6 7 8 9 0 1

Version	IHL	Type of Service	Total Length	
Identification			Flags	Fragment Offset
Time to Live		Protocol	Header Checksum	
Source Address				
Destination Address				
Options				
Data				

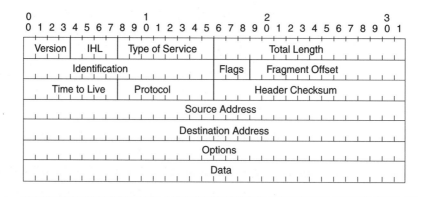

Illustration 2-1 Example of Internet Datagram Header

Address Terminology, Notation, and Numbering

Before going into the details of IP addressing, it is important to learn the terminology that will be used throughout this book. You should become familiar with the following terms.

- *Bit* (binary digit): The smallest addressable unit of data on a computer. A bit has one of two possible states, often represented as 1 and 0.
- *Byte:* Usually a unit of data that is 8 bits in length. In the past a byte was a unit of data in which a computer word could be divided. This definition resulted in bytes being other than 8 bits in length. (I worked with a computer system in the mid-1970s that used an 18-bit computer word; the character set (XS-3) it used had bytes that were 6 bits in length.)
- *Octet:* A unit of data that is *always* 8 bits in length. The 32-bit IP address is frequently referred to as 4 octets in length.
- *All ones* (all 1s): The condition when the data unit, IP address, or address portion being referenced is filled entirely with bits with a value of 1.
- *All zeros* (all 0s): The condition when the data unit, IP address, or address portion being referenced is filled entirely with bits with a value of 0.
- *High order:* This term is synonymous with "most significant," but throughout this text if it helps to remember that high order is the same as leftmost, go with it.
- *Low order:* Same as "least significant." Rightmost.
- *Most significant:* Technically, the bit or octet in a data unit that, if you were to take away or change the value from a 1 to a 0 (or all 1s to all 0s), would have the greatest impact on the data unit's value. This is best shown with an example. Assume an octet that has a value of all 1s as shown:

1 1 1 1 1 1 1 1	This octet has a decimal value of 255.

Now change the rightmost bit to a 0:

11111110	This octet has a decimal value of 254.

Now look at the original octet with the leftmost bit altered to a 0:

01111111	This octet has a decimal value of 127.

It is clear that changing the leftmost bit had the greatest impact on the value of the octet. The leftmost bit is thus the most significant bit in an octet. Similarly, the leftmost octet is the most significant octet in an IP address:

11111111	11111111	11111111	11111111

(Value: 4,294,967,295)

Voiding (zeroing out) the rightmost octet:

11111111	11111111	11111111	00000000

(Value: 4,294,967,040)

Voiding the leftmost octet:

00000000	11111111	11111111	11111111

(Value: 16,777,215)

- *Least significant:* The bit or octet that, if changed from a value of 1 (or all 1s) to a 0 (or all 0s), would have the least impact on the value of the entire data unit. In IP the rightmost bits are the least significant bits.
- *Dotted decimal notation:* The most common representation of a TCP/IP address. Take the 32-bit IP

address and divide it into four octets. Convert each octet from binary into decimal. Put a "." (dot) between each of the four decimal numbers. Even though the numbers are now in decimal, each number is still referred to as an octet, since its value must be in the valid range of an 8-bit number (0 to 255). An example of this follows:

00001010	00000001	10011100	01011011

(Decimal Value: 167,877,723)

00001010 00000001 10011100 01011011

The first octet, the high-order octet, converts to 10.

The second octet converts to 1.

The third octet converts to 156.

The fourth octet, the low-order octet, converts to 91.

The dotted decimal notation for the IP address in this example is

10.1.156.91

- *Hexadecimal notation:* Although much less common than dotted decimal, this notation still abounds. Start the same way as you would converting from a 32-bit IP address. Divide it into four octets and then divide each octet in half again so that you have eight 4-bit groups. Convert each group of 4 bits into their hexadecimal equivalents. Concatenate the resulting hexadecimal digits. It is common to prepend a hexadecimal number with a "0x" to indicate that it is a base-16 (hexadecimal) number. For instance:

10101100	00010000	10110110	00010011

(Decimal Value: 2,886,776,339)

10101100		00010000		10110110		00010011	
1010	1100	0001	0000	1011	0110	0001	0011
A	C	1	0	B	6	1	3

The hexadecimal notation for the IP address in this example is:

0xAC10B613 (sometimes written as AC.10.B6.13)

Determining the Class of an IP Address

Every IP address, with the exception of a handful of special-purpose addresses, has a classification associated with it. To determine the class of an IP address, examine the four high-order bits of the address. Remember, these are the leftmost bits, also known as the four most significant bits of the IP address. Use the flowchart in Illustration 2-2 to determine the class.

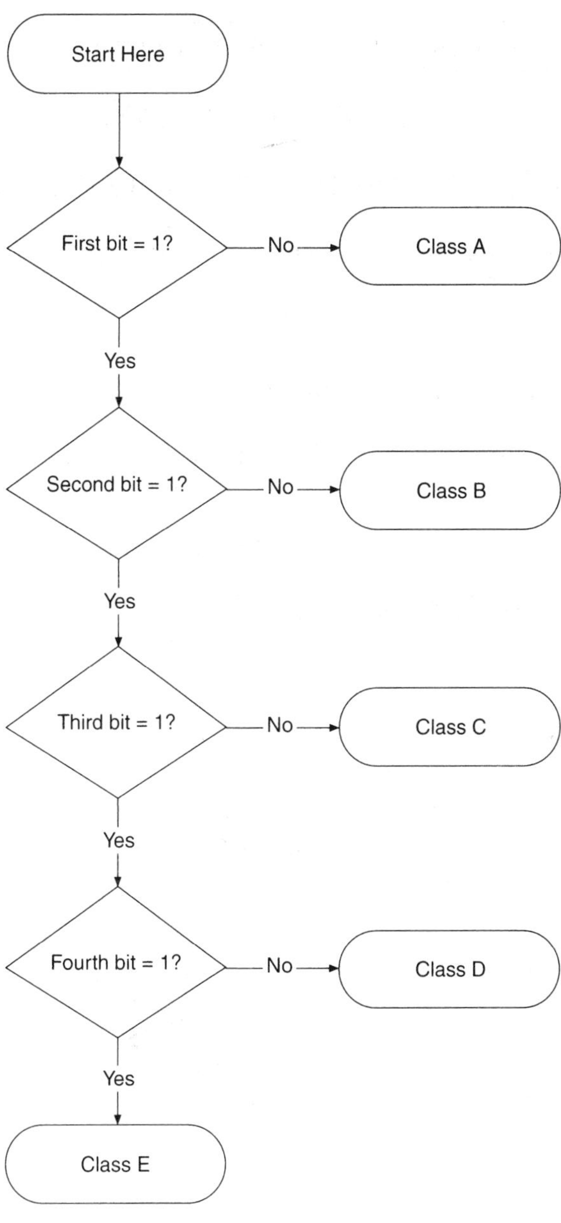

Illustration 2-2 IP Address Class Determination Chart

As previously discussed, the class of an IP address is one mechanism used to determine the split between the number of bits used for the network portion and the host portion of an IP address. The following sections discuss each of the IP address classes and the network/host split that each classification implies.

Class A

A Class A IP address has a 0 in the most significant bit position. If the high-order octet of the IP address has a 0 for its most significant bit, it is a Class A IP address no matter what the value of any other octet in the address. This could be represented graphically as

0xxxxxxxxxxxxxxxxxxxxxxxxxxxxxxx

where x = "don't care."

If all the bits marked as "don't care" were set to 0 and the IP address were converted to dotted decimal notation, the IP address would be 0.0.0.0. If all the bits marked as "don't care" were set to 1 and converted to dotted decimal notation, the IP address would be 127.255.255.255. Without applying any special rules (which we eventually will), it can be seen that Class A IP addresses will invariably fall in the range 0.0.0.0 to 127.255.255.255, inclusive.

You were forewarned that the class of an IP address dictates a minimum number of bits allocated to the network portion. In fact, a Class A IP address reserves the entire first octet for use as the network portion. Since any bits not used explicitly for the network portion are used for the host portion of the IP address, the three low-order octets of a Class A IP address are available as host addresses.

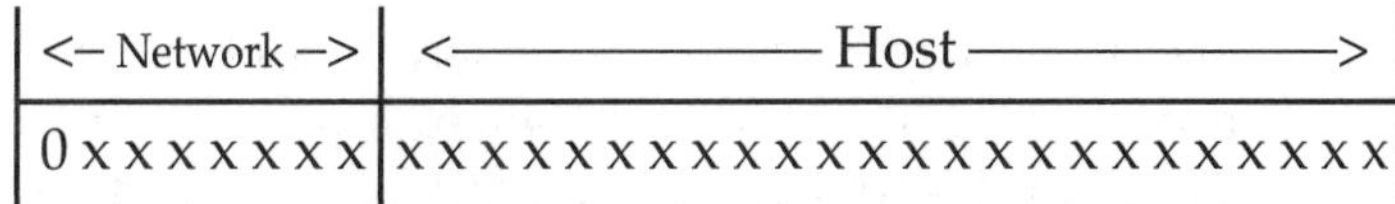

The implication is that there are 128 Class A networks (0 to 127). Each Class A network can have 16,777,216 (2^{24}) unique host identifiers! There will be special cases that restrict the total number of hosts available. These will be discussed later; the objective for now is to form the foundation of understanding on which IP addresses are derived.

Class B

A Class B IP address has a "10" in the two most significant bit positions. This could be represented graphically as

10xxxxxxxxxxxxxxxxxxxxxxxxxxxxxx

where x = "don't care."

If all the bits marked as "don't care" were set to 0 and the IP address were converted to dotted decimal notation, the IP address would be 128.0.0.0. If all the bits marked as "don't care" were set to 1 and converted to dotted decimal notation, the IP address would be 191.255.255.255. It can be seen that Class B IP addresses will fall in the range 128.0.0.0 to 191.255.255.255, inclusive.

A Class B IP address reserves the entire two high-order octets for use as the network portion. Since any bits not used explicitly for the network portion are used for the host portion of the IP address, the two low-order octets of a Class B IP address are available as host addresses.

As a result, there are 16,384 Class B networks (128.0 to 191.255). Each Class B network can have a possible 65,536 (2^{16}) unique host identifiers, assuming that we are not applying any special rules yet.

<—— Network ——>	<—— Host ——>
10xxxxxx xxxxxxxx	xxxxxxxx xxxxxxxx

Class C

A Class C IP address has a "110" in the three most significant bit positions. This could be represented graphically as

110xxxxxxxxxxxxxxxxxxxxxxxxxxxxx

where x = "don't care."

If all the bits marked as "don't care" were set to 0 and the IP address were converted to dotted decimal notation, the IP address would be 192.0.0.0. If all the bits marked as "don't care" were set to 1 and converted to dotted decimal notation, the IP address would be 223.255.255.255. It can be seen that Class C IP addresses will fall in the range 192.0.0.0 to 223.255.255.255, inclusive.

A Class C IP address reserves the entire three high-order octets for use as the network portion. Since any bits not used explicitly for the network portion are used for the host portion of the IP address, only the low-order octet of a Class C IP address is available for host addresses.

<—— Network ——>	<— Host —>
110xxxxxxxxxxxxxxxxxxxxx	xxxxxxxx

As a result, there are 2,097,152 Class C networks (192.0.0 to 223.255.255)! Each Class C network can have a possible 256 (2^8) unique host identifiers, assuming that we are not applying any special rules.

Class D

A Class D IP address is defined as an IP address that has a "1110" in the four most significant bit positions. This could be represented graphically as

1 1 1 0 x x x x x x x x x x x x x x x x x x x x x x x x x x x x

where x = "don't care."

If all the bits marked as "don't care" were set to 0 and the IP address were converted to dotted decimal notation, the IP address would be 224.0.0.0. If all the bits marked as "don't care" were set to 1 and converted to dotted decimal notation, the IP address would be 239.255.255.255. It can be seen that Class D IP addresses will fall in the range 224.0.0.0 to 239.255.255.255, inclusive.

Class D IP addresses differ from Classes A, B, and C IP addresses. Class D addresses are reserved for multicast group usage. There is no relevance to network and host portions in multicast operations. Multicast will be discussed in more detail in a later chapter. For now, let's simply state that one or more hosts can belong to a group, by assignment or by joining, and can share data with all members of that group through the use of a single Class D IP address. There is a potential for having 268,435,456 unique multicast groups!

Class E

A Class E IP address has a "1111" in the four most significant bit positions. This could be represented graphically as

1111xxxxxxxxxxxxxxxxxxxxxxxxxxxx

where x = "don't care."

If all the bits marked as "don't care" were set to 0 and the IP address were converted to dotted decimal notation, the IP address would be 240.0.0.0. If all the bits marked as "don't care" were set to 1 and converted to dotted decimal notation, the IP address would be 255.255.255.255. It can be seen that Class E IP addresses will fall in the range 240.0.0.0 to 255.255.255.255, inclusive. You will soon see, however, that the address of 255.255.255.255 has a special use.

Class E IP addresses are not available for general use. They have been reserved for future use.

Unicast Addresses

Classes A, B, and C, as defined previously, are used for unicast addresses. A *unicast address* is one that refers to a single source or destination. This is not to say that all destination addresses that you might find in an IP datagram are unicast addresses if they qualify as Class A, B, or C through examination of the first three bits. There are special-case addresses, as we will see, that would qualify as Class A, B, or C addresses under the strict rules cited earlier that would not be unicast addresses.

Subnetting

If there were no mechanism for being able to divide the IP address into network and host portions and if there were not a separate and distinct field in the IP header for the two functions, the address architecture would be flat; there would be no means by which an administrator could develop a hierarchical network. In fact, this would be almost no different from the architecture that we would have at the link layer (hardware addresses), with the exception that we would be putting an additional layer of complexity into the protocol for the purpose of hiding the hardware implementations.

Luckily this is not the case; the three unicast classes of IP addresses provide some capability to develop hierarchical networks. We will see what is meant by a hierarchical topology in subsequent chapters. Unfortunately, the granularity of network-to-host divisions is not conducive to efficient use of IP address space. That is, relying solely on the class of the IP address to define the network portion would lead to a tremendous waste.

Take, for example, a fictitious midsized company with 400 computers (TCP/IP hosts). Three hundred of the hosts are at the company's central headquarters, and there are two satellite plants with 50 hosts apiece. Since we have determined to this point that a Class C network can have a possible 256 unique host numbers and this company's central site has 300 hosts, there are two options. Two Class C networks could be used at the central site and deal with the technical problems of having two separate logical networks on the same physical network, or a single Class B network could be used for the central site. Let's say that the Class B option was chosen by the network administrator because it would require less work to set up and maintain. The two remote sites are well served by having their own Class C network. Thus we have one Class B and two Class C networks used to internetwork three sites with a total of 400 sites among them.

	Available Space	**Used Space**
Class B	65,536 hosts	300 hosts
Class C	256 hosts	50 hosts
Class C	256 hosts	50 hosts
Total	66,048 hosts	400 hosts

Here is the math:

Utilization (%) = (used space/available space) $\times$ 100

Utilization (%) = (400 hosts/66,048 hosts) $\times$ 100 = .6%

Waste (%) = 100% $-$ .6% = 99.4%

Naturally I had the ability to define the numbers in this example to suit my purpose. Using only six-tenths of a percent of the available address space does seem like an awful waste. Even if the poor utilization is acceptable, the use of one Class B and two Class C networks would exaggerate the routing tables of the Internet if they were connected. The point, however contrived, is that without some other mechanism to enable us to optimize the use of the available host portion, the IP address would be entirely too inefficient to be effective, and routing tables would become too large and cumbersome.

Such a mechanism, called a *subnet,* was formalized in 1985 by J. Mogul and J. Postel in RFC 950, "Internet Standard Subnetting Procedure." This RFC discussed the difficulties that might be encountered when implementing this third level of hierarchy and further defines the "strongly recommended" method for subnetting. There are several factors beyond inefficiency and routing table growth that would motivate an organization to implement IP subnets. RFC 950 discusses these factors:

- *Different technologies:* Especially in a research environment, there may be more than one kind of LAN in use; e.g., an organization may have some equipment that supports Ethernet and some that supports a ring network.
- *Limits of technologies:* Most LAN technologies impose limits, based on electrical parameters, on the number of hosts connected and on the total length of the

cable. It is easy to exceed these limits, especially those on cable length.

- *Network congestion:* It is possible for a small subset of the hosts on a LAN to monopolize most of the bandwidth. A common solution to this problem is to divide the hosts into cliques of high mutual communication and to put these cliques on separate cables.
- *Point-to-point links:* Sometimes a "local area," such as a university campus, is split into two locations too far apart to connect using the preferred LAN technology. In this case high-speed point-to-point links might connect several LANs.

Point-to-point links have traditionally been one of the most wasteful uses for IP addressing. With a point-to-point link, there are exactly two hosts participating on the network. Even with the most restrictive subnet mask, there is a 50 percent waste of address space on this type of network. This will be explained in detail later. Some fairly recent developments have enabled the use of *unnumbered IP interfaces* on point-to-point networks. This also will be explained in detail later.

The addition of the subnet level of hierarchy to a network address, beyond the inherent class of the network, permits network administrators to more effectively utilize their address space. A single IP network, such as the Class A network 10.0.0.0, can be chopped up into smaller networks through the use of a subnet mask that delineates the structure of the subnet addressing used within the control of the local network administrator.

Subnet Masks

IP subnets are implemented by borrowing a portion of the local part of the IP address and extending the concepts used in defining the network portion. This is done with a *mask.* Masks were in use in other areas long before they were applied to data communications. For example, photographers use masks in their darkroom work. Whenever photographers have an image that is especially well suited for their needs but the background is inappropriate, they use a mask to isolate the subject they want to keep from the rest of the picture. For instance, Illustration 2-3 depicts the original photograph of a little girl.

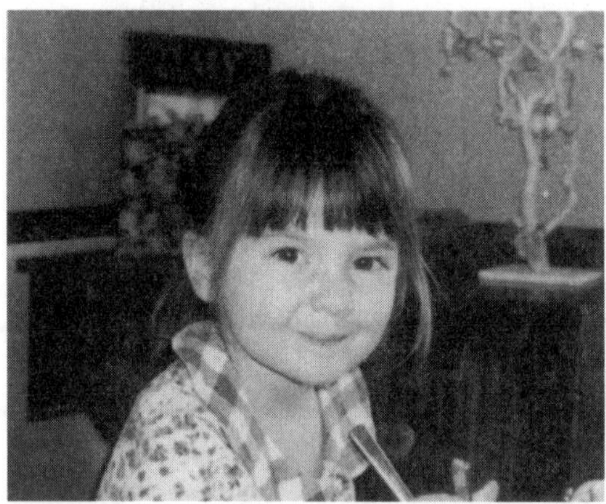

Illustration 2-3 Original Photograph

A photographer would create a mask that would be placed between the negative and the photographic paper on the enlarger. The mask is opaque where the image's background is to be filtered out and transparent where the foreground, the little girl, is to pass through to the photographic paper, as shown in Illustration 2-4. In this illustration, the black portion is opaque and the white portion is transparent. The result is an image of the little girl with the background removed; she has been effectively isolated from the other parts of the original photograph (Illustration 2-5).

Illustration 2-4 Image Mask

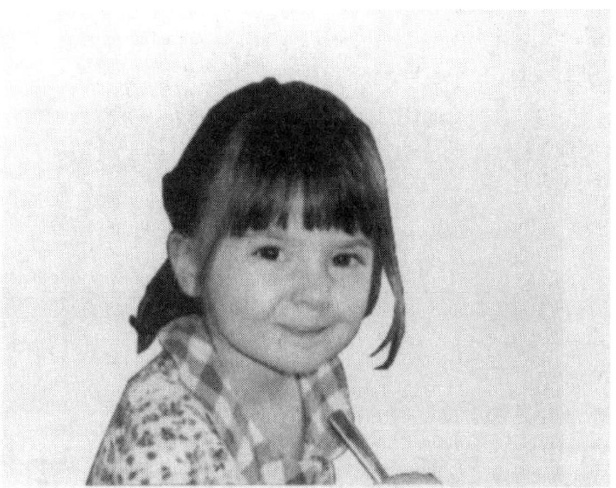

Illustration 2-5 Resulting Masked Photograph

Subnet masks work in essentially the same way. Let's start with the binary representation of the IP address 172.16.182.19:

10101100 00010000 10110110 00010011

Original IP Address

We can create a mask the same length as the address itself:

11111111 11111111 11111111 00000000

Network Mask

Think of the 1s portion as transparent and the 0s portion as opaque in the photograph analogy. Wherever there is a 1 in the network mask, the original IP address can "project" through. Wherever there is a 0 in the network mask, the original IP address is "filtered out." The resulting masked address is

10101100 00010000 10110110 00000000

Resulting Masked Address

Note that the leftmost three octets are the same as the original IP address but the fourth octet, where the mask was "00000000," has been altered.

Mask Mathematics

Now that the concept has been illustrated, let's dispose of the photograph analogy and look at the mask mathematically. Boolean algebra is the mathematical study of logic. It deals with "proofs" through the application of logic — algebraic operations on the values "true" and "false." The same mathematical principles used in Boolean algebra can be applied to binary numbers. In fact, these binary operations are the basis for all mathematics implemented in digital computing devices. Although that is way beyond the scope of this book, we should discuss a few operations to fully understand how masks are implemented.

The AND operator results in a TRUE if *and only if* the two operands (variables) are both TRUE. Thus the following statements are correct.

TRUE	AND	TRUE	=	TRUE
TRUE	AND	FALSE	=	FALSE
FALSE	AND	TRUE	=	FALSE
FALSE	AND	FALSE	=	FALSE

Assuming that a binary 1 is TRUE and a binary 0 is FALSE, the table would look like the following:

1	AND	1	=	1
1	AND	0	=	0
0	AND	1	=	0
0	AND	0	=	0

This can be represented with the following logic tables.

AND	TRUE	FALSE
TRUE	TRUE	FALSE
FALSE	FALSE	FALSE

OR

AND	1	0
1	1	1
0	0	0

The NOT operator is a unary operator. This means that it has only a single operand. The NOT operator always results in the logical opposite of the operand. Thus the following statements are correct.

NOT TRUE = FALSE

NOT FALSE = TRUE

Assuming that a binary 1 is TRUE and a binary 0 is FALSE, the table would look like the following.

NOT 1 = 0

NOT 0 = 1

This can be represented with the following logic tables.

NOT	
TRUE	FALSE
FALSE	TRUE

OR

NOT	
1	0
0	1

Those are the only two logical operators that you need to be acquainted with to understand the mask operation. The following is a piece of *metacode* that implements the mask operation.

For $n = 0$ to 31,

$$N_n = A_n \text{ AND } M_n$$

$$H_n = A_n \text{ AND } (\text{NOT } M_n)$$

next n

where
N_n is the n bit of the network identifier (network portion) after masking

H_n is the *n* bit of the host identifier (host portion) after masking
A_n is the *n* bit of the IP address before masking
M_n is the *n* bit of the network mask

Although the process is not normally performed in a loop, I have chosen to use a loop for ease of explanation. The metacode is explained as follows. A loop is executed 32 (0 to 31, inclusive) times, with the variable *n* being incremented at the completion of each iteration. The loop is executed 32 times due to the number of bits in the IP address. The variable *n* is representative of the bit position:

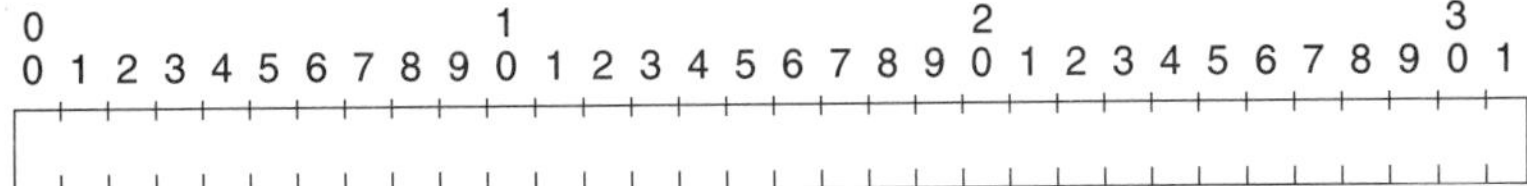

Each iteration of the loop sets a bit in both the network ID and the host ID. The network ID bit is set by performing a logical AND operation on the address bit (same position) and the mask bit. The host ID is a little more complicated. The mask bit must be inverted since we are now interested in letting the host portion through and filtering out the network portion. To invert the bit, the NOT operation is performed on the mask bit. Then an AND operation is performed on the result of the NOT operation and the address bit. The result is the host ID bit for that iteration of the loop. At the completion of 32 iterations of the loop, both the network ID and host ID are completely constructed and separated from each other as specified by the mask used.

Contiguous Mask Bits

RFC 950 specified that since subnets were described through the use of a mask, there was nothing to prevent anybody from setting up a specialized subnet procedure, such as the use of the low-order bits in the local portion of the address or every other bit of the local portion. It was recommended that the subnet mask be derived from the high-order bits of the local portion and that the bits be contiguous, but still it was only a recommendation.

Even though masks constructed from noncontiguous and non-high-order bits were allowed, I don't know of any hardware vendor that permitted such a configuration. I am sure that some did — I just don't know who they are. However, common practice was to subnet using the high-order bits of the host portion of the address. Subnetting in a manner other than that was foolish, and no serious networking professional that I know of would consider it. A pragmatic reason for not doing so is that most vendors do not permit anything but contiguous, high-order bits in the subnet mask. In fact, every vendor that I currently know of has this restriction. I used to hold it against them that they should be so brazen as to neglect the possibility of noncontiguous bits. Someplace along the way, I got a bit wiser and took the attitude of "So what? Why should they cater to the absurd?" I would be happy to rescind those thoughts if someone would give me a strong illustration of why anything other than contiguous, high-order subnet masks should be permitted.

Things have been revised with respect to this, anyway. It is now a requirement that if you are going to use subnets, the mask should be contiguous and occupy the high-order bits of the local address portion.

Subnet Terminology

There are some specific ways to refer to addresses and masks throughout the industry. Some are defined in RFCs, and others have become *de facto* standard terms. This section introduces you to some of what is used in the industry and in this text.

- Class A Mask — 255.0.0.0: The mask that would be used to describe a Class A network without subnetting.
- Class B Mask — 255.255.0.0.
- Class C Mask — 255.255.255.0.
- *n-bit network mask:* The high-order *n* bits of the mask are set to 1. For instance, using a "24-bit network mask" means that the mask is 255.255.255.0.
- *n-bit subnet mask:* The mask that uses the high-order *n* bits of the local address portion. You must know the class of the IP network for the statement "I use a 10-bit subnet mask" to be meaningful.

Consider the following examples:

10.1.1.254 with a 16-bit subnet mask	Mask = 255.255.255.0
172.16.182.19 with a 10-bit subnet mask	Mask = 255.255.255.192
Class C with a 6-bit subnet mask	Mask = 255.255.255.252

- *n-host bits:* Only the low-order *n* bits are not used for the mask. For instance, someone who has "4 host bits" is using a mask of 255.255.255.240.
- */n:* A written notation with the same meaning as "*n*-bit network mask." For instance, the notation "172.18.250.3/24" is the same as saying "24-bit network mask" and means that the mask is 255.255.255.0. This is often called CIDR notation (discussed later).

- *Network mask:* All the bits used for masking the IP address.
- *Subnet mask:* Only the mask bits below the natural network mask. For instance, if I had a Class B address and a network mask of 255.255.255.192, the subnet mask would be the low-order 10 bits of the network mask, or 0.0.255.192.
- *Natural, or inherent network, mask:* The mask that would be used to describe an address without subnetting. The mask that is defined by the class of the address.
- *Network ID:* The result of an AND operation of the network mask with an IP address.
- *Subnet ID:* The result of an AND operation of the subnet mask with an IP address.
- *Subnet Prefix* (also called Prefix): All addressing bits defined by the subnet mask bits. Refers to an IP subnet or to a collection of IP subnets. This term is used extensively in IPv6 discussions.
- *Host ID:* The result of a NOT operation of the network mask, then an AND operation of the prior result with an IP address. Please see the "Mask Mathematics" section to clarify this awkward and terse explanation.

Of the many ways to refer to subnets, the most accurate is to specify how many bits are in the network mask. Many people use the "*n*-bit subnet mask" terminology, but this is falling out of favor. The force behind this change is classless interdomain routing (CIDR), which is a short-term strategy for the depletion of Internet address space. CIDR is discussed in Chapter 7.

Regardless of what the complete mask might be, a single octet within the mask might have from 0 to 8 bits used for a part of that entire mask. Table 2-1 should help you get acquainted with the octet numbering for cases in which only part of the octet is used for mask bits. Remember, only the high-order bits of the octet will be used for the mask.

Graphical Depiction	Number of Masking Bits in Octet	Decimal Value
00000000	0	0
10000000	1	128
11000000	2	192
11100000	3	224
11110000	4	240
11111000	5	248
11111100	6	252
11111110	7	254
11111111	8	255

Table 2-1 Octet Numbering When Portion Used for Mask Bits

Special-Case Addresses

The previous discussions of individual classes of addresses commonly had some sort of disclaimer, such as "This is assuming that we are not applying any special rules yet that might restrict the total." In writing this book, I had to make a decision: I could be like most people and tell you the final result — jump to the bottom line — or I could show you. I chose to show you. The result of showing is that there are some intermediate steps where there are inaccuracies. When I said that a Class C address had address space to support 256 unique hosts, that was correct because an 8-bit number can have 256 unique values and that particular 8-bit number is used for host IDs. It was also incorrect, due to some special cases that cannot be counted as available host IDs. I am now going to make it correct.

A 0 in any of the octet fields of an IP address means that the octet contains all 0 bits. A "−1" in any field means that the field contains all 1 bits. The general meaning of all 1s is "all" and is used in broadcasts. Any IP address that has a field of all 1s can legally be used only as a destination IP address. The general meaning of all 0s is "this" and is often used when a host is uncertain of its IP address and needs to be informed of all or part of it. An IP address that has a field of all 0s can legally be used only as a source IP address.

The following are special-case IP addresses:

- {Network ID = 0, Host ID = 0}: This host on this network. In the BOOTP process a host that does not yet know its IP address will send out a BOOTP request and use an IP address of all 0s for its source. Example: IP address = 0.0.0.0 (mask is irrelevant)
- {Network ID = 0, <Host-number>}: Specified host on this network. Can be used only as a source address.

Potentially used in the BOOTP process. Example: IP address = 0.0.0.5/24 = "host #5 on this network"

- {Network ID = –1, Host ID = –1}: Limited broadcast. Can be used only as a destination address. The IP datagram that has a destination IP address of all 1s is sent as a broadcast to all hosts on the same physical media as the originator of the limited broadcast datagram. The packet should not be forwarded by any host. Example: IP address = 255.255.255.255 (mask is irrelevant)
- {<Network-number>, Host ID = –1}: Directed broadcast to specified network. Also used only as a destination address. The datagram that has this as a destination address should be forwarded to the specified network number and then broadcast to all hosts on that network. Example: IP address = 192.168.1.255/24 = "all hosts on network 192.168.1.0"
- {<Network-number>, <Subnet-number>, Host ID = –1}: Directed broadcast to specified subnet. Can be used only as a destination address. The datagram that has this as a destination address should be forwarded to the specified subnet and then broadcast to each host on that subnet. Example: IP address = 10.1.1.255/24 = "all hosts on subnet 10.1.1.0 of the 10.0.0.0 network"
- {<Network-number>, Subnet ID = –1, Host ID = –1}: Directed broadcast to all subnets of a specified subnetted network. Can be used only as a destination address. The intent was to provide a mechanism for broadcasting on all subnets of the specified network. RFC 1812, "Requirements for IPv4 Routers," reports that this broadcast feature was "broken" and of limited utility. It is being recommended for future omission. Example: IP address = 10.255.255.255 = "all hosts on all subnets of the 10.0.0.0 network"

- {Network ID = 127, Host ID = <any>}: Internal host loopback address. A packet with an IP address that has a 127 in its first octet should never be seen outside of the host (on the network). It is used primarily when a service resides on the same host that the client is on. In general, the standard loopback address used on a host is 127.0.0.1.

IP Addressing Revisited

Now that the special-case IP addresses have been covered, let's discuss the limitations that are imposed on the IP addressing as a result of the special cases.

- *A Host ID of all 1s:* This special case is used for broadcasts. It reduces the number of available hosts in a subnet by 1.
- *A Host ID of all 0s:* This special case is used for "this host." It also reduces the number of available hosts in a subnet by 1.
- *A Network ID of all 1s:* This special case is used by broadcasts. This reduces the address space available to the Class E addresses. Little current impact.
- *A Network ID of all 0s:* This special case is used for "this network." Because the prefix technically falls into the Class A space, it reduces the number of Class A networks by 1.
- *A Network ID of 127:* This special case is used for the loopback interface. Since the network 127.0.0.0 falls into Class A address space, this reduces the number of Class A networks by 1.

- *A Subnet ID of all 1s:* This special case is used for subnet broadcasts. It reduces the number of subnets by 1. Since it was "broken" and is being omitted in the future, there eventually will be no impact to subnet numbering. Some vendors still prevent a subnet with an ID of all 1s from being used as a valid network. Eventually this feature will converge, and everyone will permit the use of all subnets. Test the waters, but be wary of interoperability.

The Straight Skinny of IP Address Space: A Summary

Now that we have applied the special cases to our previously "perfect" world, let's go to the bottom line. How much host space do we really have?

- *Class A addresses:* There are 126 Class A networks possible. Remember that 0 and 127 are taken away by the special-case addresses. In a Class A network, there is room for a maximum of 16,777,214 hosts; we lost two hosts due to special-case addresses.
- *Class B addresses:* There are 16,384 Class B networks (128.0 to 191.255). No Class B addresses were lost due to special-case addresses. Each Class B network can have a possible 65,534 hosts. Two lost.
- *Class C addresses:* There are 2,097,152 Class C networks (192.0.0 to 223.255.255). No Class C networks were lost. Each Class C network can have a possible 254 unique host identifiers. Two lost.
- *Subnets:* Whenever subnetting is used, you may or may not lose one or two of the subnet IDs due to the

all-1s case and the all-0s case. The all-0s case was not specified as a special case in the list just reviewed; however, RFC 950 extended the use of the all-0s "this" to the concept of subnets. I am not certain whether it was ever used; but its relevance has since been dropped from the special-case addresses, if it ever was used. The point is that if you want to use the all 1s or all 0s subnet, you will have to verify the correct operation and interoperability of all equipment in the intranet. Further, the implication of all this is that the minimum number of subnet bits (other than 0) that can be used is either 1 or 2. You may use a 1-bit subnet mask (e.g., 172.16.0.0 255.255.128.0) if you verify that everything functions normally with an all-1s and all-0s subnet ID. Otherwise, you will have to use 2 bits to support two subnets since the all-1s and all-0s would not be available.

- *Hosts:* You will always lose two host IDs per subnet. The minimum number of host bits that you can use is two. You would lose the all-1s and all-0s host ID (11 and 00), and you would have two host IDs for use (10 and 01). The bottom line is that the smaller the number of host bits (i.e., the larger the subnet mask), the greater the impact a loss of two host IDs per network will have.

Practice Questions

1. For the following IP addresses, identify the inherent network mask.

Address	Mask
150.1.1.1	____________
1.1.1.1	____________

Address	Mask
200.1.1.1	________
128.0.0.1	________
224.1.1.1	________

2. Assuming a Class A address, provide the mask that provides the requirement most optimally for each host quantity listed. For example, if I needed 20 hosts, I would use a netmask of 255.255.255.224. This netmask accommodates 30 hosts. The next-lower subnet accommodates only 14 hosts, which is clearly not enough.

Quantity of Hosts	Mask
140	________
61,325	________
2	________
300	________
1200	________

3. What mask would you use if you wanted to divide a Class B address into 64 equal-size subnets?
4. What mask would you use if you wanted to divide a Class B address into 250 networks of 32 hosts per network?
5. How many usable addresses are available in the 10.1.1.128/26 subnet?
6. How many Class C networks are there? Approximately how much of the total IPv4 address space do Class C addresses account for?

chapter

3

Network Devices

In this chapter we begin to build an essential base of knowledge that will eventually assist you in the process of designing an efficient IP address scheme. Specifically, this chapter will introduce you to devices that you might find on a TCP/IP network. The devices are defined categorically by function, with a few references to manufacturers for illustrative purposes only. This book does not endorse any particular manufacturer.

Hosts

In TCP/IP, a *host* is basically any device that has an IP address on the network. Traditionally, a host is thought of as a central general-purpose computer; a mainframe like an IBM 3090 is a host. Put those notions aside. In TCP/IP almost *everything* is a host. If it has an IP address, it is a host. There are special types of hosts, such as a *router* or a TCP/IP to "something" *gateway.* These will be discussed in this chapter. Another type of host, called a *multihomed host,* has more than one IP address defined on it.

For the most part — in this book, anyway — a reference to a host is a reference to a general-purpose computer, such as a user's workstation. The next sections will define some other devices, most of them special-purpose computers, that can be found in TCP/IP networks.

A Reference Model

The ISO (International Organization for Standardization) defined an Open System Interconnection (OSI) reference model on which it would develop a set of protocols, commonly known as the OSI protocols. These protocols have not been generally well accepted or implemented, for reasons well beyond the scope of this book. The reference model has endured and is often used in discussions that deal with layered protocols. Illustration 3-1 shows what the OSI reference model looks like.

OSI Reference Model	TCP/IP Protocol Layers
Application	Application
Presentation	
Session	
Transport	Transport
Network	Network
Link	Link
Physical	Physical

Illustration 3-1 Comparison of OSI and TCP/IP Protocol Layers

Some layers of the OSI reference model function almost identically to the layers of TCP/IP. Even though small differences exist in the functions provided by the layers, let's generalize that the physical layer (layer 1) through the transport layer (layer 4) of the OSI model are enough like the TCP/IP model that we can say we have discussed them already (in Chapter 1) and they do not warrant much further discussion at this time. For the sake of continuity, however, here is a summary:

- *Physical layer (layer 1):* The physical network medium. Unshielded twisted pair (UTP), coaxial cable, optical fiber, and radio frequency are examples.
- *Link layer (layer 2):* The protocol standards for interfacing with the physical network medium. Ethernet, IEEE 802.3, Token Ring, PPP, and Frame Relay are examples.
- *Network layer (layer 3):* The protocols for establishing end-to-end routing. IP, ICMP, and IGMP are examples.
- *Transport layer (layer 4):* The protocols for end-to-end transport of data with a given level of service (reliable or unreliable). TCP and UDP are examples.
- *Session layer (layer 5):* The protocols for maintenance of end-to-end sessions.
- *Presentation layer (layer 6):* The protocols used for conversion of data from one format to another, such as from ASCII to EBCDIC.
- *Application layer (layer 7):* The user applications.

Of course, the big difference is that TCP/IP stops at the transport layer. Anything above the transport layer in TCP/IP is considered to be the application layer. The session and presentation layer functions are built into the applications if they require the use of the function. An example of this is the TN3270 (Telnet-3270) application, which allows a user of a TCP/IP workstation to establish a terminal session with an IBM 3270–based system. On the surface that does not sound too bad, but the TN3270 application has to be able to convert from ASCII, which the TCP/IP workstation uses, to EBCDIC, which the 3270 terminal requires. In the OSI protocol, the application would be oblivious to the two different character sets since the conversion would be handled at the OSI presentation layer.

Repeaters

The physical networks typically have some sort of electrical or optical limitation associated with them that generally will translate into a distance limitation. For instance, a station on one end of a coaxial cable would be able to communicate effectively with a station on the remote end under normal conditions only if the cable were a certain length or less. Ethernets and Token Rings are subject to limitations like this. To overcome some of these limitations, we use a special type of amplifier, known as a *repeater,* to boost the signal and to get additional distance on the physical medium. See Illustration 3-2.

In the OSI reference models, a repeater works only at layer 1 — the physical layer. There is no concern for hardware addresses; in fact, a repeater has no hardware address. The signal may simply be amplified or, if it is a digital signal, regenerated. A repeater can be used only to a join two networks with the same physical characteristics, i.e., both are 10base2 CSMA/CD networks.

Illustration 3-2 Network with Repeater

Bridges

Sometimes when the network will not need to be made to handle greater distances, but additional devices cannot be added because the specification for the maximum number of devices per segment is on the verge of being exceeded, a *bridge* can be useful. Bridges operate at layer 2, the link layer, of the OSI reference model. As a layer 2 device a bridge receives a frame and checks for the hardware address in the "forwarding database" to determine whether the destination of the frame is on the physical network that the bridge received it from or whether it has knowledge of an interface that it should send it out of. Bridges typically are used to join two networks of the same type; however, there are bridges that can join an Ethernet and a Token Ring at the link layer. These bridges are known as *translational bridges,* since they have the ability to convert the byte ordering of the Token Ring hardware address to that of Ethernet and vice versa.

Bridges are also useful in applications other than when the physical network is on the verge of exceeding its connection capacity. For example, bridges can be used to segment "high talkers and listeners" — transmit and receive station pairs — into cliques. The traffic would be passed to the other network only if the bridge detected that the destination was not local. Bridges are also one of the few networking choices for traffic that cannot be routed. Examples of nonroutable traffic are Netbios, Netbeui, and DEC LAT. There are tricks to handling these, such as tunneling of the traffic in a routable protocol, but these protocols are more often bridged.

Bridges may have an IP address associated with them, typically for management purposes. The Simple Network Management Protocol (SNMP) requires a device to have an IP address to be able to poll it for status or, at the least, "alive" status through PING (Packet Internet Groper) functionality.

TCP/IP traffic can be bridged; it does not have to be routed. If TCP/IP is being bridged throughout an organization, the IP addressing would be set up as if it were a single IP network (no need to subnet), with all hosts in the enterprise being homed to that one network. Bridges would have only a single IP address associated with them since its only purpose would be for management.

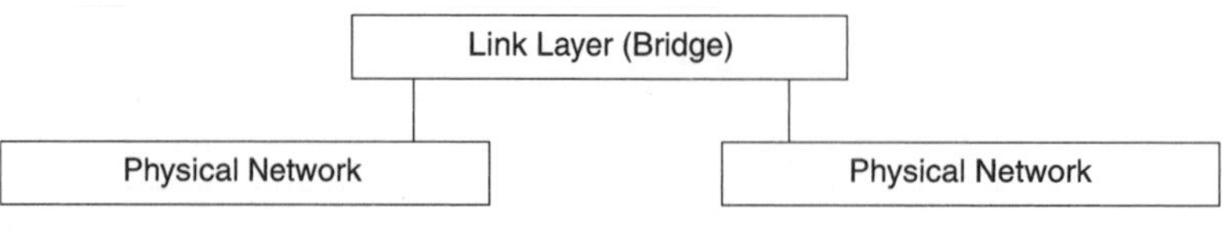

Illustration 3-3 Network with Local Bridge

Bridges may be implemented so that they span a wide area network (WAN) link. The bridge in Illustration 3-3 is termed a *local bridge.* A bridge used to interconnect two networks over a WAN link is called a *remote bridge* and must be implemented in pairs. See Illustration 3-4.

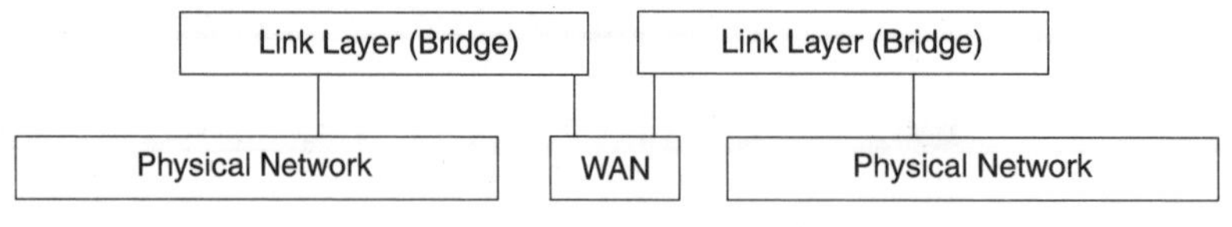

Illustration 3-4 Network with Remote Bridges

Bridges do have shortcomings, including the following.

- The forwarding decisions are not very sophisticated. In the absence of an entry in its forwarding database for the destination hardware address of the packet it has received, a bridge will forward the packet onto all connected interfaces except the one it received the packet from.

- Loops cannot exist in a bridged network. A protocol called Spanning Tree must be run on the bridges if there is any possibility that loops exist. The Spanning Tree Protocol does not require much background traffic to support it, but it can take more than just a few seconds before the network can converge after a link failure.
- Broadcast traffic is sent throughout the network. Any time a link layer broadcast is sent from a station, it must traverse the entire network. In a large network, broadcast traffic can be significant.
- Bridges normally are used only to join networks that are of the same type. The exception is the translational bridge.

Routers

If a protocol has an address at the network layer (layer 3), it is a candidate for routing. Some of the protocols that can be routed include TCP/IP, Novell IPX, DECnet, and AppleTalk. Routers, although they have their own inherent shortcomings, have some advantages over bridges.

- The forwarding decisions that a router makes can be extremely sophisticated or fairly simplistic. The decision belongs to the network designers and implementers. The basis for the decisions will be covered in the next chapter.
- In a routed network, loops are not only permitted but encouraged. In a bridged network, loops have to be "broken" so that traffic is not passed over redundant links. The routing protocol in a routed network determines how traffic should be forwarded. Routing

loops can occur, and they can be detrimental to the health of the network. However, safeguards such as split horizon and "count to infinity" reduce the likelihood that routing loops will occur and lessen their impact when they do occur.

- Link layer broadcast traffic is not forwarded across a router. Most broadcasts at the network layer are also not forwarded. The all-1s destination IP address is known as a limited broadcast and is kept local to the network on which it is originated. In a bridged IP network, these broadcasts would be forwarded across the bridge.
- Disparate network types can be joined using routers. Any network on which TCP/IP can be run can be joined with another network running TCP/IP through the use of bridges. Typical examples would be Token Ring, Ethernet, and serial networks.

Illustration 3-5 shows a routed network. Unlike bridges, which would typically have only one IP address per physical device for administration purposes only, a router by definition must have at least two IP addresses. This makes a router a special instance of a multihomed host. In fact, a router must have an IP address for each logical TCP/IP network that it wishes to participate in and route data between. There are cases in which a router would have many IP addresses on a single physical port. More on that in Chapter 5. Illustration 3-5 would require at least two IP addresses to be defined on the router, one for each network.

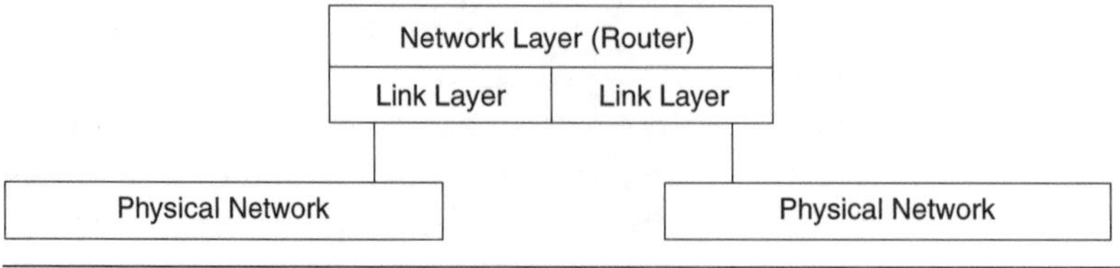

Illustration 3-5 Network with Local Router

Routers can also span a wide area network (WAN), as shown in Illustration 3-6. The illustration depicts two routers, each with a local network, being spanned with a WAN link. Sometimes the WAN link between the two routers does not require an IP address on the routers' ports. However, a worse case is being shown in Illustration 3-6, where there are three TCP/IP networks: The local network on the far left is being joined to the local network on the far right over a WAN link that is also running TCP/IP. The general case is that both routers would have different host numbers but would have identical network/subnet numbers on the link that joins them (the WAN). Therefore, there are three IP networks being shown; only the WAN is common to both routers.

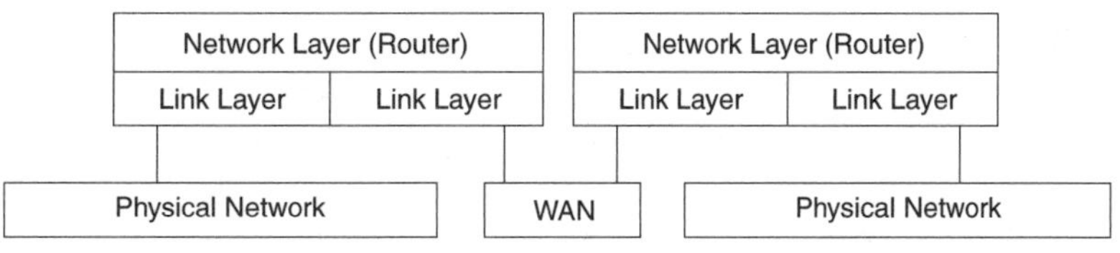

Illustration 3-6 Network with WAN Router

Gateways

Repeaters, bridges, and routers have an increasing level of sophistication and provide a higher degree of network packet-forwarding sophistication with each jump. Repeaters work at layer 1, the physical layer; bridges work at layer 2, the link layer; and routers work at layer 3, the network layer. Another type of device that might be found in a network is known as a *gateway*. In a somewhat obsolete usage, routers were called gateways in the earlier days of the Internet. Nowadays a gateway has come to be known as a device that operates at layers above the network layer, layers 4 through 7 in the OSI reference model. Gateways perform some level of translation, usually protocol translation, such as TCP/IP to IBM SNA.

Network Address Translation relies on Application Level Gateways (ALG) to perform address translation inside of the IP packet's payload. (See the section on Network Address Translation in Chapter 8 for more information on ALGs.) There is no need for a discussion of gateways in this book beyond this cursory clarification of the term.

Network Management Systems

Most networks have a computer system that serves a special purpose. This *network management system* (NMS) monitors the health of the connected network devices. Network management systems can be implemented on any operating system but are commonly found on UNIX, DOS, Windows, and OS/2. Apple Macintosh versions can be found as well. Network management functions can be implemented in custom-developed software or in off-the-shelf software. Prices range from a few hundred dollars to hundreds of thousands of dollars.

In a TCP/IP environment network management is most often implemented through the Simple Network Management Protocol (SNMP). TCP/IP network devices that support SNMP include an SNMP agent in the software. This SNMP agent "listens" for requests on UDP port 161. These requests ask for information about the network device. The device answers with an SNMP reply and includes information about the requested piece of information. SNMP devices may also be able to send SNMP *traps* to the network management station. Traps provide the NMS with unsolicited status about the device, such as "link down, interface 1."

SNMP network management systems are very useful in the monitoring of a network and the determination that a network problem exists. They have the ability to plot trends, such as packets or octets, through an interface over time. They are also useful for providing a graphical view of the network and connectivity.

Network Analyzers

Network management systems aid in the determination that a problem exists in a network. They work well for identifying failed hardware components or network circuits, but they often do little for isolating protocol problems. This is the domain of the *network analyzers,* also called protocol analyzers. Like network management systems, these analyzers are implemented on a variety of platforms under a variety of operating systems. They are commonly stand-alone devices, usually portable, but can be simple software that can make a normal PC listen passively to a network and record the packets. Network analyzers can provide information on all layers of all protocols or can be used exclusively for certain layers and specific protocols.

Once the packets have been captured, and sometimes during the capture, they can be decoded to provide a human-readable interpretation of the contents of the packets. Some analyzers have the ability to "suggest" the nature of network problems through software called an *inference engine.* This is a rule-based system that suggests, or infers, a condition, based on the satisfaction of rules in a knowledge database.

A *remote monitor* (RMON) is special type of network analyzer used in conjunction with a network management system. An RMON can be a stand-alone piece of equipment typically placed at strategic points in a network and generally left there.

It can also be implemented in network devices, such as routers. An RMON is specifically designed to allow an NMS to set up packet captures and decodes, as well as some other network analyzer functions.

A point of clarification: Network analyzers generally do not actively participate, protocol-wise, in any way on the network that is being monitored. There are exceptions to this, such as the Distributed Sniffer System by Network Associates, which uses TCP/IP to transport testing information to a central control console. RMON devices must use TCP/IP, typically on the same network as is being monitored, for the transport of the testing information to a network management system. Note that I was careful to say that network analyzers do not generally participate in the *protocols* of the network; they *do* participate in the network electrically. I have seen cases in which network WAN problems have cleared up as a result of the insertion of the analyzer in the circuit!

Summary

This chapter provided a brief introduction to the layered protocols of the OSI reference model and correlated the layers of TCP/IP to the model. This chapter also introduced the network devices that can be found in a network and illustrated the utility of each of the devices through the OSI reference model.

An important definition discussed in this chapter is the TCP/IP host. From TCP/IP's perspective a host is any device that has a IP address assigned to it. A special type of host that has more than one IP address associated with it is the multihomed host.

As far as the contents of this book are concerned, the most important device discussed is the router. The router makes packet-forwarding decisions, based on the destination IP address found in a TCP/IP packet, or specifically, the IP datagram. The router is said to work at layer 3, the network layer. A router must have at least two IP addresses defined on it. A physical port on a router may have more than one IP address bound to it.

Other device types, such as the repeater, bridge, and gateway, were also discussed. The intent was to provide a better understanding of the router with a discussion of the other devices and the function within the OSI reference model.

Other types of devices can be found in a TCP/IP network. Some are used specifically for the transmission of the data at the physical layer. These include modems, CSU/DSUs, transceivers, and line drivers, which mostly relate only to local networking media and do not directly affect IP internetworking. Others are specific implementations of repeaters, bridges, and routers, such as wiring hubs, Token Ring media access units (MAUs), and Layer 2 and Layer 3 Ethernet switches. These devices are for the most part commonplace. New variations are being introduced continually. To get more information on the wealth of network devices that are available, contact a reputable networking reseller.

Practice Questions

1. What layer does an Ethernet router use to make forwarding decisions?
2. What layer does a 10base2 repeater use to make forwarding decisions?
3. What layer does a Token Ring bridge use to make forwarding decisions?
4. What type of a device can bridge a Token Ring LAN with an Ethernet LAN?

chapter

4

Routing

In this chapter, we continue to build the base of knowledge begun in Chapter 3, which discussed network devices commonly found in a TCP/IP network. Although other devices were discussed, focus was given to bridges and routers. With a bridged TCP/IP network, all hosts are found on a single IP network, with each host having a unique host address on that network, as in Illustration 4-1. Take note that the bridge only has a single IP address: 192.168.1.1. This works fine for small networks with only a few sites, but since it is nonhierarchical, it presents serious scalability consequences. The optimal choice for all networks, big or small, is to route the TCP/IP traffic. This requires the network to be partitioned into multiple TCP/IP networks, with each host interface common to each TCP/IP network having a unique host address. See Illustration 4-2.

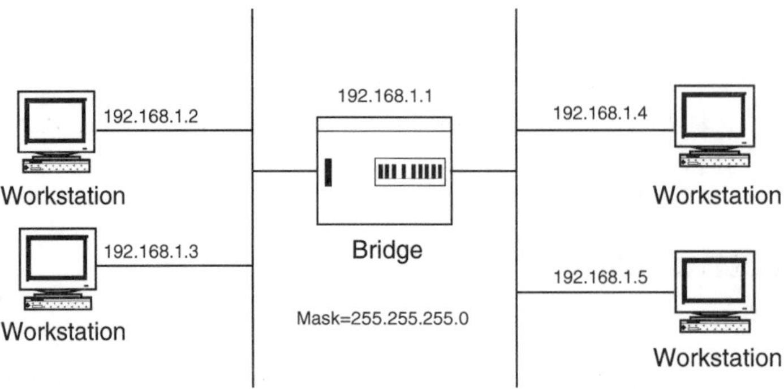

Illustration 4-1 Example of a Bridged Network

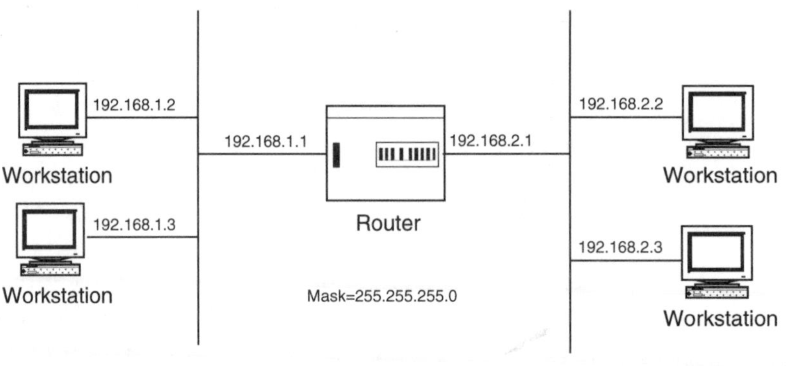

Illustration 4-2 Example of a Routed Network

In the routed network, two Class C networks — 192.168.1.0 and 192.168.2.0 — are being used. Note that the router has two IP addresses associated with it. The router is multihomed since it is connected to both of the networks. The router has the ability to take traffic off the network on the left and forward it to the network on the right (and vice versa), based on the destination address found in the IP datagram. The router makes this decision with the aid of a *route table,* also called a *forwarding information base* (FIB).

This chapter deals with the router's process of determining how a datagram should be forwarded. It is critical to understand this to develop an optimal address scheme.

The Route Table

The format for a route table varies with each manufacturer; however, the content is almost universal. I have included excerpts from two IP routers and one UNIX workstation in Tables 4-1, 4-2, and 4-3.

Destination	Route Mask	Next Hop	Port	Metr	Typ	Src	Age
0.0.0.0	0.0.0.0	172.16.3.65	J3.1	1	REM	MGMT	0
172.16.3.0	255.255.255.192	172.16.3.1	J5	0	DIR	LOC	72177
172.16.3.64	255.255.255.192	172.16.3.126	J3.1	0	DIR	LOC	68994
172.16.3.128	255.255.255.192	172.16.3.190	J1	0	DIR	LOC	72184
172.16.3.192	255.255.255.192	172.16.3.254	J1	0	DIR	LOC	72184
172.16.4.0	255.255.255.192	172.16.3.4	J5	115	REM	OSPF	29766
172.16.4.64	255.255.255.192	172.16.3.4	J5	90	REM	OSPF	13662
172.16.4.128	255.255.255.192	172.16.3.4	J5	100	REM	OSPF	29766
172.16.6.64	255.255.255.192	172.16.3.65	J3.1	576	REM	OSPF	17268
172.16.8.0	255.255.255.192	172.16.3.65	J3.1	90	REM	OSPF	68985
172.16.8.64	255.255.255.192	172.16.3.65	J3.1	130	REM	OSPF	13662
172.16.8.128	255.255.255.192	172.16.3.65	J3.1	75	REM	OSPF	68985
172.16.25.0	255.255.255.192	172.16.3.62	J5	50	REM	OSPF	71289
172.16.25.128	255.255.255.192	172.16.3.62	J5	35	REM	OSPF	71294
172.16.25.192	255.255.255.192	172.16.3.62	J5	35	REM	OSPF	71294

Table 4-1 Advanced Computer Communications Route Table

O	E2	172.16.3.0	255.255.255.0
		[110/2] via 172.17.253.30, 01:27:31, TokenRing0	
O		172.16.67.64	255.255.255.192
		[110/548] via 172.17.253.30, 01:27:31, TokenRing0	
O		172.16.65.64	255.255.255.192
		[110/548] via 172.17.253.30, 01:27:31, TokenRing0	
O	IA	172.16.71.64	255.255.255.192
		[110/142] via 172.17.253.30, 01:27:31, TokenRing0	
O	IA	172.16.4.0	255.255.255.192
		[110/257] via 172.17.253.30, 01:27:31, TokenRing0	
O	E2	172.16.8.0	255.255.255.0
		[110/2] via 172.17.253.30, 01:27:31, TokenRing0	
O	IA	172.16.8.0	255.255.255.192
		[110/102] via 172.17.253.30, 01:27:31, TokenRing0	

Table 4-2 Cisco Systems Route Table

Destination	Gateway	Genmask	Flags	Metric	Ref	Use	Iface
172.16.8.0	0.0.0.0	255.255.255.192	U	0	0	246846	eth0
127.0.0.0	0.0.0.0	255.0.0.0	U	0	0	163840	lo
0.0.0.0	172.16.8.1	0.0.0.0	UG	0	0	224692	eth0

Table 4-3 UNIX Route Table

Each of the route tables shown has a destination, a route mask, a next hop (gateway), a metric, and an interface (port) field. The routers also indicate the routing protocol that is the source of the routing entry and the age of the route. The UNIX route table provides some statistics on the number of packets that have traversed the route, as well as whether the route is direct (the destination IP network is directly defined on that workstation's interface) or indirect (the destination IP network must be reached through a router). Workstations may or may not have a route mask field. For the remainder of the book, I will illustrate my examples with route tables from Advanced Computer Communications (ACC) routers unless otherwise stated. The issue being illustrated will apply almost universally to all routers and most workstations.

Four general types of routes can be found in a route table:

- *Host routes:* A route to a specific host system. This type of route is most easily identified by a route mask of all 1s (255.255.255.255).
- *Hierarchical network prefix routes:* A route to a specific network. This type of route has a route mask with a length greater than or equal to 1 bit and less than or equal to 30 bits.
- *Default route:* A route to be used for any destination when a more specific route does not exist. This type of route has a destination and a route mask of all 0s (0.0.0.0). A route table may have multiple instances of a default route with different next hops or metrics.
- *Loopback route:* On a UNIX workstation this is the route defined and used by the loopback interface. A loopback route has a destination of 127.0.0.0 in the route table.

Let's revisit the ACC route table (Table 4-1) and discuss some of the specifics. The following is an explanation of each of the fields.

- *Destination:* The IP address of the destination network or host.

- *Route mask:* The mask that defines which bits of the destination IP address are significant in the route decision.
- *Next hop:* The IP address of a router that is the next hop to the destination network.
- *Port:* The physical port that the TCP/IP packet must be sent out of to reach the next hop router.
- *Metric:* A value assigned to the route to assist in determining the routing preferences.
- *Type:* A value that refers to the type of route. DIR = direct (the router is directly connected to the destination network), REM = remote (the destination is reachable through another router).
- *Source:* The routing protocol that caused the route to be created. MGMT = management (static routes), LOC = Local (direct routes), ICMP (dynamic route created by ICMP), RIP (dynamic route created by RIP), OSPF (dynamic route created by OSPF).
- *Age:* The amount of time in seconds since the route was last updated.

The Forwarding Process

On receiving a packet, a router verifies that the IP header was not corrupted, performing a checksum of the IP header and comparing it to the value in the datagram checksum field. Provided that the checksum is determined to be valid, the destination IP address is examined. If the packet is not destined for the router — i.e., the destination address is not equal to one of the router's IP interfaces — the packet is queued for forwarding.

Assuming that the packet must be forwarded, three possibilities exist:

- The destination address is a unicast address. The address is a Class A, B, or C address and is not a special-case broadcast address.
- The destination address is a broadcast address.
- The destination address is a multicast address. The address is a Class D address.

If the destination address falls into the first category (unicast address), the router determines which interface the datagram should be sent out of and what the IP address is for the next-hop router (if any). The time-to-live (TTL) field is decremented and verified that it is not equal to 0. The packet is discarded if TTL equals 0. The datagram is fragmented if necessary, and the hardware address of the link layer destination is determined. A link layer header is built to encapsulate the IP datagram for transmission on the physical medium.

If the destination address falls within the second category (broadcast address), the router must determine whether the broadcast is a limited broadcast or is a directed broadcast. If it is a limited broadcast (255.255.255.255), the packet cannot be forwarded out to another interface, but it might be used by the router itself. It is queued for local delivery to the router. If the datagram is a directed broadcast, it is treated as a unicast address for forwarding to the network, where it will be broadcast to all stations. That is, the router determines, through examination of the destination's network prefix and the routing table, which interface the datagram should be forwarded out of and the IP address of the next-hop router (if any). The TTL field is decremented and checked for packet discard eligibility. The datagram is fragmented if necessary, and the hardware address of the link layer destination (possibly link layer broadcast) is determined. A link layer header is constructed to encapsulate the IP datagram on the physical medium.

The case in which the destination address is a Class D address (multicast address) will be discussed in chapter 11.

Determining the Optimal Route

Once a packet has arrived at a router and is determined to be a unicast or a directed broadcast that must be forwarded, it is necessary to determine the interface it should be sent out of and the next-hop router's IP address. There may not be a next-hop router in all instances. When a packet is destined for a network that is directly defined on one of the router's interfaces, the packet is sent from the router directly to the destination IP address without traversing an additional router.

In many cases, the "direct versus remote" decision has been incorporated into the route table, and the interface and next-hop decisions are made in the same way as for all other forwarded packets. In instances when the decisions are separated, the router's IP interfaces must be examined and compared to the destination address of the datagram to be forwarded. For each IP interface defined on the router, the network mask must be applied to the router's IP address and the packet's destination IP address. If the network portion of each address is identical, the destination network of the datagram is considered local and the router does not need to forward the packet to another router for delivery. The router must, in that case, cross-reference the IP address to the hardware address of the destination device and forward the packet out of the identified port using the hardware address at layer 2.

In cases when the route table implements these decisions or when the IP datagram must be sent to a next-hop router, a procedure is defined to find the most appropriate port and next-hop address. These procedures reduce the entire set of route table entries to a subset of routes consisting of zero, one, or more than one viable route alternative for the datagram. These procedures, outlined next, are generally known as *pruning rules.*

- *Rule 1: Basic Match.* Prior to the application of this rule, the working set of route entries is equal to the entire route table. For each entry in the route table, the route mask is applied to both the destination IP address of the datagram and the corresponding destination field in the route table. All route entries except the ones in which the masked portion of the destination address and the destination route are identical are removed from the working set of route entries. Default routes are the exception; they are always included in the working set of route entries.

  Consider Table 4-4. Before the Basic Match pruning rule is applied, this route table is the working set of route entries. Assuming that an IP datagram arrives destined for 172.16.8.66, the working set of route entries after the Basic Match pruning rule is applied as shown in Table 4-5.

Destination	Route Mask	Next Hop	Port	Metr	Typ	Src	Age
0.0.0.0	0.0.0.0	172.16.3.65	J3.1	1	REM	MGMT	0
172.16.0.0	255.255.0.0	172.16.3.65	J3.1	1	REM	MGMT	0
172.16.3.0	255.255.255.192	172.16.3.1	J5	0	DIR	LOC	72177
172.16.3.64	255.255.255.192	172.16.3.126	J3.1	0	DIR	LOC	68994
172.16.3.128	255.255.255.192	172.16.3.190	J1	0	DIR	LOC	72184
172.16.3.192	255.255.255.192	172.16.3.254	J1	0	DIR	LOC	72184
172.16.4.0	255.255.255.192	172.16.3.4	J5	115	REM	OSPF	29766
172.16.4.64	255.255.255.192	172.16.3.4	J5	90	REM	OSPF	13662

Destination	Route Mask	Next Hop	Port	Metr	Typ	Src	Age
172.16.4.128	255.255.255.192	172.16.3.4	J5	100	REM	OSPF	29766
172.16.6.64	255.255.255.192	172.16.3.65	J3.1	576	REM	OSPF	17268
172.16.8.0	255.255.255.0	172.16.3.65	J3.1	621	REM	OSPF	29766
172.16.8.0	255.255.255.192	172.16.3.65	J3.1	90	REM	OSPF	68985
172.16.8.64	255.255.255.192	172.16.3.65	J3.1	130	REM	OSPF	13662
172.16.8.64	255.255.255.192	172.16.3.62	J5	720	REM	OSPF	52002
172.16.8.128	255.255.255.192	172.16.3.65	J3.1	75	REM	OSPF	68985
172.16.25.0	255.255.255.192	172.16.3.62	J5	50	REM	OSPF	71289
172.16.25.128	255.255.255.192	172.16.3.62	J5	35	REM	OSPF	71294
172.16.25.192	255.255.255.192	172.16.3.62	J5	35	REM	OSPF	71294

Table 4-4 Route Table to Search

Destination	Route Mask	Next Hop	Port	Metr	Typ	Src	Age
0.0.0.0	0.0.0.0	172.16.3.65	J3.1	1	REM	MGMT	0
172.16.0.0	255.255.0.0	172.16.3.65	J3.1	1	REM	MGMT	0
172.16.8.0	255.255.255.0	172.16.3.65	J3.1	621	REM	OSPF	29766
172.16.8.64	255.255.255.192	172.16.3.65	J3.1	130	REM	OSPF	13662
172.16.8.64	255.255.255.192	172.16.3.62	J5	720	REM	OSPF	52002

Table 4-5 Route Table after Basic Match

- *Rule 2: Longest Match.* After the Basic Match pruning rule has been applied, the working set of route entries is examined to see which entry (entries) has the longest (most specific) route mask. All routes in the working set that have a shorter (more general) route mask are discarded. Even though the default route has a zero-length route mask, the Longest

Match pruning rule applies to it as well. Had the working set of route entries prior to the application of the Longest Match pruning rule contained only a default route, the working set of route entries afterward would have just the default route in it. The previous example would be reduced to the working set of route entries after the application of the Longest Match pruning rule, as shown in Table 4-6.

Destination	Route Mask	Next Hop	Port	Metr	Typ	Src	Age
172.16.8.64	255.255.255.192	172.16.3.65	J3.1	130	REM	OSPF	13662
172.16.8.64	255.255.255.192	172.16.3.62	J5	720	REM	OSPF	52002

Table 4-6 Route Table after Longest Match

- *Rule 3: Weak Type of Service.* This pruning rule applies to pre-DiffServ usage only. Most routers do not support this function, even though some modern routing protocols have the capability to support Type of Service routing. OSPF is an example of a routing protocol that can support Type of Service routing. The IP header has a field identified as "Type of Service (TOS)" that spans the second octet of the header and that supports two distinct functions, precedence and type of service. The high-order three bits of the field are the Precedence field, and the next four bits are the Type of Service flags. These TOS flags can influence how routing decisions are made for the packet being examined. The flags are

  D Delay

  T Throughput

  R Reliability

  C Cost

They are set to bias a potential routing decision in favor of their respective factor.

The three bits that represent the Precedence field influence the treatment of the packet while it is in queue in a router. Congestion in routers results in a growth of queues and delays associated with traversing the queues. The Precedence field permits the router to select certain packets for earlier transmission over other, less time-sensitive packets. Since the Precedence affects only queueing, it should not be used to influence the routing decision.

Each route in the routing table may have a Type of Service field associated with it. When the Weak TOS pruning rule is applied, the TOS flags (bits 3–6 of the TOS field) of the datagram are compared to the TOS field of all the candidate routes in the working set. If a match is made, all routes except those that match are discarded from the working set. If no match is made, all routes except the ones that have a Type of Service equal to 0000 are discarded from the working set of route entries.

Routers and routing protocols that do not support Type of Service routing will set the Type of Service flags in the route table to 0000. The pruning rule still applies.

- *Rule 4: Best Metric.* Each route in the working set of route entries is ordered according to the metric field. The lower the metric, the better. The route(s) with the best metric are retained, and the other routes are discarded from the working set of candidate routes. The earlier example would be reduced down to the working set of route entries shown in Table 4-7 after the application of the Best Metric pruning rule. The route with a metric of 720 has been removed from the working set of routes in favor of the route with a metric of 130.

Destination	Route Mask	Next Hop	Port	Metr	Typ	Src	Age
172.16.8.64	255.255.255.192	172.16.3.65	J3.1	130	REM	OSPF	13662

Table 4-7 Route Table after Best Metric

- *Rule 5: Vendor Policy.* In many cases the working set of route entries would have been reduced down to a single candidate route by this point; however, it is possible to end up with a set of candidate routes all with equal metrics. The Vendor Policy pruning rule leaves the choice to the router vendor as to how to handle this condition. Possibilities include selection of the route that was less recently used (load splitting), administrative preference, and first in list (discard others). The Vendor Policy pruning rule can be very sophisticated or extremely simplistic.

After the application of the pruning rules, there should be either no routes in the working set of route entries or one route. If the working set is empty, the packet should be discarded and an appropriate ICMP error generated. Otherwise, the packet should be wrapped in a link layer protocol, using the hardware address of the next hop and queued for forwarding.

Even though guidelines on interpreting a route table exist, sometimes a device on the network does not "play by the [pruning] rules," so to speak. I ran into a host system several years ago that needed to be statically routed. After its tables were built, it became obvious that nonoptimal routes were being taken by the workstation when it sent packets out but that the packets were returning by an optimal path. It turned out that the way the workstation interpreted its routing table was incorrect: It was using the first route from the top that satisfied the Basic Match pruning rule — the default route. Make sure you understand the algorithms that each routing-decision device uses to choose the next hop for the packet.

Dynamic Routing Protocols

Two classifications can be used with routing protocols: (1) interior routing protocols and exterior routing protocols and (2) link-state protocols and distance-vector protocols. The first, interior versus exterior, is a distinction based on an *autonomous system*. An autonomous system is an area of routing that is under a common administrative control. Network administrators have the ability to define the address scheme and routing protocols within an autonomous system. The routing protocols that are designed for optimal operation within an autonomous system fall into the category of *interior routing protocols*. Those protocols that are designed to route between autonomous systems are called *exterior routing protocols*. Exterior Gateway Protocol (EGP) and Border Gateway Protocol-4 (BGP-4) are examples of exterior routing protocols.

Exterior routing protocols are used to route packets within the Internet between autonomous systems (ASs). In the recent past they provided routing only between classes of networks. Currently, we use the BGP-4 exterior routing protocol to advertise routing information between autonomous systems. No capabilities were provided to discriminate between subnets inside of each domain. Since you or I can do very little to affect the efficiency of the routing tables in the Internet, this book deals primarily with interior routing protocols. Remember, within an autonomous system the network administrator has control over subnetting and routing architectures.

The second routing protocol category, distance-vector and link-state, defines the underlying routing architecture. A distance-vector routing protocol keeps track of distances (hop-count or cost) to each network and the physical interface to use to get to the network. A link-state protocol keeps track of direct neighbors and sends updates of its neighbor information to each of its neighbors. Eventually, a router has all the information required to depict the network. The route table is computed using this topology data.

Several interior routing protocols are in use today in a TCP/IP network. They include RIP (RIPv1), RIPv2, OSPF, IS-IS, IGRP, and E-IGRP. RIP and OSPF are the most common standard routing protocols but IS-IS has been increasing in popularity as of late. RIP and OSPF are opposites in many regards. RIP is a distance-vector routing protocol, whereas OSPF is a link-state routing protocol. RIP does not include subnet information; OSPF does include subnet mask information. These and other features of the routing protocols greatly affect the addressing scheme chosen within an autonomous system.

RIP (RIP Version 1)

RIP stands for Routing Information Protocol. The first version of the protocol was formally defined in RFC 1058 (June 1988). It is one of the most widely used interior routing protocols. This comes as a result of the following factors:

- *Ease of use and implementation:* There are generally three steps to running RIP in a network. First, set the route broadcast update interval (or accept the default). Second, specify the neighboring routers. Third, turn on RIP routing. There is not much else that can be done or configured. It just starts working.
- *Age:* RIP was in use in TCP/IP networks even before RFC 1058 was written. RIP was the most popular, if not the only, dynamic interior routing protocol for a long time.

It is easiest to understand the operation of RIP through an illustration. Consider the network in Illustration 4-3. This TCP/IP network has three Class C networks in use. The mask of 255.255.255.0 is being used throughout. The networks are 192.168.1.0, 192.168.2.0, and 192.168.3.0.

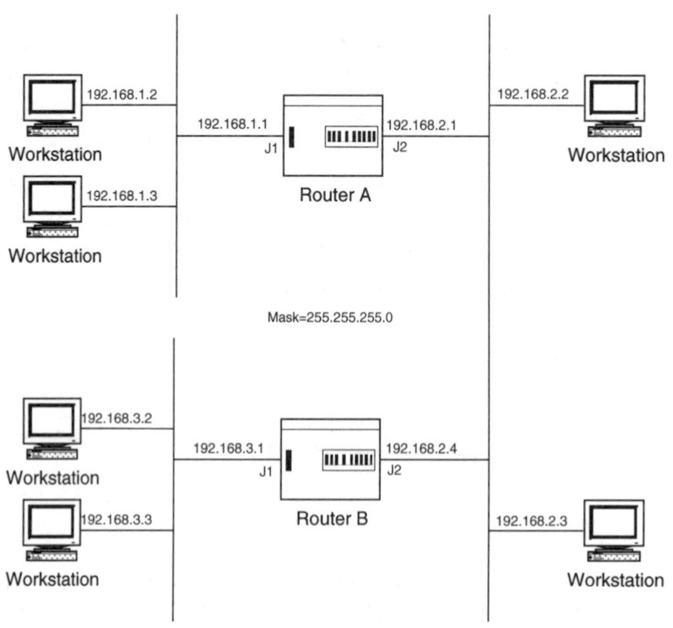

Illustration 4-3 Mechanics of RIP

To configure RIP routing, Router A would need to be told to listen to updates from Router B. This would enable RIP updates on the network in common between Router A and Router B (192.168.2.3), as well as define the *trusted neighbor.* Router B would need to be told that Router A is a trusted neighbor. This means that Router B trusts the route advertisements coming from Router A. The RIP update interval has a default value of 30 seconds, but in most routers this can be set to a different value. Assuming the default update interval is all right, RIP can be enabled.

Henceforth at the expiration of each update interval, Router A will send a limited broadcast (UDP port 520) on port J2, telling the network and any routers running RIP about network

192.168.1.0. Router B, trusting the RIP update from Router A, installs the route in its route table if it does not already have the entry in it. If Router B does already have a route entry for the 192.168.1.1, it will check to see whether the metric for the newly arrived route is better than the current route entry's metric. If it is better, the old route entry is replaced with the new route. If the newly received update exactly describes a route that is in the route table, the age of the existing route entry is reset to 0.

Router B also broadcasts route updates on its port J2 to tell all the RIP routers about network 192.168.3.0. Router A receives the update and installs the route entry or updates the timer for the route. Table 4-8 is Router A's route table during normal operation in the network shown in Illustration 4-3.

Destination	Route Mask	Next Hop	Port	Metr	Typ	Src	Age
192.168.1.0	255.255.255.0	192.168.1.1	J1	0	DIR	LOC	3569
192.168.2.0	255.255.255.0	192.168.2.1	J2	0	DIR	LOC	3569
192.168.3.0	255.255.255.0	192.168.2.4	J2	1	REM	RIP	25

Table 4-8 Route Table on Router A under Normal Operation

RIP is notorious for its slow network convergence (how long it takes for all routing in the network to stabilize on a correct routing table after a network change). This is greatly affected by the update interval. If Router A stops hearing a route update from Router B, the route for network 192.168.3.0 will start to age. After six update intervals, the route is marked as unusable, with a metric of 16. The route is purged shortly thereafter. Using the default values, the route would not be marked as invalid in Router A's route table for 180 seconds following the "failure" of Router B. Certain mechanisms help speed things up under the right circumstances. One such mechanism is route poisoning, which halts the use of a route in a remote router.

The major thing to know about RIP is how it handles of network mask information: RIP does not pass information about the network masks in its route update. So long as you are aware of this and its effects, you can avoid the pitfalls and possibly even take advantage of some side effects. RIP infers a route mask for a network route entry, based on the inherent class of the IP address, unless the router receiving the update has an interface configured for a subnet of the same IP network. In that case, the subnet mask in effect on the router will be used. Because of the reasons stated above, RIPv1 is known as a "class-full" routing protocol.

To get a better handle on all this, let's look at some specific examples.

RIP Example 1. Consider Illustration 4-4. The route mask has changed from the previous illustration. The mask now being used (255.255.255.240) would allow each Class C network to be divided into 14 or 16 subnetworks, each with 14 hosts per subnet. The illustration does not try to explain what on earth the network administrator was thinking in devising this scheme; it serves only to make a point. Instead of explaining the mechanics up front, let's look at Router A's route table (Table 4-9) and take note of a peculiarity.

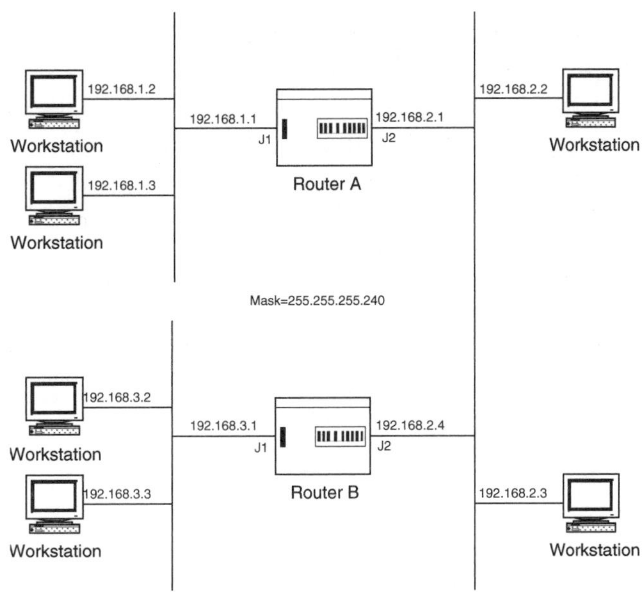

Illustration 4-4 RIP Example I

Destination	Route Mask	Next Hop	Port	Metr	Typ	Src	Age
192.168.1.0	255.255.255.240	192.168.1.1	J1	0	DIR	LOC	3569
192.168.2.0	255.255.255.240	192.168.2.1	J2	0	DIR	LOC	3569
192.168.3.0	255.255.255.0	192.168.2.4	J2	1	REM	RIP	13

Table 4-9 Route Table on Router A for RIP Example I

Why does entry 192.168.3.0 have a route mask that is different from the others? Router A does not have network 192.168.3.0 defined on any of its interfaces. Therefore, if Router A receives an update with a route 192.168.3.0, it can assume only that the route mask is the inherent class of the network. In this case it is assumed that the mask should be the normal Class C mask of 255.255.255.0. As far as this example is concerned, the mis-masked route entry is "no big deal." Since Router B is the only place that any subnets of the Class C network 192.168.3.0 can be reached from, Router A can send any IP datagram with a destination address having 192.168.3 as the first three octets to Router B, and it will know how to deliver them. Certainly, it would be nice if Router A knew that it could route only packets destined for the first subnet of that Class C address, but that's not the way RIP works.

RIP Example 2. What would the route table on Router A, example 1 look like if the same subnet mask (255.255.255.240) were used but the first and second octet of all the IP addresses were changed from "192.168" to "172.16"? The answer is shown in Table 4-10.

Destination	Route Mask	Next Hop	Port	Metr	Typ	Src	Age
172.16.1.0	255.255.255.240	172.16.1.1	J1	0	DIR	LOC	3569
172.16.2.0	255.255.255.240	172.16.2.1	J2	0	DIR	LOC	3569
172.16.3.0	255.255.255.240	172.16.2.4	J2	1	REM	RIP	13

Table 4-10 Route Table on Router A for RIP Example 2

The route mask for entry 172.16.3.0 is 255.255.255.240 because the network has changed from being based on subnetting of three Class C networks to subnetting of a single Class B network. As such, all routers have a subnet of that one Class B network defined on them. Router A inferred the mask, based on its local interface's IP addresses and masks.

RIP Example 3. When the mask was incorrectly identified in RIP Example 1, it worked out that everything would function despite the mistake. See if you can figure out what's going to happen to routing between Router A and Router C. Can Router A PING Router B? What about routing between Host A and Host C? Can they PING each other? See Illustration 4-5, and for a hint, examine Router B's route table in Table 4-11.

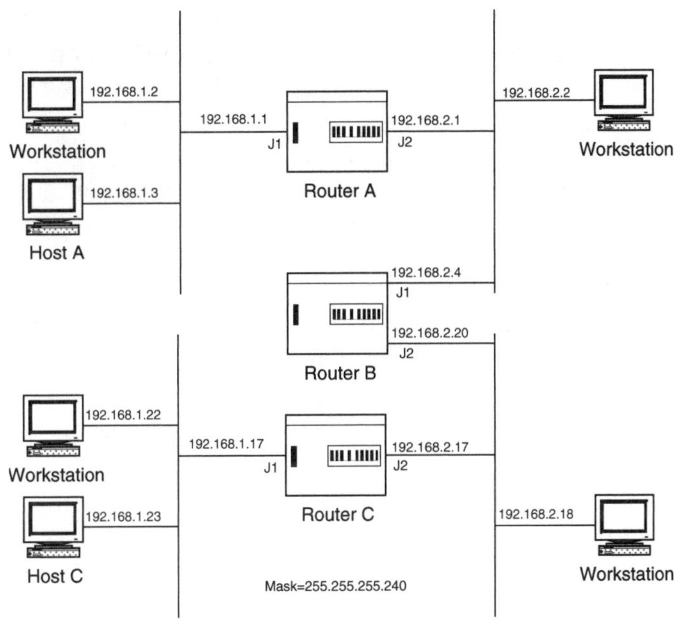

Illustration 4-5 RIP Example 3

Destination	Route Mask	Next Hop	Port	Metr	Typ	Src	Age
192.168.2.0	255.255.255.240	192.168.2.4	J1	0	DIR	LOC	3569
192.168.2.16	255.255.255.240	192.168.2.20	J2	0	DIR	LOC	3569
192.168.1.0	255.255.255.0	192.168.2.1	J1	1	REM	RIP	13
192.168.1.0	255.255.255.0	192.168.2.17	J2	1	REM	RIP	4

Table 4-11 Route Table on Router B for RIP Example 3

Router A (192.168.2.1) can PING Router C (192.168.2.17). Host A (192.168.1.3) cannot PING Host C (192.168.1.23). Routers A and C can PING each other because all the routers, including Router B, have IP subnets from the Class C network 192.168.2.0 defined on them. So long as Router A uses a destination IP address of 192.168.2.17 and a source address of 192.168.2.1 for the PING packet, there can be no confusion regarding the routing. Remember, with the mask that is being used, the addresses 192.168.2.1 and 192.168.2.17 reflect the same host ID (1) on different IP networks.

A problem occurs when Router B receives a RIP update from Router A. Router B sees the IP network 192.168.1.0 in the update. Not having an interface with that Class C defined on it, Router B infers that the route mask to be used is the inherent mask of the network. In this case a Class C mask is used, and the route is installed in the route table. Router C sends an update to Router B for network 192.168.1.16 (the all-0s host portion for the second subnet), but because Router B still has no way of knowing what the actual mask should be, it assumes the inherent Class C mask. The routes have different next hops, so the route is installed.

Router B sends an update to Router A. In that update Router B includes the route to network 192.168.1.0 with the next hop of 192.168.2.17. Router A rejects the route because it already has a 192.168.1.0 entry in its route table. Further, the network is a local route, indicating that it is directly defined on Router A. There can be no better route than the one it already has.

Assume that Host A sends a PING packet to Host C. As soon as the PING packet arrives at Router A, it is discarded because Router A has no route to that particular subnet in its routing table. The PING fails.

There is also a desirable side effect of the mismasking of route entries. This will be discussed in the Addressing to Achieve Route Table Efficiency section of Chapter 7.

Open Shortest Path First (OSPF)

OSPF is a much more complicated routing protocol than RIP. Configuration of RIP is brief and simple; only a few parameters can be changed. OSPF offers many more configuration options. These include:

- OSPF areas
- Area route summarization
- Enabling OSPF on a router or on specific interfaces
- Virtual links
- Costs (metric)
- Importation of routing information from other routing protocols
- Exportation of routing information to other routing protocols
- OSPF interface timers, such as the hello interval and the dead interval
- Authentication

OSPF is a complicated, yet extremely powerful and efficient routing protocol. This section will not cover OSPF in depth; please refer to one of the many excellent references, including RFC 2178, "OSPF Version 2," that discuss the details of the protocol. It is necessary, however, to cover portions of the OSPF protocol to point out the aspects that have to do with IP addressing. So here's a quick overview of OSPF.

OSPF is a link-state routing protocol. Whenever a new router joins with a network running OSPF, the router will exchange a database with another router on the network. This database represents the network topology to the router. From the information in this link-state database, the router is able to compute an optimal route table. The new router is now capable of effective routing. From this point on the router must maintain contact with each of its neighbors. If it loses contact, the neighbor will imminently sense that it has lost contact and will flood an advertisement out to all OSPF routers that the connection has been lost. All routers update their respective link-state databases with the information from the recent link-state advertisement and force a recomputation of the route table. One huge advantage over RIP is that the link-state database contains information on all the subnets that the routes use. Let's look at the same network that gave RIP trouble, shown again in Illustration 4-6.

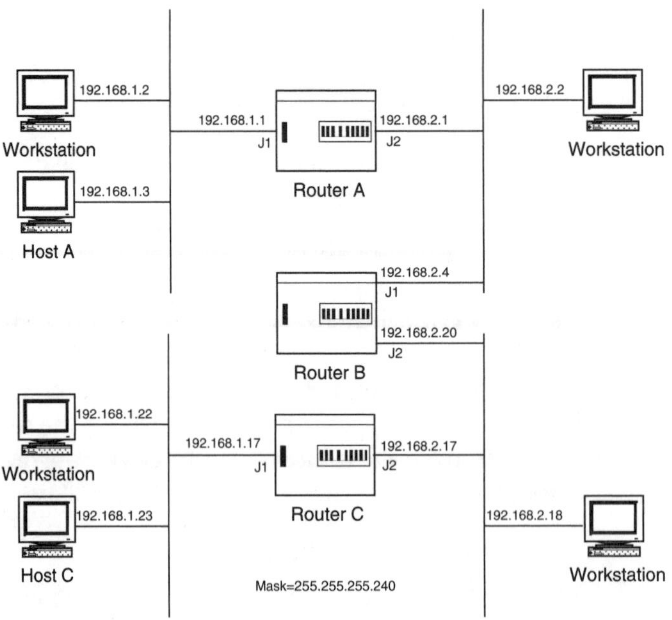

Illustration 4-6 OSPF Example I

OSPF Example 1. Because RIP could not pass subnet mask information in the route update, Router B assumed that the route update for network 192.168.1.0 used a mask of 255.255.255.0, which prevents the packet from passing correctly between the 192.168.1.0/28 network and the 192.168.1.16/28 network. (See Illustration 4-6.) OSPF would construct a route table on Router B like the one in Table 4-12.

Destination	Route Mask	Next Hop	Port	Metr	Typ	Src	Age
192.168.2.0	255.255.255.240	192.168.2.4	J1	0	DIR	LOC	3569
192.168.2.16	255.255.255.240	192.168.2.20	J2	0	DIR	LOC	3569
192.168.1.0	255.255.255.240	192.168.2.1	J1	1795	REM	OSPF	2184
192.168.1.16	255.255.255.240	192.168.2.17	J2	1795	REM	OSPF	2662

Table 4-12 Route Table on Router B for OSPF Example 1

On Router C the route table would look like Table 4-13. It is clear from the route tables that all four networks in the illustration are represented. There can be no problem determining the next hop of a packet at any point in the network.

Destination	Route Mask	Next Hop	Port	Metr	Typ	Src	Age
192.168.1.16	255.255.255.240	192.168.1.17	J1	0	DIR	LOC	3002
192.168.2.16	255.255.255.240	192.168.2.17	J2	0	DIR	LOC	3569
192.168.1.0	255.255.255.240	192.168.2.20	J2	3590	REM	OSPF	72184
192.168.2.0	255.255.255.240	192.168.2.20	J2	1795	REM	OSPF	3569

Table 4-13 Route Table on Router C for OSPF Example 1

In an error-free OSPF network, very little overhead traffic is required to maintain the routing. Each router sends an OSPF Hello packet to its neighbors at the expiration of the hello interval (usually 10 seconds). If the dead interval (usually 40 seconds) expires before receipt of the next hello, the link is marked down. This represents the worst case on the amount of time that OSPF requires to determine link failure. If a router determines that one of the physical ports that an OSPF interface is defined on fails, the router can advertise that the link is down. This triggers a flurry of route table recalculation on each router that receives the link-state advertisement (LSA). This LSA is small; it takes only about 40 octets for the largest link-state advertisement above the IP layer. (OSPF is implemented on top of IP.) When an OSPF router rejoins, the process starts over again, with an exchange of OSPF link-state information.

It is easy to see that in a stable network little overhead is associated with OSPF. A flapping link — a tentative interface that continues to cycle between operable and inoperable — can cause the greatest impact to an OSPF network. In fact, not only is the link-state advertisement being flooded to all routers with each transition, but the routers are also forced to recalculate the route table. This calculation is not an insignificant computation, and it tends to cascade within each set of routers in a series. In fact, it tends to have the greatest impact on the routers at the edge of the network whose computational power is nearly consumed by the forwarding of packets alone.

To minimize the impact of the flooding and recalculation, the concept of *areas* was developed. An area is the boundary for flooding of link-state advertisements. An OSPF router within an area will have a complete map of the topology only within the area to which it belongs, plus some summary information about the OSPF topology beyond its borders. This information is summarized by a special-purpose router called an *area border router*. This router serves as a gateway between the backbone area (area 0.0.0.0, commonly called area 0) and another, non-backbone area. The backbone area must be contiguous in an OSPF network, and all areas must connect to the backbone area via an area border router.

The area border router has the ability to summarize link-state advertisements received from one area and to send only a summary link advertisement into the adjoining area. The advantage to this can be significant or minimal, depending on how well that addressing scheme was laid out. See where I was going? It all boils down to addressing in the long run.

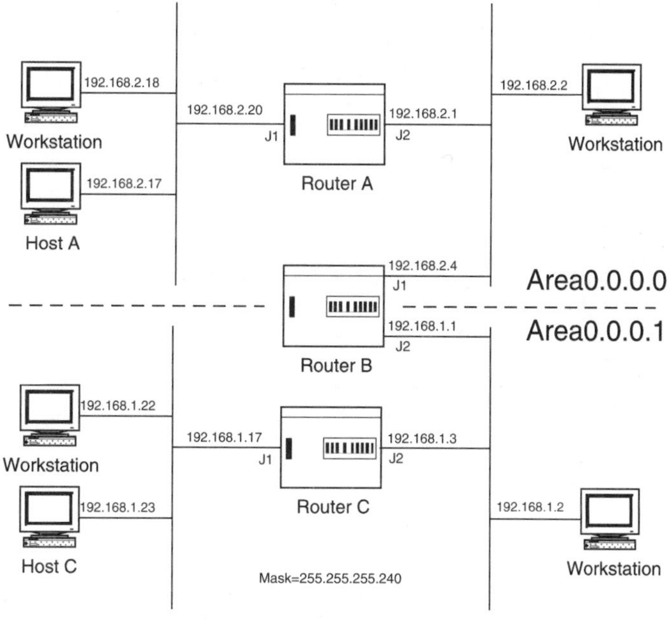

Illustration 4-7 OSPF with Areas

Consider Illustration 4-7. The illustrated network consists of three routers in two different areas, area 0 and area 1. All of Router A and the 192.168.2.4 IP interface of Router B are in the backbone area, area 0. The 192.168.1.1 IP interface of Router B and all of Router C are in area 1. If the J1 port on Router A fails, Router A will detect that the link is down and will flood a link-state advertisement to all routers in the area. Router B receives the LSA, applies any summarization rules, and creates a summary link-state advertisement, if necessary, to be flooded into area 0.0.0.1.

Route summarization can also occur at an area border router. All the networks in each of the areas that it adjoins can be summarized into only a few route entries if the addressing scheme permits. Summarization will be discussed in chapter 7.

Static Routing

RIP and OSPF are examples of dynamic routing protocols. Information must be exchanged between the routers. This information exchange is the basis for route table construction. A *static route* is configured by the network administrator and, once installed, usually will not change except through manual intervention. A static architecture might be worth consideration for a number of reasons.

- *No traffic overhead due to static routing:* The routing update in a RIP network can get rather large. Even though the running average might suggest a small percentage of total bandwidth over the course of a day, keep in mind that the update is sent out at 30-second intervals (default). At the expiration of the update interval, the route update will be transmitted. For some amount of time, depending on the link speed and the size of the update, the link may be saturated.
- *Dial media (ISDN):* Routers have the ability to evaluate the destination address of a packet, determine which remote site needs to have a connection established, and place "the call" to pass the traffic. This

could be a local call and might be subject to a usage fee, based on the connect time. Or the call could be across the country and thus subject to the long-distance carrier's tariffs. In either case, you wouldn't want a call to be placed every time a route update is sent.

- *Import into dynamic routing:* Static routes can be imported into OSPF routing and other routing protocols. This means that you can statically define a portion of your network and import those routes into a dynamic portion of the network.
- *Route efficiency:* Static routing can lead to some sophisticated route schemes. The network administrator has the ability to design a routing strategy that considers many different factors when biasing a route decision. This is known as *traffic engineering* and allows the network architect to balance IP load across many links to relieve congestion. The administrator also has the ability to set up route aggregation schemes.

There are also a few reasons not to do static routing.

- *Static is static:* In the event of a failure, static routing cannot recover well by shifting traffic loads to compensate. Those are capabilities of a dynamic routing protocol.
- *Configuration is a pain:* All the initial configuration, the maintenance and updates, and the continuous redesign are manual operations.
- *You just don't want that ISDN line to drop:* By running a dynamic routing protocol across an ISDN line, you can sieze the line for your exclusive use. Not recommended for areas that meter usage.

ICMP Routing

Many people in this industry do not consider ICMP to be a routing protocol, but in many ways, it is. ICMP, the Internet Control Message Protocol, has a message type that redirects routing from a nonoptimal route to one that is more optimal. This message is known as an ICMP Redirect. The format for an ICMP Redirect is shown in Illustration 4-8 and has the following values.

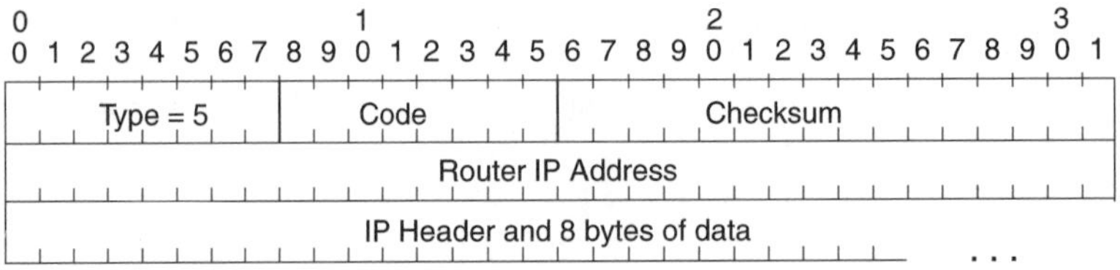

```
0                   1                   2                   3
0 1 2 3 4 5 6 7 8 9 0 1 2 3 4 5 6 7 8 9 0 1 2 3 4 5 6 7 8 9 0 1
+-+-+-+-+-+-+-+-+-+-+-+-+-+-+-+-+-+-+-+-+-+-+-+-+-+-+-+-+-+-+-+-+
|   Type = 5    |     Code      |           Checksum            |
+-+-+-+-+-+-+-+-+-+-+-+-+-+-+-+-+-+-+-+-+-+-+-+-+-+-+-+-+-+-+-+-+
|                       Router IP Address                       |
+-+-+-+-+-+-+-+-+-+-+-+-+-+-+-+-+-+-+-+-+-+-+-+-+-+-+-+-+-+-+-+-+
|               IP Header and 8 bytes of data                   ...
+-+-+-+-+-+-+-+-+-+-+-+-+-+-+-+-+-+-+-+-+-+-+-+-+-+-+
```

Illustration 4-8 ICMP Redirect

- *Type:* Value is 5 for a Redirect message.
- *Code:* Values are 0 for Network Redirect, 1 for Host Redirect, 2 for TOS (Type of Service) and Network Redirect, and 3 for TOS and Host Redirect.
- *Checksum:* Self-explanatory.
- *Router IP address:* The IP address of the router that has a better route to the destination than was originally used.

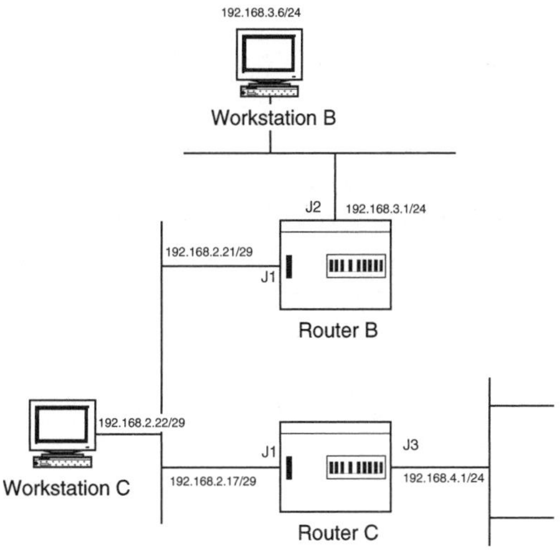

Illustration 4-9 Classic ICMP Redirect Scenario

Illustration 4-9 shows the classic example of when a Redirect occurs. Workstation C's route table is shown in Table 4-14, and Router C's route table is shown in Table 4-15.

Destination	Gateway	Genmask	Flags	Metric	Ref	Use	Iface
192.168.2.22	0.0.0.0	255.255.255.248	U	0	0	246846	eth0
127.0.0.0	0.0.0.0	255.0.0.0	U	0	0	163840	lo
0.0.0.0	192.168.2.17	0.0.0.0	UG	0	0	224692	eth0

Table 4-14 Route Table on Workstation C

Destination	Route Mask	Next Hop	Port	Metr	Typ	Src	Age
192.168.2.16	255.255.255.248	192.168.2.17	J1	0	DIR	LOC	540
192.168.3.0	255.255.255.0	192.168.2.21	J1	75	REM	OSPF	245
192.168.4.0	255.255.255.0	192.168.4.1	J3	0	DIR	LOC	540

Table 4-15 Route Table on Router C

Workstation C has a default route to Router C. When Workstation C wishes to communicate with Workstation B, it sends its packets to Router C. Router C sees that the next hop for getting to the 192.168.3.0/24 network is 192.168.2.21 and is reachable through the same interface that the original packet was received on. This triggers an ICMP Redirect from Router C to Workstation C, telling of the more optimal path. In the future when Workstation C sends data to Workstation B, it should send the packets directly to 192.168.2.21 (Router B).

There are many other types of messages and functions for ICMP, such as ICMP Echo, commonly known as PING. RFC 792 defines ICMP.

Direct Routing (ARP and ARP Variants)

Whenever a router or a workstation sends a packet to a device on an IP network that has been defined locally on the router or workstation, it must translate the IP address of the destination to the destination's hardware address. On a physical network that permits multiple access (such as Ethernet, Token Ring, and Frame Relay for example), there must be some mechanism for cross-referencing the IP address to the hardware address and vice versa. On Ethernet, the protocols for maintaining the cross-reference are Address Resolution Protocol (ARP) and Reverse ARP (RARP). Other types of networks may have similar functionality or may require a manual mapping of the address resolution.

IP routers forward packets based on information about IP networks in their routing tables. Once a router determines that a packet must be forwarded to another router (next hop), the router must encapsulate the IP datagram into an appropriate link layer header and use the hardware address of the next hop as the link layer destination. This is also true if a router has the destination network locally defined and the packet is to be delivered to a host on that network. The router must find out the hardware address of the host for the link layer header.

Proxy ARP is an interesting variation of ARP. Prior to the adoption of RFC 950 (Internet Standard Subnetting Procedure), subnets were not permitted. A class C network could have 254 hosts and could not be subdivided as we can do today. RFC 1027, "ARP and Transparent Subnet Gateways" (Oct 1987), documented a procedure that was used to divide a single network of hosts into multiple networks. The hosts were addresses as if they were on a single IP network (no subnets permitted yet) and they were split apart by a gateway (router) as shown in Illustration 4-10.

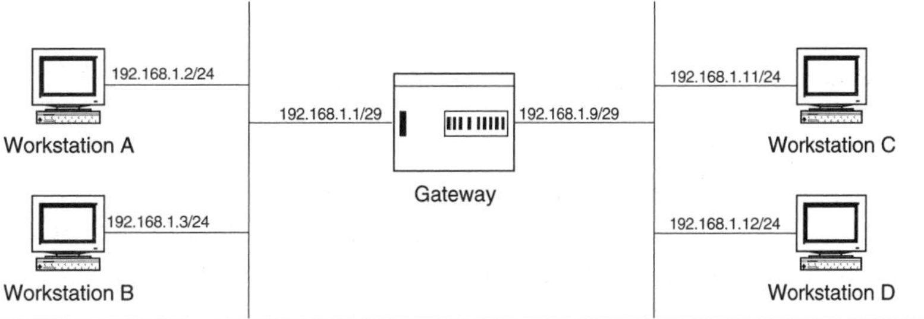

Illustration 4-10 Example of Proxy ARP

Before the introduction of the gateway into the network, Workstation A could communicate with Workstation C simply by ARPing for the hardware address of the device with an IP address of 192.168.1.4 and then using the returned hardware address to transmit packets directly to the workstation. When the network got too big, it needed to be divided up into smaller groups. Gateways were added that supported both RFC 950 and Proxy ARP. This was easier to do than updating the software on the hosts to support RFC 950 subnetting. You need to keep in mind that this is the Internet of the early years and not the one that we are familiar with now. In fact, if you want to get an idea of what the folks architecting that version of the Internet were dealing with, take a look at the "motivation" section of RFC 1027. The University of Texas at Austin had a large Ethernet "connecting over 10 buildings" and had "more than 100 hosts connected to it"!

Here is how Proxy ARP works. If Workstation A ARPs to find the hardware address for Workstation C, the gateway sees the request and examines the packet to see what network the ARP packet originated on and what network the packet is destined for. If the source and the destination IP address are on the same network, the gateway does nothing since the two hosts can communicate without the intervention of the gateway. If the hosts are on different networks and the gateway has interfaces in both of the networks, the gateway will answer the ARP request using its own hardware address of the interface on the originating network. Workstation A will believe that the gateway is actually Workstation C and forward the packet to the gateway. The gateway knows that the packet does not belong to it because it has a different destination IP address than is bound to any of its interfaces. So the gateway ARPs for Workstation C's hardware address and forwards the packet from Workstation A to Workstation C.

While this may seem to be "old news" and no longer relevant, Proxy ARP has found new uses in today's IP networks. It is used by Mobile IP, dial-up remote access concentrators, and other tunnel servers such as Realm Specific IP servers to "attract" traffic for forwarding to a host that is using a temporary address allocated from a pool. See the sections on Mobile IP (Chapter 12) and addressing for remote access concentrators (Chapter 7) for more information.

The mechanics of ARP and RARP are beyond the scope of this book. RFC 826 defines ARP, RFC 903 defines RARP, RFC 1293 defines Inverse ARP, and RFC 1735 defines NBMA (non-broadcast, multiple access) ARP used on Frame Relay and X.25 networks. ATM ARP functionality is discussed in the sections on IP over ATM in Chapter 5.

Hand Tracing a Route

When routing does not seem to be working correctly, one of the best ways to diagnose a problem is to hand trace the routing from source to destination *and back* since routing may not dictate the same path in both directions. Starting at the source of the IP datagram, use the pruning rules that are applicable for the platform, determine the next hop, and follow the path all the way to the destination. Make sure that you get *all* the candidate routes when you apply the Basic Match pruning rule. It is easy to forget some subnets! Hand trace the routing for the path from the destination to the source address as well. Just because you have routing to get from the source to the destination address, it does not mean that you could get back to the source from the destination.

Illustration 4-11 is an example of hand tracing. Tables 4-16 through 4-20 show the corresponding route tables on each of the workstations and routers.

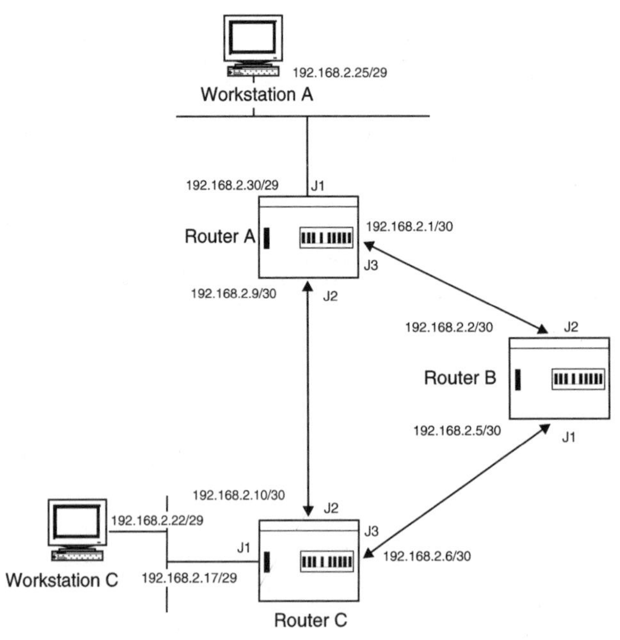

Illustration 4-11 Example Network for Hand Tracing a Route

Destination	Gateway	Genmask	Flags	Metric	Ref	Use	Iface
192.168.2.25	0.0.0.0	255.255.255.248	U	0	0	246846	eth0
127.0.0.0	0.0.0.0	255.0.0.0	U	0	0	163840	lo
0.0.0.0	192.168.2.30	0.0.0.0	UG	0	0	224692	eth0

Table 4-16 Workstation A

Destination	Gateway	Genmask	Flags	Metric	Ref	Use	Iface
192.168.2.22	0.0.0.0	255.255.255.248	U	0	0	246846	eth0
127.0.0.0	0.0.0.0	255.0.0.0	U	0	0	163840	lo
0.0.0.0	198.168.2.17	0.0.0.0	UG	0	0	224692	eth0

Table 4-17 Workstation C

Destination	Route Mask	Next Hop	Port	Metr	Typ	Src	Age
192.168.2.0	255.255.255.252	192.168.2.1	J3	0	DIR	LOC	467
192.168.2.4	255.255.255.252	192.168.2.10	J2	75	REM	OSPF	452
192.168.2.8	255.255.255.252	192.168.2.9	J2	0	DIR	LOC	492
192.168.2.16	255.255.255.248	192.168.2.10	J2	20	REM	OSPF	452
192.168.2.24	255.255.255.248	192.168.2.30	J1	0	DIR	LOC	492

Table 4-18 Router A

Destination	Route Mask	Next Hop	Port	Metr	Typ	Src	Age
192.168.2.0	255.255.255.252	192.168.2.2	J2	0	DIR	LOC	455
192.168.2.4	255.255.255.252	192.168.2.5	J1	0	DIR	LOC	456
192.168.2.8	255.255.255.252	192.168.2.1	J2	75	REM	OSPF	441
192.168.2.8	255.255.255.252	192.168.2.6	J1	75	REM	OSPF	441
192.168.2.16	255.255.255.248	192.168.2.6	J1	75	REM	OSPF	450
192.168.2.24	255.255.255.248	192.168.2.1	J2	75	REM	OSPF	449

Table 4-19 Router B

Destination	Route Mask	Next Hop	Port	Metr	Typ	Src	Age
192.168.2.0	255.255.255.252	192.168.2.9	J2	75	REM	OSPF	245
192.168.2.4	255.255.255.252	192.168.2.6	J3	0	DIR	LOC	478
192.168.2.8	255.255.255.252	192.168.2.10	J2	0	DIR	LOC	540
192.168.2.16	255.255.255.248	192.168.2.17	J1	0	DIR	LOC	540
192.168.2.24	255.255.255.248	192.168.2.9	J2	20	REM	OSPF	463
192.168.2.25	255.255.255.255	192.168.2.5	J3	2	REM	MGMT	0

Table 4-20 Router C

In this example, users have complained that the workstations can reach one another, but the response time is off from what is expected. The physical port statistics on the routers indicate nonoptimal routing. What's the problem? To start with, look at the route table on Workstation A and verify that the default gateway and the IP interfaces were configured with the correct mask. Everything looks fine; the default gateway is 192.168.2.30. Telnet to Router A (192.168.2.30). If Workstation A were sending packets to Workstation C, the destination IP address would be 192.168.2.22, and the source address would be 192.168.2.25. The route in Router A's route table that would provide the next hop is the fourth one down; 192.168.2.22 falls into a six-host network, 192.168.2.16/29. The next hop is 192.168.2.10, port J2 on Router C. Telnet to Router C. Examining its route table reveals that the 192.168.2.16/29 network is locally attached. The packet can be routed directly to Workstation C from Router C, since they share an Ethernet connection.

Now we have to do the same thing for the reverse direction since Workstation C must respond to Workstation A's packet. Look at Workstation C's route table. The default gateway is 192.168.2.17 and the IP interfaces are configured correctly. Telnet to 192.168.2.17. Now the destination IP address that we are looking for is 192.168.2.25. The route table reveals a host route (denoted by the route mask 255.255.255.255) to the host 192.168.2.25, and the next hop is configured for 192.168.2.5! Now I remember! I had installed a bunch of static routes a few weeks ago, trying to troubleshoot a different problem. I must have left one in. I'll bet that if I remove it, everything will be fine again.

Hand tracing a route from source to destination and back can take some time but will invariably reveal flaws in a routing architecture. Luckily, some tools such as *traceroute* can help speed the process. Traceroute's function is to show you the hops taken to get from a source to a destination. It does this through the use of both ICMP and UDP. The following is the result of a traceroute from Router C to Router A:

```
hop 1: 192.168.2.17
hop 2: 192.168.2.5
hop 3: 192.168.2.9
Target (192.168.2.25) reached on hop 4, round-trip time 280 ms.
```

It is easy to see that the second hop was not as expected: The packet should have been routed from 192.168.2.17 to 192.168.2.9. Traceroute does not indicate the reason for this, so it's back to the hand tracing of the routing. This time, however, I can start at 192.167.2.17 on the return path. Traceroute can save time in the debugging process, but it won't do the complete analysis for you.

Summary

This chapter dealt with the fundamentals of routing. Foremost, a person must have an understanding of the route table elements and how next hops are selected for the packet being routed. The route table pruning rules, which a router uses to select the packet's next-hop destination, are

Rule 1	Basic Match
Rule 2	Longest Match
Rule 3	Weak Type of Service
Rule 4	Best Metric
Rule 5	Vendor Policy

Not all devices choose a next hop in the same manner as IP version 4 routers. Make sure that you understand the algorithms used in your network for choosing next-hop destinations.

Routing protocols can be interior or exterior. Interior routing protocols handle routing within an autonomous system (a system under a single administrative control) that is capable of making decisions about subnetting and routing policies. Two examples of interior routing protocols are RIP and OSPF. Exterior routing protocols handle routing between autonomous systems. EGP and BGP are exterior routing protocols.

Routing protocols also can be link-state or distance-vector. OSPF is an example of a link-state protocol. OSPF permits the use of variable subnet masks by including the route mask information in the link-state database. OSPF converges rapidly after a network change. If a link fails in the network, it is possible to converge to a stable state in only a few seconds. OSPF also introduces the concept of areas. An area is the boundary for flooding of link-state advertisements and for summarizing routing information. It can be complicated getting OSPF operational.

RIP is an example of a distance-vector routing protocol. RIP does not convey information about route masks in its route update broadcasts. As such, it must infer the route mask to use from the inherent class of the address and whether that network has a subnet defined on one of the router's interfaces. The route mask chosen is sometimes wrong and can lead to unexpected routing results. RIP relies on the receipt of routing updates at a regular interval (usually every 30 seconds). If it fails to get a route update for a previously known route, the route will eventually get marked as unusable and shortly afterward be flushed from the route table. A route could be marked as up for a long time after an outage. RIP is known for slow network convergence but is simple to implement.

Other routing protocols, such as IGRP, EIGRP, and RIPv2, were not discussed. There are similarities and differences among these routing protocols and RIP or OSPF. I chose RIP because of its widespread use and OSPF because it is a strong, modern, standards-based protocol.

Practice Questions

1. Using the route table in Table 4-1, what is the age of the route entry used to forward a packet to the following destinations?

Destination	Age
172.16.4.142	___
172.16.6.130	___
172.16.5.3	___

2. Using the route table in Table 4-4, what is the age of the route entry used to forward a packet to the following destinations?

Destination	Age
172.16.8.5	___
172.16.5.3	___
172.16.8.66	___

3. What's the difference between a link-state routing protocol and a distance-vector routing protocol? Name examples of each.
4. Name two examples of a classfull routing protocol.
5. Name two examples of a classless routing protocol.
6. What type of device in OSPF does route summarization?
7. What is the Area ID for the OSPF backbone area?

IP Address Layout

section

Everything up to this point has been to provide you with background and motivation that support the discussion on the design or redesign of IP addressing schemes. This is where the rubber meets the road. Indeed, sometimes you have to redesign the addressing architecture because of inappropriate planning or address administration or as a result of changes in infrastructure. Address redesign is healthy, and so is a visit to the dentist.

Address-Needs Assessment

Renovation of an addressing scheme is often a painful process. In fact, the first time you do it will probably be brutal. The second time you do it, you should be only slightly uncomfortable. Renovation becomes necessary because the birth of a network is seldom planned. It just happens, and it propagates. When a network is started, it is typically within a single workgroup. Then others in the company or office take notice and say, "We want that, too." So they get added, then others get added, and so on. Eventually people start to see the network performance decline. The network administrator answers with more bandwidth here and there, and the problem goes away. The network expands some more, and performance declines again. The network administrator adds more bandwidth and another router. Several subnets lose their routing within the network, and the network administrator adds a few host routes to fix the problem. And so on.

That is how an address scheme typically develops. Nowhere during the evolution did anyone say, "What if we needed to change the addressing? How difficult would that be?" At this point a redesign looks pretty much like an initial design. (To be honest, any large-scale network change makes me pucker. IP readdressing is no different.) There may be a few extra considerations, such as saving pools of addresses to avoid complete readdressing, network outages, interim steps, and project management.

With the playing field leveled between design and redesign, let's look at the points that should be considered when (re)designing an IP address scheme.

- *Network topology:* Different network topologies, such as ethernet, point to point and frame relay networks, require different IP addressing architectures. *Chapter 5.*
- *Internet connection:* This is one of the biggest issues when determining the address scheme. How many hosts are going to require an address directly on the Internet? None, just a few, or all? Is there ever going to be a desire to connect to the Internet? How will that be done? Legal IP address or not? How many networks were you allocated? *Chapter 6.*
- *Size of routing tables:* Routing efficiency is improved with the reduction of entries in the route table. In

Chapter 4 we discussed the pruning rules a router uses to select a next-hop destination. If the working set of routes at the start of the pruning process is all routes in the route table, it makes sense that the Basic Match pruning process would be improved if the table were smaller and fewer routes had to be examined to determine whether a basic match existed. *Chapter 7.*

- *Address efficiency:* Registered Internet addresses seem to be at a premium these days. The prevailing IP address allocation authority evaluates all requests for an address allocation carefully to determine whether the applicant really needs "that many addresses." The motto of the day is "Do more with what you have." Efficiency of address utilization is important in cases like this. *Chapter 8.*
- *Ease of administration:* One of the goals in designing an address scheme should always be to make the address scheme easy to use and understand and to make future changes easier. *Chapter 9.*
- *Anticipated growth and unanticipated change:* An addressing scheme should permit growth and change within the constraints of desired address efficiency. Growth that is anticipated should always be a major consideration of an address design. *Chapter 10.*

chapter 5

Common Topology Addressing

This chapter provides an overview of general IP addressing issues associated with common network topologies. The topologies presented here include Ethernet and Token Ring, point-to-point connections, dial-in pooled access, Frame Relay, and ATM. Others such as FDDI and X.25 are currently in use. The general addressing issues discussed with respect to the subset presented in this chapter are universal.

Introduction to the IP Address Worksheet

I have developed a system that I use when designing an address plan. This and subsequent chapters in this section will all use this system to explain concepts as they are introduced. Illustration 5-1 shows a portion of the IP address worksheet. The entire worksheet is contained in Appendix C. Please feel free to copy the worksheets out of the appendix and to cut and paste (real scissors, real glue) them together for use in this and subsequent chapters.

.0/24	.128/25	.192/26	.224/27	.240/28	.248/29	.252/30
0	0	0	0	0	0	0
1	1	1	1	1	1	1
2	2	2	2	2	2	2
3	3	3	3	3	3	3
4	4	4	4	4	4	4
5	5	5	5	5	5	5
6	6	6	6	6	6	6
7	7	7	7	7	7	7
8	8	8	8	8	8	8
9	9	9	9	9	9	9
10	10	10	10	10	10	10
11	11	11	11	11	11	11
12	12	12	12	12	12	12
13	13	13	13	13	13	13
14	14	14	14	14	14	14
15	15	15	15	15	15	15
16	16	16	16	16	16	16
17	17	17	17	17	17	17
18	18	18	18	18	18	18
19	19	19	19	19	19	19
20	20	20	20	20	20	20
21	21	21	21	21	21	21
22	22	22	22	22	22	22
23	23	23	23	23	23	23
24	24	24	24	24	24	24
25	25	25	25	25	25	25
26	26	26	26	26	26	26
27	27	27	27	27	27	27
28	28	28	28	28	28	28
29	29	29	29	29	29	29
30	30	30	30	30	30	30
31	31	31	31	31	31	31

Illustration 5-1 Portion of IP Address Worksheet

The worksheet represents the subnetting that is possible with an 8-bit host partition, as in the case of a Class C address. The concepts can all be extended to Class A or Class B addresses; the worksheet just gets bigger, that's all. For a Class C address the worksheet has 256 rows, not including the header. The rows are numbered consecutively, starting at 0 and ending at 255. The rows represent all the possible addresses for a Class C network. The columns represent the subnet mask.

.0/24	.128/25	.192/26	.224/27	.240/28	.248/29	.252/30

For a Class C network 192.168.1.0, the network mask 255.255.255.0 would be represented by the leftmost column. This could be represented in this text more easily through the use of the alternative "/*n*" CIDR notation. The representation 192.168.10.5/28 would indicate that the Class C address specified is subnetted with a mask of 255.255.255.240.

Note the two types of shading on the IP address worksheet. Boxes shaded in light gray, as in the first row and in the rightmost column of rows 4 and 8, indicate that the address is not available to be used as a host address. These are addresses that have an all-0s host portion and are special-case addresses. Boxes shaded in dark gray, as in the last row of the full worksheet (Appendix C) and in the rightmost column of rows 3 and 7, also indicate that the address is not available to be used as a host address. These are addresses that have an all-1s host portion and are special-case addresses as well.

Take a look at the rightmost column of the worksheet. The header indicates that this column applies to a mask of 255.255.255.252 (a CIDR notation of /30). For the Class C network 192.168.1.0, the addresses in the range 192.168.1.0 to 192.168.1.31 can be subdivided, using a mask of 255.255.255.252, into eight separate networks:

192.168.1.0

192.168.1.4

192.168.1.8

192.168.1.12

192.168.1.16

192.168.1.20

192.168.1.24

192.168.1.28

Note that these eight addresses are shaded light gray in the worksheet to indicate that they are the special-case all-0s addresses.

The broadcast addresses for each of these networks are

192.168.1.3

192.168.1.7

192.168.1.11

192.168.1.15

192.168.1.19

192.168.1.23

192.168.1.27

192.168.1.31

These addresses are shaded dark gray to indicate that they are the all-1s addresses on the network.

All columns have a number of consecutively grouped unshaded cells. These represent all of the potential valid host addresses for a given subnet. There are only two hosts available per subnet when using a mask of 255.255.255.252. All legitimate subnets will have the lowest address in the range shaded in light gray and the highest address in the range shaded in dark gray.

Addresses in the range 192.168.1.0 to 192.168.1.31 can be subdivided into any of the following.

- 8 networks using a mask of 255.255.255.252 (/30)
- 4 networks using a mask of 255.255.255.248 (/29)
- 2 networks using a mask of 255.255.255.240 (/28)
- 1 network using a mask of 255.255.255.224 (/27)

The entire Class C network 192.168.1.0 can be subdivided into any of the following (or many combinations thereof).

- 64 networks of 2 hosts using a mask of 255.255.255.252
- 32 networks of 6 hosts using a mask of 255.255.255.248
- 16 networks of 14 hosts using a mask of 255.255.255.240
- 8 networks of 30 hosts using a mask of 255.255.255.224
- 4 networks of 62 hosts using a mask of 255.255.255.192
- 2 networks of 126 hosts using a mask of 255.255.255.128
- 1 network of 254 hosts using a mask of 255.255.255.0

Consider the two-router network in Illustration 5-2. Assume that we can use only IP addresses from 192.168.1.0 to 192.168.1.31.

Also assume that we must use numbered IP interfaces on the routers, which would require a two-host network for connecting Router A to Router C on the point-to-point link. We need 5 IP addresses for the Ethernet at the remote branch office, 13 IP addresses for the Ethernet at the corporate office, or three networks with a total of 20 IP addresses. Should be doable. If we use fixed-length subnet masks, we could divide the address space in half by using a 28-bit network mask (255.255.255.240), with each half consisting of 14 hosts (Illustration 5-3). This is not viable, because we need at least three networks due to the point-to-point link having to use numbered interfaces. If we use a 29-bit network mask, we can divide the host space into four equal-sized networks with six hosts per network (Illustration 5-4).

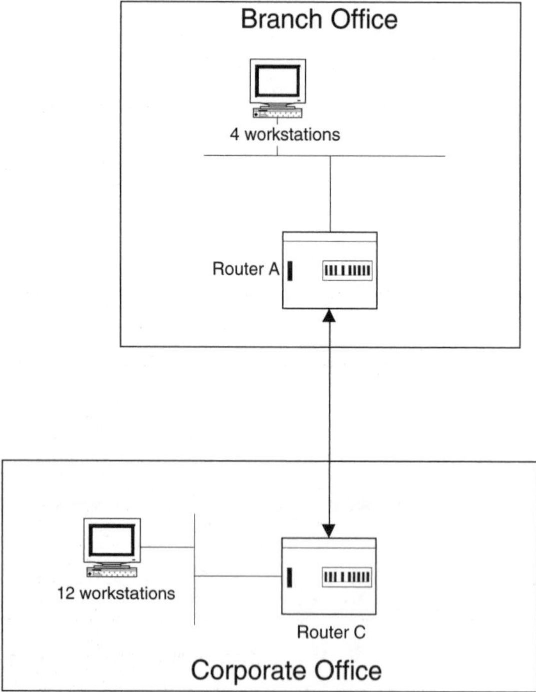

Illustration 5-2 Example Network

.0/24	.128/25	.192/26	.224/27	**.240/28**	.248/29	.252/30
0	0	0	0	**0**	0	0
1	1	1	1	**1**	1	1
2	2	2	2	**2**	2	2
3	3	3	3	**3**	3	3
4	4	4	4	**4**	4	4
5	5	5	5	**5**	5	5
6	6	6	6	**6**	6	6
7	7	7	7	**7**	7	7
8	8	8	8	**8**	8	8
9	9	9	9	**9**	9	9
10	10	10	10	**10**	10	10
11	11	11	11	**11**	11	11
12	12	12	12	**12**	12	12
13	13	13	13	**13**	13	13
14	14	14	14	**14**	14	14
15	15	15	15	**15**	15	15
16	16	16	16	**16**	16	16
17	17	17	17	**17**	17	17
18	18	18	18	**18**	18	18
19	19	19	19	**19**	19	19
20	20	20	20	**20**	20	20
21	21	21	21	**21**	21	21
22	22	22	22	**22**	22	22
23	23	23	23	**23**	23	23
24	24	24	24	**24**	24	24
25	25	25	25	**25**	25	25
26	26	26	26	**26**	26	26
27	27	27	27	**27**	27	27
28	28	28	28	**28**	28	28
29	29	29	29	**29**	29	29
30	30	30	30	**30**	30	30
31	31	31	31	**31**	31	31

Illustration 5-3 Networks with 14 Hosts per Network

.0/24	.128/25	.192/26	.224/27	.240/28	**.248/29**	.252/30
0	0	0	0	0	**0**	0
1	1	1	1	1	**1**	1
2	2	2	2	2	**2**	2
3	3	3	3	3	**3**	3
4	4	4	4	4	**4**	4
5	5	5	5	5	**5**	5
6	6	6	6	6	**6**	6
7	7	7	7	7	**7**	7
8	8	8	8	8	**8**	8
9	9	9	9	9	**9**	9
10	10	10	10	10	**10**	10
11	11	11	11	11	**11**	11
12	12	12	12	12	**12**	12
13	13	13	13	13	**13**	13
14	14	14	14	14	**14**	14
15	15	15	15	15	**15**	15
16	16	16	16	16	**16**	16
17	17	17	17	17	**17**	17
18	18	18	18	18	**18**	18
19	19	19	19	19	**19**	19
20	20	20	20	20	**20**	20
21	21	21	21	21	**21**	21
22	22	22	22	22	**22**	22
23	23	23	23	23	**23**	23
24	24	24	24	24	**24**	24
25	25	25	25	25	**25**	25
26	26	26	26	26	**26**	26
27	27	27	27	27	**27**	27
28	28	28	28	28	**28**	28
29	29	29	29	29	**29**	29
30	30	30	30	30	**30**	30
31	31	31	31	31	**31**	31

Illustration 5-4 Four Networks with Six Hosts per Network

The problem is that one network needs to have 13 IP addresses, and this subnet permits a maximum of only six hosts per network. Even using two of these six host networks would fall short of the total hosts required. It appears that there is no solution if we use fixed-length masks. We could use variable-length masks, but that would require extreme caution if we wanted to use RIP routing. Remember, RIP routing does not include route masks in the routing updates. We could use OSPF, though. So let's look at how the networks might be divided up using variable-length subnet masks (Illustration 5-5).

The first network, 192.168.1.0/30, has two available hosts. This network will be used for the point-to-point network between Router A and Router C. The second network, 192.168.1.8/29, can have six hosts in it. The branch office requires four workstations and one router address (five total host addresses). This network would fit the requirement, with one host address to spare. The third network, 192.168.1.16/28, can have 14 hosts. Since the corporate office requires only 13 host addresses, this network will fit the requirement and also have one host address to spare. Overall there isn't too much left over; the one left over network, 192.168.1.4/30, can be considered "room to grow" (nothing is ever *wasted*).

Illustration 5-6 shows what the network looks like with addresses assigned. Since we restricted ourselves to use only the first 32 addresses in the 192.168.1.0 Class C address, seven-eighths of all the address space in that one Class C network is still available. That's enough space to install another seven networks just like it!

.0/24	.128/25	.192/26	.224/27	.240/28	.248/29	.252/30
0	0	0	0	0	0	**0**
1	1	1	1	1	1	**RTR A 1**
2	2	2	2	2	2	**RTR C 2**
3	3	3	3	3	3	**3**
4	4	4	4	4	4	4
5	5	5	5	5	5	5
6	6	6	6	6	6	6
7	7	7	7	7	7	7
8	8	8	8	8	**8**	8
9	9	9	9	9	**RTR A 9**	9
10	10	10	10	10	**10**	10
11	11	11	11	11	**WS A 11**	11
12	12	12	12	12	**WS B 12**	12
13	13	13	13	13	**WS C 13**	13
14	14	14	14	14	**WS D 14**	14
15	15	15	15	15	**15**	15
16	16	16	16	**16**	16	16
17	17	17	17	**RTR C 17**	17	17
18	18	18	18	**18**	18	18
19	19	19	19	**WS A 19**	19	19
20	20	20	20	**WS B 20**	20	20
21	21	21	21	**WS C 21**	21	21
22	22	22	22	**WS D 22**	22	22
23	23	23	23	**WS E 23**	23	23
24	24	24	24	**WS F 24**	24	24
25	25	25	25	**WS G 25**	25	25
26	26	26	26	**WS H 26**	26	26
27	27	27	27	**WS I 27**	27	27
28	28	28	28	**WS J 28**	28	28
29	29	29	29	**WS K 29**	29	29
30	30	30	30	**WS L 30**	30	30
31	31	31	31	**31**	31	31

Illustration 5-5 Variable-Length Subnet Mask Solution

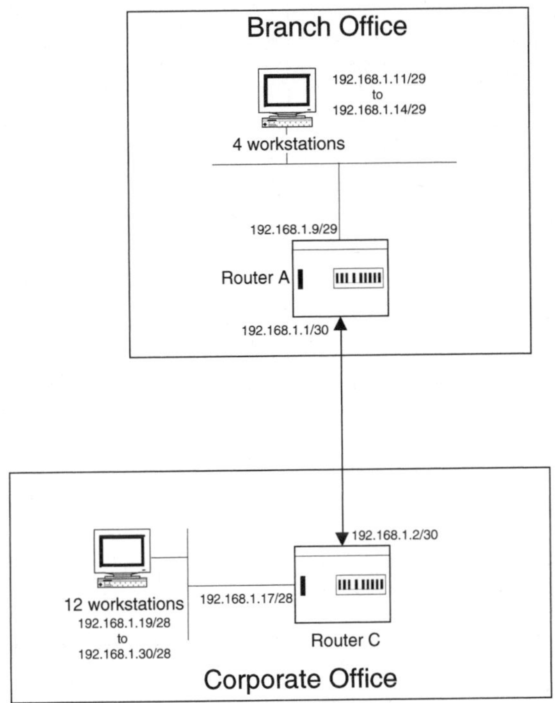

Illustration 5-6 Example Network with Addresses

Additional examples will be provided for designing an appropriate address scheme taking efficiency of routing and address utilization, administrative ease of use, and management, growth, and Internet connectivity into consideration. The IP addressing worksheet in Appendix C divides the host portion of a Class C address into subnets and lets you see clearly where each network begins and ends when a specific mask is used.

Broadcast-Capable, Multiple-Access Networks: Ethernet and Token Ring

There are several options for addressing on an Ethernet or a Token Ring. One strategy is to have a single IP network sufficient in size to be able to provide address space for the hosts that need connectivity through that medium. The address space should include some reserved IP addresses that will be allocated as the network grows. Illustration 5-7 depicts a single Ethernet using only a portion of the address space for a Class C network.

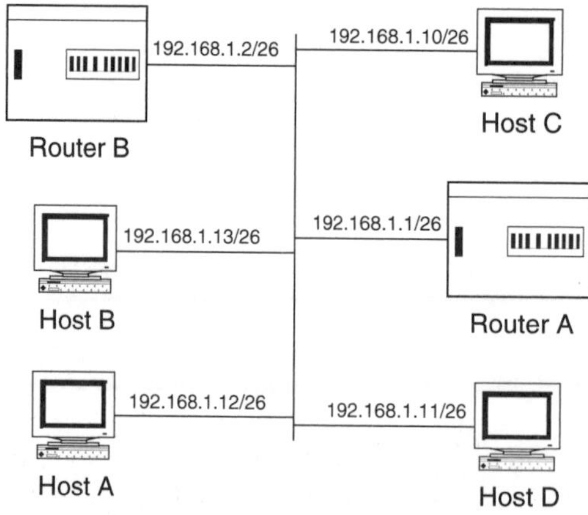

Illustration 5-7 IP Addressing on a LAN (Single Network)

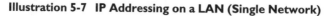

The Class C network, 192.168.1.0, is subnetted with a mask of 255.255.255.192. This network is capable of supporting 62 hosts, so there is plenty of room for expansion. The most popular network sizes for an Ethernet or a Token Ring permit from 14 to 254 hosts.

Another addressing scheme involves the division of an Ethernet into workgroups, or cliques. Each workgroup should have the majority of its needed resources internal (including disk space, printers) to the workgroup. Illustration 5-8 shows a Token Ring with two workgroups. A 29-bit network mask (255.255.255.248) permits a maximum of six hosts per network.

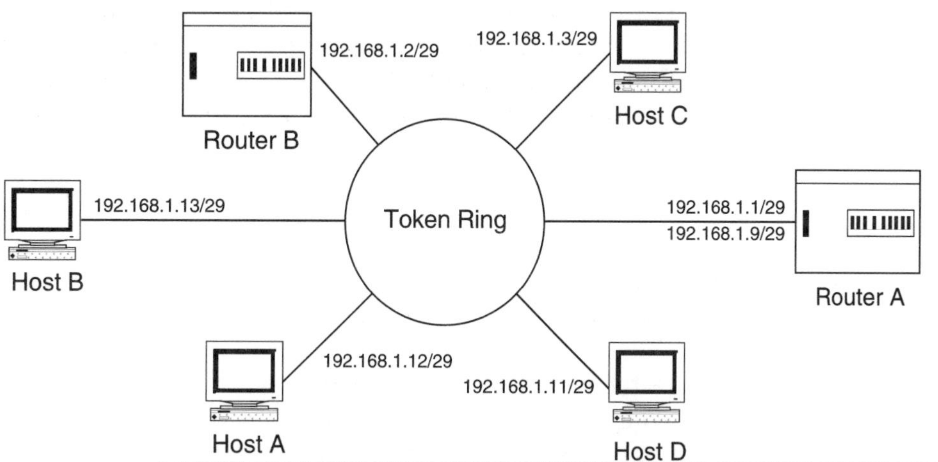

Illustration 5-8 IP Addressing in a LAN (Multiple Networks)

The first workgroup — Router B, Host C, and Router A — is using the 192.168.1.0/29 network. The second workgroup — Host B, Host A, Host D, and Router A — all participate on the 192.168.1.8/29 network. When Host C wishes to exchange a file with Host A, a router must forward the traffic between the two networks. Router A is multihomed; it has IP interfaces on both workgroup networks. Router A will forward the traffic from 192.168.1.3/29 to 192.168.1.12/29.

Occasionally members of workgroups change in their traffic patterns and use the router too much to facilitate their communications. In this case, there are essentially three options:

Move one of the hosts into the other host's workgroup;

Multihome the hosts in both workgroups; or

Abolish hopes of achieving a workgroup addressing scheme and flatten out the IP architecture.

LAN Transit Networks

I was amazed to find a bastion of networks out there are still predominantly non-TCP/IP networks. I was at a site recently where they were routing IPX (heavily) and bridging IP for management (Telnet console access or SNMP). Administration was divided into the Novell group, which supported LAN applications, and the WAN group, which managed interconnections. I have seen cases in which a LAN group resisted having TCP/IP on its network. In one case that I know of, the LAN group permitted a network of only two TCP/IP hosts to participate on its IPX LAN. I thought it was worth showing Illustration 5-9. Router A and Router B share the same IP network, 192.168.1.0/30. That network can have only two hosts so it looks very much like a point-to-point link, which is what it logically is. The LAN is used only for TCP/IP connectivity across some distance, although its main purpose is to service IPX workstations and servers.

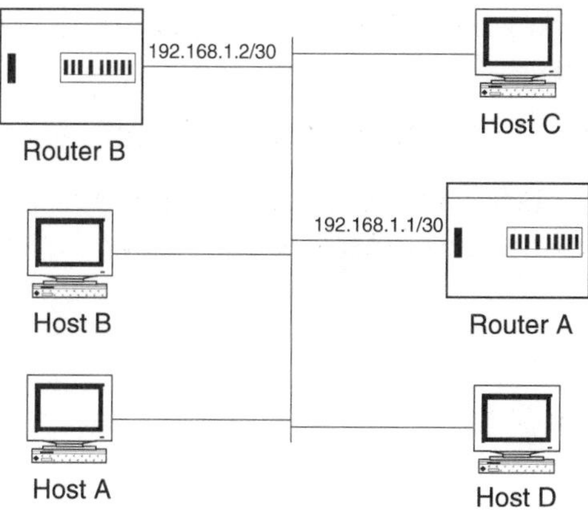

Illustration 5-9 IP LAN Transit Network

Another technology is worth mentioning at this time. Virtual LAN or VLAN is a technology made possible by LAN switches. In a nutshell, all hosts in a VLAN are numbered as if they belong to a single IP subnet. The LAN switch divides these hosts into broadcast domains that can be secure and are easily modified so that a clique of users can be grouped almost ad-hoc into a workgroup. It used to be that proponents of VLANs would cite the adage "switch when you can, route when you must" as a way to keep the network running as fast as possible. This is not as true these days as it once was. We now have wire-speed routers and layer 3 switches that permit both a hierarchical IP model (VLAN requires a flat IP model) and line rate forwarding.

Point to Point (Numbered)

Some router manufacturers do not offer an option for an unnumbered IP interface. If this is the case, each end of a point-to-point link must have an IP address. Since there can be only two hosts on a point-to-point link, it would be a waste to use a network that could support more than two hosts. In Illustration 5-10 the routers have a point-to-point link between them. They are configured to use network 192.168.2.0/30, one of the subnets that supports only two hosts. In a RIP environment, the damage can be much more severe. Whenever you are restricted to using a fixed-length subnet mask, the number of hosts allocated to a point-to-point link would be the same as what is allocated to an Ethernet or vice versa.

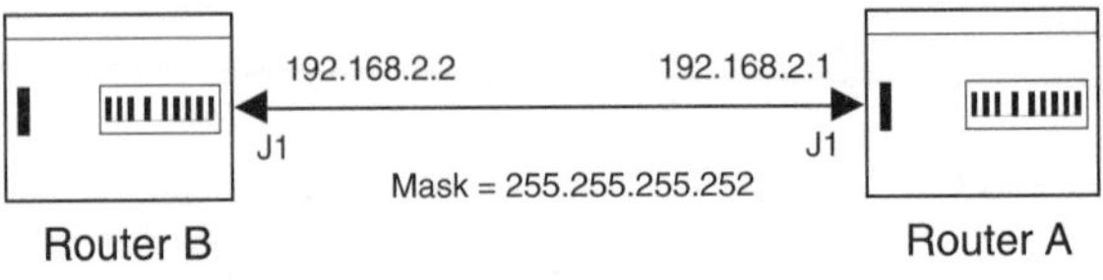

Illustration 5-10 Point-to-Point (Numbered)

Point-to-Point (Unnumbered)

The good news is that many routers do support unnumbered IP on point-to-point links. This is not as big a boon to OSPF as it is to RIP, since OSPF can support variable-length subnet masks, but it is a savings and has some big rewards. For instance, you don't need to be configured for every network that could possibly be at the other end of the link. This is especially nice for the dial-backup application, as well as ISDN remote dial-in applications. The routers are able to support unnumbered interfaces because they use an identifier for each end point, the router ID. Illustration 5-11 shows an unnumbered IP network between Router A and Router B.

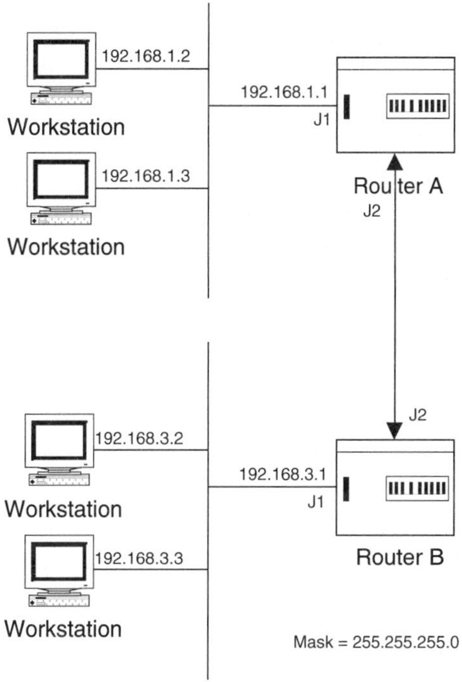

Illustration 5-11 Point-to-Point Network (Unnumbered)

As mentioned, ISDN (and other dial-up services) is a special type of point-to-point connection. When it is up, it looks and behaves just like a digital leased line. Routers typically run PPP across the ISDN link. What makes an ISDN line different is that it also behaves like a telephone. Through the use of the D-channel signaling, a router can place a call with ISDN as simply as a computer can dial and connect with a modem. It is a very powerful feature that allows a router to "place a call" over ISDN and to begin routing based on the destination IP address within a packet. After a period of inactivity, the router can tear down the call and be ready to place the next one. Unnumbered IP interfaces work nicely on any point-to-point dial connection, since it would be cumbersome to configure the interfaces to be able to use the same network as all the remotes use. The alternative is to multihome the router with an address from each one of the remote location's IP networks.

Pooled Dial-In Access

There are many ways of doing dial-in access. This section shows a few of the more common methods and focuses primarily on methods that terminate 23 or more narrowband users cost effectively. Devices that I consider to be in this class are Terminal Servers, Remote Access Servers, high-density Remote Access Concentrators, and ISDN PRI routers. This section gives a brief overview of addressing with respect to these dial-in access methods.

Pooled dial-in access links should be treated as individual point-to-point links that are mass terminated on a single device or multiple devices. The links could be addressed using a 2-bit host ID, or the PPP links could use unnumbered IP with the host being provided a single IP address for identity. Illustration 5-12 shows a small network where there are two hosts and a dial router connected to a central Remote Access Server. We'll make a few assumptions for use in our example. First, we'll say that Hosts A and B are dialing in from a remote residence using analog modem technology. The Dial Router is located in a small office and is dialing out over an ISDN Basic Rate Interface (BRI). The Remote Access Server (RAS) has an ISDN Primary Rate Interface (PRI) over which all modem and ISDN calls are being presented as dial-in users. In this situation, most likely found in enterprise networks where security is paramount, the links use numbered PPP and the numbers are assigned to the end points of the WAN link on a static basis. Host A connects the RAS using the 192.168.2.0/30 IP network, which permits only two host addresses. The RAS can advertise each network as individual route entries, or it can aggregate these networks into one or just a few routes to Router A using route aggregation methods discussed in Chapter 7. Hosts and the routers dialing into the RAS must match IP networks with what is defined on the RAS. That is, since Host A has an IP address of 192.168.2.2, when it dials in, the RAS must configure the port that it connects to as 192.168.2.1 for communications to succeed. This is not so difficult where every remote user has their own port to dial into using a specific telephone number, but it does become more complex when there is a pool of incoming ports that service all calls to a single hunt group. In this case, a mechanism is needed to detect the identity of the user during PPP negotiation to associate a configuration profile with an inbound port.

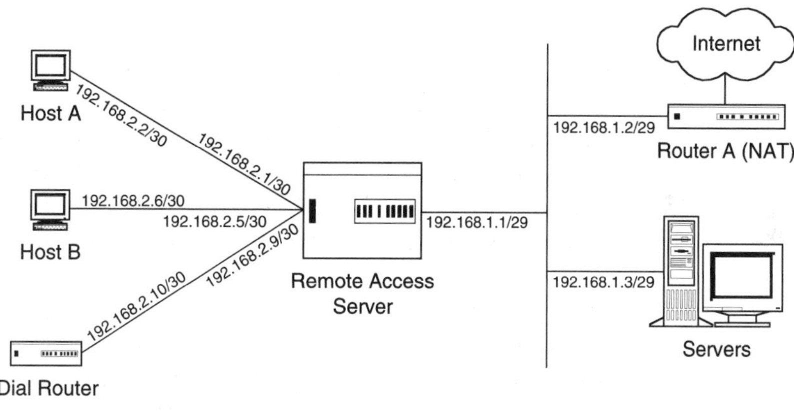

Illustration 5-12 Pooled Dial-In Access Using Numbered PPP Links

A more realistic and up-to-date method for setting up remote access is shown in Illustration 5-13. In this scenario, the dial-in hosts and routers are not configured in advance for a specific IP address on the WAN link. In fact, the WAN link will use IP Control Protocol (IPCP) of PPP to receive an IP address from the Remote Access Server. The actual WAN link itself will use unnumbered IP. The IP address provided via IPCP to the remote device will be used as an ID only to terminate the IP packets. In this scenario, I have also introduced a Remote Authentication Dial In User Service (RADIUS) server. Instead of having each user profile defined on each Remote Access Server, the user profiles are defined on one or more centrally located RADIUS servers that validate the remote device's User-name and Password and then return a set of attributes that the RAS will use to configure the link for correct communications. Of course, there usually is nothing to prevent all or some of the user profiles from being defined on the RAS. Small installations may not opt for a RADIUS server. Large installations may rely on both RADIUS for normal user authentication and "back-doors" (system administrator profiles) that are locally defined on the RAS. In the event that the RADIUS server becomes unavailable, an administrator can still dial into the RAS for diagnostic purposes.

The RADIUS Framed-IP-Address attribute is used to tell the RAS what IP address should be used for that specific user. There are two special addresses that can be returned to the RAS in the Framed-IP-Address attribute. If Framed-IP-Address is configured as 255.255.255.254, this signals the RAS to make the IP address assignment from the Remote Access Server's pool of IP addresses. If Framed-IP-Address is configured as 255.255.255.255, this signals the RAS to allow the remote user to "suggest" an IP address to be used during PPP negotiation. The Framed-IP-Address could also contain a specific IP address that the RADIUS server wants the RAS to issue to the user with IPCP. This last option is useful if a specific user is to get a specific IP address whenever they dial into the RAS. It is also useful if the RADIUS server maintains the pool of IP addresses instead of the RAS.

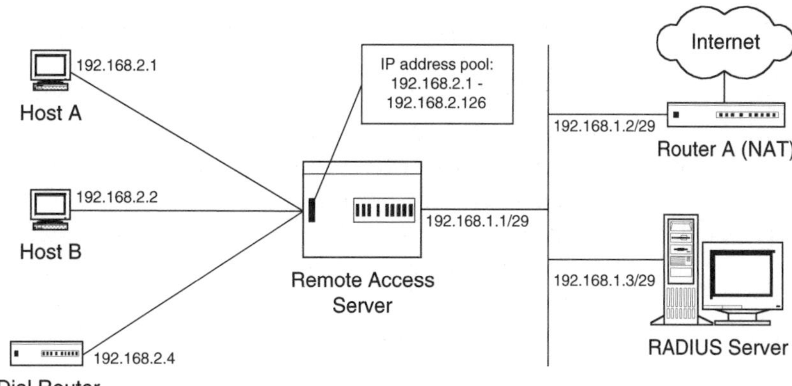

Illustration 5-13 Pooled Dial-In Access Using RAS Maintained Address Pool

In our current discussion, the RAS is making the IP assignments to dial-in users from its internal IP address pools. This means that when RADIUS authenticates the user, it must return the Framed-IP-Address=255.255.255.254. The administrator of the RAS has the following options

- *Inject a host route into the dynamic routing system for each IP address that is allocated:* The RAS will create host routes in its routing table for each address allocated. These routes would naturally be included in the routing updates being sent by the RAS to Router A in Illustration 5-13.
- *Advertise a single IP route that subsumes all host IP addresses that are in the pool:* This can be done in a couple of ways. One way is to let the RAS be an area border router in OSPF and summarize all the host routes into a single route. Another way is to not run a dynamic routing protocol on the 192.168.1.0/29 network in Illustration 5-13. Router A (now being

used as a corporate core router instead of the indicated Internet router) could be running OSPF and import the static route to 192.168.2.0/65 (next hop 192.168.1.1) into the dynamic routing system.

- *Permit Proxy ARP to attract the traffic to the RAS for forwarding to the host or dial router:* Look at Illustration 5-14 to see how this works. (If you need to, refer back to Direct Routing, Chapter 4, for additional information on Proxy ARP.) Note in the illustration how the Ethernet is addressed using a full Class C network of 192.168.2.0/24. Also note that the IP address pool uses 192.168.2.1 through 192.168.2.126 (which are the host addresses for the network 192.168.2.0/25). The Ethernet is carefully numbered using IP addresses from 192.168.2.128/25, the other half of the 192.168.2.0/24 network. If Router A were to receive an IP packet for Host A (192.168.2.1), it would believe — based on the network mask bound to its 192.168.2.129 interface — that Host A is a host on the Ethernet, which it is not. Router A checks its ARP cache for the hardware address of Host A. There is no entry because it the first time since the ARP cache was flushed that Router A has needed to deliver data to 192.168.2.1. Router A sends an ARP request and the RAS responds for 192.168.2.1 with the Remote Access Server's own hardware address. Router A sends the data to the RAS thinking that it was actually Host A. The RAS knows how to forward that data to the actual Host A, and the transmission is completed.

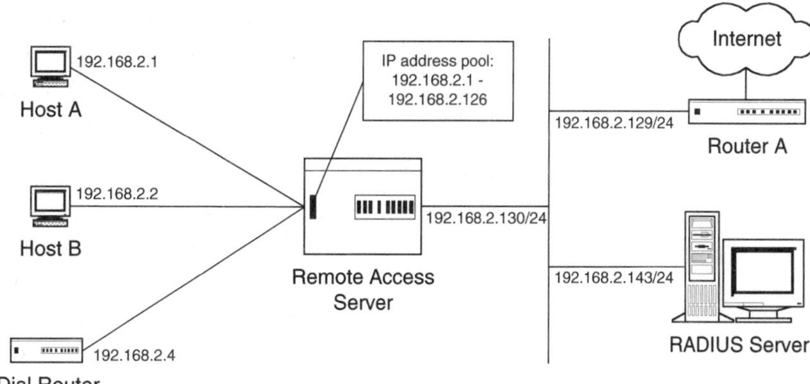

Illustration 5-14 Pooled Dial-In Access Using RAS Maintained Address Pool and Proxy ARP

I discussed the ability of the RADIUS server to allocate the IP addresses to the dial-in users earlier in this section. The RADIUS server can be configured with a pool of IP addresses as shown in Illustration 5-15. When the user's attributes are returned to the RAS, it includes a Framed-IP-Address with a value equal to the IP address allocated to that remote user. For this to work well and scale so that it can handle many users dialing into many sites, the RADIUS server must be able to allocate from unique pools of IP addresses depending on the Remote Access Server's identity. In other words, the solution does not scale well if the RADIUS server can only make allocations out of a single IP address pool. Host routes would not be able to be aggregated because of the haphazard allocations all over the network. If the RADIUS server can maintain an IP address pool for each RAS (or cluster of RASs), the RADIUS server becomes a nice, centralized tool for managing the IP address pools deployed in the network. Without this capability, a small ISP with multiple RASs and a single block of IP addresses would still find this method desirable.

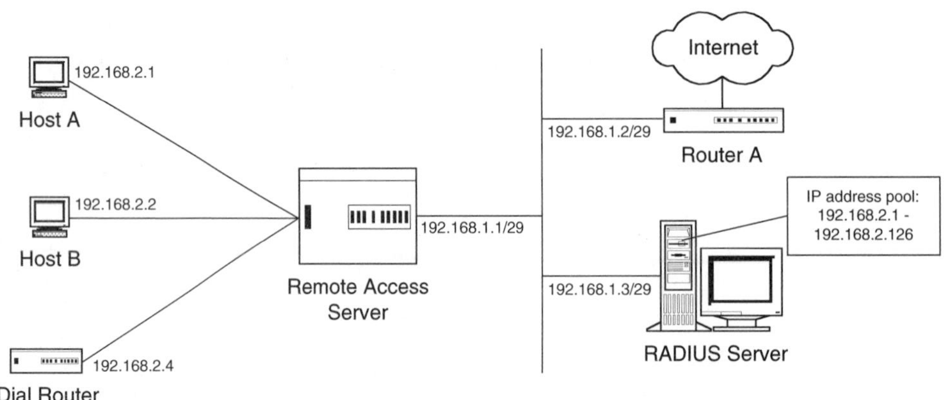

Illustration 5-15 Pooled Dial-In Access Using RADIUS Maintained Address Pool

Nonbroadcast Multiple-Access Networks: Frame Relay

Frame Relay, ATM, and X.25 are examples of networks that permit multiple devices (more than two) to connect and communicate but do not have the capability to support broadcast. To avoid a clamor of calls and e-mail, let me say that I do understand that Frame Relay was designed to look just like a local area network and to support broadcast capability. I have never seen a carrier offer any kind of broadcast or multicast capability, but I am sure that some must support it. In this text, which should be fairly close to "real world," I will discuss Frame Relay as if there were no broadcast capability. See Illustration 5-16.

A typical Frame Relay network would have a number of routers, each with a single physical interface into the Frame Relay network or "cloud." To the Frame Relay subscriber it would appear that they are the only devices on the network — a virtual private network. Each site that needs to communicate directly with another site would require a permanent virtual circuit (PVC). The end points of the PVC are identified with a data link connection identifier (DLCI). Even though a router may have more than one PVC that is terminated on it to allow direct access to multiple sites, it still may require only one physical connection to the carrier.

It is important to note that Frame Relay is based on the premise that modern digital networks are nearly error free. As such, some of the functions that were essential in X.25 have been removed, their functions handled by the higher-layer protocols. Another interesting distinction is the way in which bandwidth is sold and allocated. A subscriber will pay for a guaranteed data rate, called the *committed information rate* (CIR). As long as the subscriber keeps the data flowing into the cloud at a rate equal to or less than the CIR, the carrier agrees not to discard any packets. The subscriber may burst above the CIR and all the data may be allowed through; however, under conditions of congestion the Frame Relay service provider may discard any packets that make up the excess above the CIR.

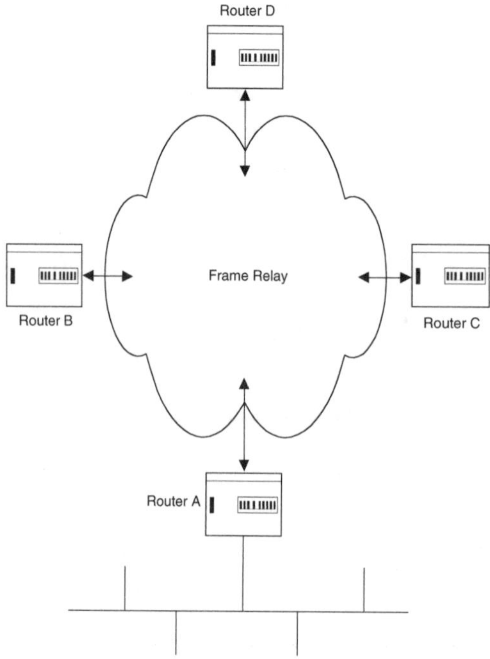

Illustration 5-16 Logical Frame Relay View

Frame Relay (Full-Mesh)

One way to configure a Frame Relay network is to provision each site with a PVC to every other site. This is known as a full-mesh configuration (Illustration 5-17). Carriers typically charge for the presence of the PVC and for the CIR the PVC is provisioned to use. As a result, the full-mesh Frame Relay configuration is typically the more expensive configuration. Sometimes it is not cost-prohibitive, though, so it pays to ask the carrier's account manager.

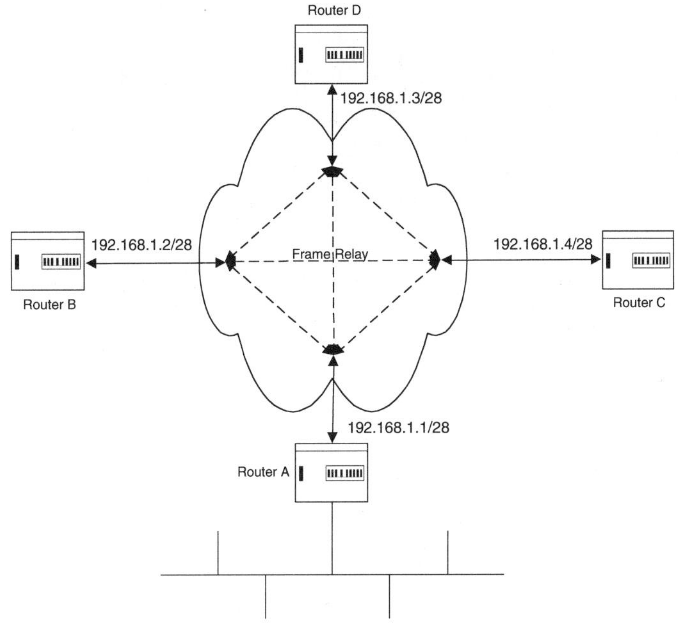

Illustration 5-17 Full-Mesh Frame Relay (View 1)

In Illustration 5-17, Router B knows that to pass traffic to Router D, it must use the link layer address — the DLCI — that corresponds to Router D. The Frame Relay switch will use the path specified by the permanent virtual circuit to deliver the frame to Router D. IP addressing is simple in a full-mesh network: Pick a network size sufficient to accommodate the number of devices internetworked — using the Frame Relay service plus some growth — and assign a host ID from the chosen subnet to each router's Frame Relay interface, as shown in Illustration 5-17. An address scheme that uses only a single IP network for addressing all of the devices on the Frame Relay network is known as a *cloud model.* All hosts are in the single IP network cloud.

The number of PVCs required to provision a network in a full-mesh configuration is equal to $N*(N-1)/2$, where N is the number of nodes in the Frame Relay network. A network with four sites would require six PVCs to interconnect them. This is shown in Illustration 5-18. Can you imagine what a 20-site full-mesh network would look like if it were drawn out similar to the 4-site network in the illustration?

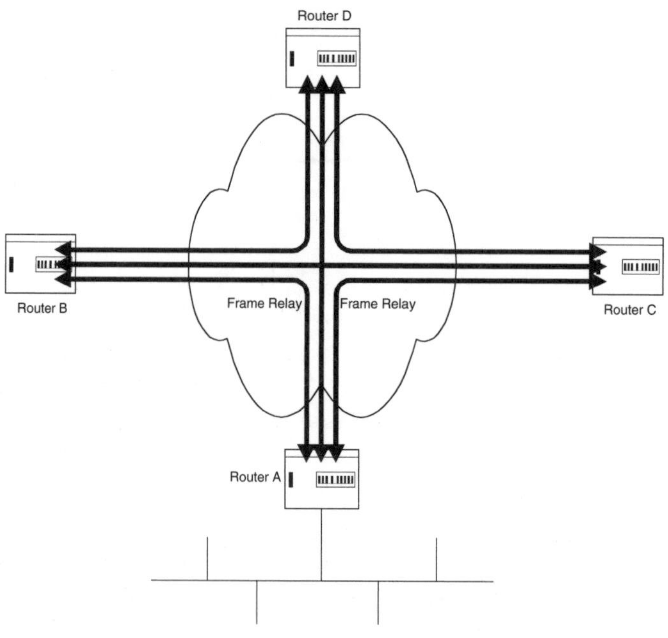

Illustration 5-18 Full-Mesh Frame Relay (View 2)

Both RIP and OSPF work well in a full-mesh Frame Relay network using the cloud model for IP addressing. In fact, OSPF works best when implemented in this way. OSPF relies on constant contact with its neighbors and since each router in a full-mesh Frame Relay network has a PVC between itself and any other router in the Frame Relay network, these adjacencies are easily maintained. In actuality, only one router per network needs to maintain these neighbor relationships with all the other routers in the network. This router is known as the *designated router* (DR). In a full-mesh Frame Relay network, it may not matter which of the routers on the IP network becomes the designated router.

Frame Relay (Hub-and-Spoke)

A Frame Relay configuration that is far more popular than the full-mesh configuration is a topology commonly called *hub-and-spoke*. One central Frame Relay hub router has a PVC to each of the remote sites. Each remote site has a PVC to only one location, the Frame Relay hub router. Where N equals the number of nodes in a frame relay network, there will be exactly $(N-1)$ PVCs used in a hub-and-spoke Frame Relay network. One reason to configure this type of network is that the nonhub routers are truly remote offices that need some resources that are centrally located (at the same site where the hub router is located), and the remote sites seldom communicate with one another. The remote sites can communicate with one another, but they must, in all cases, do this through the hub router.

One of two different IP addressing models may be used for a hub-and-spoke Frame Relay network: the cloud model, which we have already discussed, and the point-to-point model. Again, the cloud model would have a single IP network. Each router's Frame Relay interface would be assigned a host address from that network. This is in contrast to the point-to-point model, which allocates an IP network for each PVC, and each end point has a host address in that network assigned to it. Illustration 5-19 depicts a point-to-point addressing model in a hub-and-spoke Frame Relay network.

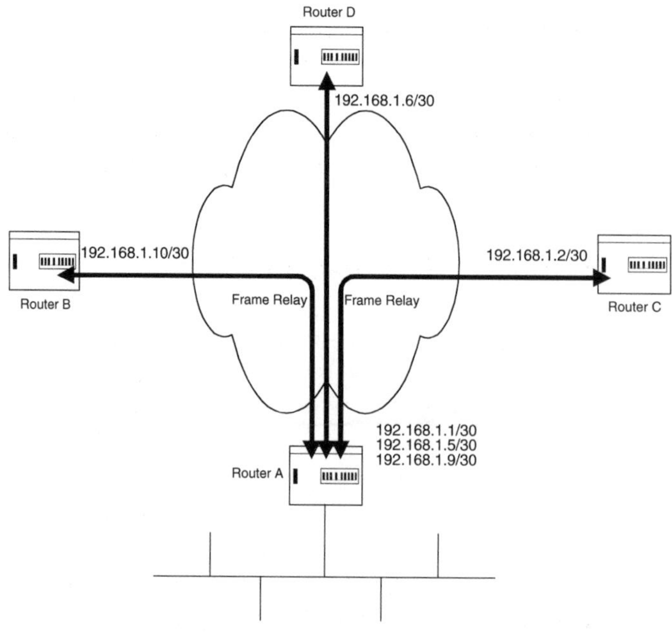

Illustration 5-19 Point-to-Point Addressing of Hub-and-Spoke Frame Relay

RIP typically can operate in either IP addressing model in a hub-and-spoke Frame Relay network. OSPF, because of the way it needs to maintain adjacencies, dictates a point-to-point addressing model. The designated router on a given IP network can always maintain its adjacencies since there are always at most two routers on a point-to-point Frame Relay IP network. If you use a cloud model on a hub-and-spoke Frame Relay network and run RIP, it is possible to convert over to OSPF without having to change the IP addressing to the point-to-point model. It is kind of a cheat, but I have done it effectively. The key is that the hub router must be forced into being the designated router. Another router will become the backup designated router and it won't be able to maintain its adjacencies, but that has never been a problem. If the hub router fails, there will be bigger problems to worry about than what the backup designated router is. Use this approach with caution; there are no guarantees how another router would handle the situation or even if it would allow a router to be ineligible to become the designated router. The best policy for Frame Relay addressing for OSPF routing is to use the point-to-point address model.

Frame Relay (Partial-Mesh)

Sometimes a company starts either with a full-mesh Frame Relay network and cuts back on its meshing based on usage or with a hub-and-spoke and adds PVCs because certain sites seem to "collaborate" with each other. The result is something less than a full-mesh network and more than a hub-and-spoke network. This is known as a *partial-mesh Frame Relay network.*

For RIP routing, either the cloud or point-to-point address model will work. For OSPF, the cloud will not work. Generally there are no guarantees as to whether a single router will have a PVC to each of the other routers. In Illustration 5-20 Router E does not have a PVC to Router A, so it is necessary to define a network for each PVC and to allocate addresses accordingly.

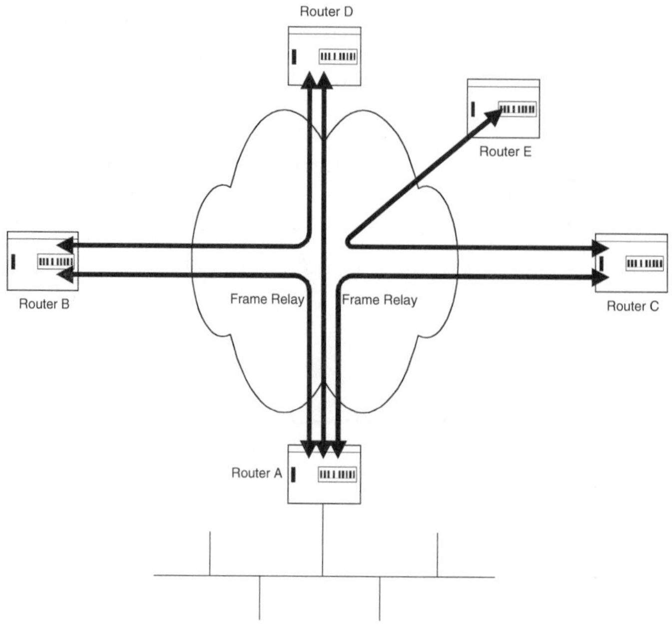

Illustration 5-20 Partial-Mesh Frame Relay

Nonbroadcast Multiple-Access Networks: ATM

ATM is pretty similar to Frame Relay in terms of the IP addressing used to identify hosts and subnets. As mentioned before, neither are broadcast capable and as a result must add server-based functionality to support broadcast functionality. Of course, this section is only intended to introduce ATM and IP addressing of an ATM-based internetwork. Should you want to explore the details of IP over ATM mechanisms, please consult one of the many books dedicated to that purpose.

Like a Frame Relay Network, a service provider's ATM network supports many customers (corporations and institutions)

kbone fabric. It is very common for service
ion these connections using ATM perma-
(PVCs), although ATM supports switched
Cs) as well. Where Frame Relay used DLCIs
points of the virtual circuits, ATM uses Vir-
rs (VPIs) and Virtual Channel Identifiers
he virtual circuit. In this discussion, I will
e circuits as PVCs and SVCs. The difference
l an SVC is pretty simple: A PVC is config-
d remains intact until it is deprovisioned by
the word *permanent.* An SVC, like a normal
POTS network, has a call setup and tear-
VC is established between a pair of ATM
d and torn down when no longer needed. A
rk with an overlay IP network would have a
rs, each with a single physical interface into
or cloud. Even though a router may have
C that is terminated on it to allow direct
sites, it still may require only one physical
TM carrier.

y, which has a variable-length frame, ATM
ells of 53 bytes (48 bytes of payload and 5
rhead). In Frame Relay, it is possible that an
fit into the variable-length payload without
nted into multiple frames. In ATM, because
l and because of adaptation layer overhead
d here), it is very likely that IP packets will be
fragmented among multiple cells. This is important to understand — IP packets going into an ATM cloud will likely get segmented and therefore must be reassembled at the exit point of the ATM cloud. This process is called *segmentation and reassembly,* or SAR. I will get back to this point later in this chapter.

Also unlike Frame Relay, which only has congestion management, ATM has Quality of Service (QoS) built into the protocol. This QoS will permit the network engineer to provision a guaranteed data rate, a minimum bit rate, or to use whatever bandwidth is available on any specified PVC or SVC. This will result in the cell being assigned a certain cell loss priority that will determine the order in which packets are discarded in the event of congestion.

ATM circuits are connection-oriented. PVCs and SVCs are virtual point-to-point circuits that are being passed over a shared infrastructure. ATM switches use label swapping in the forwarding process. A cell arrives in one interface of an ATM switch, the VPI/VCI field is examined and compared to a cross-reference table, and a new VPI/VCI is put into the cell. The cell is then forwarded out of a specified interface of the ATM switch. The cross-reference table is populated (built) when the PVC is provisioned or during call setup for an SVC. ATM presents some interesting problems when IP is run over the top of ATM and specifically when it is run over SVCs. This is due to the connectionless orientation of IP and the lack of integration of the IP and the ATM routing mechanisms.

In the next few sections, I will introduce three mechanisms that are currently being used for IP over ATM. They are LAN Emulation (LANE), Classical IP (CIP or CLIP), and Multiprotocol over ATM (MPOA). Again, these are introductions — each mechanism could warrant an entire book. I will focus mainly on the IP addressing implications.

ATM–LAN Emulation (LANE)

LAN Emulation was created when ATM was first being deployed to ease customers in their migration from Ethernet and Token Ring to ATM-based LANs. LANE allows an ATM-attached (with an ATM network interface card) host to communicate with Ethernet or Token Ring hosts seamlessly at layer 2. The issue here, of course, is that both Ethernet and Token Ring are connectionless, broadcast-capable networks and ATM is a connection-oriented network not inherently capable of broadcast. The communication is made possible by the use of three external (not a network service) servers called the LANE Configuration Server (LECS), Broadcast and Unknown Server (BUS), and the LANE Server (LES). These are capable of being implemented on a separate ATM-attached host but are most commonly implemented in ATM hubs and switches, alleviating the need for the extra server(s) in the emulated LAN (ELAN). These three servers, sometimes collectively called LANE services, combine to perform the emulation of a LAN over an ATM cloud. For instance, if a station — a LANE Client (LEC) — needs to send a layer 2 broadcast, the BUS server receives the broadcast from the originating station and sends the broadcast to the other hosts in the emulated LAN using ATM SVCs, essentially setting up point-to-point circuits from the BUS to all LECs (not to be confused with the LECS — the LANE Configuration Server). The LES, among other things, maintains a cross-reference of ATM to MAC addresses used for address translation.

As stated before, LANE is a layer 2 mechanism. As such, it supports any protocol that can run over Ethernet or Token Ring including IP, IPX, Appletalk, and DecNet to name a few. When supporting IP, an emulated LAN would look like Illustration 5-21. Here we see four ATM-attached hosts (Hosts A through D) and two Ethernet-attached hosts. Each of the four ATM-attached hosts, as well as the bridge and LES/BUS/LECS server, are LAN Emulation Clients. They have interfaces on the emulated LAN. Each LEC has an Ethernet MAC address as well as an ATM address. Whenever a LEC needs to communicate with another LEC, it must know the MAC address of the client on the receiving end. If Host A wanted to send a frame to Host B, Host A would need to "ask" the LES what ATM address is being used by Host B using Host B's MAC address. The LES also does ATM-to-MAC address resolution. When Host A wants to send a frame to Host E, the ATM address of the bridge will be returned by the LES and the packet will be forwarded onto the Ethernet by the bridge.

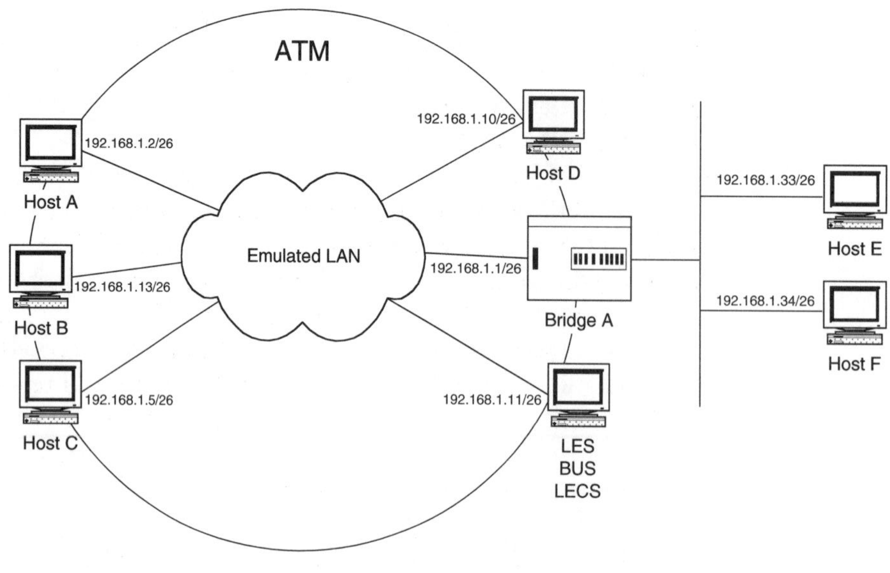

Illustration 5-21 IP over LAN Emulation

Notice that all of the IP addresses are allocated out of a single IP subnet, 192.168.1.0/26. This is called a Logical IP Subnet (LIS). There can be more than one LIS, but the example shown only depicts a single LIS. Each LIS must have its own LAN Emulation Services and must use a single IP subnet. Multiple logical IP subnets must have an IP router, in order to join them. Ethernet and Token Ring hosts must be bridged into an emulated LAN if they use the same IP address space as the ATM-attached hosts. They can be routed into the LIS if they use a different IP address space.

ATM–Classical IP (CIP or CLIP)

Classical IP operates at layer 3. It does not support any protocol other than IP; hence this is not a multiprotocol solution. Like IP in a LANE environment, hosts are divided up into Logical IP Subnets (LISs). Illustration 5-22 shows two LISs as well as an

IP Ethernet. Logical IP Subnet 1 uses IP addresses allocated from the subnet 192.168.1.0/28. Logical IP Subnet 2 uses IP addresses from 192.168.1.16/28. The Ethernet uses IP addresses from 192.168.1.32/28.

Whereas in LANE we need a LES, BUS, and LECS server for ATM-to-MAC addresses, Classical IP uses an ATMARP server for IP-to-ATM address resolution. Each LIS must have its own ATMARP server. At least this is true when SVCs are used in the ATM cloud to interconnect the hosts. When PVCs are used with Classical IP, the ATMARP server is not needed because Inverse ARP can resolve the ATM-to-IP addresses. In reality, the ATM switches or hubs will likely implement the ATMARP server needed in an SVC environment.

Here's the kicker. When using Classical IP with PVCs, the IP network must be fully meshed. That is, each IP host *must* have a PVC to each and every other host in the LIS. Obviously, this does not scale well as there must be $(n*(n-1))/2$ PVCs to support n number of hosts. As the number of hosts grows, the number of PVCs required grows exponentially! Thus to keep the number of PVCs down to a manageable level, the hosts must be divided up into Logical IP Subnets, but this division comes at a price. Pretend that Illustration 5-22 uses PVCs instead of SVCs (mentally remove the ATMARP server). When Host A wants to communicate with Host B, it send the IP packet to Host B's ATM address directly. However, when Host A wants to send an IP packet to Host E in a different LIS, it must send the packet to Router B, which must reassemble the IP packet from several cells, read the IP header information, determine the best IP route (in this case it needs to go out the 192.168.1.30 interface), and then segment that IP packet into multiple ATM cells for forwarding to 192.168.1.18. This SAR function slows down the packet delivery significantly. Keep in mind that all the ATM-attached hosts in the illustration are on the same ATM network and that if native ATM were used they could communicate directly with each other. Of course, this situation could be mitigated if SVCs were used in the ATM network, but most service providers deploy PVCs for ATM WAN interconnect circuits.

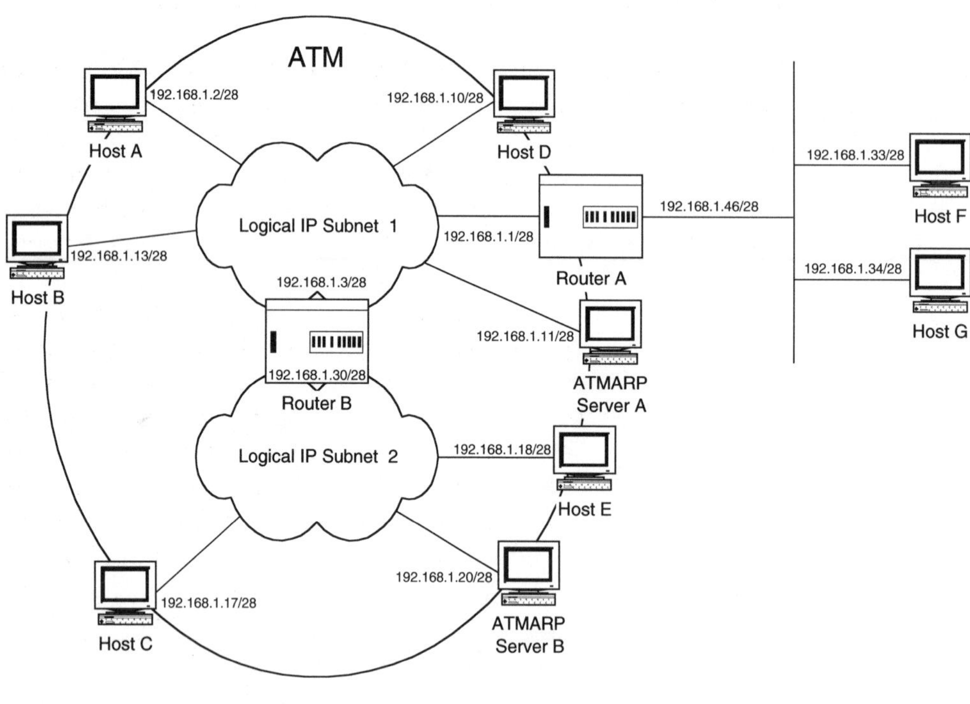

Illustration 5-22 Classical IP

One case that I have not shown is the case where ATM is used as a replacement for point-to-point leased lines. The service provider will build PVCs from one site to another site and typically terminate the ATM on a router. This is really a variant of the situation previously discussed where each end point is assigned an IP address allocated out a single subnet. In this case, a mask of 255.255.255.252 is usually used. This actually looks very much like Illustration 5-19, which was presented in the

Frame Relay section. By replacing the label "Frame Relay" in the cloud with "ATM," the illustration can be used here as well.

ATM–Multiprotocol over ATM (MPOA)

In the previous section, I pointed out that one of the downsides of Classical IP is that any time a router is used to forward packets across a Logical IP Subnet, the cells must be reassembled into an IP packet, which is routed and then resegmented for transmission on the next LIS. MPOA introduces an alternative called Next Hop Resolution Protocol (NHRP), which has the ability to cut through the normal IP routed path if the source and destination host are on the same ATM network. NHRP — through the use of Next Hop Servers deployed in each Logical IP Subnet — will tell the source host the ATM address of the destination host, and packets can be sent directly without using the routers. Unfortunately, it is not always economical (in one sense or another) to establish these cut-through SVCs for every IP packet in the network. Only flows that exceed a specified threshold will have cut-through paths established; all other traffic must traverse the IP routed path to get to the destination.

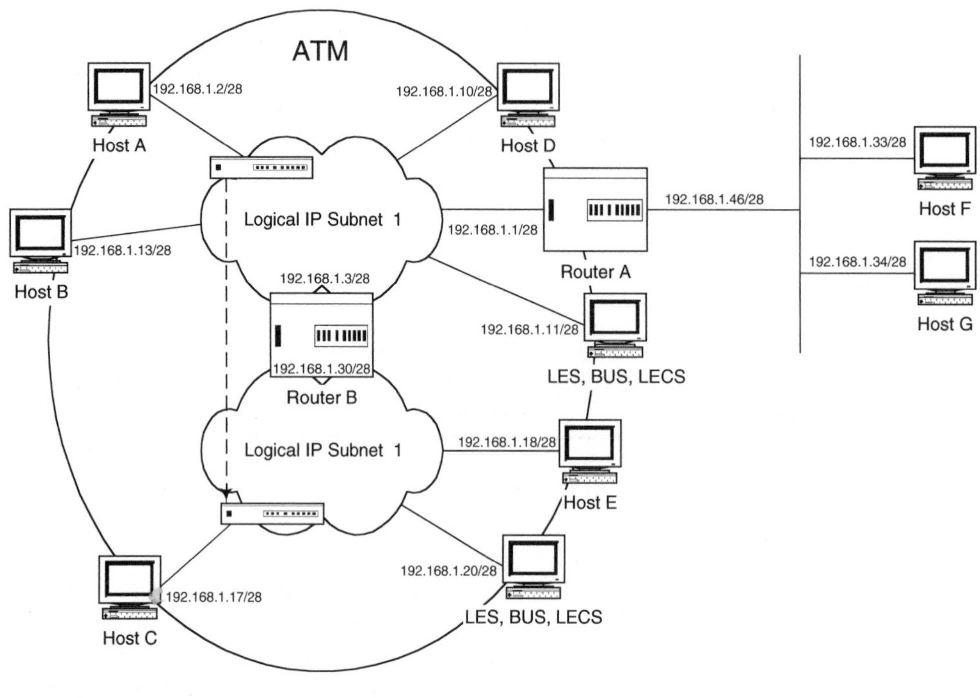

Illustration 5-23 Multiprotocol over ATM

MPOA uses LANE (actually a superset of LANE) for layer 2 forwarding. If Classical IP were used, the solution would be relevant only for IP traffic. But because MPOA uses LANE, any layer 3 protocol could be used. In Illustration 5-23, there are three IP subnets being used: 192.168.1.0 is used in LIS 1, 192.168.1.16 is used in LIS 2, and 192.168.1.32 is used for the Ethernet. When Host A sends packets to Host D, normal LANE function prevails and the LES and BUS are used to resolve the address. When Host A sends a PING packet to Host E, the packet is forwarded via Router B to Host E and the packet is subject to segmentation and reassembly. When Host A sends a file transfer to Host C, it is determined that the flow warrants a cut through SVC and NHRP provides Host A with the ATM address of Host C to build the SVC and transfer the file. When

Host A transfers a file to Host F, the file transfer *must* pass through Router A and is subject to reassembly in one direction (toward Host F) and segmentation in the other direction (toward Host A from Host F).

Summary

Many different topologies can be found in a modern TCP/IP network. This chapter summarized some of the more common topologies and discussed the addressing schemes that could be used with each. The following were discussed in the chapter:

- *Ethernet and Token Ring:* Examples of broadcast-capable, multiple-access networks. It is typical to use a single IP network on each segment or ring and to allocate addresses for hosts out of that network. VLANs were also introduced in this section. VLAN technology dictates the use of a flat (nonhierarchical) IP model within the switched core, and routing is only performed at the edge.
- *Point-to-point links:* There are exactly two hosts per point-to-point link: "this" end and "that" end. Therefore, the IP interfaces for those hosts can be configured to use unnumbered IP interfaces or numbered IP interfaces. If an IP address must be assigned to the hosts, it is common to use a network defined with a 30-bit network mask. These networks have enough host addresses to support only two hosts.
- *Pooled dial-in access:* These are treated in roughly the same manner as point-to-point links except that the pooling device will often serve as a point of route aggregation. Users and routers dialing into a central remote access concentrator are authenticated using

RADIUS, which decides how the terminal will be provided with an IP address. The IP Control Protocol of PPP actually handles the negotiation of the address and assigns an address to the terminal if needed.

- *Frame Relay:* This is an example of a nonbroadcast multiple-access network. Frame Relay topologies are commonly configured as hub-and-spoke. Other possibilities are full-mesh and partial-mesh. Depending on the Frame Relay topology and the routing protocol used in the intranet, the addressing scheme can be in the format of the cloud model (one network, many hosts) or the point-to-point model (many networks, two hosts per network).
- *ATM:* This is another example of a nonbroadcast multiple-access network. There are three common mechanisms for IP over ATM. They are LAN Emulation, which operates at layer 2 and permits any protocol that runs over Ethernet to be run over ATM; Classical IP, which operates at layer 3 with PVCs or SVCs; and Multiprotocol over ATM (MPOA), which uses LANE for layer 2 forwarding and Next Hop Resolution Protocol (NHRP) for cut-through forwarding across Logical IP Subnets.

Practice Questions

1. How many subnets can go in a Class C network if the subnet mask is 255.255.255.248?
2. List the networks that are created if the Class B network 172.16.1.0 is subnetted using the CIDR notation "/18." Assume fixed-length subnet masks are used.
3. How many subnets can go in a Class B network if the subnet mask is 255.255.255.192?

4. Which of the following network types are not non-broadcast multiple-access networks?

Frame Relay X.25 Token Ring ATM Point to Point

5. What network mask is best to use with OSPF on a Frame Relay link if the topology is a partial mesh but not hub-and-spoke?
6. Which RFC defines the operation of Proxy ARP?
7. What three methods were discussed for IP over ATM?

chapter 6

Addressing for Internet Connections

The addresses used within an autonomous system are greatly dependent on whether the hosts within that system must have direct connections to the Internet. The reason for this is that if the hosts are to have direct Internet connections, then the addresses must be unique among all the hosts connected to the Internet. To ensure this uniqueness, address-assignment agencies screen requests for addresses and make allocations. There are also guidelines for choosing an addressing scheme if an entity wishes to use TCP/IP for data transport but has no intention of connecting to the Internet. These topics are discussed in this chapter.

The Internet Connection

The Internet has become explosively popular in the recent years. More and more companies are offering information about their company or their products to people using the

Internet and giving their employees access to the resources of the Internet. It is easy to get information published on the Internet and thus available to the masses. Typically, a phone call to the local Internet service provider (ISP) is all that it takes to get the ball rolling. The ISP will get a domain name, such as motive.net, allocated and set up a Web server with the desired content on it. How to get all of a company's employees access to the Internet can be a bit more daunting. The details for making the decision to do so are well beyond the scope of this book. Let's assume for the moment that the decision is black or white. That is, we will assume that if a company wants to make all the Internet's resources available to all people and systems in the organization, it must get a "legal" Internet address allocation. This is really not the case, but we'll save the discussion of the gray areas for the end of the chapter.

So what is a "legal" address? A *legal address* is one for which a company has, at one time or another, petitioned a legitimate Internet address-allocation authority for a network number and the authority was obliged to grant the request (or at least offer a partial allocation). The petitioning entity is provided with an IP network number (or more than one) that is registered exclusively for its use. No other entity may connect to the Internet and advertise routing to those addresses except for the organization to which it is registered. In short, a legal address is an address for which the user is the registered owner.

In the earlier days of the Internet, it was not so difficult to get an IP network allocated to an organization that had much more addressing space than the organization could possibly require. If a company could justify a requirement for more than the number of hosts that a Class C address could provide, it could (almost) easily request and receive a Class B network number. It was unheard of that multiple Class C networks would be allocated to an entity if a single Class C were insufficient. This was in part due to the fact that if two Class C networks were allocated, the Internet backbone's route table would increase by two routes, whereas a Class B allocation would only increase it by only one route. Further, it was beyond expectation that the Internet—which at that time was used to link universities, government agencies, and research firms—would ever become a consumer product and reach into the homes of millions of people.

Class B networks are difficult to get today, although quite a few are still available. To be sure, you must be able to justify a significant efficiency of address space utilization if there is to be any hope of getting a Class B network allocation, assuming that there are some networks that have yet to be divvied out. Today, if you petition for a network allocation, you are much more likely to get more than one Class C address if the petition justifies the need for that much address space. Even so, chances are good that the address requirement will be scrutinized and the request reduced to a more "realistic" allocation. Don't let the possibility of having part of your petition rejected deter you from requesting the "realistic" amount of addresses that you think you will need now and in the foreseeable future. Class C allocations of more than one network are being made in such a way that the route tables will no longer grow by the number of networks that are allocated to a single entity. Attempts are being made to allocate networks in such a way that Internet route tables increase by only one route with the addition. This is known as *supernetting* and will be discussed in Chapter 7.

Petitioning for a registered IP network number is usually not very difficult. ARIN recommends that you request IP address space from upstream provider. If that does not work out, you can request IP address space from your provider's provider. Only then, after trying the first two suggestions, can you request IP address space directly from ARIN. But the minimum block of IP address space assigned by ARIN is a /20. Multi-homed organizations can request a /20 allocation if they can prove they have efficiently utilized a /21 allocation. If /20 (equivalent of 16 class C networks) is more address space than you can justify, you must go to your upstream provider for an allocation.

Appendix A provides the current template from ARIN to be used by ISPs. Appendix B provides the end-user IP number request template. To register with ARIN for a network number, you must fill out the information in the template and file the request. All the information for how to do this is found in the template document. There are recurring fees for ownership of IP network numbers, as well as domain names. When the IP network number allocation is made, you will be notified of the IP network that has been registered for your exclusive use. The success of CIDR (explained later) depends, however, on getting network allocations directly from your Internet service provider, except in extenuating circumstances. Check with your local ISP for a network allocation.

Private IP Network Allocation

An entity that does not have any intention of providing Internet access to the desktops of its employees yet wishes to use TCP/IP on its networks has a several choices. It can use a registered IP network number that they own, any valid IP network number(s) even though they may be registered under another organization ("illegal" addresses), or network numbers specifically allocated for use by private IP networks.

Obtaining a registered IP network number is not a bad choice, especially if there is a glimmer of hope that some day (within the next year) Internet service will be offered to the desktops. There are some drawbacks, though. First, the IP address-allocation authority will not happily grant a frivolous request. There is a shortage of address space as it is; if every company using TCP/IP required unique addressing, the shortage would be even greater. Second, the address space allocated to the entity would be "tight." That is to say, the addresses would have to be used efficiently, with little room for administrative amenities (discussed in Chapter 9).

If the Internet will not be offered to the desktops, there are better choices than the use of a legal IP network for addressing. Although not recommended, you can use any valid IP network in the construction of your addressing plan, even if it is registered to another entity. TCP/IP is suite of protocols. IP addresses can have a first octet that ranges from 1 to 255. The value of the first octet determines that class of the network, which in turn determines the address space that can be used. All this was covered in Chapter 2. The point is that TCP/IP does not define the Internet or the global usage of the addresses. It does require that in a TCP/IP internetwork all addresses be unique. Many first-time or even second-time TCP/IP network implementers will decide on the quantity of hosts that a network will have in it and will choose one of the many IP network numbers that will fulfill the host requirements. More often than not, the network number is chosen for its appearance on paper or for its euphonic qualities (how it rolls off the tongue). In a pure sense this is not an incorrect way of choosing the network number for an organization; however, it has some problems. Mistakes happen. Everyone knows that. Be aware that if you are the administrator of a network that uses someone else's registered IP network and— somehow— that network is advertised to the Internet and its traffic is rerouted to you, you will definitely hear about it.

The best option is to use a set of IP networks that have been set aside specifically for use in private IP networks. RFC 1918, "Address Allocation for Private Internets," delineates a group of networks that, if they were inadvertently advertised on the Internet, would not harm anybody's routing. The private IP network allocations include one Class A network, 10.0.0.0; 16 Class B networks, 172.16.0.0–172.31.0.0, and 256 Class C networks, 192.168.0.0–192.168.255.0. This RFC sets aside quite a bit of host space. Almost all of the examples in this book are illustrated using these private IP networks.

Although you can combine all of the networks set aside in RFC 1918, depending on your requirement, it is more common to choose either the Class A network, the Class B networks, or the Class C networks and to use just that one set of allocations throughout your network. Which one should you choose? It depends on the objective you set for your addressing scheme. After you have read Chapter 7, you will see that there are ways of using RIP routing and achieving route aggregation if you can take advantage of the assumptions that a router makes with regard to network masks in the route updates. This would typically require the use of the Class B or Class C allocations. If the goal is to design a scheme that is easy to administer and that uses OSPF, the Class A allocation would work extremely well.

Network Address Translators

You might number your networks with private IP addresses and then, whether planned or not, still need to provide Internet access to internal resources. You can do this with *network address translation* (NAT). In fact, this is a strategy that has relieved some of the stress on the IP network allocation demand. The concept is fairly simple: Get a small allocation of registered addresses that are globally unique. Use private IP networks as defined in RFC 1918 for addressing within the autonomous system. Use a firewall, a router, or a dedicated piece of hardware that implements a *network address translator* function at the boundary between the Internet and the autonomous system. This device will map an address in one realm to an address in another, statically or dynamically.

There are actually several slightly different variations of NAT that warrant some discussion. Network address translation is a blanket term for a technique in which addresses within one addressing realm (usually deploying addressing from the private IP allocation defined in RFC 1918) are replaced or translated into one or more addresses in another addressing realm (usually composed of globally unique addresses). There are several scenarios that will dictate how NAT is actually deployed but there are really two main variants: traditional network address translation and network address port translation.

Traditional Network Address Translation

Traditional NAT is also called *Outbound NAT*. This is where an entity such as a corporation has set up TCP/IP networks using the private IP allocation and needs to access the Internet. While there may be 5000 hosts in the corporate IP realm, it might be determined that at any one given time, only a small percentage of that total are actively accessing the resources of the Internet. For example, it might be that of those 5000 hosts, only about 50 are actually accessing the Internet at any given time. Consider Illustration 6-1. The left side is the enterprise network. This is a private realm in that the IP address plan is under the management of a single entity and they may be using private address allocations, "illegal" IP addresses, or legal addresses but not wishing outside visibility into the structure of the internal networks. The right side is an external address realm. When used with globally unique addresses, this state is sometimes called the "public" state. The external address realm can also be comprised of private IP addresses, as we will see shortly.

The example shows the private realm being addressed using the private IP allocations. There are two hosts being shown in addition to the router. The cloud labeled "remainder of Corp network" serves to remind us that there are another 4998 hosts besides hosts A and B. The external realm is composed of globally unique addresses. I have chosen to use 200.200.0.0/16 in the illustration. (I always try to avoid using real IP networks in my examples, but this is one case where it cannot be avoided.) One interface of Router A, all of Router B, and Hosts C and D are in the external realm. Note that there is a pool of IP addresses allocated to Router A, which it will use for address translations. This pool, 200.200.1.0/26, is composed of a block of addresses from the external realm and is made up from hosts out of the subnet 200.200.1.0/26, which has room for 64 addresses. While it is possible to use disparate IP addresses to make up the pool, each time a new IP address is used out of the pool, a host route will be added to the routing mechanism. It is better to use a single subnet as the IP address pool since only one route would need to be advertised by the NAT-enabled router to provide routing information for the private realm hosts. In fact, routing can be done in one of many ways. Router A could advertise the 200.200.1.0/26 subnet in its routing updates, or Router B could have a static route pointing to Router A for 200.200.1.0/26 and inject this route into the dynamic routing protocol. I would prefer the first; however, there may be a need to impose a demarcation between the private and the external realm where no dynamic routing protocols are permitted. Either way, since we are routing to a subnet instead of individual hosts, the first and last host in the subnet are generally not usable since they are the all-1s and all-0s cases and have special meaning in the IP protocol. The remaining 62 hosts are available for address translation.

In traditional NAT, if Host A wishes to communicate with any other host inside the corporate network (within the private realm), it does so in a normal manner. When Host A wishes to communicate with any host inside the external realm, it must do so with the aid of a network address translator. The fundamental reason for this is that the addresses used within the private realm are not globally unique and therefore they cannot be routed toward. As mentioned before, another reason for doing

NAT might be that the administrators of the private realm might not want the topology of the network to be visible from the exterior. This will be discussed in greater detail later in this chapter.

Again considering Illustration 6-1, suppose Host A in the private realm needs to communicate with Host C (maybe a Web server) in the public realm. Host C is known in the domain name service (DNS) as hostc.motive.net. Whenever Host A refers to Host C by this name (and not by its IP address), Host A must do a DNS lookup to convert Host C's name to its IP address. After this, Host A can send data packets directly to Host C. When the first packet from Host A goes out into the public realm, Router A, being NAT enabled, examines the pool of available IP addresses to determine if there are resources available to create a new association. An *association* or *binding* in traditional NAT is made up of the private realm's source address and the IP address from the pool. Of course, there must be some state information included to assist in the teardown of

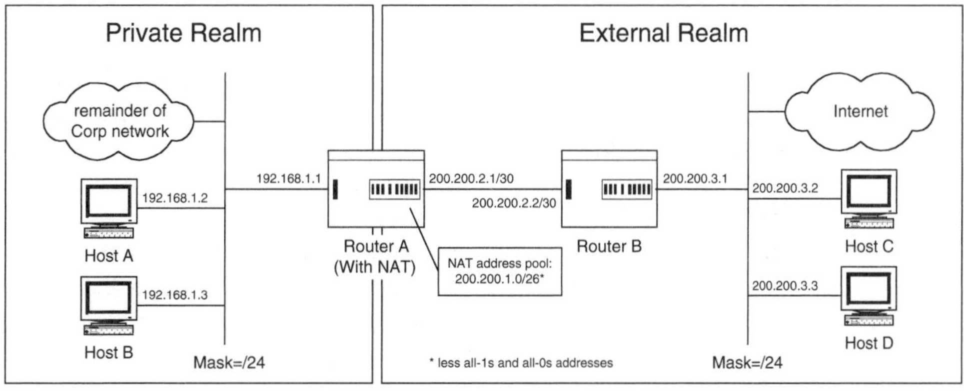

Illustration 6-1 Traditional Network Address Translation

the association but this detail requires only a mention at this time. Assume the binding shown in Table 6-1.

Private Realm IP Address	External Realm IP Address
192.168.1.2	200.200.1.1

Table 6-1 Example NAT Binding Table

Whenever Host A sends packets to Host C, Router A (NAT) will replace the source address of 192.168.1.2 with 200.200.1.1, recompute the header checksum, and forward the packet on to Router B for delivery to the destination address 200.200.3.2. When Host C responds to Host A, it swaps the source and destination addresses in the IP packet and sends it to Router B. Router B forwards the packet to Router A, which is advertising reachability to 200.200.1.0/26. Router A is the NAT box. It looks to see if it has an active binding for 200.200.1.1. If it does, it gets the private realm IP address of Host A and replaces the destination address of 200.200.1.1 with 192.168.1.2, recomputes the header checksum, and forwards the packet on toward 192.168.1.2 in the corporate network.

This describes a pretty simple address translator that works much of the time. One of the problems that immediately comes up is when the application places a private realm IP network or address within the packet's payload. File Transfer Protocol (FTP) and Simple Network Management Protocol (SNMP) are examples of protocols that could have a private realm IP address in its payload. Network address translation uses the concept of *application-level gateways* (ALGs) to perform application-specific translation functions. Some protocols such as IPSec cannot have network address translation performed on it. IPSec prevents the source or destination IP addresses from being altered; attempts to do so would result in failure to communicate.

It is not easy to determine when a binding should be torn down in a NAT router. Most network address translators allow the administrator to set a timer that upon expiration will cause the binding to be deleted. This timer is restarted whenever a NAT operation is performed for the corresponding binding. After the binding has been deleted, a packet arriving at the NAT router that uses an unbound address will be silently discarded by the NAT. It is possible to forward packets meant for one binding that has been deleted to a newly formed binding that used the same IP address from the NAT pool. This can be reduced by having more addresses available in the pool than is anticipated to be used at the same time or by having a reuse timer that prevents reuse of an address immediately after its binding is deleted.

Some or all of the bindings can be permanent. A permanent binding will not be torn down after a specified period of inactivity. This can be useful for providing a service in the private realm to users in the external realm. Mail servers and Web servers are examples where an administrator would rather make a service available on a regular basis using the same IP address. A single permanent binding can support all different types of services since the port numbers in the TCP and UDP packets are not affected by traditional NAT.

Network Address Port Translation

Network address port translation (NAPT), sometimes simply called *port address translation* (PAT), allows a single IP address to be used by many hosts. As each TCP and UDP packet has a port number in its header that can be mapped back to a specific host, it is possible to use only one IP address to represent many hosts in the private realm. Remember from Chapter 1 that the TCP and UDP port fields are 16-bit integer values ranging from 0 to 65,535. NAPT implementations will usually allow ports 1024 and up to be used in the available pool. This permits a maximum of about 64,000 sessions to be multiplexed onto a single IP address. The quantity actually permitted by the NAPT platform may be significantly less due to the processing power of the platform.

Network address port translation is often deployed to connect small offices to the Internet using an ISDN or analog modem router dialing the ISP using a single residential type account. This is shown in Illustration 6-2. The private realm consists of three hosts on a LAN. Also on the LAN is a small ISDN router that has been programmed to dial into an Internet service provider (ISP). The router is set up to dial on demand, which means that when a packet arrives that must be routed over the default route, the router will dial an access server at the ISP. The remote access server (RAS) at the ISP accepts the connection as if it were a user dialing in via an ISDN terminal adapter using PPP. During PPP establishment, the remote access concentrator will assign the dial-in user (in this case, the small ISDN router) an IP address to be used during the connection. This is also the IP address that will be used in NAPT. Since there is only one IP address for use in the external realm and there are three hosts that might simultaneously like to use the Internet, the NAPT device must use additional protocol information to demultiplex the three devices' traffic and deliver it to the correct host. For ICMP, the ICMP query ID serves to discriminate traffic. For TCP and UDP, the binding in NAPT consists of the private IP address, the private TCP/UDP port, the public IP address, and the public TCP/UDP port. For instance, see Table 6-2.

Private Realm IP Port	Private Realm Port	External Realm IP	External Realm
192.168.1.2	2023	200.200.2.1	1028
192.168.1.4	4058	200.200.2.1	1033

Table 6-2 Example NAPT Binding Table

Any time traffic arrives at the NAPT device from the private realm, the NAPT router will replace the source IP address of

192.168.1.4 and TCP port of 4058 with 200.200.2.1 and 1033, respectively, before recomputing the checksums and forwarding the revised packet out to the RAS at the ISP. Packets arriving into the NAPT device from the external realm will have the destination IP address of 200.200.2.1 and destination TCP port of 1028 changed to 192.168.1.2 and 2023, respectively. Like traditional NAT, application-level gateways are required for applications that transmit private realm IP addresses and TCP/UDP ports within the body of the payload.

One more thing to note about NAPT is the difficulty of offering services to the external realm from within the private realm. In Illustration 6-2, if Host B is running an FTP server and Host D is needing access, Host D would need to know the IP address of Host B. The FTP service is available through two different well-known TCP ports (20 and 21). Assume that the ISDN router is dialed in at the time Host D attempts to FTP to Host B (although this might not be the case all the time). Router B obtained an IP address for itself and for NAPT via IPCP during PPP establishment. Lacking a more dynamic method, the network administrator for the private realm needs to be able to query the router and determine the IP address assigned to it. This information

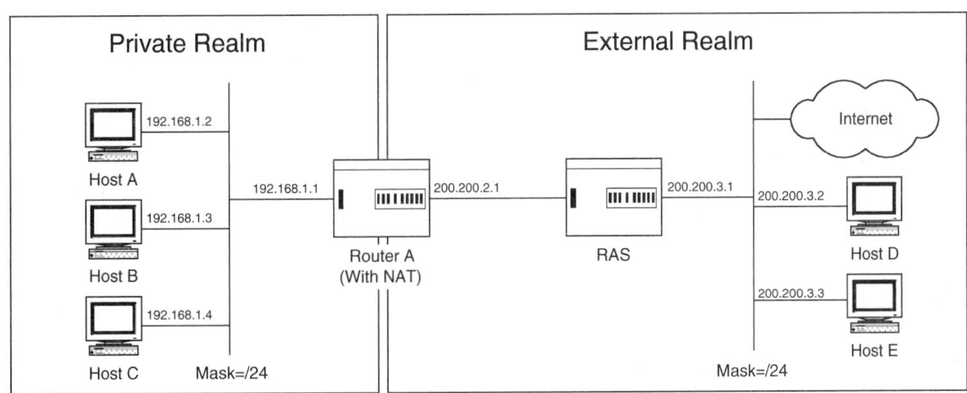

Illustration 6-2 Network Address Port Translation

would need to be passed on to the operator of Host D since the service is being offered through a NAPT device. The Host D operator fires up FTP and enters the IP address of the host as 200.200.2.1 and accepts the default port assignment of 20 and 21 (assuming that this is even an option). The NAPT device must have a permanent binding in place, such as that shown in Table 6-3, to be able to vector off specific protocols to a specific host. This being the case, the Host D user will connect to the Host B FTP server and download files.

Private Realm IP Port	Private Realm Port	External Realm IP	External Realm
192.168.1.3	20	200.200.2.1	20
192.168.1.3	21	200.200.2.1	21

Table 6-3 NAPT Permanent Binding Table

One important thing to note is that only one host in the private realm can host a well-known service such as WWW, Telnet, FTP, and TFTP. The permanent bindings shown in Table 6-4 are permitted.

Private Realm IP Port	Private Realm Port	External Realm IP	External Realm
192.168.1.3	20	200.200.2.1	20
192.168.1.3	21	200.200.2.1	21
192.168.1.4	20	200.200.2.1	2020
192.168.1.4	21	200.200.2.1	2021

Table 6-4 Permanent Binding Table for a Well-Known Service

Both Host B and Host C are offering FTP services. Users in the public realm can access the services being offered by 192.168.1.3 (Host B) by FTPing to 200.200.2.1. Users that wish to access the FTP server on Host C must alter their FTP client settings to use ports 2020 and 2021 instead of the defaults 20 and 21, respectively.

Some Interesting NAT Examples

By now, you should understand the basics of network address translation and how it differs from network address port translation. This section shows a few examples that are not only interesting but relevant as well. The first example involves two corporations whose networks are as shown in Illustration 6-3. For now, assume they are separate entities, completely independent of each other. The first corporation is wholly contained within private IP addressing Realm A as is the second corporation in Private Realm B. Both corporations connect to the Internet via a NAT-enabled router. Both corporations use the 192.168.0.0/16 private address allocation within their respective private realms. I have obviously emphasized the fact that there are overlaps in the address space in the two private realms, but that is not a problem because the two Internet NAT boxes are doing address translation for each private realm into the external realm.

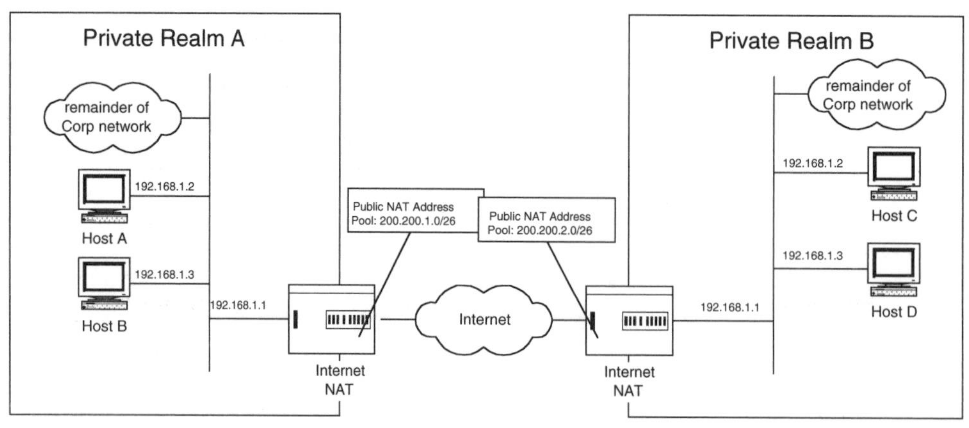

Illustration 6-3 Two-Way Network Address Translation Scenario

Now let's mix things up a bit. Let's say that the two completely independent corporations in the above illustration decide to form a close partnership such as a software development outsourcing arrangement. They want to link the two corporate computing networks together. They don't want to use the Internet as a VPN for this purpose due to security and intolerance to inconsistency (they want to dabble in voice-over IP services). Because of this, they run a point-to-point circuit between the two data centers. On each end of this circuit are NAT-enabled routers: Router A and Router B in Illustration 6-4. Router A has a NAT address pool using 172.16.1.0/28. Router B uses 172.16.2.0/28 for its pool of addresses. Assume that Routers A and B have the bindings shown in Table 6-5 and 6-6, respectively.

Private Realm IP Address	External Realm IP Address
192.168.1.2	172.16.1.1
192.168.1.3	172.16.1.2

Table 6-5 Router A Bindings

Private Realm IP Address	External Realm IP Address
192.168.1.2	172.16.2.1
192.168.1.3	172.16.2.2

Table 6-6 Router B Bindings

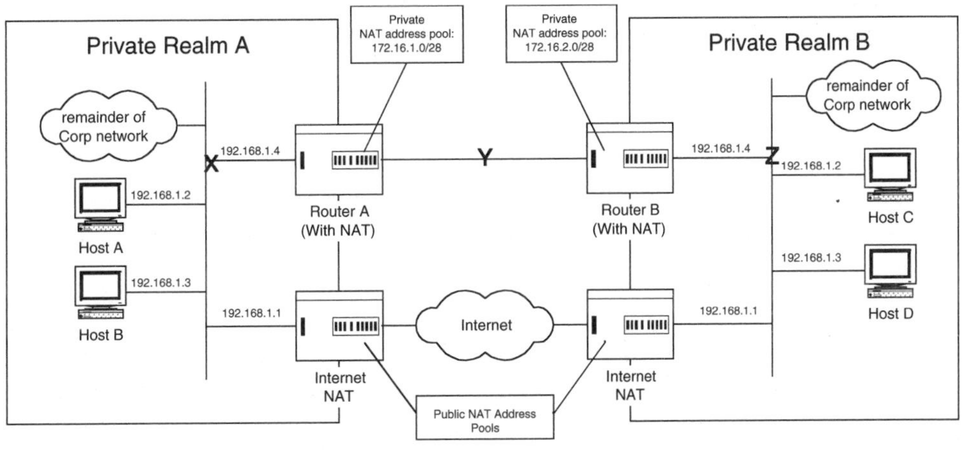

Illustration 6-4 Two-Way Network Address Translation Scenario

Let's now say that Host A wants to Telnet to Host C. By virtue of DNS, Host A knows that Host C is 172.16.2.1. There are three specially labeled points—X, Y, and Z—where we will take a "snapshot" of the packet as it travels from Host A to Host C. (Assume this is not the first packet sent from Host A to Host C, so Host A knows that it needs to send packets for Host C to Router A for forwarding. Host C also knows how to forward packets destined for Host A.) So, Host A sends a packet to Host C. At point X, the packet's addressing looks like this:

Source IP		Destination IP	
192.168.1.2	. . .	172.16.2.1	. . . data, etc.

Remember that the destination IP address in the packet is the external realm IP address that is bound to Host C in private realm B. You get the idea. The packet now goes through the NAT function in Router A. Stating it simply, the packet's source address is translated according to Router A's NAT bindings. This results in a packet at point Y that looks like this:

Source IP		**Destination IP**	
172.16.1.1	. . .	172.16.2.1	. . . data, etc.

Now the packet enters Router B and its NAT function translates the destination IP address in the packet so that it is compatible with private realm B's addressing. The packet, now at point Z, looks like this:

Source IP		**Destination IP**	
172.16.1.1	. . .	192.168.1.2	. . . data, etc.

This packet is correctly routable to Host C by Router B. Host C now responds to Host A's transaction by sending a packet back to Host A. At point Z, the packet looks like this:

Source IP		**Destination IP**	
192.168.1.2	. . .	172.16.1.1	. . . data, etc.

Router B translates the source IP address so that, at point Y, the packet looks like this:

Source IP		**Destination IP**	
172.16.2.1	. . .	172.16.1.1	. . . data, etc.

Finally, Router A translates the destination IP address for the packet entering the private realm. At point X, as the packet is being delivered to Host A, it looks like this:

Source IP	...	Destination IP	
172.16.2.1	...	192.168.1.2	... data, etc.

Here is an interesting observation. The private NAT address pool configured on Router B must be allocated from Private Realm A's address plan. Likewise, the private NAT address pool configured on Router A must be allocated from Private Realm B's address plan. There cannot be an overlap in address usage inside a private realm with the other private realm's NAT address pool. Router A advertises the route to 172.16.2.0/28 as being reachable via Router B to all hosts and routers in Private Realm A.

A note of caution. When looking at traditional NAT by itself (not in the above scenario), private addressing is typically on the interior of the private realm and globally unique addresses in the external realm (the Internet). Since the globally unique IP addresses must also be unique within the private realm, there is no need to alter the globally unique address in the IP packet as it traverses the NAT device. This is good for security in that you always know the IP address of the host that is accessing your network via NAT. You have an audit trail in the event that somebody in the external realm has less than noble intentions. However, the above example has two NAT boxes working in series with the output from one being the input to the other, which causes both the source and the destination IP address to be altered as a packet goes from one private realm to the other. This introduces a degree of insecurity since you can never be sure who is accessing your network. Thus it is important to record bindings along with timestamps in an audit log to improve this situation.

Here's another interesting use for NAT. Illustration 6-5 shows a problem that arises when a corporation fails to address their internal networks using the private IP address allocations defined in RFC 1918. The corporation used the addresses from

200.200.0.0/16 for its networks even though those addresses had already been legally allocated to someone else and were currently in use within the Internet. Of course, this is not a problem until the "illegal" user of the 200.200.0.0 networks wants to connect to the Internet. Illustration 6-5 shows the scenario with emphasis that the 200.200.3.0/24 network is used in the private realm and in the external realm (the Internet). If Host A needs to communicate with Host B, it does so in a normal manner without using the NAT box. If Host A wants to communicate with 222.222.0.1 (apologies to the legal owner of the network), it does so through the NAT box having its private realm address of 200.200.3.2 replaced with an address out of the 200.200.1.0/26 address pool. A problem becomes obvious when Host A wishes to communicate with Host D. Host A sends a packet with a source address of 200.200.3.2 and a destination address of 200.200.3.3. The packet is routed to Host B and not to Host D as intended.

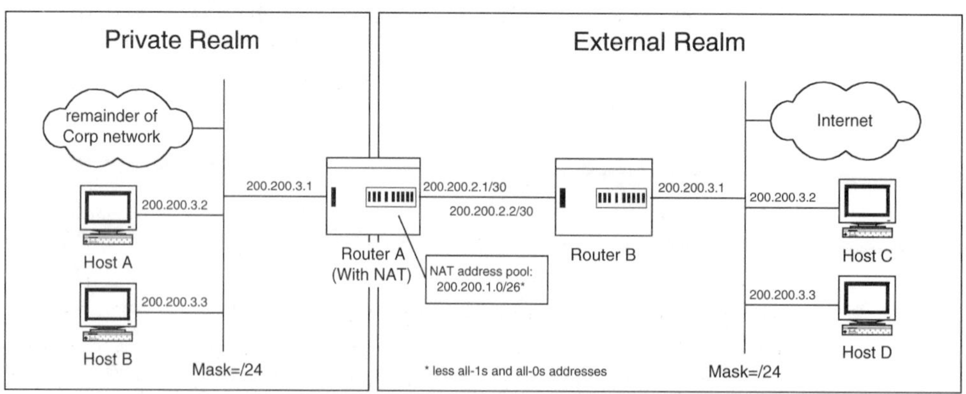

Illustration 6-5 Example NAT Issue

Good news! There is a type of NAT, called *Twice NAT,* that resolves this problem. Essentially, Twice NAT does the same function as the two NAT boxes described in the previous example (Illustration 6-4) where the output of one NAT box is fed into the input of another NAT box. Both the source and the destination addresses are replaced as it traverses the Twice-NAT-enabled router, as shown in Illustration 6-6. Router A is performing Twice NAT, and it has a DNS application-level gateway doing DNS lookup conversion from the external realm into the private realm. If Host A wants to access a service from hostd.motive.net, the first thing it must do is resolve the name into an IP address. It does a DNS lookup as usual, but the DNS ALG on Router A intercepts the lookup and sends its own DNS lookup for hostd.motive.net. When it gets a response to the DNS lookup, it creates a binding using an IP address out of the private NAT address pool (172.16.1.0/26) such as that shown in Table 6-7.

Private Realm IP Address	External Realm IP Address
172.16.1.1	200.200.3.3

Table 6-7 Inside Bindings

Then it formats a reply to the initial query by Host A using the private realm IP address (172.16.1.1) instead of the real Host D address of 200.200.3.3. At this point, Host A knows that the IP address to be used to reach Host D is 172.16.1.1 and that address is completely reachable from inside the private realm. When Host A sends a packet to 172.16.1.1, it is sent to Router A because it is advertising a route to 172.16.1.0/26. Router A makes sure that there is still a binding for 172.16.1.1 and, if it exists, replaces the destination IP address of 172.16.1.1 with the real external realm IP address for Host D, 200.200.3.3. Since the Host A's source address of 200.200.3.2 cannot be routed to or from Host D, the NAT router must create a binding for the private realm source address of 200.200.3.2 with an address from the public NAT address pool (200.200.1.0/26). The binding might look like Table 6-8.

Private Realm IP Address	External Realm IP Address
200.200.3.2	200.200.1.1

Table 6-8 Outside Bindings

The source address in the packet is altered from 200.200.3.2 to 200.200.1.1, the checksum is recomputed, and the packet is forwarded into the external realm. The response from Host D has the destination IP address changed from 200.200.1.1 to 200.200.3.2 according to the outside bindings. The source IP address is changed from 200.200.3.3 to 172.16.1.1 according to the inside bindings in Router A. This is pretty much what was done in Illustration 6-4, except that it is being done in a single NAT router that has two bindings tables instead of two NAT routers each with one bindings table.

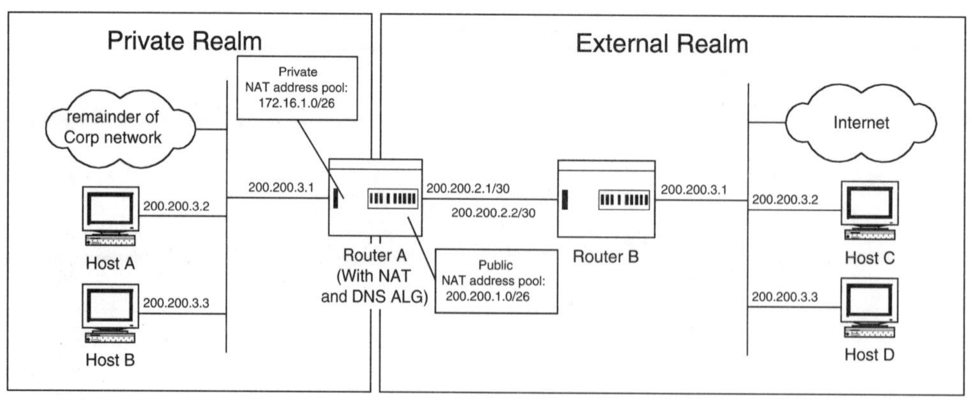

Illustration 6-6 Twice Network Address Translation

The next two illustrations have been added to reinforce the concepts of Twice NAT. Illustration 6-7 shows how the network looks from the perspective of a host in the private realm. Note that where there are overlaps in the addressing, the 172.16.1.0/26 network is used instead of the overlapped 200.200.3.0/24 network. Illustration 6-8, on the other hand, shows how the network looks from the perspective of a host in the external realm. The private realm network is represented entirely by the 200.200.1.0/26 network within the external realm.

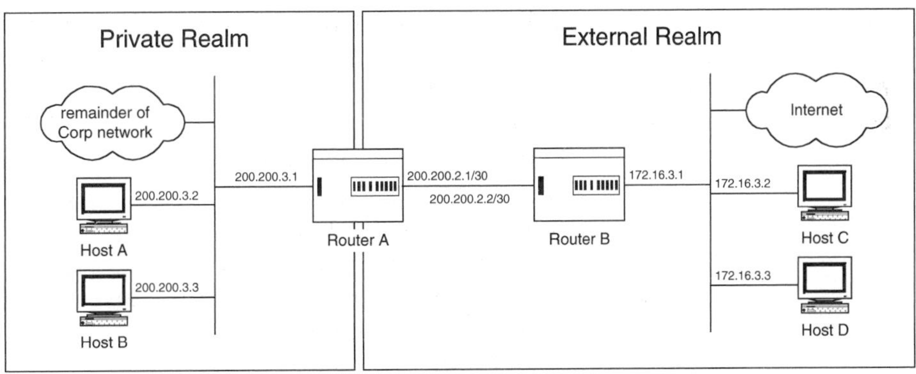

Illustration 6-7 Private Realm View after Twice NAT

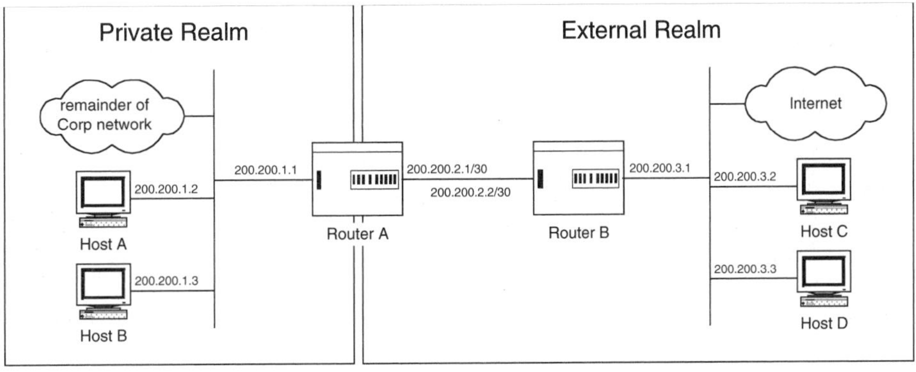

Illustration 6-8 External Realm View after Twice NAT

NAT Wrap-Up

Network address translation has some very nice and desirable qualities. Primarily, it allows an organization of many networked hosts and routers to be addressed using the private IP allocation yet still permit connection to the Internet or to other similarly addressed organizations. It does this without the hosts at either end of the communications having to be aware that translation is occurring. This, however, is not easy because each application that uses IP addresses (and possibly TCP/UDP port numbers) in the packet payload must be handled by a specific application-level gateway to ensure end-to-end transparency. No special client software is required for NAT.

One of the benefits of NAT is that it saves globally unique addresses. The only devices that need to be mapped are the ones that need access to or by the Internet. Devices such as routers do not need to be mapped at all. Further, those devices in the autonomous system that initiate connections to Internet resources are able to share a pool of globally unique addresses instead of being allocated a constant globally unique address. It turns out that this saving of address space is really just a short-term measure to relieve the pressures of address depletion. The long-term solution is clearly in the adoption of IPv6 (see Chapter 13).

One of the downsides of NAT is that it breaks TCP's end-to-end connection and that it does so without the user's knowledge. Thus, since IPSec, for example, is a protocol that requires end-to-end integrity of the data, it is not possible to run IPSec through a NAT box.

Realm Specific IP

So we have determined that NAT is effective but has a nasty little habit of violating IP's end-to-end connections. The IETF has traditionally frowned on the interruption of the end-to-end integrity of TCP. Perhaps that is why there is another proposal being considered by the IETF to solve the types of problems that NAT is currently dealing with. This new protocol is called *Realm Specific IP* (RSIP). RSIP requires the client to be RSIP-aware and to use RSIP to request the use of an external realm IP address.

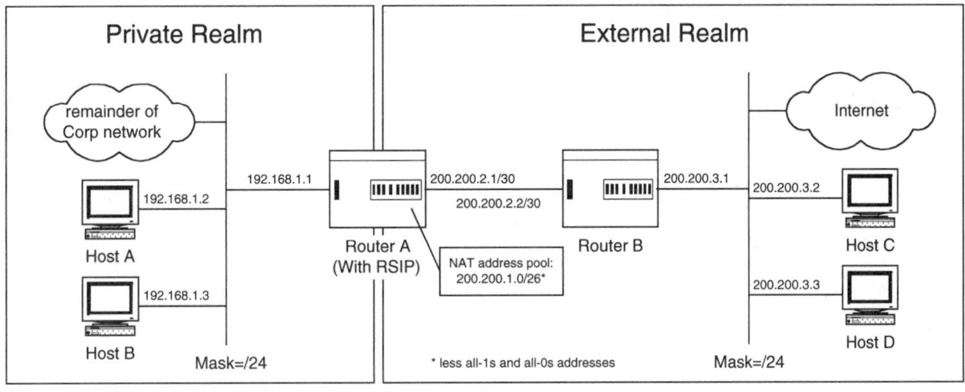

Illustration 6-9 Realm Specific Address IP

Take a look at Illustration 6-9 as I outline the operation of RSIP. This network was introduced in the coverage of traditional NAT (Illustration 6-1), except there was a NAT-enabled router instead of a RSIP-enabled router. As before, the left side of the illustration is the private realm where the example corporation used IP addresses from the private allocation defined in RFC 1918. The right side is the external realm, which for now can be considered to be the Internet where only globally unique addresses are routable. The flavor of RSIP that allocates unique

IP addresses from a pool of available IP addresses is called *Realm Specific Address–IP* (RSA-IP), which is analogous to NAT.

The big difference between NAT and RSIP is that with RSIP, the host must be able to negotiate what IP address it will use for the duration of its connection to the external realm. NAT is completely transparent to the host. With RSIP, the host must request an IP address from the RSIP gateway (Router A)—allowing that there is an IP address available for it to use—and the RSIP client (Host A) must request a tunnel to be established between the client and the gateway. The IP address is assigned to Host A and represents the tunnel end point. The RSIP protocol allows for several tunnel types, including Generic Router Encapsulation (GRE), IP-IP, and Layer 2 Tunneling Protocol (L2TP). IP addresses are "leased" by the client for a specified period of time, in a manner similar to that within the Dynamic Host Configuration Protocol (DHCP).

The RSIP gateway is essentially a tunnel server with a control protocol for requesting resources. When the request comes in for an IP address lease, the RSIP gateway creates a binding similar to the ones in NAT except that the entries are the IP address assigned from the RSIP pool and the tunnel identifier, which is a virtual interface that looks like a point-to-point link. An example is shown in Table 6-9.

Tunnel Identifier	IP Address
tunnel_host_a	200.200.1.1
tunnel_host_b	200.200.1.3

Table 6-9 Example RSIP Binding Table

This binding table serves not as a matrix for how a packet's source or destination address should be altered but as a route table for associating the virtual tunnel interface with the destination IP address of the packet. The packet, from source to destination, does not get altered. This alleviates the need for the application-level gateways used in NAT for ensuring the applications such as FTP and SNMP work. IPSec, which cannot run through a NAT box, has no problem working in an RSIP environment.

Just as Realm Specific Address–IP (RSA-IP) is similar to network address translation (NAT), Realm Specific Address and Port–IP (RSAP-IP) is similar to network address port translation (NAPT). Illustration 6-10 is used to introduce RSAP-IP. This network, first introduced in Illustration 6-2, shows a small office of three hosts dialing into an ISP's remote access server using a personal account over an ISDN circuit. The ISDN router, Router A, is also an RSIP gateway. The three hosts are configured to request IP address resources from the RSIP gateway, Router A. Router A was given an IP address for its use for the duration of the connection during PPP negotiation. RSAP-IP allows multiple hosts to access the external realm using only a single IP address (that provided by the RAS to Router A). The bindings in RSAP-IP must include enough information for the correct demultiplexing of the RAS-to-Router A data stream and for getting the packets forwarded into the tunnel corresponding to the correct host. This would look something like Table 6-10.

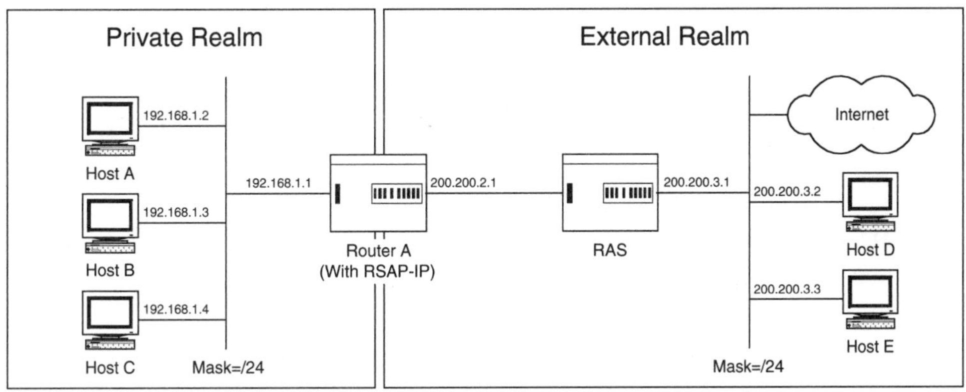

Illustration 6-10 Realm Specific Address and Port IP

Tunnel Identifier	IP Address	Port
tunnel_host_a	200.200.1.1	1064
tunnel_host_b	200.200.1.1	2031
tunnel_host_b	200.200.1.1	2034

Table 6-10 Example RSAP-IP Binding Table

Whenever Host B needs to start a new IP session, it must request resources (IP address and TCP/UDP port) from the RSIP gateway. If the gateway has resources, it will respond by granting the resources and by creating a new binding. The host that was allocated the resource will use that address and port as the source IP address and source port number for all packets in that session. For details on how RSIP deals with ICMP and IPSec packets in the bindings, please refer to the current Internet Draft or RFC on Realm Specific IP. The current revision at the time of this writing is "Realm Specific IP: Framework" <draft-ietf-nat-rsip-framework-04.txt> dated March 2000.

Again, the RSIP server function in the router does not alter the packet in transit. The RSIP gateway is responsible for routing packets onto tunnels that terminate at a specific host. With RSAP-IP, the routing decision cannot be made only using the IP address but must also consider the TCP/UDP port number in the destination fields of the IP and TCP or UDP headers.

Summary

The biggest decision to be dealt with when determining what the addressing plan will be for an enterprise is whether Internet service will be offered to the desktop. In the past, a company that required Internet access typically used registered IP network numbers in the autonomous system. This is still a popular choice, as evidenced by the quantity of network number requests that the Internet number assignment authorities process on a monthly basis.

Companies that are implementing TCP/IP networks with no intention of connecting to the Internet still may be able to get and implement the addressing using registered IP network numbers, but this is becoming more and more uncommon with the requirements that the InterNIC is placing on address-utilization efficiency. Instead, it is good practice to design the addressing within an autonomous system that will not connect to the Internet around the private IP address allocations set aside in RFC 1918. They are

- *Class A:* 10.0.0.0 through 10.255.255.255
- *Class B:* 172.16.0.0 through 172.31.255.255
- *Class C:* 192.168.0.0 through 192.168.255.255

If addressing is designed to use an unregistered IP network number or one or more of the private IP network numbers, there is technology that provides Internet access to hosts within the autonomous system. One such technology is network address translation (NAT). NAT makes this possible by mapping registered, globally unique addresses to the private or unregistered addresses in use within the autonomous system. There are some downsides of using NAT, including the requirement for application-level gateways to obtain address translation within the IP payload.

An alternative technology that is being developed by the IETF is Realm Specific IP (RSIP). RSIP hosts must have special software for tunneling to the edge of the domain where the server can request IP addresses for use during the connection. Whereas NAT is transparent to the host, RSIP is transparent to the application.

Practice Questions

1. List the three private network allocations set aside by RFC 1918.
2. What organization oversees IP number allocations in your country?
3. Name a TCP/IP protocol or application that requires an application-level gateway to pass through a NAT.
4. Name a protocol that cannot run through NAT.
5. What tunnel types are supported by RSIP?

chapter 7

Addressing to Achieve Route Table Efficiency

A route table can be judged on its precision for delivering packets in the shortest period of time, with the least number of hops, or for the least amount of money. Whatever the metric is that determines the routing decisions, *the route table has to be searched in its entirety to perform the Basic Match pruning rule.* Each unicast packet received by a router must have a next hop identified for it. The larger the initial working set of routes, the more time it takes to search for the next hop. So the smaller the initial working set of routes, the better.

There are two aspects to achieving route table efficiency. First, you have to plan for route reduction in the IP addressing scheme. It does not happen naturally, even if you do everything else right. Second, the routing architecture must be able to summarize routes.

The concepts of route aggregation have recently been extended to the Internet backbone itself. This is discussed later in this chapter.

Addressing for Route Aggregation: An Example

Route aggregation, summarization, reduction, and collapsing all mean about the same thing. It is the representation of more than one route with a single route—sometimes even hundreds or thousands of routes with a single route entry. The classic example is a workstation that has the route table shown in Table 7-1.

Destination	Gateway	Genmask	Flags	Metric	Ref	Use	Iface
172.16.8.0	0.0.0.0	255.255.255.192	U	0	0	246846	eth0
127.0.0.0	0.0.0.0	255.0.0.0	U	0	0	163840	lo
0.0.0.0	172.16.8.1	0.0.0.0	UG	0	0	224692	eth0

Table 7-1 Example Route Aggregation Route Table

This workstation has a route entry for its locally defined IP interface and for the loopback address, and it has a default gateway. The default route stands for all routes not explicitly defined in the route table. This one route entry can represent an entire intranet or the entire Internet.

Remember the example used to illustrate the utility of the IP address worksheet in Chapter 5? Let's add a third router to the mix. Let's say that in our example a large regional corporation that wanted to take its success to a national level bought several smaller companies that were prominent in other regions. Our example company was one of these purchased companies. The new corporate office wants to be connected to each of the new regional offices. Illustration 7-1 depicts the corporate office router's connection to our example company's regional office.

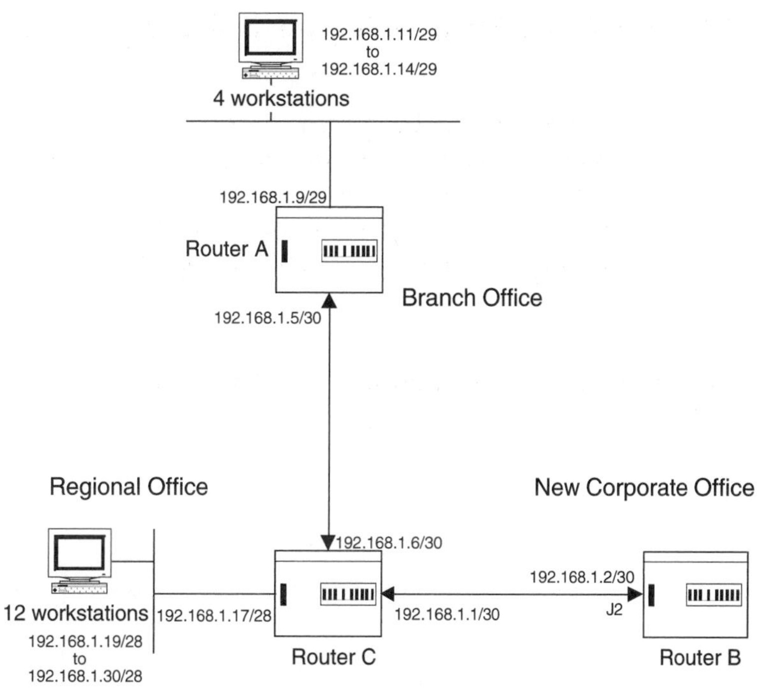

Illustration 7-1 Example Corporate Network

Illustration 7-2 shows how the IP address worksheet looks with the addition of Router B. Note that we have done a pretty good job of packing all the IP addresses to the left of Router B into a small area in the IP address worksheet. In fact, it is within the boundary of the 192.168.1.0/27 network, as denoted by the thick black lines bracketing it in the .224/27 column. This network can support a maximum of only 30 hosts. From Router B's perspective, you can get to any host in the 192.168.1.0/27 network by going out the J2 interface on Router B. As you can see in Table 7-2, the route table for Router B is small. The route entry on the second line of the route table summarizes all four network routes. The first entry in the route table is there because the IP address of 192.168.1.2 is defined on the J2 interface of Router B.

.0/24	.128/25	.192/26	.224/27	.240/28	.248/29	.252/30
0	0	0	0	0	0	**0**
1	1	1	1	1	1	**RTR C 1**
2	2	2	2	2	2	**RTR B 2**
3	3	3	3	3	3	**3**
4	4	4	4	4	4	**4**
5	5	5	5	5	5	**RTR A 5**
6	6	6	6	6	6	**RTR C 6**
7	7	7	7	7	7	**7**
8	8	8	8	8	**8**	8
9	9	9	9	9	**RTR A 9**	9
10	10	10	10	10	**10**	10
11	11	11	11	11	**WS A 11**	11
12	12	12	12	12	**WS B 12**	12
13	13	13	13	13	**WS C 13**	13
14	14	14	14	14	**WS D 14**	14
15	15	15	15	15	**15**	15
16	16	16	16	**16**	16	16
17	17	17	17	**RTR C 17**	17	17
18	18	18	18	**18**	18	18
19	19	19	19	**WS A 19**	19	19
20	20	20	20	**WS B 20**	20	20
21	21	21	21	**WS C 21**	21	21
22	22	22	22	**WS D 22**	22	22
23	23	23	23	**WS E 23**	23	23
24	24	24	24	**WS F 24**	24	24
25	25	25	25	**WS G 25**	25	25
26	26	26	26	**WS H 26**	26	26
27	27	27	27	**WS I 27**	27	27
28	28	28	28	**WS J 28**	28	28
29	29	29	29	**WS K 29**	29	29
30	30	30	30	**WS L 30**	30	30
31	31	31	31	**31**	31	31

Illustration 7-2 IP Address Worksheet for Route Aggregation I

Destination	Route Mask	Next Hop	Port	Metr	Typ	Src	Age
192.168.1.0	255.255.255.252	192.168.1.2	J2	0	DIR	LOC	3569
192.168.1.0	255.255.255.224	192.168.1.1	J2	1	REM	MGMT	0

Table 7-2 Route Table for Route Aggregation 1, Router B, etc.

Had there been other devices out to the right of Router B, they would need to know only that to get to anything in 192.168.1.0/27, they would send it to Router B. The network as it looks to Router B is shown in Illustration 7-3.

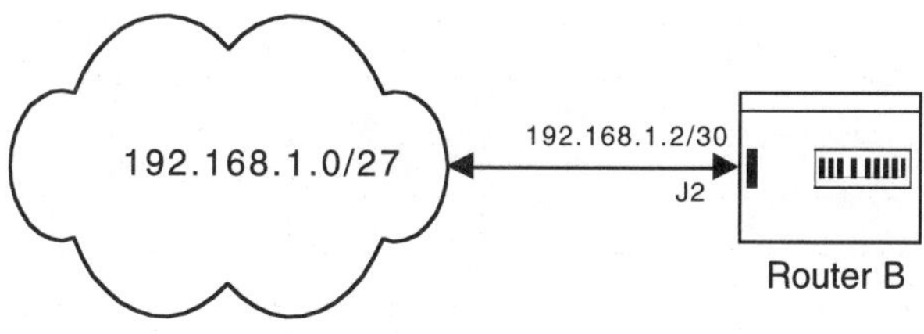

Illustration 7-3 Network Route to Router B

The company that purchased our little example company also bought seven other regional companies. The CIO liked the job that the network administrator did on the IP addressing at our example company, adopting the IP addressing architecture and using it on the other sites. Since the network administrator was so frugal in the use of IP addresses, there was room left over in the 192.168.1.0 Class C network, enough for seven more regional offices. What a coincidence! Now the network might look like the one in Illustration 7-4 and Router B's route table might look like Table 7-3.

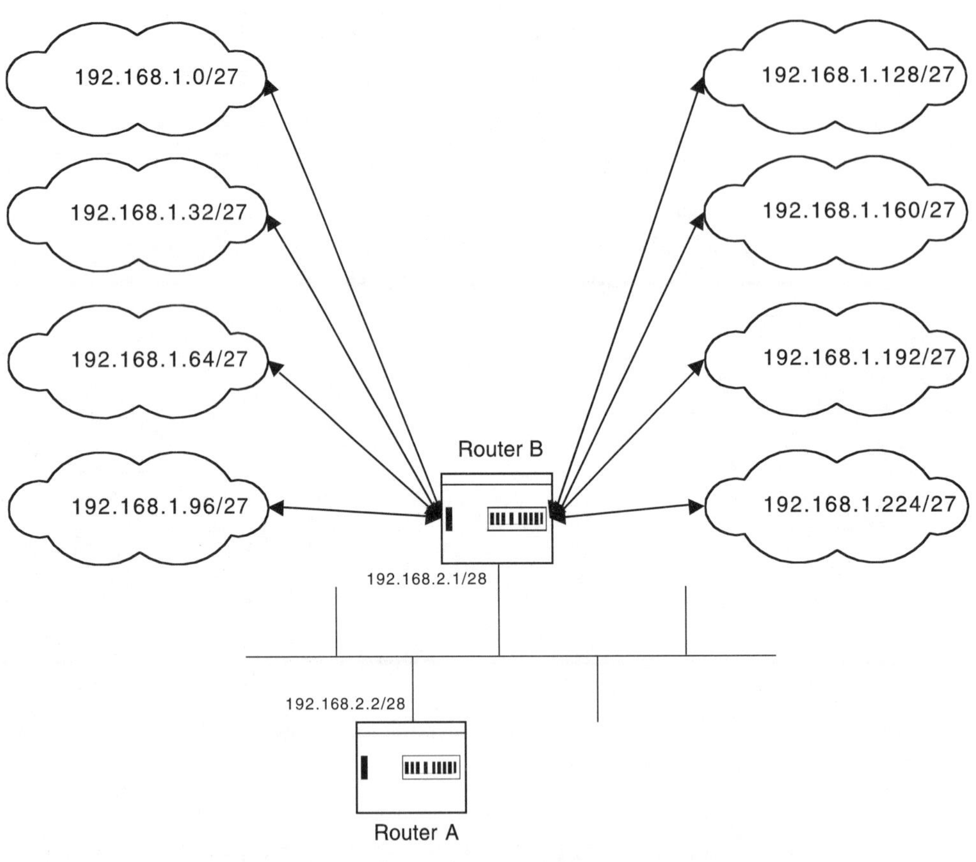

Illustration 7-4 Example Network with Route Aggregation 2

Destination	Route Mask	Next Hop	Port	Metr	Typ	Src	Age
192.168.2.0	255.255.255.240	192.168.2.2	J1	0	DIR	LOC	3569
192.168.1.0	255.255.255.252	192.168.1.2	J2	0	DIR	LOC	3569
192.168.1.0	255.255.255.224	192.168.1.1	J2	1	REM	MGMT	0
192.168.1.32	255.255.255.252	192.168.1.34	J3	0	DIR	LOC	3569
192.168.1.32	255.255.255.224	192.168.1.33	J3	1	REM	MGMT	0
192.168.1.64	255.255.255.252	192.168.1.66	J4	0	DIR	LOC	3569
192.168.1.64	255.255.255.224	192.168.1.65	J4	1	REM	MGMT	0
192.168.1.96	255.255.255.252	192.168.1.98	J5	0	DIR	LOC	3569
192.168.1.96	255.255.255.224	192.168.1.97	J5	1	REM	MGMT	0
192.168.1.128	255.255.255.252	192.168.1.130	J6	0	DIR	LOC	3569
192.168.1.128	255.255.255.224	192.168.1.129	J6	1	REM	MGMT	0
192.168.1.160	255.255.255.252	192.168.1.162	J7	0	DIR	LOC	3569
192.168.1.160	255.255.255.224	192.168.1.161	J7	1	REM	MGMT	0
192.168.1.192	255.255.255.252	192.168.1.194	J8	0	DIR	LOC	3569
192.168.1.192	255.255.255.224	192.168.1.193	J8	1	REM	MGMT	0
192.168.1.224	255.255.255.252	192.168.1.226	J9	0	DIR	LOC	3569
192.168.1.224	255.255.255.224	192.168.1.225	J9	1	REM	MGMT	0

Table 7-3 Route Table for Route Aggregation 2, Router B, etc.

If Router B had a specific route to each network, it would have more than 30 routes in its route table. Since the routes were designed to collapse into a fewer number of routes, Router B needs to know about only 17 routes (9 specific routes and 8 general routes)—about half of what would have been required if all networks were represented by a specific route.

Router A's route table for the second route aggregation might look like Table 7-4.

Destination	Route Mask	Next Hop	Port	Metr	Typ	Src	Age
192.168.2.0	255.255.255.240	192.168.2.2	J2	0	DIR	LOC	3569
192.168.1.0	255.255.255.0	192.168.2.1	J2	1	REM	MGMT	0

Table 7-4 Route Table for Route Aggregation 2, Router A

This table has only two routes; 32 routes were collapsed into a single route entry! Router A needs to know only that any packet with a destination whose first three octets (determined by route mask) are 192.168.1 should be forwarded to Router B as the next hop.

Planning for Aggregation

Now that you have seen an example of route aggregation, let's go back to the excerpt from the IP addressing worksheet. Look at with network 192.168.1.16/30 in Illustration 7-5. This is a specific network in a hypothetical address plan. This network, along with 192.168.1.20/30, can be aggregated by a general route of 192.168.1.16/29. This route and up to two additional routes (192.168.1.24/30 and 192.168.1.28/30 *or* 192.168.1.24/29) also can be subsumed (another term for aggregated) by a more general route, 192.168.1.16/28. Route 192.168.1.0/27 can subsume any route with more than 27 bits of network mask in the range 192.168.1.0 to 192.168.1.31. Route 192.168.1.0/24 can subsume any route to any network in the 192.168.1.0 Class C network.

.0/24	.128/25	.192/26	.224/27	.240/28	.248/29	.252/30
0	0	0	0	0	0	0
1	1	1	1	1	1	1
2	2	2	2	2	2	2
3	3	3	3	3	3	3
4	4	4	4	4	4	4
5	5	5	5	5	5	5
6	6	6	6	6	6	6
7	7	7	7	7	7	7
8	8	8	8	8	8	8
9	9	9	9	9	9	9
10	10	10	10	10	10	10
11	11	11	11	11	11	11
12	12	12	12	12	12	12
13	13	13	13	13	13	13
14	14	14	14	14	14	14
15	15	15	15	15	15	15
16	16	16	16	16	16	16
17	17	17	17	17	17	Start 17
18	18	18	18	18	18	Here 18
19	19	19	19	19	19	19
20	20	20	20	20	20	20
21	21	21	21	21	21	21
22	22	22	22	22	22	22
23	23	23	23	23	23	23
24	24	24	24	24	24	24
25	25	25	25	25	25	25
26	26	26	26	26	26	26
27	27	27	27	27	27	27
28	28	28	28	28	28	28
29	29	29	29	29	29	29
30	30	30	30	30	30	30
31	31	31	31	31	31	31

Illustration 7-5 IP Address Worksheet Showing Route Aggregation

If it were just that simple, there would be no problem. However, network topologies must have the right "shape" to allow for route aggregation. Typically the network should have *funnels,* or bottlenecks (not be be confused with capacity bottlenecks), to be able to take advantage of aggregation. If there are other paths for the routing, the specific network routes might have a chance to get into the route tables. In addition, with alternative paths it becomes difficult to use RIP and let the networks aggregate naturally. This is discussed later in this chapter. In Illustration 7-4, Router B is the funnel. Everything at the top of the illustration was part of network 192.168.1.0/24, and everything at the bottom was part of 192.168.2.0/24—two distinct Class C networks.

Funnels appear throughout the modern intranet. Frame Relay lends itself to route aggregation when used in the popular hub-and-spoke topology. Dial-in remote-access modem pools are excellent points for route aggregation, as is an ISDN Primary Rate interface.

RIP and Route Aggregation

Some interesting side effects can be achieved by using RIP routing. Due to the fact that RIP (version 1) does not pass subnet information in its route updates, RIP must make assumptions about the network masks. This was presented in Chapter 4. If a router receives a RIP route update and the router does not have an interface configured for the class of that network, it will use the natural mask for the route. If it does have a network defined on one of the router's interfaces, it will use the mask defined for that interface.

For example, assume the following network route update is sent out:

Destination = 192.168.1.0   Metric = 1

Suppose a router (Router 1) that has the following addresses defined directly on its interfaces receives the route update.

Address	**Subnet**
192.168.2.1	255.255.255.192
192.168.4.129	255.255.255.192

The router will have a route entry installed, as shown in Table 7-5.

Destination	Route Mask	Next Hop	Port	Metr	Typ	Src	Age
192.168.2.0	255.255.255.192	192.168.2.1	J2	0	DIR	LOC	3569
192.168.4.128	255.255.255.192	192.168.4.129	J3	0	DIR	LOC	3569
192.168.1.0	255.255.255.0	192.168.2.23	J2	1	REM	RIP	0

Table 7-5 Route Table with RIP Update, Router 1

However, suppose that the same route were received by a different router (Router 2) with the following interfaces defined on it.

Address	Subnet
192.168.2.1	255.255.255.192
192.168.1.129	255.255.255.192

Then the route table would look like Table 7-6.

Destination	Route Mask	Next Hop	Port	Metr	Typ	Src	Age
192.168.2.0	255.255.255.192	192.168.2.1	J2	0	DIR	LOC	3569
192.168.1.128	255.255.255.192	192.168.1.129	J3	0	DIR	LOC	3569
192.168.1.0	255.255.255.192	192.168.2.23	J2	1	REM	RIP	0

Table 7-6 Route Table with RIP Update, Router 2

The only difference between the two routers is that Router 2 has a subnet of the Class C network 192.168.1.0 on one of its interfaces. This forces the router to use the same subnet mask as is used for the 192.168.1.128/26 network. In some cases, this would cause incorrect routing choices to be made by the router. Look at the example in Illustration 7-6, where this is *not* the case.

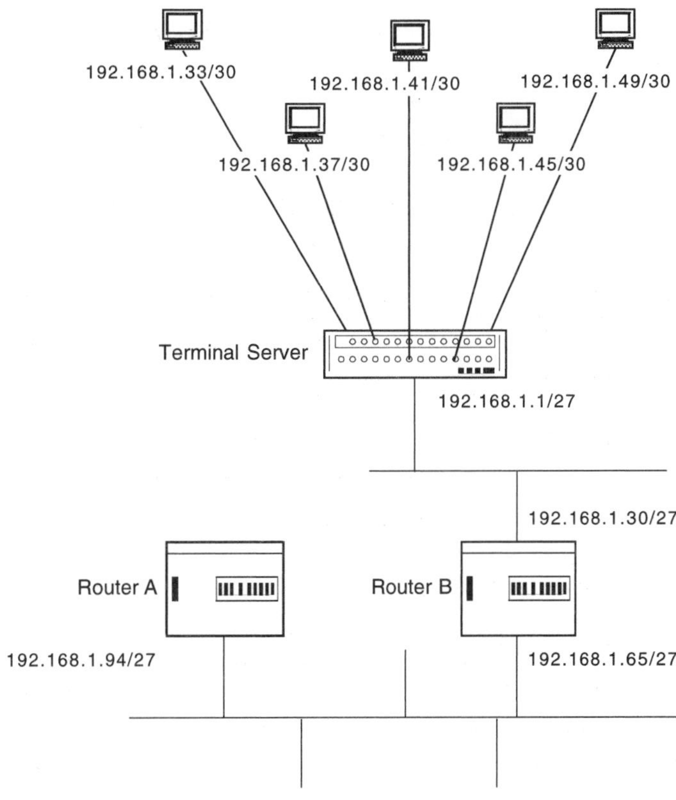

Illustration 7-6 Example Network with RIP Aggregation I

At the top of the illustration are five hosts connected to a terminal server. Each host is assigned an address in one of the point-to-point IP networks. The terminal server also has a host ID in each of the point-to-point IP networks, although these addresses are not shown in the illustration. For instance, for the point-to-point IP network 192.168.1.32/30, the workstation is the 192.168.1.33/30 address and the terminal server is the 192.168.1.34/30 address. In addition to the IP addresses required for the five point-to-point IP networks, the terminal server has an IP address assigned to its Ethernet port but it is in a network defined by a smaller mask (permits more hosts).

Terminal servers often have the ability to run RIP routing. Suppose we turn RIP routing on for both Router A and Router B and for the terminal server. The terminal server would have the route table shown in Table 7-7.

Destination	Route Mask	Next Hop	Port	Metr	Typ	Src	Age
192.168.1.0	255.255.255.224	192.168.1.1	J2	1	DIR	LOC	812
192.168.1.32	255.255.255.252	192.168.1.34	J1.1	0	DIR	LOC	812
192.168.1.36	255.255.255.252	192.168.1.38	J1.2	0	DIR	LOC	812
192.168.1.40	255.255.255.252	192.168.1.42	J1.3	0	DIR	LOC	812
192.168.1.44	255.255.255.252	192.168.1.46	J1.4	0	DIR	LOC	812
192.168.1.48	255.255.255.252	192.168.1.50	J1.5	0	DIR	LOC	812
192.168.1.64	255.255.255.224	192.168.1.30	J2	1	REM	RIP	17

Table 7-7 Route Table for the Terminal Server

This is expected. We get a pleasant surprise when we examine the route table for Router B (Table 7-8).

Destination	Route Mask	Next Hop	Port	Metr	Typ	Src	Age
192.168.1.0	255.255.255.224	192.168.1.30	J1	0	DIR	LOC	359
192.168.1.32	255.255.255.224	192.168.1.1	J1	1	REM	RIP	18
192.168.1.64	255.255.255.224	192.168.1.65	J2	0	DIR	LOC	358

Table 7-8 Route Table for Router B

The five point-to-point networks on the terminal server have been subsumed by a single IP route entry of 192.168.1.32/27! This is an example in which the assumptions that a router makes regarding the network mask can work in your favor.

There are times, however, when such assumptions can just as easily be wrong. For instance, look at Illustration 7-7. This network is very much like the one we just discussed, except that the Ethernet between Router A and Router B has been readdressed. The route table for Router A is shown in Table 7-9.

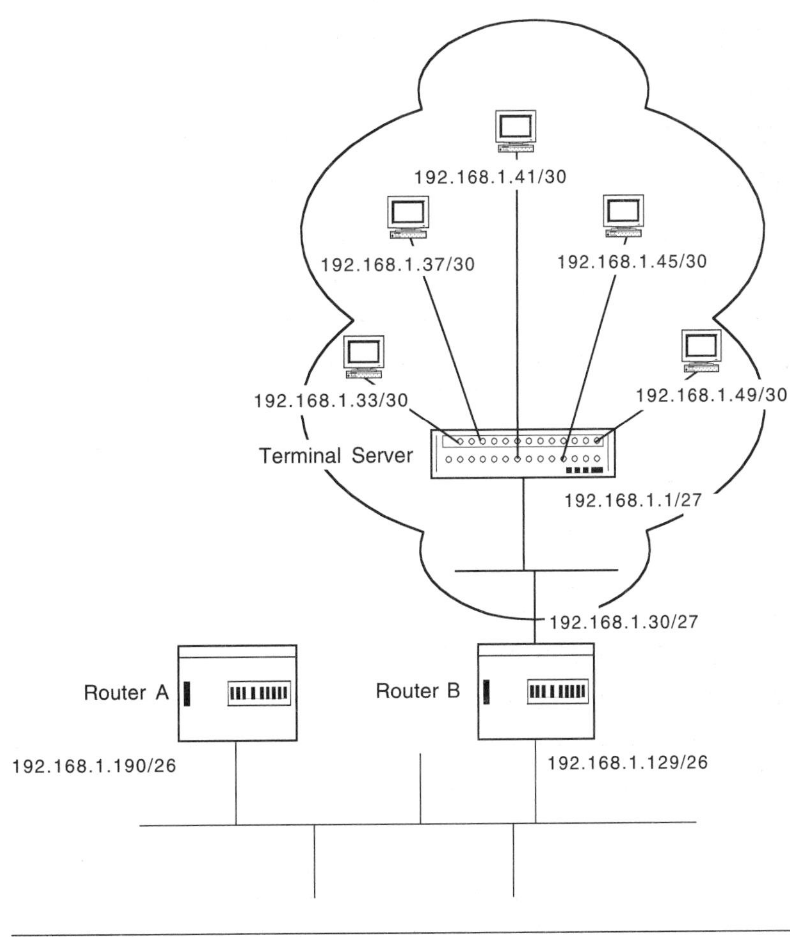

Illustration 7-7 Example Network with RIP Aggregation 2

Destination	Route Mask	Next Hop	Port	Metr	Typ	Src	Age
192.168.1.0	255.255.255.192	192.168.1.129	J1	1	REM	RIP	18
192.168.1.128	255.255.255.192	192.168.1.190	J1	0	DIR	LOC	358

Table 7-9 Route Table for Router A

There is a route entry for the locally defined IP address, as well as a RIP route to the network 192.168.1.0/26. This route has also subsumed all the other routes on Router B. The route table for Router A couldn't be better.

Now let's look at the route table for the terminal server (Table 7-10). The terminal server has a route entry for 192.168.1.128, but look at the route mask—it is wrong. The mask should have been 255.255.255.192. Any addresses from 192.168.1.59 to 192.168.1.190 would not be reachable from the terminal server, as a result of the wrong mask being assumed for the route. The terminal server should issue an ICMP Destination Unreachable notification.

Destination	Route Mask	Next Hop	Port	Metr	Typ	Src	Age
192.168.1.0	255.255.255.224	192.168.1.1	J2	0	DIR	LOC	812
192.168.1.32	255.255.255.252	192.168.1.34	J1.1	0	DIR	LOC	812
192.168.1.36	255.255.255.252	192.168.1.38	J1.2	0	DIR	LOC	812
192.168.1.40	255.255.255.252	192.168.1.42	J1.3	0	DIR	LOC	812
192.168.1.44	255.255.255.252	192.168.1.46	J1.4	0	DIR	LOC	812
192.168.1.48	255.255.255.252	192.168.1.50	J1.5	0	DIR	LOC	812
192.168.1.64	255.255.255.224	192.168.1.30	J2	1	REM	RIP	17
192.168.1.128	255.255.255.224	192.168.1.30	J2	2	REM	RIP	24

Table 7-10 Route Table for the Terminal Server

Here is an alternative. Let's use a different Class B or Class C network for each grouping of networks, as is shown in Illustration 7-8. Three different Class C networks are being used in this example. Network 192.168.1.0/24 is being used in the rightmost terminal server cloud. Network 192.168.2.0/24 is being used in the leftmost terminal server cloud. Network 192.168.8.0/24 is being used on the Ethernet shared by Routers A, B, and C. The route tables for the three routers are shown in Table 7-11 through 7-13.

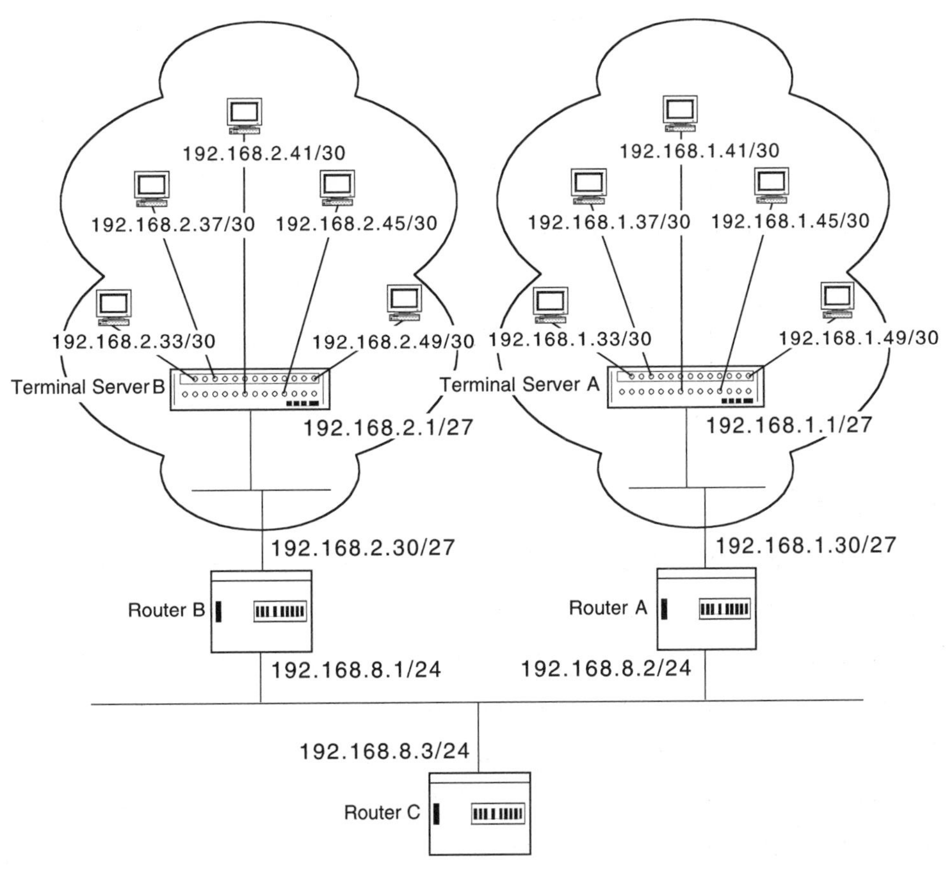

Illustration 7-8 Example Network with RIP Aggregation 3

Destination	Route Mask	Next Hop	Port	Metr	Typ	Src	Age
192.168.1.0	255.255.255.224	192.168.1.30	J1	0	DIR	LOC	359
192.168.1.32	255.255.255.224	192.168.1.1	J1	1	REM	RIP	18
192.168.2.0	255.255.255.0	192.168.8.1	J2	1	REM	RIP	5
192.168.8.0	255.255.255.0	192.168.8.2	J2	0	DIR	LOC	358

Table 7-11 Router A

Destination	Route Mask	Next Hop	Port	Metr	Typ	Src	Age
192.168.1.0	255.255.255.0	192.168.8.2	J2	1	REM	RIP	6
192.168.2.0	255.255.255.224	192.168.2.30	J1	0	DIR	LOC	359
192.168.2.32	255.255.255.224	192.168.2.1	J1	1	REM	RIP	19
192.168.8.0	255.255.255.0	192.168.8.1	J2	0	DIR	LOC	358

Table 7-12 Router B

Destination	Route Mask	Next Hop	Port	Metr	Typ	Src	Age
192.168.1.0	255.255.255.0	192.168.8.2	J2	1	REM	RIP	6
192.168.2.0	255.255.255.0	192.168.8.1	J2	1	REM	RIP	24
192.168.8.0	255.255.255.0	192.168.8.3	J2	0	DIR	LOC	358

Table 7-13 Router C

Router C has no IP interface defined with any subnet of the Class C networks 192.168.1.0/24 or 192.168.2.0/24, therefore the best assumption that Router C can make is that the mask should be the inherent mask for the Class C networks (255.255.255.0). This would indicate that the entire Class C network can be reached via the next hop specified in the route table. In this case, it is true.

Using the quirks of RIP routing to lead to a smaller, more compact route table can be rewarding. It can reduce the size of the route tables throughout the intranet significantly. However, it does require planning and it can leave you scratching your head about why routing works to "these sites" but not to "those sites."

OSPF and Route Aggregation

Unlike RIP, OSPF includes the route mask information in its route updates (link-state advertisements). The manner in which we were able to get some route summarization with RIP is not available for use with OSPF. There is, however, a way to summarize routes in OSPF.

Recall from Chapter 4 that an area in OSPF is a group of IP networks in which the routers share the same link-state databases. The OSPF backbone area (area 0.0.0.0) is required in every autonomous system running OSPF. This may be the only area in the domain, or it may be one of many. Area 0.0.0.0 is always used to join any other areas. For that reason, area 0 must always be contiguous. In places where it is not possible for it to be physically contiguous, virtual links are used to join the two or more portions of the backbone area into a logically contiguous area.

Area border routers serve as the conduit between different areas, usually the backbone area and any other area. The area border router maintains a link-state database for each area in which it participates. All routing in or out of an area passes through the area border router(s). The area border router can be viewed as a funnel for traffic into and out of the areas. Since funnels are excellent places to get route aggregation, area border routers are capable of summarizing routes into and out of areas.

Illustration 7-9 depicts OSPF route aggregation. Router B is the area border router between the backbone area 0.0.0.0 and area 0.0.0.1. If route summarization is configured for Router B, it will collapse the routes it receives from the backbone area and will send a summary of the routes to Router C in area 0.0.0.1. Likewise, it can collapse the routes that it receives from area 0.0.0.1 and summarize them into the backbone area. The summarization rules, which define the summary address and mask to be applied to incoming route information, are defined on the area border router. Whenever a route falls into the range defined for summarization, the summary route information will be sent instead of the specific route information. If Router B were configured to collapse the routes to the inherent network mask, Router C's route table would look like Table 7-14.

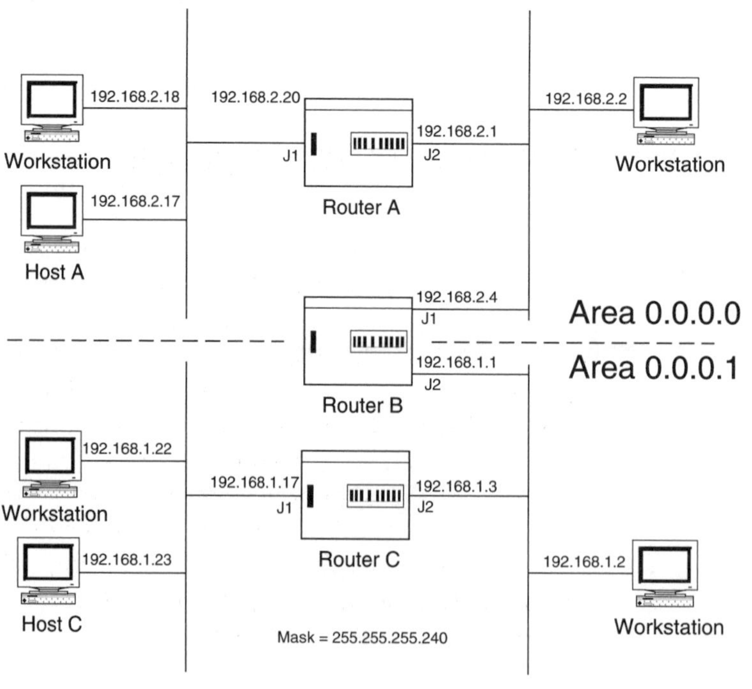

Illustration 7-9 Example Network with OSPF Route Aggregation

Destination	Route Mask	Next Hop	Port	Metr	Typ	Src	Age
192.168.1.0	255.255.255.240	192.168.1.3	J2	0	DIR	LOC	358
192.168.1.16	255.255.255.240	192.168.1.17	J1	0	DIR	LOC	358
192.168.2.0	255.255.255.0	192.168.1.1	J2	258	REM	OSPF	24

Table 7-14 Route Table for Router C

Using the summarization capability of the area border router can be powerful, but the addressing plan must have been developed to support it. If the addressing scheme does not collapse into a compact representation at the border router, network perturbations on the other side of the area border router will probably trigger route table recalculations. Calculating a route table in a large OSPF network can be CPU intensive.

Static Routing and Route Aggregation

Setting up a network to be completely static has its advantages and disadvantages. One advantage is that the network architect can perform traffic engineering to get the most efficient route tables possible. The disadvantage is that the network does not react well to changes in topology; rerouting must be manually effected. Many people believe that static routing is an administrative nightmare that should not be considered; I am not among them. This is not to say that I would design a completely static network. But I would certainly consider a hybrid routing network such as OSPF and static routing. OSPF (and some implementations of RIP) permit static routes to be imported into the dynamic routing system.

In the next example, static routing will be mixed with OSPF to illustrate several points. Illustration 7-10 shows the network under normal conditions. Tables 7-15 through 7-19 are the route tables for several of the routers.

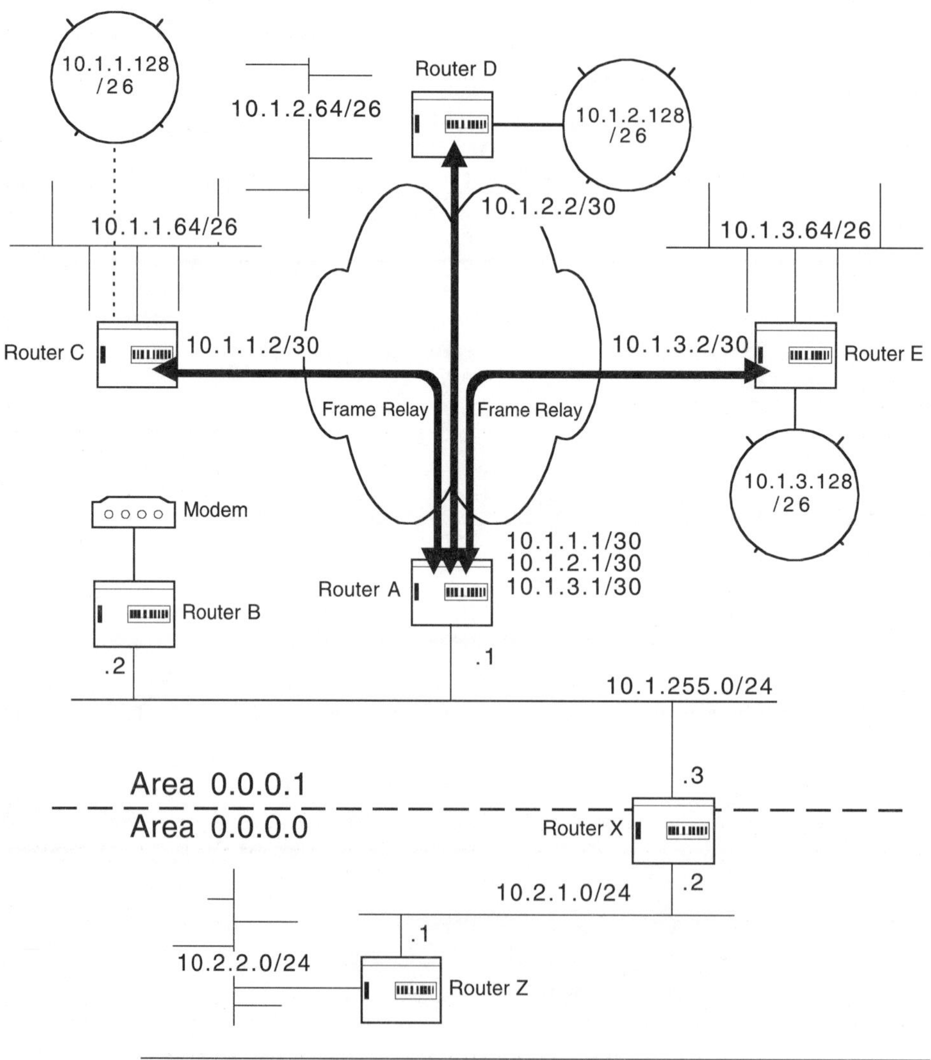

Illustration 7-10 Example Network with Static and OSPF Routing I

Destination	Route Mask	Next Hop	Port	Metr	Typ	Src	Age
10.1.1.0	255.255.255.0	10.1.1.2	J2	1	REM	MGMT	0
10.1.1.0	255.255.255.252	10.1.1.1	J2	0	DIR	LOC	358
10.1.2.0	255.255.255.0	10.1.2.2	J2	1	REM	MGMT	0
10.1.2.0	255.255.255.252	10.1.2.1	J2	0	DIR	LOC	358
10.1.3.0	255.255.255.0	10.1.3.2	J2	1	REM	MGMT	0
10.1.3.0	255.255.255.252	10.1.3.1	J2	0	DIR	LOC	358
10.1.255.0	255.255.255.0	10.1.255.1	J1	0	DIR	LOC	420
10.2.0.0	255.255.0.0	10.1.255.3	J1	62	REM	OSPF	24

Table 7-15 Router A

Destination	Route Mask	Next Hop	Port	Metr	Typ	Src	Age
10.1.1.0	255.255.255.0	10.1.225.1	J1	1	REM	OSPF	32
10.1.2.0	255.255.255.0	10.1.225.1	J1	1	REM	OSPF	34
10.1.3.0	255.255.255.0	10.1.225.1	J1	1	REM	OSPF	31
10.1.255.0	255.255.255.0	10.1.255.2	J1	0	DIR	LOC	420
10.2.0.0	255.255.0.0	10.1.255.3	J1	62	REM	OSPF	24

Table 7-16 Router B

Destination	Route Mask	Next Hop	Port	Metr	Typ	Src	Age
0.0.0.0	0.0.0.0	10.1.1.1	J1	1	REM	MGMT	0
10.1.1.0	255.255.255.252	10.1.1.1	J1	0	DIR	LOC	358
10.1.1.64	255.255.255.192	10.1.1.65	J2	0	DIR	LOC	358
10.1.1.128	255.255.255.192	10.1.1.129	J3	0	DIR	LOC	358

Table 7-17 Router C

Destination	Route Mask	Next Hop	Port	Metr	Typ	Src	Age
10.1.1.0	255.255.255.0	10.1.255.1	J2	1	REM	OSPF	523
10.1.2.0	255.255.255.0	10.1.255.1	J2	1	REM	OSPF	126
10.1.3.0	255.255.255.0	10.1.255.1	J2	1	REM	OSPF	442
10.1.255.0	255.255.255.0	10.1.255.3	J2	0	DIR	LOC	1420
10.2.1.0	255.255.255.0	10.2.1.2	J1	0	DIR	LOC	1420
10.2.2.0	255.255.255.0	10.2.1.1	J1	63	REM	OSPF	352

Table 7-18 Router X

Destination	Route Mask	Next Hop	Port	Metr	Typ	Src	Age
10.1.0.0	255.255.0.0	10.2.1.2	J1	0	REM	OSPF	128
10.2.1.0	255.255.255.0	10.2.1.1	J1	0	DIR	LOC	1421
10.2.2.0	255.255.255.0	10.2.2.1	J2	0	DIR	LOC	1421

Table 7-19 Router Z

Router A serves as the Frame Relay hub router. The Frame Relay network is using a point-to-point addressing model, as denoted by the fact that the Frame Relay connection uses a network with a mask of 255.255.255.252, which has room for only two unique host identifiers. Static routing has been used between the Frame Relay hub router and the remote sites. Each remote site has two networks (10.1.x.64/26 and 10.1.x.128/26), plus the point-to-point IP network. If dynamic routing were used on this link, the Frame Relay hub router would have two dynamic route entries for each of the remote local area networks for each static route that subsumes them (10.1.x.0/24). The Frame Relay hub router imports these static routes into OSPF so that other routers, such as Router B and Router X, can route to the remote sites.

Router B is the dial-backup hub router. Whenever a network outage occurs that requires a remote site to establish an alternative connection, such as loss of Frame Relay service, the remote site will connect to Router B with a dial-up link. Router B has an adequate amount of interfaces that use unnumbered IP for the connection. Router B is running OSPF on all interfaces.

Router C is an example of one of the remote sites. It has three networks configured on it (10.1.1.0/30, 10.1.1.64/26, and 10.1.1.128/26) and one unnumbered interface (J4), which is used for dial-backup. The unnumbered interface is the only interface configured for OSPF, although it is operational only when the primary port is inoperative. Router C has a default route (0.0.0.0) configured to send any traffic that it does not have a more specific route for to the Frame Relay hub router.

Router X, an area border router, is configured to summarize 10.1.x.x routes from area 0.0.0.1 as a route entry of 10.1.0.0 255.255.0.0 into area 0.0.0.0. Similarly, Router X is configured to summarize 10.2.x.x routes from area 0.0.0.0 as a route entry of 10.2.0.0 255.255.0.0 into area 0.0.0.1.

Router Z is a backbone router because it is internal to area 0.0.0.0 and has no other areas defined on its interfaces. Router Z has only one dynamic route in its routing table (10.1.0.0 255.255.0.0), which is the route that was created by the summarization at Router X.

Now let's look at what happens when the Frame Relay connection to Router C is lost. See Illustration 7-11 and Tables 7-20 through 7-24.

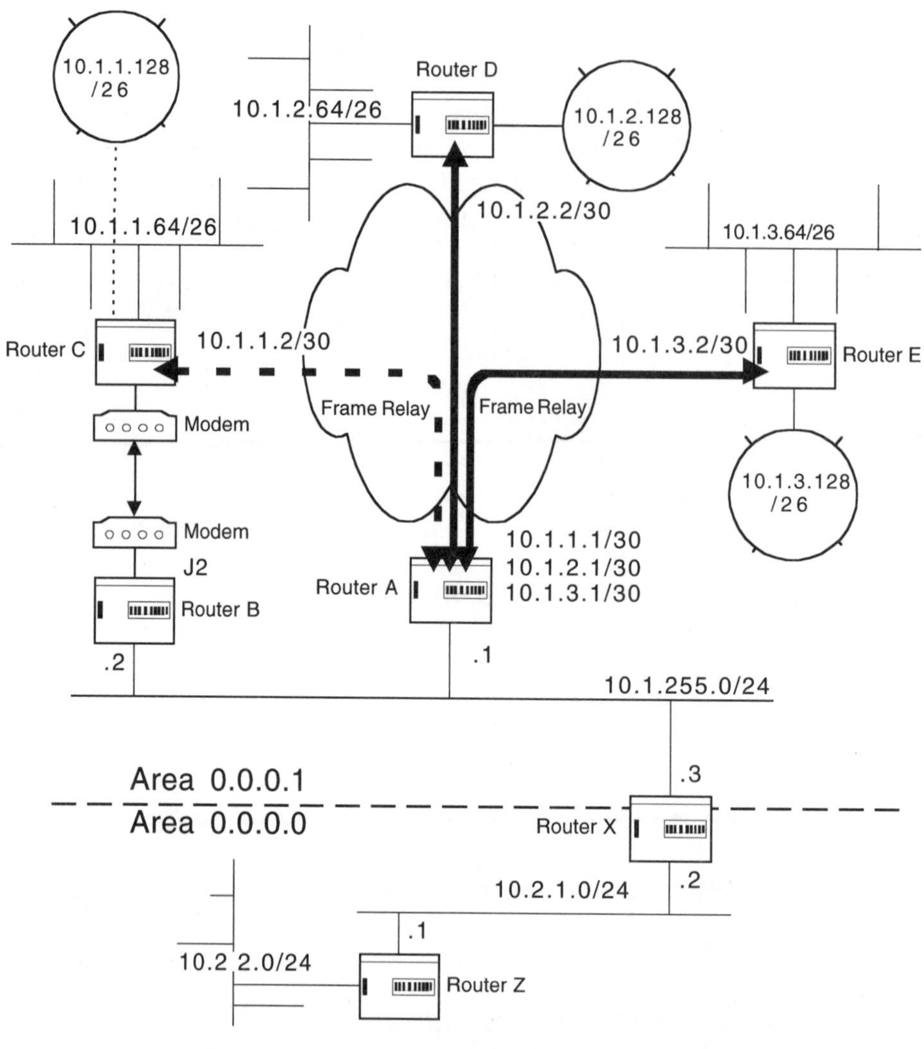

Illustration 7-11 Example Network with Static and OSPF Routing 2

Destination	Route Mask	Next Hop	Port	Metr	Typ	Src	Age
10.1.1.0	255.255.255.0	10.1.1.2	J2	1	REM	MGMT	0
10.1.1.0	255.255.255.252	10.1.1.1	J2	0	DIR	LOC	358
10.1.1.64	255.255.255.192	10.1.255.2	J1	53	REM	OSPF	243
10.1.1.128	255.255.255.192	10.1.255.2	J1	53	REM	OSPF	243
10.1.2.0	255.255.255.0	10.1.2.2	J2	1	REM	MGMT	0
10.1.2.0	255.255.255.252	10.1.2.1	J2	0	DIR	LOC	358
10.1.3.0	255.255.255.0	10.1.3.2	J2	1	REM	MGMT	0
10.1.3.0	255.255.255.252	10.1.3.1	J2	0	DIR	LOC	358
10.1.255.0	255.255.255.0	10.1.255.1	J1	0	DIR	LOC	420
10.2.0.0	255.255.0.0	10.1.255.3	J1	62	REM	OSPF	24

Table 7-20 Router A

Destination	Route Mask	Next Hop	Port	Metr	Typ	Src	Age
10.1.1.0	255.255.255.0	10.1.255.1	J1	1	REM	OSPF	34
10.1.1.64	255.255.255.192	10.1.255.2	J2	25	REM	OSPF	243
10.1.1.128	255.255.255.192	10.1.255.2	J2	25	REM	OSPF	243
10.1.2.0	255.255.255.0	10.1.255.1	J1	1	REM	OSPF	32
10.1.3.0	255.255.255.0	10.1.255.1	J1	1	REM	OSPF	34
10.1.255.0	255.255.255.0	10.1.255.2	J1	0	DIR	LOC	420
10.2.0.0	255.255.0.0	10.1.255.3	J1	62	REM	OSPF	24

Table 7-21 Router B

Destination	Route Mask	Next Hop	Port	Metr	Typ	Src	Age
0.0.0.0	0.0.0.0	10.1.1.1	J1	1	REM	MGMT	0
10.1.1.64	255.255.255.192	10.1.1.65	J2	0	DIR	LOC	358
10.1.1.128	255.255.255.192	10.1.1.129	J3	0	DIR	LOC	358
10.1.2.0	255.255.255.0	J4	J4	75	REM	OSPF	32
10.1.3.0	255.255.255.0	J4	J4	75	REM	OSPF	34
10.1.255.0	255.255.255.0	J4	J4	53	REM	OSPF	124
10.2.0.0	255.255.0.0	J4	J4	53	REM	OSPF	59

Table 7-22 Router C

Destination	Route Mask	Next Hop	Port	Metr	Typ	Src	Age
10.1.1.0	255.255.255.0	10.1.255.1	J2	1	REM	OSPF	523
10.1.1.64	255.255.255.192	10.1.255.2	J2	1	REM	OSPF	521
10.1.1.128	255.255.255.192	10.1.255.2	J2	1	REM	OSPF	492
10.1.2.0	255.255.255.0	10.1.255.1	J2	1	REM	OSPF	126
10.1.3.0	255.255.255.0	10.1.255.1	J2	1	REM	OSPF	442
10.1.255.0	255.255.255.0	10.1.255.3	J2	0	DIR	LOC	1420
10.2.1.0	255.255.255.0	10.2.1.2	J1	0	DIR	LOC	1420
10.2.2.0	255.255.255.0	10.2.1.1	J1	63	REM	OSPF	352

Table 7-23 Router X

Destination	Route Mask	Next Hop	Port	Metr	Typ	Src	Age
10.1.0.0	255.255.0.0	10.2.1.2	J1	0	REM	OSPF	128
10.2.1.0	255.255.255.0	10.2.1.1	J1	0	DIR	LOC	1421
10.2.2.0	255.255.255.0	10.2.2.1	J2	0	DIR	LOC	1421

Table 7-24 Router Z

When Router C comes up on the dial-backup link, it exchanges the link-state database (OSPF's routing information) with Router B. Router C learns the routing information for the rest of the network and is able to install routes that are more specific than the general default route that it had been using prior to the dial-backup connection.

Router B learns about the networks from Router C and passes the link-state advertisements to all the routers that it exchanges information with. This routing information is flooded throughout area 0.0.0.1.

Router A receives the link-state advertisements from Router B and recomputes its route table. It installs two routes, 10.1.1.64/26 and 10.1.1.128/26, in the route table. These routes are more specific than the 10.1.1.0/24 route and will therefore be used to route traffic to the two local area networks at the Router C site.

Router X, the area border router between area 0.0.0.1 and area 0.0.0.0, receives the link-state advertisements for the routes and does two things. It recomputes its route table and summarizes the routing information for flooding into area 0.0.0.0. Since the summary information is subsumed by the existing summary information already being used in area 0.0.0.0, the link-state advertisement is not sent to each of the routers in area 0.0.0.0.

Router Z, the router internal to area 0.0.0.0, is unaffected by the change in topology in area 0.0.0.1. Its routing table is not recomputed.

The one thing to watch out for in this routing setup is the condition that occurs when Router B is not in a dial-backup condition and either the Ethernet (or the Token Ring) at the Router C site fails. Any packet that arrives at Router A for a destination that is homed to the failed Ethernet segment is routed according to the 10.1.1.0/24 route to Router C. Router C determines that its route to that network is down but that it has a default route to

Router A that might be able to determine another route to the destination. Router C sends the packet back to Router A. Router A sends the packet to Router C. This is a *routing loop*, one of the hazards of static routing. The solution is to let the packet be discarded as a result of the TTL, but this is wasteful and the cycle will repeat with every packet sent to that destination. Another alternative, supported by most modern routers, is to establish a filter that discards all packets going out of Router C on the Frame Relay interface whose destination would otherwise be local to Router C.

Classless Interdomain Routing (CIDR)

The Internet Advisory Board determined a few years back that unless some measures were taken to stave it off, the Internet was in danger of catastrophe. The globally unique address space was being allocated at unprecedented rates. The Internet had won the favor of the masses and was growing. Resources that once seemed limitless started to look insufficient. In particular, registered Internet networks that once seemed plentiful were thinning out. The Class B networks were about to be completely allocated. As the networks were allocated, they were put into service on the Internet. For almost every network that was allocated, a route was added to the Internet route tables. At the same time that the Internet was experiencing the pains from a shortage of available addresses, it was suffering from the unexpected increases to its route tables.

Supernetting

The Internet Advisory Board needed both a short-term and a long-term solution. As the short-term solution, a strategy was devised that would permit aggregation of multiple smaller networks into a single larger network. This is roughly analogous to the way in which an inverse multiplexor works to take several low-bandwidth channels and combine them into a single logical channel of larger bandwidth. Making a single network out of smaller contiguous networks is known as *supernetting.* Thank goodness that it did not get the moniker of "inverse subnetting."

Up until this point, network allocations were made from one of three pools of networks. The Class A pool had 126 networks, each with room for 16,777,214 hosts. The Class B pool had 16,384 networks with room for 65,534 hosts per network. The Class C pool had 2,097,152 networks with room for 254 hosts in each network. Except for really small or really large organizations, almost everybody wanted a Class B network. It was perceived that Class B networks were for organizations that had plans that required more than 254 and fewer than 65,534 hosts. Of course, it was possible to get allocations for multiple Class C networks, but every one of the Class C networks would increase the Internet route table, and multiple Class C networks could be cumbersome to administer.

Now, with the *classless interdomain routing* (CIDR) aggregation strategy, multiple Class C networks can be aggregated to form a network that supports a quantity of hosts somewhere between a Class C and a Class B. In essence, CIDR has removed the significance of the network class. Illustration 7-12 shows how I have taken the IP address worksheet and modified it to illustrate supernetting.

.0/16	.128/17	.192/18	.224/19	.240/20	.248/21	.252/22	.254/23	.255/24
0	0	0	0	0	0	0	0	0
1	1	1	1	1	1	1	1	1
2	2	2	2	2	2	2	2	2
3	3	3	3	3	3	3	3	3
4	4	4	4	4	4	4	4	4
5	5	5	5	5	5	5	5	5
6	6	6	6	6	6	6	6	6
7	7	7	7	7	7	7	7	7
8	8	8	8	8	8	8	8	8
9	9	9	9	9	9	9	9	9
10	10	10	10	10	10	10	10	10
11	11	11	11	11	11	11	11	11
12	12	12	12	12	12	12	12	12
13	13	13	13	13	13	13	13	13
14	14	14	14	14	14	14	14	14
15	15	15	15	15	15	15	15	15
16	16	16	16	16	16	16	16	16
17	17	17	17	17	17	17	17	17
18	18	18	18	18	18	18	18	18
19	19	19	19	19	19	19	19	19
20	20	20	20	20	20	20	20	20
21	21	21	21	21	21	21	21	21
22	22	22	22	22	22	22	22	22
23	23	23	23	23	23	23	23	23
24	24	24	24	24	24	24	24	24
25	25	25	25	25	25	25	25	25
26	26	26	26	26	26	26	26	26
27	27	27	27	27	27	27	27	27
28	28	28	28	28	28	28	28	28
29	29	29	29	29	29	29	29	29
30	30	30	30	30	30	30	30	30
31	31	31	31	31	31	31	31	31

Illustration 7-12 Portion of CIDR Aggregation Worksheet

If you had a requirement for address space equivalent to multiple Class C addresses, you would be allocated a single network derived from Class C networks. It might look like Table 7-25.

Address Requirement	Class C Networks	Network Allocated
1 to 254	192.168.0.0	192.168.0.0/24
255 to 510	192.168.0.0 to 192.168.1.0	192.168.0.0/23
511 to 1022	192.168.0.0 to 192.168.3.0	192.168.0.0/22
1023 to 2046	192.168.0.0 to 192.168.7.0	192.168.0.0/21
2047 to 4094	192.168.0.0 to 192.168.15.0	192.168.0.0/20
4095 to 8190	192.168.0.0 to 192.168.31.0	192.168.0.0/19

Table 7-25 Single Networks Derived from Multiple Class C Networks

If you had a requirement for 6000 host addresses, you could be allocated a network such as 192.168.0.0/19, which would be a composite of 32 Class C addresses. Depending on how you intended to engineer the subnetting, you could possibly make a case for an allocation of a Class B network. The point is, however, that even though 32 Class C networks were allocated, only one route, 192.168.0.0/19, was added to the Internet route tables. Further, the utilization of the 192.168.0.0/19 supernet is as high as 0.73, whereas if a Class B network were allocated for the demand, it would achieve a utilization of only 0.09. Supernetting is clearly a much more efficient utilization of address space.

Classless Addressing

The name "classless interdomain routing" suggests that this classless strategy is applied to the Internet backbone where interdomain routing takes place. Since the goal of reducing the route table within the Internet is embodied in the CIDR strategy, it follows that support for supernetting must be built into the exterior routing protocols. Older exterior routing protocols, such as EGP and BGP-2, lack support in the route table for a network mask. The updates themselves do not carry network mask information but derive the mask from the class of network being advertised. BGP-4, on the other hand, supports masks different from the one implied through the inherent class of the network. Typically, this would be a smaller mask than the inherent mask of the network; however, all the principles apply to cases of larger masks. This is good from the perspective that Class C address space, which accounts for less than a quarter of all address space, may be consumed faster than expected by allocation of supernets. The supernet 192.168.8.0/21 supports the same number of hosts as the subnet 172.16.8.0/21. If the Class C address space were consumed faster than expected, a single Class A network could be split up into as many as 256 Class B equivalent networks, 65,536 Class C equivalent networks, or any combination necessary. Not all of the Class A networks have been allocated. In fact, half of all the Class A networks were reserved by the IANA. This is roughly 25 percent of all globally unique address space.

Subnetting and supernetting strategies work fine for modern exterior gateway routing protocols, but what about the interior routing protocols? In the past (and in many places, the present), routers have relied on classes for assumptions about what configurations should be allowed. For instance, although CIDR permits a network such as 192.168.8.0/21 to be defined, an interior router might have difficulty with it. In reality, validity checks that once prevented a user from incorrectly configuring a network interface with an address of 192.168.9.21 using a network mask of 255.255.248.0 must be removed to permit such a configuration. The notion of classes must be removed from routers.

This is not so difficult if you are using a modern routing protocol such as OSPF. RIP version 1 is a different story. Remember that RIP makes some assumptions to compensate for the absence of subnet mask information in the route updates. These assumptions should be kept in mind when using a supernet allocation. If a RIP router were to receive an update such as 192.168.8.0 (/21), it would likely install the route in its tables and use a mask of 255.255.255.0, which would be wrong. This is not too different from the way some of the older exterior routing protocols mentioned earlier would react.

Address Allocation

The real factor that initiated the CIDR movement was that the Internet unexpectedly grew quite popular. As more organizations became connected, more and more addresses were being assigned by the allocation authorities. The address space became depleted and the route tables bloated. The route tables would benefit slightly from supernetting; however, the route tables would greatly benefit from a large-scale route aggregation plan. RFC 1518, "An Architecture for IP Address Allocation with CIDR," provides the framework for such a plan. The essence of the architecture is similar to the concepts discussed earlier in this chapter. The exception is that earlier portions of this chapter studied aggregation within an autonomous system; RFC 1518 applies aggregation techniques to the Internet backbone.

In the plan presented in RFC 1518, an entity—such as an Internet service provider or a government—is allocated a number of IP networks or supernets. Subscribers come to a provider for Internet access, and the subscriber is allocated networks from the provider's allocation. The subscriber maintains the IP network for the duration of the business agreement. A subscriber who wishes to change providers relinquishes the IP networks belonging administratively to the provider. This is an important point. Under this architecture, the end users would "lease" their IP addresses from the provider. If it were a purchase arrangement, the end users would take their allocation with them to a new provider. This would defeat the purpose of the aggregation strategy since each segment of the initial provider allocation that is rehomed would have to be advertised separately on the Internet backbone in addition to the provider's aggregated route advertisement. The more this situation occurs, the less efficient the scheme becomes. The best policy for ensuring the highest degree of aggregation is to "rent" the IP addresses. It is important to note, however, that the CIDR specification does not *require* users to relinquish their IP networks if they change their Internet service provider. This requirement would have to be dictated by the ISP as a part of the service contract. Illustration 7-13 depicts an architecture as detailed in RFC 1518 and Illustration 7-14 show a sample worksheet for that architecture.

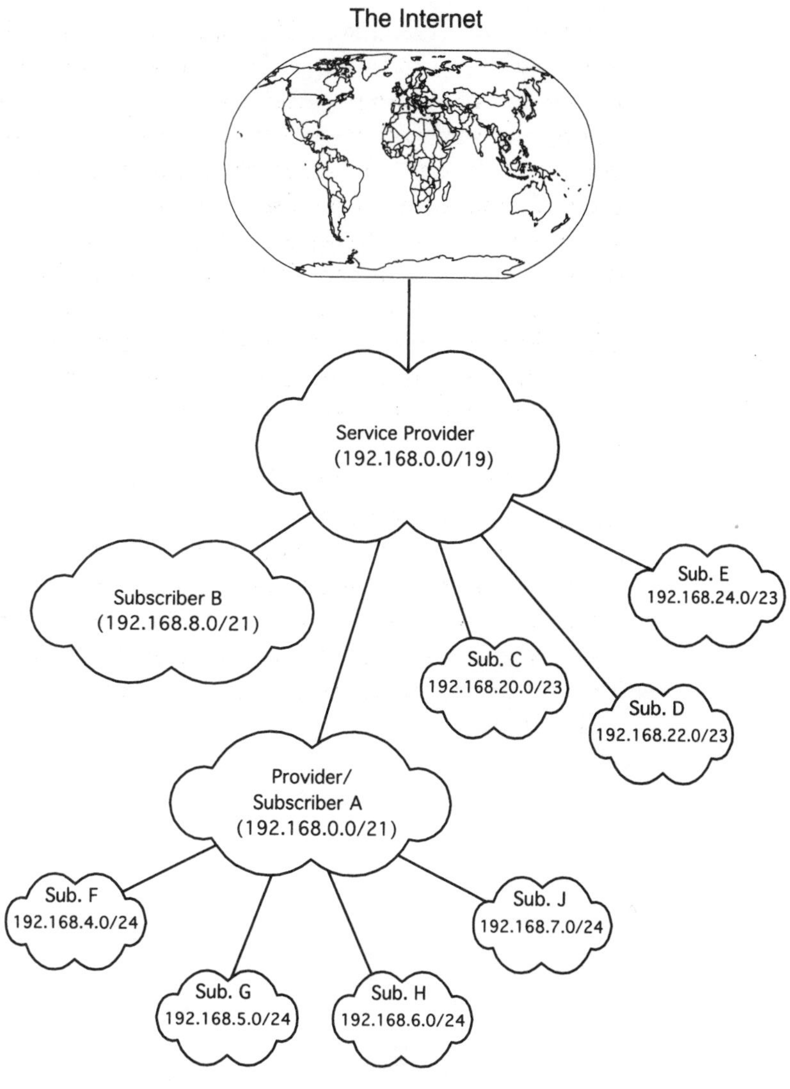

Illustration 7-13 Example Allocation for Internet Route Optimization

.0/16	.128/17	.192/18	.224/19	.240/20	.248/21	.252/22	.254/23	.255/24
0	0	0	**SvcProv** 0	0	**Sub A** 0	0	0	0
1	1	1	1	1	1	1	1	1
2	2	2	2	2	2	2	2	2
3	3	3	3	3	3	3	3	3
4	4	4	4	4	4	4	4	4
5	5	5	5	5	5	5	5	5
6	6	6	6	6	6	6	6	6
7	7	7	7	7	7	7	7	7
8	8	8	8	8	**Sub B** 8	8	8	8
9	9	9	9	9	9	9	9	9
10	10	10	10	10	10	10	10	10
11	11	11	11	11	11	11	11	11
12	12	12	12	12	12	12	12	12
13	13	13	13	13	13	13	13	13
14	14	14	14	14	14	14	14	14
15	15	15	15	15	15	15	15	15
16	16	16	16	16	16	**Avail.** 16	16	16
17	17	17	17	17	17	17	17	17
18	18	18	18	18	18	18	18	18
19	19	19	19	19	19	19	19	19
20	20	20	20	20	20	20	**Sub C** 20	20
21	21	21	21	21	21	21	21	21
22	22	22	22	22	22	22	**Sub D** 22	22
23	23	23	23	23	23	23	23	23
24	24	24	24	24	24	24	**Sub E** 24	24
25	25	25	25	25	25	25	25	25
26	26	26	26	26	26	26	**Avail.** 26	26
27	27	27	27	27	27	27	27	27
28	28	28	28	28	28	**Intrnl** 28	28	28
29	29	29	29	29	29	29	29	29
30	30	30	30	30	30	30	30	30
31	31	31	31	31	31	31	31	31

Illustration 7-14 Class C Supernet Worksheet: ISP to Subscriber

In this example the Internet service provider (ISP) has been allocated supernet 192.168.0.0/19, which is a composite of 32 Class C networks, from 192.168.0.0 to 192.168.31.0. The ISP reserves the supernet 192.168.28.0/22, a block of four Class C networks, for its own internal use. The remainder of the 192.168.0.0/19 supernet has been suballocated to five organizations, subscribers to the connectivity service that the ISP is providing. They are denoted as Subscribers A through E in Illustrations 7-13 and 7-14. Two blocks of networks are not currently allocated, 192.168.16.0/22 and 192.168.26.0/23.

Interestingly, Subscriber A is also a provider. Subscriber A has received an allocation of Class C networks that, when considered together, comprise the supernet 192.168.0.0/21. This provider has chosen to reserve the supernet 192.168.0.0/22 for internal purposes. The remaining four Class C networks from the initial allocation have been suballocated by Provider/Subscriber A to four organizations as individual Class C networks, 192.168.4.0/24 through 192.168.7.0/24, as shown in Illustration 7-15.

.224/19	.240/20	.248/21	.252/22	.254/23	.255/24
SvcProv 0	0	**Sub A** 0	**Intrnl** 0	0	0
1	1	1	1	1	1
2	2	2	2	2	2
3	3	3	3	3	3
4	4	4	4	4	**Sub F** 4
5	5	5	5	5	**Sub G** 5
6	6	6	6	6	**Sub H** 6
7	7	7	7	7	**Sub J** 7

Illustration 7-15 Suballocation of Networks from Provider/Subscriber A

It is possible to add another layer of hierarchy and aggregation. This is referred to as *continental aggregation* and could happen, for instance, if all of the Internet service providers within the United States were given their allocations out of the same supernet of Class C networks. Other geographic areas would be assigned their own supernet from which they could make sub-allocations to Internet service providers and subsequently to the end users.

One last note regarding subscriber-to-provider aggregation is depicted in Illustration 7-13. This architecture works particularly well when the provider is the sole Internet service provider for a particular subscriber. If a subscriber has more than one connection to the Internet, this architecture may prove inadequate. A single autonomous system would not be likely to take an address allocation from more than one ISP. There are several choices for how the IP addressing should be derived for organizations that have more than one Internet ingress/egress. Among the choices are for the organization to request a globally unique address allocation from only one of the Internet service providers. The other Internet service providers may advertise more specific routes than the ISP that provided the allocation, but the situation would not be any worse than if the organization requested its IP network allocations from the InterNIC or some other authority.

Summary

The route table is the central database used to determine the next-hop address to be used in the forwarding process. It is likely that the entire database must be searched to derive a list of candidate routes during the Basic Match pruning rule. The smallest and most compact route table will be more quickly and efficiently searched than will a large and cumbersome route table.

This chapter dealt with designing an IP address scheme that will result in as small a route table as possible, given the network architecture and interior routing protocol employed in the autonomous system. Route aggregation was discussed as it pertains to RIP, OSPF, and static routing. In a RIP environment, automatic route aggregation is a side effect of RIP updates not including a subnet mask and the assumptions that a router makes when trying to assign a route mask to a received network route update. In an OSPF environment in which the subnet mask information is passed in the link-state updates, route aggregation is performed at an area border router. In a static routing environment, route aggregation can be set up as elaborately as the network administrator cares to set it up. Static routing can be one of the best ways to achieve an efficient route table. Static routing can also be used in conjunction with a dynamic routing protocol whereby the static routes are imported into a dynamic routing architecture such as OSPF. This can lead to additional levels of route aggregation.

A new concept, called supernetting or classless interdomain routing (CIDR), is much more than supernetting, however. It is a strategy for curbing the growth of the route tables within the Internet and for utilizing remaining address space more efficiently.

Practice Questions

1. What is the smallest network that subsumes each of the following subnets? In other words, what is the smallest route that aggregates the listed networks?

a. 192.168.1.0/30	192.168.1.8/30	192.168.1.12/30
b. 192.168.1.0/30	192.168.1.8/29	192.168.1.16/29
c. 192.168.1.0/28	192.168.1.16/30	192.168.1.20/30
d. 192.168.1.0/24	192.168.2.0/24	
e. 192.168.1.8/29	192.168.1.40/29	192.168.1.52/30

f. 192.168.1.56/29	192.168.1.112/28	192.168.1.80/28
g. 192.168.1.64/26	192.168.1.32/28	192.168.1.56/30
h. 192.168.1.0/24	192.168.3.0/24	192.168.5.0/24
i. 172.16.0.0/16	172.24.0.0/16	172.28.0.0/16

2. (Bonus) What single route subsumes all the Class B and all the Class C networks but not the Class A networks?

chapter 8

Addressing for High Utilization of Address Space

As we have seen in previous chapters, it is important that globally unique IP networks be utilized efficiently. This due in part to the recent boom in Internet popularity and is exacerbated by inadequate granularity in the addressing mechanisms. That is, there are essentially three classes of unicast addresses that can support discrete numbers of host addresses. A Class A network can support 16,777,216 hosts, a Class B network can support 65,534 hosts, and a Class C network can support 254 unique host addresses. These are the maximum numbers of hosts that each class of address could support if the network were not subnetted and all hosts were on the single IP network. This is rarely the case, due to the traffic and media constraints. For all practical purposes, it is necessary to subnet the network into manageable units and, at the same time, maintain a high degree of address utilization.

Estimating Address Assignment Efficiency

In 1994, Christian Huitema wrote RFC 1715, "The *H* Ratio for Address Assignment Efficiency," to document an approach for estimating the efficiency of an addressing scheme. In RFC 1715 the *H ratio* is defined as

$$H = \log(\text{number of objects})/\text{available bits}$$

Note that the formula uses a base-10 log function instead of a base-2 log function. I prefer to present the formula first from a base-2 perspective since I believe that it is easier to understand than the base-10 equivalent.

$$H = \log_2(\text{number of objects})/\text{available bits}$$

To state it as simply as possible, the log base 2 of a number is, when rounded up to the nearest integer, equal to the number of bits required to represent the magnitude of the number in binary. For instance, the log base 2 of 16 is equal to exactly 4. That is, to represent 16 levels in binary would require 4 bits. The log base 2 of 38 is approximately 5.25. Rounding up to the nearest integer, it would require 6 bits to represent 38 levels in binary. It is easy to see from looking at the log base 2 formula that if you had 8 bits to work with and you had 256 objects, this would render an *H* ratio equal to 1 since the log base 2 of 256 is exactly 8. You require 8 bits and you have 8 bits available to use; therefore you have 100 percent efficiency.

The interpretation of the formula starts to get a little difficult for values of *H* less than 1. For instance, would an *H* ratio of 0.875 be equivalent to 87.5 percent efficiency? The answer is *no.* To illustrate, let's assume that you have 8 bits of address space available and 128 objects that need addresses. We know that you could represent 256 objects with 8 bits of address space; 128 objects in a space that could accommodate 256 objects indicates a 50 percent utilization, but our *H* ratio is 0.875! If you had 2 objects in the same address space, you would get an *H* ratio of 0.125, even though you have less than 0.8 percent address space utilization.

Now back to the formula given in RFC 1715:

$$H = \log(\text{number of objects})/\text{available bits}$$

This formula uses the log base 10 of the number of objects. The reason cited is "because they are easier to compute mentally." I'm not going to argue with someone who computes logarithms mentally! I do have a calculator that computes log base 10 functions but not log base 2 functions naturally, so perhaps the RFC 1715 formula would be easier for me to use. Let's take a look at a few of the calculations we worked earlier, but now let's use the log base 10 formula. If you had 256 objects and 8 bits of address space available, the RFC 1715 *H* ratio would be 0.301. The maximum value possible for the RFC 1715 *H* ratio is 0.301 and is equivalent to a 100 percent utilized address space. But 128 objects and 8 bits available renders an *H* ratio of 0.263 and a utilization of only 50 percent.

Table 8-1 shows a comparison of the log base 2 *H* ratio, the log base 10 *H* ratio, and utilization for various numbers of hosts with 8 bits of address space available.

Number of Hosts(%)	H Ratio ($\log_2$)	H Ratio ($\log_{10}$)	Utilization %
256	1.0	0.301	100
128	0.875	0.263	50
64	0.75	0.225	25
32	0.625	0.188	12.5
16	0.5	0.151	6.25

Number of Hosts(%)	H Ratio (log_2)	H Ratio (log_{10})	Utilization %
8	0.375	0.113	3.125
4	0.25	0.075	1.56
2	0.125	0.038	0.781

Table 8-1 Comparison of log_2 and log_{10} *H* Ratios and Their Utilization Percents

From the table you can see that a log base 10 *H* ratio of 0.20 will render a utilization between 12.5 percent and 25 percent. One of the examples provided in RFC 1715 is the Internet address space. In 1994 there were approximately 3 million hosts connected to the Internet, which has an address space of 32 bits. The log base 10 *H* ratio is 0.202, which, as we just saw, would fall somewhere between 12.5 percent and 25 percent utilization. Now remember that a Class A network can accommodate about 16.7 million addresses, a Class B network can accommodate about 65 thousand addresses, and a Class C network can accommodate 254 addresses. The total potential address space for the Internet is more than 3.72 billion addresses. That means that 3 million addresses out of more than 3 billion potential addresses is less than 0.1 percent utilization. How can this be? Take a 32-bit address space: To get a 100 percent utilization, you would require approximately 4.3 billion objects. To get 12.5 percent utilization, you would require about 537 million objects. Now compute the *H* ratio (log_{10}) for 537 million objects with 32 available bits. The *H* ratio is equal to 0.273. Well, now I am really confused! The same utilization (12.5 percent) with 8 bits of available space rendered an *H* ratio of 0.188.

Calculating Address Assignment Efficiency

The reason for the confusion is that the *H* ratio is a ratio based on the number of bits. As the number of bits increases, so too does the significance of the highest-order bit. In fact, it increases exponentially. For instance, in an 8-bit representation the 7th bit has a decimal value of 64 and the 8th bit has a value of 128, a difference of 64. In a 16-bit representation the 15th bit has a value of 16,384 and the 16th bit has a value of 32,768, a difference of 16,384. The *H* ratio cannot be used to indicate the utilization efficiency of an address space unless the number of bits representing the address space is a constant. Besides, who needs to work logarithms to estimate the efficiency of an addressing scheme? To me, the bottom line is how many hosts I can address with the networks I am allocated and how many addresses I use from the potential space:

$$\text{Utilization} = \text{addresses used} / \text{addresses possible}$$

To represent this as a percentage, I simply multiply the result by 100. The "addresses possible" portion of this formula can refer to the allocated network(s), all subnets of the allocated network, or a single subnet of the allocated network. For instance, if you had a Class C address allocated to you and you wanted to determine the utilization of your addressing scheme, you would simply count the number of allocated addresses on that Class C network and divide that quantity by 254, the maximum number of hosts possible. Some folks could argue that you should divide by 256, since that is the number of addresses possible with an 8-bit field. This would suggest that the maximum utilization of a Class C address is 0.992. I believe that it is unnecessary to "dock" you for the loss of the all-0s and all-1s addresses from the start. (If you noticed that the example in Chapter 2 used 256 hosts per Class C and 65,536 hosts per Class B, let me remind you that I had not discussed the special-case all-0s and all-1s addresses at that time.)

Now suppose that you have a Class C address divided into four equal-sized subnets. Each subnet has the capacity to have 62 hosts per subnet. The maximum number of hosts would be 248 (62 4). If all addresses in each of the subnets were allocated, the utilization of the Class C network would be

Utilization of Class C network = 248/254 = 0.976

On the other hand, the utilization with respect to all subnets would be

Utilization of all subnets = 248/248 = 1.0

When you calculate the utilization of the network, you are including the loss of efficiency due to subnetting. When you calculate the utilization with respect to all subnets, you are calculating the efficiency you have achieved within the bounds of the subnetting your network requires. To illustrate, consider the case in which you have a Class C network allocated to you and you must allocate 64 point-to-point IP networks out of it. Since there are exactly two hosts on a point-to-point IP network, there will be exactly 128 addresses used out of the possible 254 addresses possible on the Class C network. The utilization of the Class C network that you were allocated is 0.504. The utilization with respect to all subnets, however, is 1.0.

Addressing Efficiency and Routing Protocols

Chapter 4 discussed routing and the way that different routing protocols deal with addressing. Remember from the discussion that RIP does not convey subnet mask information in the routing updates. Conversely, OSPF does reflect the masks in the link-state advertisements. It would follow that OSPF would tend to allow better address space utilization than RIP would give. Let's revisit a previous example. The network in Illustration 8-1 reflects two sites joined by a point-to-point numbered IP network. The corporate office site must permit at least 13 addresses on its Ethernet (12 hosts and 1 router). The point-to-point IP network requires two host addresses (one for each router), and the branch office requires five addresses on its Ethernet.

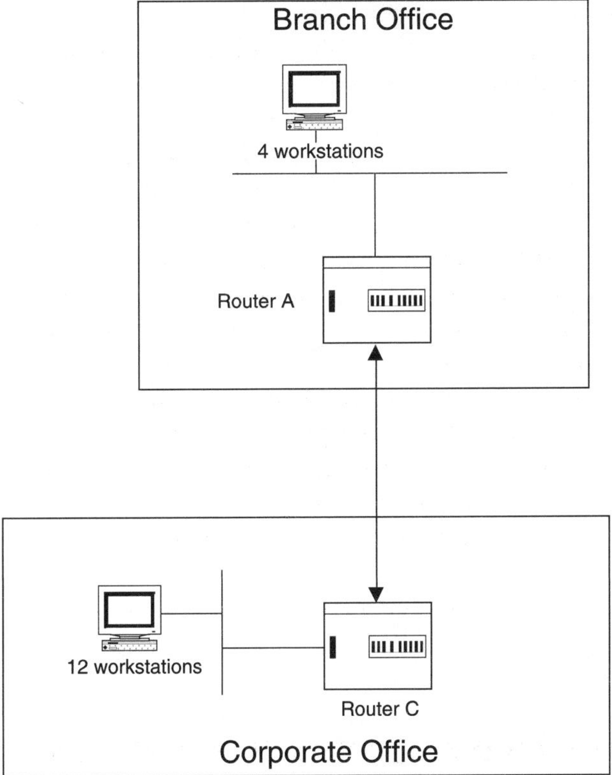

Illustration 8-1 Example Network

In a RIP routing environment, we are constrained to have fixed-length subnet masks. The network that has the largest address requirement is the Ethernet at the corporate office. It requires a 28-bit network mask to accommodate 13 hosts (it can handle up to 14 hosts). For our addressing we would need to allocate three subnets that can each accommodate 14 hosts (42 total hosts), even though we need to provide for only 20 addresses. The utilization with respect to all subnets is

Utilization (subnets) = 20/42 = 0.476

In an OSPF environment you can create subnets, depending on your networking needs. In our example the point-to-point IP network required the use of a subnet that could potentially accommodate 14 hosts. That subnet alone had a utilization of only 0.143! The best choice for a point-to-point (numbered) IP network is a two-host subnet with a mask of 255.255.255.252.

Illustration 8-2 shows how addressing might be set up in an OSPF environment. This addressing scheme has three subnets with a total capacity for 22 addresses. Since 20 addresses are used, the utilization with respect to all subnets is

Utilization (subnets) = 20/22 = 0.909

.0/24	.128/25	.192/26	.224/27	.240/28	.248/29	.252/30
0	0	0	0	0	0	**0**
1	1	1	1	1	1	**RTR A 1**
2	2	2	2	2	2	**RTR C 2**
3	3	3	3	3	3	**3**
4	4	4	4	4	4	4
5	5	5	5	5	5	5
6	6	6	6	6	6	6
7	7	7	7	7	7	7
8	8	8	8	8	**8**	8
9	9	9	9	9	**RTR A 9**	9
10	10	10	10	10	**10**	10
11	11	11	11	11	**WS A 11**	11
12	12	12	12	12	**WS B 12**	12
13	13	13	13	13	**WS C 13**	13
14	14	14	14	14	**WS D 14**	14
15	15	15	15	15	**15**	15
16	16	16	16	**16**	16	16
17	17	17	17	**RTR C 17**	17	17
18	18	18	18	**18**	18	18
19	19	19	19	**WS A 19**	19	19
20	20	20	20	**WS B 20**	20	20
21	21	21	21	**WS C 21**	21	21
22	22	22	22	**WS D 22**	22	22
23	23	23	23	**WS E 23**	23	23
24	24	24	24	**WS F 24**	24	24
25	25	25	25	**WS G 25**	25	25
26	26	26	26	**WS H 26**	26	26
27	27	27	27	**WS I 27**	27	27
28	28	28	28	**WS J 28**	28	28
29	29	29	29	**WS K 29**	29	29
30	30	30	30	**WS L 30**	30	30
31	31	31	31	**31**	31	31

Illustration 8-2 Example IP Addressing Worksheet in an OSPF Environment (Continued)

You undoubtedly noticed that I did not calculate the utilization of the Class C address space. This example used only a portion of a complete Class C network. Just calculating the efficiency with respect to the subnets was sufficient to show how OSPF can facilitate efficient utilization of address space.

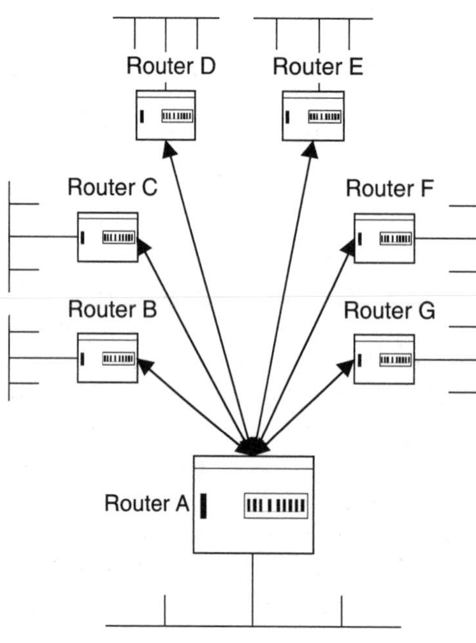

Illustration 8-3 Example Network with Six Remote Sites

Now let's look at a little different scenario, as shown in Illustration 8-3. In this example six remote sites are connected via point-to-point links to the central (hub) site. Each of the seven sites has 10 workstations connected to the Ethernet at the site. Assuming that one Class C network is available for the addressing and that point-to-point numbered IP networks must be used, let's look at how the network could be addressed, first using RIP and then with OSPF.

In a RIP environment, in which you are constrained to a fixed-length subnet mask, the minimum mask that will handle at least 10 hosts (plus the router IP address) is 255.255.255.240 (28-bit mask), which can accommodate up to 14 hosts. A Class C network can be divided into 16 of these subnets. The number of addresses required in this topology is

Ethernet addresses = 7 (10 w/s + 1 router) = 77

Point-to-point addresses = $6 \times 2 = 12$

Total addresses = 89

Of the possible 16 subnets that the Class C network could be divided into, 13 were actually used (7 Ethernets and 6 point-to-point links), and 3 were "wasted"—excuse me, "reserved for future growth." These 16 subnets can accommodate 14 host addresses each, for a total capacity of 224 host addresses. The utilization with respect to all subnets is 0.397, but when you consider only the subnets that addresses are allocated from, the utilization can be said to be 0.489. You might want to calculate the utilization in this way, seeing that there are indeed three subnets unused and that they could support one more remote site like the others. The utilization of the Class C network is calculated as follows:

Utilization (Class C network) = 89/254 = 0.35

Addressing for the same example network using OSPF, we can pick subnet sizes as appropriate for the type of network and number of hosts. The point-to-point networks would use the traditional point-to-point numbered IP network mask of 255.255.255.252. There are six subnets of this size. The Ethernets could use a 255.255.255.240 subnet, as we used for RIP in this example. The number of host addresses in this example remains the same, at 89 host addresses. The utilization with respect to the subnets that addresses were allocated from is

Utilization (allocated subnets) = 89/110 = 0.809

The utilization with respect to all subnets cannot be calculated for this example because of the number of subnet combinations that the remaining address space can be divided into. A little over half of the address space from the Class C network is available for future growth. The utilization of the Class C network address space is the same as for RIP, 0.35.

The Class C network utilization is the same for RIP as it is for OSPF in the example. The key difference is that the utilization of the subnets is much higher for OSPF than for RIP. More important, the RIP network has room to grow equal to one more remote site. The OSPF network, on the other hand, has room to grow equal to five more remote sites!

Cheating RIP to Achieve Efficiency

Now let's discuss an option for improving the address utilization in a fixed-length subnet environment. Although it is possible to get involved in an OSPF network design using fixed-length subnet masks, let's aim primarily at RIP routing.

Consider the simple scenario shown in Illustration 8-4. It is common for the equivalent of a Class C network to be allocated to a given remote site. In this example, the point-to-point connection and the remote Ethernet should have addresses allocated from the same Class C network. There are two physical networks: the point-to-point network and the Ethernet. Traditionally, we would cut the address space in half and give the Ethernet 126 host addresses in the x.x.x.0/25 network and the point-to-point 126 hosts in the x.x.x.128/25 network, with 124 host addresses on that network being wasted (*really* wasted this time.) What we can do instead is allocate more subnets with fewer hosts per subnet, allocate one of the subnets to the point-to-point network, and allocate the remaining subnets to the

Ethernet. Table 8-2 reflects the maximum number of Ethernet host addresses and efficiency attainable when dividing the address space of a Class C network into these multiple fixed-length subnets.

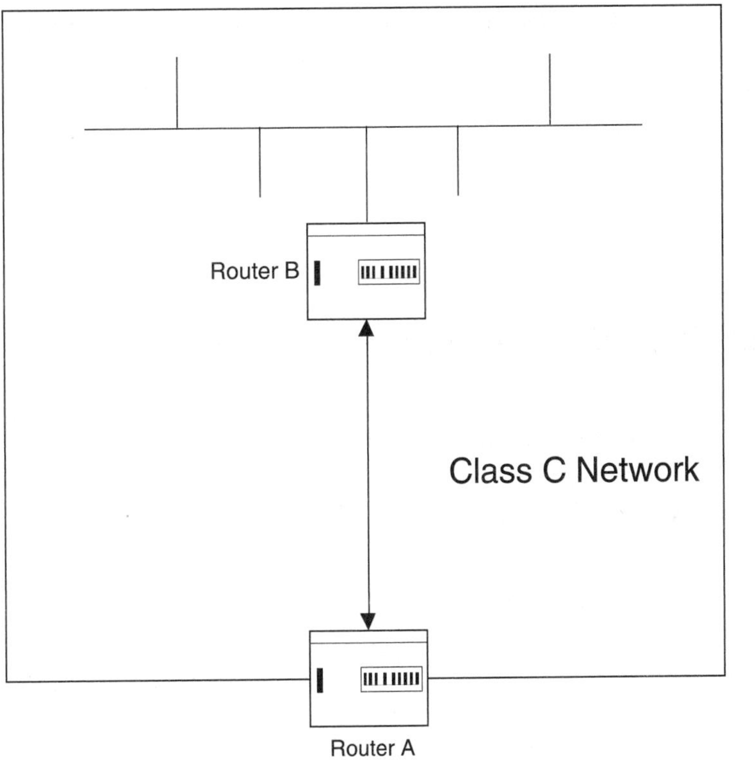

Illustration 8-4 Fixed-Length Subnet Masks and Utilization

Number of Subnet	Hosts/ Subnets	Max. Ethernet Hosts	Max. Utilization
2	126	126	0.504
4	62	186	0.740
8	30	210	0.835
16	14	210	0.835
32	6	186	0.740
64	2	126	0.504

Table 8-2 Maximum Utilization with Fixed-Length Subnet Masks

It is clear that the number of host addresses that can be placed on the physical Ethernet can be increased by more than 80 and that the total address utilization can get as high as 0.835. For this to work, however, the network must be divided up into cliques, with interclique communications handled by the multihomed router. The router must have an address in each of the clique networks for the cliques to share information and resources. Even though the maximum Ethernet hosts and utilization are the same for the cases in which the address space is divided into 8 or 16 subnets, it is more than likely that a larger clique size is desirable since there would potentially be fewer interclique communications necessary.

Network Mask Deception: Another Trick

Network mask deception is a trick that I have tried and found to work in the instances that I have attempted. I cannot tell you whether there are conditions in which this would fail to work. It warrants a mention in this book because of the benefit it can provide. Implement it with caution!

Consider an Ethernet that has a single network allocated to it and addressing divided into multiple subnets. In other words, it has been partitioned into cliques, as was just discussed. If a host in one of the cliques is to communicate with a host in any other clique, it must be facilitated by the router, as shown in Illustrations 8-5 and 8-6.

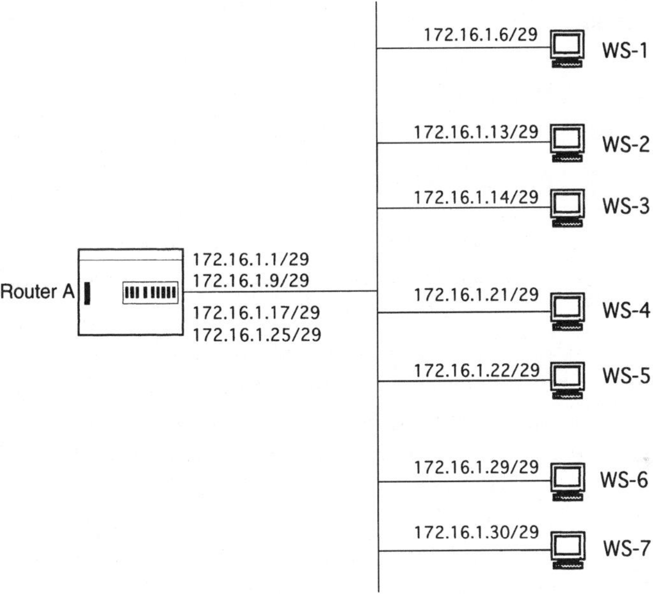

Illustration 8-5 Dividing a LAN into IP Cliques

.0/24	.128/25	.192/26	.224/27	.240/28	**.248/29**	.252/30
0	0	0	0	0	**0**	0
1	1	1	1	1	**RTR-A 1**	1
2	2	2	2	2	**2**	2
3	3	3	3	3	**3**	3
4	4	4	4	4	**4**	4
5	5	5	5	5	**5**	5
6	6	6	6	6	**WS-1 6**	6
7	7	7	7	7	**7**	7
8	8	8	8	8	**8**	8
9	9	9	9	9	**RTR-A 9**	9
10	10	10	10	10	**10**	10
11	11	11	11	11	**11**	11
12	12	12	12	12	**12**	12
13	13	13	13	13	**WS-2 13**	13
14	14	14	14	14	**WS-3 14**	14
15	15	15	15	15	**15**	15
16	16	16	16	16	**16**	16
17	17	17	17	17	**RTR-A 17**	17
18	18	18	18	18	**18**	18
19	19	19	19	19	**19**	19
20	20	20	20	20	**20**	20
21	21	21	21	21	**WS-4 21**	21
22	22	22	22	22	**WS-5 22**	22
23	23	23	23	23	**23**	23
24	24	24	24	24	**24**	24
25	25	25	25	25	**RTR-A 25**	25
26	26	26	26	26	**26**	26
27	27	27	27	27	**27**	27
28	28	28	28	28	**28**	28
29	29	29	29	29	**WS-6 29**	29
30	30	30	30	30	**WS-7 30**	30
31	31	31	31	31	**31**	31

Illustration 8-6 IP Address Worksheet Showing IP Cliques

This example shows a single IP network, 172.16.1.0/27, that has been partitioned into four cliques: networks 172.16.1.0/29, 172.16.1.8/29, 172.16.1.16/29, and 172.16.1.24/29. Illustrations 8-7 and 8-8 show what happens when you change the subnet mask of the workstations to 255.255.255.224 (a 27-bit network mask) and leave the router IP interfaces as previously defined, using the 29-bit network mask.

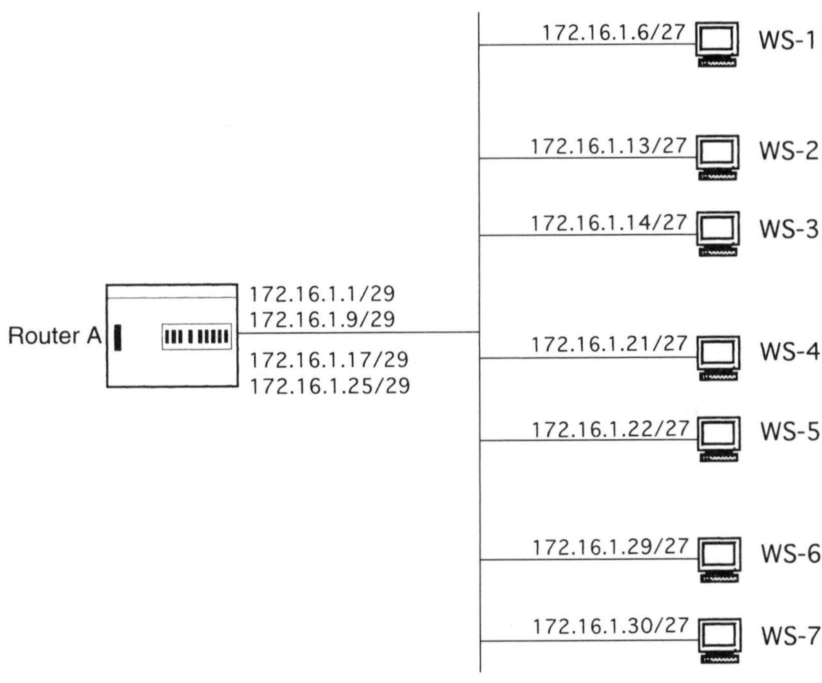

Illustration 8-7 IP Network Mask Deception

.0/24	.128/25	.192/26	.224/27	.240/28	**.248/29**	.252/30
0	0	0	**0**	0	**0**	0
1	1	1	**1**	1	**RTR-A 1**	1
2	2	2	**2**	2	**2**	2
3	3	3	**3**	3	**3**	3
4	4	4	**4**	4	**4**	4
5	5	5	**5**	5	**5**	5
6	6	6	**WS-1 6**	6	**6**	6
7	7	7	**7**	7	**7**	7
8	8	8	**8**	8	**8**	8
9	9	9	**9**	9	**RTR-A 9**	9
10	10	10	**10**	10	**10**	10
11	11	11	**11**	11	**11**	11
12	12	12	**12**	12	**12**	12
13	13	13	**WS-2 13**	13	**13**	13
14	14	14	**WS-3 14**	14	**14**	14
15	15	15	**15**	15	**15**	15
16	16	16	**16**	16	**16**	16
17	17	17	**17**	17	**RTR-A 17**	17
18	18	18	**18**	18	**18**	18
19	19	19	**19**	19	**19**	19
20	20	20	**20**	20	**20**	20
21	21	21	**WS-4 21**	21	**21**	21
22	22	22	**WS-5 22**	22	**22**	22
23	23	23	**23**	23	**23**	23
24	24	24	**24**	24	**24**	24
25	25	25	**25**	25	**RTR-A 25**	25
26	26	26	**26**	26	**26**	26
27	27	27	**27**	27	**27**	27
28	28	28	**28**	28	**28**	28
29	29	29	**WS-6 29**	29	**29**	29
30	30	30	**WS-7 30**	30	**30**	30
31	31	31	**31**	31	**31**	31

Illustration 8-8 IP Address Worksheet Showing IP Network Mask Deception

The router believes that there are four networks with hosts on each network and advertises these networks to its "rest of the world." The workstations, however, believe that there is only one network, 172.16.1.0/27, that has all the workstations and four routers on it. Each workstation has a default gateway assigned to it that is actually the router interface that would have been in its network had the more restrictive mask been used. The workstations see one another as local to their networks, due to ARP, and are able to communicate freely with one another. Any nonlocal routing would use the default gateway and would be handled by the router. The only case that I can think of that might cause problems is a BOOTP environment (see Chapter 9) or one in which the workstation does not know its network mask for its IP interface and must learn it through ICMP, Get Mask. Let me say again: *Use caution* if you try this trick!

Network Address Translation

One of the best ways to make efficient use of assigned globally unique address space is to employ network address translation (NAT). NAT was discussed in Chapter 6, so I will not go into the mechanics again. A NAT device can do two things to improve utilization of address space. First, the network administrator can set up a one-to-one mapping of globally unique addresses to private addresses. The worst case is that each host that requires Internet access has a mapped globally unique address. Since the addresses are mapped and translated at the boundary between the autonomous system and the Internet, the globally unique addresses may be assigned consecutively without addressing holes. It is possible to achieve a utilization of 1.0 using this mechanism.

The second point of efficiency improvement that NAT can offer is the use of an address pool. Typically, a one-to-one mapping, as just discussed, is configured for workstations offering services to the Internet, such as WWW and FTP servers. Those workstations in an organization that wish to access services on the Internet may be allocated a globally unique address that will endure only for the duration of the Internet access session. In this context, these addresses may be referred to as *ephemeral addresses* since they, like their TCP and UDP port namesakes, are short-lived. Pooling globally unique addresses allows for efficiencies of scale. It is possible to furnish many more workstations with access to the Internet than there are globally unique addresses, under the premise that not all workstations that can access the Internet will require simultaneous access. This is the same premise on which tenant services and PBXs are based. To get the greatest efficiency, traffic and queueing theory could be applied, complete with call arrival rates, call duration, and blocking factors. It is possible to achieve efficiencies in excess of 1.0 through the use of a dynamically allocated globally unique address pool.

Short-term IP Address Allocation (DHCP and IPCP)

Another way to efficiently utilize address space is to take advantage of the fact that devices only need IP addresses when they are turned on and connected. The *Dynamic Host Configuration Protocol* (DHCP) allocates IP addresses to hosts from a pool of addresses that it maintains. The idea is that if a host is turned off or disconnected from a local area network, it does not require an IP address. Depending on the nomadic nature of the workforce, this could render a substantial savings in address space.

The *IP Control Protocol* (IPCP) is used to negotiate IP addresses in the Point to Point Protocol (PPP). Since hosts only connect to the Internet using PPP for short durations at a time, it is unnecessary to allocate an IP address to a host full-time. It is better to maintain a pool of addresses on the remote access server or on the RADIUS server and allocate addresses to hosts for their use until they disconnect. It is possible to service as many as 2500 dial-in Internet subscribers with a single /24 network.

Summary

It is important to be efficient when assigning IP addresses, especially when the network allocation is made from globally unique address space. OSPF lends itself to addressing efficiency by virtue of being able to convey subnet mask information in its updates. RIP, which does not pass subnet mask information in its routing updates, relies on fixed-length masks. This will traditionally cause inefficiencies in networks that are irregular in size since the largest number of hosts on a single network is often used to dictate the networkwide mask. Some tricks to get greater efficiencies in a RIP environment are the use of fixed-length subnet masks and network mask deception.

Network address translation (NAT) can also be used to achieve extremely high utilization of the globally unique addresses. It is possible to exceed a utilization of 1.0 through the use of NAT, due to efficiencies of scale. DHCP and IPCP are two more ways in which efficient address space utilization can be achieved. By not giving an IP address to a computer that is powered off or is disconnected from the network, we can save IP addresses.

Practice Questions

1. What is the utilization of a /23 network that has 320 IP hosts?

2. What is the utilization of a /26 network that has 48 IP hosts?
3. What is the utilization of a /30 network that has two IP hosts?
4. What is the utilization of a /24 network that has 190 IP hosts?
5. What is the total utilization of four /30 networks with 2 hosts, two /29 networks with 5 hosts, one /28 network with 22 hosts, and one /28 network with no hosts?

chapter 9

Managing IP Addresses

One of the objectives of any IP addressing scheme should be to optimize the manageability of the addresses that are used within the TCP/IP networks. Possibly more important constraints, such as efficiency or route aggregation, are being considered that will limit the management aspects in the addressing scheme. However, it is likely that some degree of management is obtainable. Further, the assignment of addresses to TCP/IP hosts can be made significantly easier through the use of some management-enhancing mechanisms, such as BOOTP and the Dynamic Host Configuration Protocol (DHCP). In addition, it is likely that if you are designing a TCP/IP addressing architecture that deliberately accomplishes a goal such as the efficient use of globally unique networks or routing efficiency, you will want to maintain its effectiveness over time, regardless of change and growth. This chapter discusses these points.

Addressing for Management

Several methods for assigning addresses can contribute to overall management of TCP/IP addressing. The key to assigning addresses for effective management is to make the location or the utility of the address easy to remember without the need to refer to any documents. The ability to devise an optimal addressing scheme for management is often degraded by the need to devise a scheme that optimizes network address utilization. It is simply a matter of which aspect is more important. For instance, if you have a Class C address, several point-to-point networks, and a few Ethernets of various sizes, you may have to squeeze the individual subnet allocations into areas of the overall network that might not be conducive to remembering the use of the address.

In this discussion I will assume that a private network allocation is being used and that there is no concern for efficiency with regard to usage of the address space. In such a scenario I would typically choose to use the Class A network 10.0.0.0 since there is plenty of address space available for any scheme.

In a hierarchical address scheme such as a postal address, there are elements that define an area such as a country or a state, elements that define specific townships or sites within the area, and very specific addresses of people, buildings, or elements within the sites. Further, these elements are arranged in such a way that anybody, not just the postmaster or address administrator, can locate the element being addressed. In most postal addressing schemes, the odd-numbered street addresses are always on one side of the street and the even-numbered addresses on the other. Further, the addresses generally increase or decrease as you travel up or down a street. These are examples of mnemonic devices (memory aids) that assist with the management of postal addresses.

The same concepts can be applied to TCP/IP addresses. Take the following example:

10.*x*.*y*.*z*

The *x* component could be used as the network identifier or area identifier. Networks can often be divided up into buildings, townships, countries, contiguous WAN infrastructure such as X.25, or Frame Relay networks. The *x* component would be used to identify that subset of the entire network. Be cautious to ensure that the granularity of the *x* component will not cause the available identifiers to be exhausted by growth and change. For instance, it might be better to choose to reflect countries rather than municipalities with the *x* component if the network is international.

The *y* component could be used as the site identifier. Depending on how the network was subdivided using the *x* component, the *y* component would reflect a further division. For instance, if the *x* component reflected a division by state, the *y* component could reflect a specific city or group of cities within the state denoted by the value of *x*.

The last component, *z*, could be used for the host addresses required to support the site defined by the *y* component. Not all addresses must fall within the same network. There might be several IP subnets per site, divided using fixed- or variable-length masks as necessary for the situation.

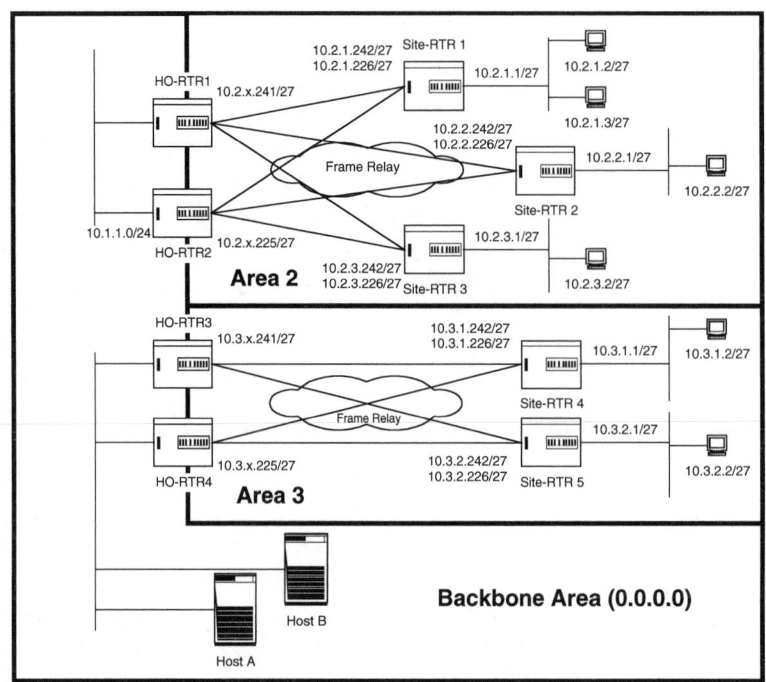

Illustration 9-1 Example of a Network Addressed for Ease of Management

Illustration 9-1 is an example of a network that is addressed using a management-oriented addressing scheme. The network uses 10.*x*.*y*.*z*, where

- *x* = *network identifier:* Initially there will be four defined and two reserved network identifiers:

0	Reserved
1	Home Office Ethernet (OSPF Backbone)
2	Frame Relay 1 (OSPF Area 2)
3	Frame Relay 2 (OSPF Area 3)

4–254	Unused
255	Reserved

- *y = site identifier:* Within each network (identified by the second octet), there can be a maximum of 256 sites (0 to 255). These are typically allocated sequentially, starting at 1 and working upward; however, the 0 value is legitimate and may be used.
- *z = site network/host:* With a 255.255.255.240 mask, the last octet of address space is split in half, with each half getting four bits. That is, the number of hosts is restricted to 14 per network. Taking into account the uses for each octet in the address, the last octet has room for 16 networks per site. Although this may be overkill, the use of the Class A address allows for a certain amount of waste. With the ability to be wasteful and inefficient, it is possible to be administratively elegant. This addressing scheme opts for administration over frugality. If each site should require another network somewhere down the road, plenty are available without sacrificing the IP address structure defined now. In the home office networks that have a mask of 255.255.255.0, there is a maximum of 254 hosts per site ID instead of the 14-host limit used in the WAN networks.

As is evident from this example, the routes will collapse into a summary at each of the OSPF border routers. The routes in area 2 will all summarize to be 10.2.0.0/16. Route table efficiency can often be a side effect of management-oriented addressing.

Another aspect of addressing for manageability is the development of a mnemonic system within each of the components of the address. This is best illustrated. In our example, the *x* component was used to define a network identifier. The home office network uses 10.1.*y*.*z*, and the Frame Relay networks use 10.2.*y*.*z* and 10.3.*y*.*z*. It is easy to see from such a scheme that 10.3.1.1 would be a host that would be found in the second Frame Relay network (OSPF area 3). Note that the second octet of the IP address also indicates the OSPF area in which the interface belongs.

Another example is where the *x* components represent states within the United States. The *x* component could be numbered consecutively from 1 to 50. The state that is first alphabetically in the list could be 10.1.0.0. Or, the state that is the furthest west could be 10.1.0.0. Or, the 13 original states of the union could be 10.1.0.0 through 10.13.0.0, and all the subsequent states would be numbered according to their admittance into the union. The point is, it does not matter what system you use, so long as you use a system and you work the system.

Develop and use a system when you are assigning host addresses, as well. The most important point is to be consistent. If possible, use the same addresses in each subnet for the router or for special workstations or hosts. Use the same range of addresses for all the user workstations. For instance, site 1 (10.2.1.*z*) in the example has five addresses defined as follows:

10.2.1.1	Router's Ethernet interface
10.2.1.13	Mary's PC
10.2.1.14	Joe's PC
10.2.1.241	Home office router Frame Relay interface
10.2.1.242	Site-RTR1 router Frame Relay interface

The first address in each of the networks is a router. The first network of the 16 networks allocated to that site is always the local Ethernet. The last addresses in the first network are always the user hosts. The last network of the 16 formed from the last octet is always the network used on the Frame Relay network. The first address in the last network is always a router. In fact, the first address is always the router IP address that is closest to the home office Ethernet in area 0.0.0.0; other routers in the same IP network would be assigned subsequent addresses, again by proximity to the home office Ethernet. Get a plan. Work the plan. Be consistent. The more address space that is available to you and the more that you can be wasteful, the more you will be able to develop an addressing scheme that is administratively easy to use.

The IntraNIC

Whenever an IP addressing scheme is developed, the objectives and the addressing rules like those detailed previously should be documented so that you and other folks will be able to understand the methodology at a later date. A lot of work and thought go into the addressing scheme; make sure that you can maintain it into the future. For instance, if a site is added while you are on vacation, somebody should have a reference that can be used to do the addressing right, so you don't have to redo it at a later time.

Along with that, there should be a log of all assigned and available addresses. This could be a database, a spreadsheet, a word processing document, or even a handwritten notebook. Make sure that it is easy to use and keep current. I call this system the *IntraNIC* after its grown-up counterpart, the InterNIC, which tracks and manages the usage of globally unique Internet addresses in the United States.

Table 9-1 shows an example of a spreadsheet implementation of an IntraNIC. The information elements defined for each row are useful data for identifying points of contact and responsible parties. Even the IP addressing worksheet is a good start for an IntraNIC. Add more columns for additional data that you want to keep on each address assigned, like what is found in Table 9-1.

IP-1	IP-2	IP-3	IP-4	Location	Owner	Equip.	Mfgr.	Host Name
10	(Net)	(Site)	(Host)					
10	1	1	1	HO	Charles	PC	Compaq	CharlesPC
10	1	1	6	HO	Charles	Host	HP	Host-A
10	1	1	7	HO	Charles	Host	HP	Host-B
10	1	1	15	HO	HO-RTR1	Amazon	ACC	HO-RTR1
10	1	1	16	HO	HO-RTR2	Amazon	ACC	HO-RTR2
10	1	1	17	HO	HO-RTR3	Amazon	ACC	HO-RTR3
10	1	1	18	HO	HO-RTR4	Amazon	ACC	HO-RTR4
10	2	1	1	Site1	Site-RTR1	Danube	ACC	Site-RTR1
10	2	1	2	Site1	Mary	PC	Compaq	MaryPC
10	2	1	3	Site1	Joe	PC	Compaq	JoePC
10	2	1	225	HO	HO-RTR2	Amazon	ACC	HO-RTR2
10	2	1	226	Site1	Site-RTR1	Danube	ACC	Site-RTR1
10	2	1	241	HO	HO-RTR1	Amazon	ACC	HO-RTR1
10	2	1	242	Site1	Site-RTR1	Danube	ACC	Site-RTR1
10	2	2	1	Site2	Site-RTR2	Danube	ACC	Site-RTR2
10	2	2	2	Site2	Don	PC	Compaq	DonPC
10	2	2	225	HO	HO-RTR2	Amazon	ACC	HO-RTR2
10	2	2	226	Site2	Site-RTR2	Danube	ACC	Site-RTR2
10	2	2	241	HO	HO-RTR1	Amazon	ACC	HO-RTR1
10	2	2	242	Site2	Site-RTR2	Danube	ACC	Site-RTR2
10	2	3	1	Site3	Site-RTR3	Danube	ACC	Site-RTR3
10	2	3	2	Site3	Sue	PC	Compaq	SuePC

Table 9-1 Example of an IntraNIC Spreadsheet

IP Management Tools and Calculators

A few companies make software for assisting in the management of an IP address and routing plan. One of these companies is Quadritek (now Lucent), who makes a piece of software called QIP that ties into large database packages such as Sybase and Oracle. This makes it possible to manage a very large organization quite easily. Just for your information, a screen shot from their software is included as Illustration 9-2.

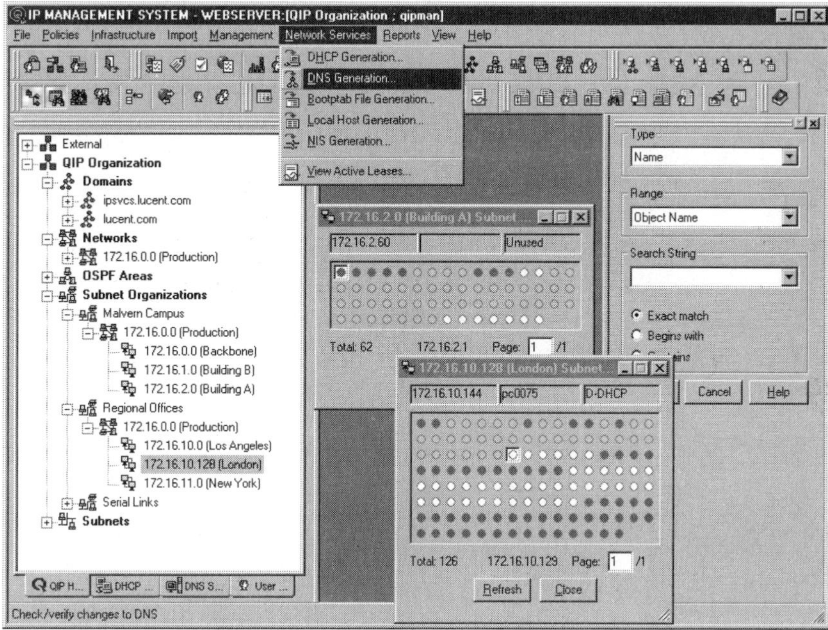

Illustration 9-2 Quadritek QIP Screen Shot

There are also several utilities that assist with the calculation of subnet masks. I had one that I included with the first edition of this book but have since discontinued. I have seen and used subnet calculators for both the PC and for the Palm PDA. You can usually find a subnet calculator by searching on the *www.tucows.com* sites.

Translation of IP Number to Name

It is possible that even if you develop an IP addressing scheme that is easy to administer, you would still choose to refer to a device with a name. There are two ways that you can configure a network so that you will not have to refer to devices solely by their IP addresses. Although this is valuable as a mnemonic device, it is also valuable for establishing independence from positional reference. That is, a device can always have a host-name of "Buck," no matter what IP network it is homed to or its geographic location.

The first mechanism is the use of the /etc/hosts file found on all UNIX hosts and many other TCP/IP hosts. The file provides a simple mapping of IP addresses to host names, such as the following:

```
10.1.1.1     CharlesPC
10.1.1.6     Host-A
10.1.1.7     Host-B
10.1.1.15    HO-RTR1
10.2.1.1     Site-RTR1
10.2.2.2     DonPC
```

A user on the workstation where the /etc/hosts file is configured can, if desired, refer to a device by its IP address. Or the user can refer to it by the name that is defined as an alias for the IP address. Instead of "Telnet 10.1.1.6" for example, it would be possible to use "Telnet Host-A."

Another means by which an IP address can be translated to a name is through the use of the domain name system (DNS). The effect is similar to the use of the /etc/hosts file; however, it is a distributed, hierarchical system that does not require each workstation's /etc/hosts file to be kept synchronized for consistency. DNS operates in a client-server model. One or more DNS servers should be run in or provide services to an autonomous system. Each workstation or device that wishes to use DNS for its translation from host name to IP address should run the DNS client.

Administration Tools

Two mechanisms in wide use today—BOOTP and DHCP—allow a network administrator to easily assign IP addresses to workstations or other network devices. These mechanisms are protocols that allow, among other things, a device to be automatically assigned an IP address for long- or short-term use. There is a very real possibility in many organizations that growth or change will render an IP addressing scheme inadequate, no matter how well it is planned. Using one of these mechanisms will make the job of readdressing the affected portion of the network much easier.

Bootstrap Protocol (BOOTP)

The *Bootstrap Protocol* (BOOTP) defines a mechanism that allows a diskless workstation to be placed on a network without any prior configuration and, through the use of a BOOTP server, acquire all IP addressing parameters and boot file parameters for it to boot up and participate on an IP network. RFC 951, "Bootstrap Protocol," is the initial RFC that defines the operation of BOOTP. Although RFC 951 defines the purpose of BOOTP as a service to diskless workstations, BOOTP has been used in many network devices, such as routers, for updating configuration files or application code. BOOTP can also provide an IP address to any workstation, not just the diskless variety.

The BOOTP server is typically run on a UNIX host. The BOOTP server process uses UDP port 67, and the BOOTP client process uses UDP port 68. The BOOTP server uses a configuration file, *bootptab,* which will instruct the service in how to service a BOOTP request from a client. The following is an example of a bootptab file:

```
global.defaults:\
      :sm=255.255.255.192:\
      :hd=/tftpboot:\
      :gw=10.1.1.15:\
      :ht=ether
CharlesPC:tc=global.defaults:ha=08000323121E:
  ip=10.1.1.1
Site-RTR1:tc=global.defaults:ha=08000325686A:
  ip=10.2.1.1:bf=sr1.scr
Site-RTR2:tc=global.defaults:ha=08000325686B:
  ip=10.2.2.1:bf=sr2.scr
```

0 1 2 3 4 5 6 7	8 9 0 1 2 3 4 5	6 7 8 9 0 1 2 3	4 5 6 7 8 9 0 1
op (1)	htype (1)	hlen (1)	hops (1)
xid (4)			
secs (2)		flags (2)	
ciaddr (4)			
yiaddr (4)			
siaddr (4)			
giaddr (4)			
chaddr (16)			
sname (64)			
file (128)			
options (312)			

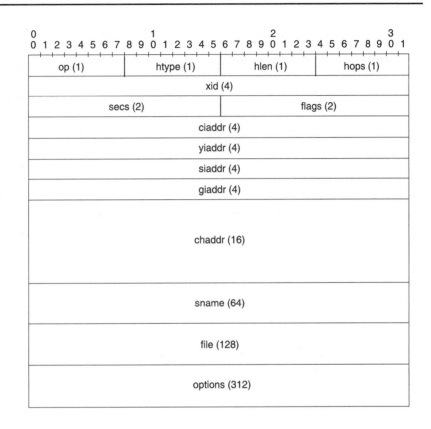

Illustration 9-3 BOOTP Packet Structure

Although the details of BOOTP are not relevant to this book, I will present a brief overview of the operation of the Bootstrap Protocol. Illustration 9-3 depicts the standard BOOTP packet. The fields are identified as follows:

- *op:* Packet op code/message type: 1 = BOOTREQUEST, 2 = BOOTREPLY
- *htype:* Hardware address type
- *hlen:* Hardware address length
- *hops:* Client sets to 0

- *xid:* Transaction ID
- *secs:* Seconds elapsed since started boot process
- *flags:* Option flags
- *ciaddr:* Client IP address
- *yiaddr:* "Your" (client) IP address
- *siaddr:* Server IP address
- giaddr: Gateway IP address
- *chaddr:* Client hardware address
- *sname:* Server host name
- *file:* Boot file name
- *vend:* Optional vendor-specific use

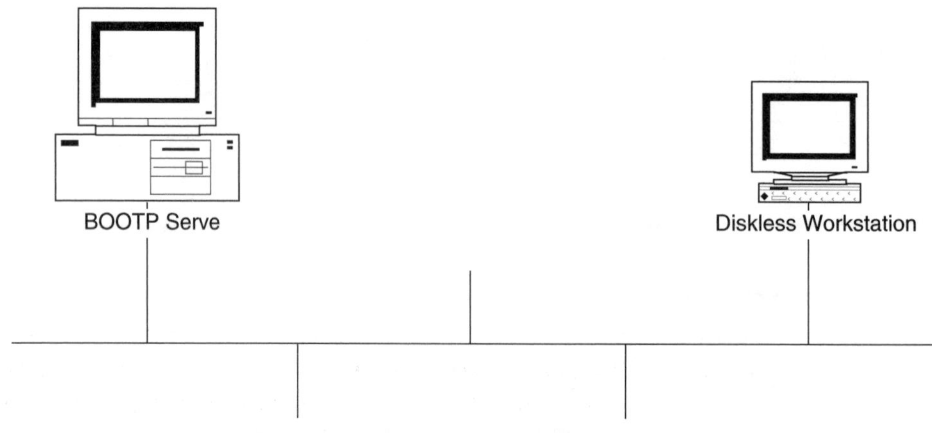

Illustration 9-4 Example BOOTP Network

Illustration 9-4 is an example of the mechanics of BOOTP. When the diskless workstation is powered on, the workstation will send out a BOOTP request packet like the following.

destip:	255.255.255.255 (limited broadcast)
srcip:	0.0.0.0 (this host, this network)
op:	1 (BOOTREQUEST)
htype:	1 (Ethernet)
hlen:	6 (Ethernet)
hops:	0
xid:	23013 (randomly set by client)
secs:	0
flags:	null
ciaddr:	0.0.0.0 (this host, this network)
yiaddr:	
siaddr:	
giaddr:	
chaddr:	08000325686B
sname:	
file:	
vend:	

Since the diskless workstation does not know the IP address of the BOOTP server, it sends the BOOTP request out as a limited broadcast, constrained to the network on which it is sent. The diskless workstation also uses the all-0s IP address as the source address in the IP datagram header.

destip:	255.255.255.255 (limited broadcast)
srcip:	172.16.1.1 (BOOTP server)
op:	2 (BOOTREPLY)

htype:	1 (Ethernet)
hlen:	6 (Ethernet)
hops:	0
xid:	23013
secs:	0
flags:	null
ciaddr:	
yiaddr:	172.16.1.21
siaddr:	172.16.1.1
giaddr:	172.16.1.1
chaddr:	08000325686B
sname:	
file:	/tftpboot/dws021
vend:	1,4,255.255.255.192

You probably noticed that the original BOOTP structure did not specify a field for subnet mask information. The use of the Vend field for this, and other purposes, is documented in RFC 1533, "DHCP Options and BOOTP Vendor Extensions."

When the diskless workstation receives this BOOTP reply from the server, it knows its IP address; however, it cannot be guaranteed that it is unique on the network. For this reason the workstation will send out three ARP requests to see whether any other device will answer up that it is the owner of the IP address 172.16.1.21. If no reply is received, in the third ARP request the diskless workstation will use a source IP address of 172.16.1.21 instead of 0.0.0.0 and announce ownership of the IP address. Then the diskless workstation sends more BOOTP requests to validate the initial response. Once satisfied that the information in the BOOTP reply is consistent, the diskless workstation initiates a TFTP file transfer of the boot file. The diskless workstation can then run the boot file and become operational.

Dynamic Host Configuration Protocol (DHCP)

The *Dynamic Host Configuration Protocol* (DHCP), can be used to provide all the parameters that a host on an IP network requires to operate and exchange information on the Internet to which it is attached. DHCP can also be used to manage the distribution of IP addresses within an autonomous system.

It should be possible to configure a DHCP server to provide all the parameters specified in RFC 1122, "Requirements for Internet Hosts—Communication Layers," and RFC 1123, "Requirements for Internet Hosts—Application and Support."

Let's take a look at the DHCP packet structure (Illustration 9-5). Comparing this structure to the BOOTP packet structure of Illustration 9-3, we see that it is identical except for the last field. The Vend field in BOOTP has come to be known as the Options field in DHCP, and more bytes are allocated to the field. DHCP allows for 312 bytes in the Option field, whereas BOOTP allowed only 64 bytes in the Vend field. In fact, you will be interested to know that UDP port 67 is used for the DHCP server and UDP port 68 for the DHCP client; these are the same numbers that BOOTP uses. The reality of the situation is that BOOTP functionality is inherent in the DHCP service. Thus it is not possible to have two different TCP/IP applications, BOOTP and DHCP, share a UDP port.

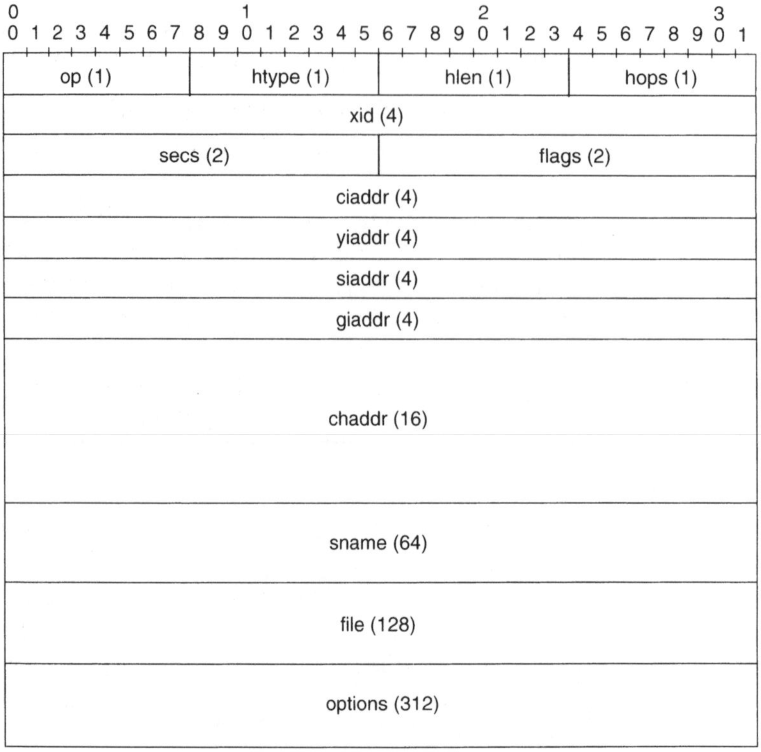

0 1 2 3
0 1 2 3 4 5 6 7 8 9 0 1 2 3 4 5 6 7 8 9 0 1 2 3 4 5 6 7 8 9 0 1

op (1) | htype (1) | hlen (1) | hops (1)
xid (4)
secs (2) | flags (2)
ciaddr (4)
yiaddr (4)
siaddr (4)
giaddr (4)
chaddr (16)
sname (64)
file (128)
options (312)

Illustration 9-5 DHCP Frame Structure

Essentially, BOOTP is a subset of the DHCP implementation. It is possible for a BOOTP client to get BOOTP services from a DHCP server. The Options field is an extension of the Vend field of the original BOOTP protocol. All extended functionality of the DHCP service is provided through essentially the same packet structure as was originally used in BOOTP.

DHCP can be used to allocate IP addresses to hosts. When a host using DHCP is powered up on a network for the first time, it negotiates with the DHCP server for an IP address. The server may provide an IP address to the requesting host under one of two premises:

- *Permanent allocation:* The DHCP server assigns an IP address to a host for its exclusive use.
- *Dynamic allocation:* The DHCP server assigns an IP address to a host for a limited time.

DHCP makes use of the term *lease,* which has a value equal to the amount of time that an IP address is assigned to a given host. In general, whenever a host first comes up, it requests an IP address good for the requested lease duration. The DHCP client and server negotiate a lease duration, and the client is assigned an IP address. It is also possible to assign a lease of 0xffffffff, which would allocate the IP address permanently to a client.

DHCP also has the ability to allocate a pool of addresses that are available for allocation within a given subnet. Address utilization can be improved by making the pool of addresses smaller than the number of potential clients. However, care should be taken to make sure that a host is not blocked from access to network resources by virtue of the address pool being depleted.

The bottom line is that if your hosts obtain their IP addresses through DHCP or BOOTP, it will be significantly easier to readdress the hosts, if necessary. Simply do a "find and replace" in the DHCP configuration file, and the hosts will come up on a different network the next time they are booted.

Summary

This chapter was concerned with the management of the allocation of IP addresses, as well as with the design of an addressing scheme to enhance management of the network devices. The keys to creating a network addressing scheme that enhances management are hierarchy and consistency. If a network is numbered such that there is a hierarchy to the IP address. such as 10.*net.site.host,* the result is not only the benefit of manageability but possibly also route aggregation. It is equally important that the host numbering scheme be consistent across similar subnets. This is exemplified by an intranet that has many point-to-point IP networks and in which the nearside router on the link always uses the odd-numbered address of the router pairings.

One efficient method for documenting the details of an IP addressing scheme is the use of an IntraNIC. An IntraNIC is a system whereby the allocation of IP addresses is managed. The IntraNIC system relies on a database (or spreadsheet) that allows an administrator to assign "ownership" of IP addresses and subnets. There are commercially available software packages to assist in the management of IP addresses.

Hosts and many network devices can be assigned IP addresses dynamically through the use of BOOTP or DHCP. BOOTP, the Bootstrap Protocol, is an older protocol that was intended to provide boot services through a network connection. DHCP, the Dynamic Host Configuration Protocol, is a superset of BOOTP. Network devices can get configuration parameters automatically on boot-up, which will permit them to communicate over their Internet. DHCP can also assign IP addresses, based on a lease request from a workstation.

Both BOOTP and DHCP allow an administrator to automatically assign IP addresses from a central server. This makes the management of IP address allocation a much simpler process. The two protocols also simplify the process of renumbering an addressing scheme.

Practice Questions

1. What UDP port does a DHCP client use?
2. What value is used in the DHCP lease field to request a permanent IP address assignment?
3. What is the name of the Unix file that provides a local mapping of name to IP address?
4. In Table 9-1, who is the owner of 10.2.1.2?

chapter 10

Addressing for Growth and Change

This chapter introduces you to a couple of small but important topics within IP addressing architecture: anticipated growth and unanticipated change. The difference between them might seem insignificant at first; however, the key to the difference lies in the terms *anticipated* and *unanticipated.*

Anticipated Growth

An addressing scheme should permit growth within the constraints of desired address efficiency. Growth that is anticipated should always be a major consideration of an address scheme design.

It almost goes without saying that if you anticipate patterns of growth within your organization, the network address scheme should allow for that growth. Excess address space should be strategically placed within the IP address plan. If I had a small branch office network (Site B) with only four IP hosts allocated, I would need an IP network with 29 bits of network mask to accommodate it (up to six hosts). If I thought that that particular branch office was likely to grow as much as 400 percent over the next few years, I doubt that it would be prudent for me to use the IP network allocation scheme shown in Illustration 10-1. The problem with such an address allocation is that when the Site B branch office begins to grow as expected, there is no overflow.

Anticipating that the Site B branch office will experience a population boom, I might opt for a scenario such as shown in Illustration 10-2. In this illustration, an entire block of 30 host addresses has been reserved for the Site B branch office. It has been blocked out so that no other allocations can be made from that group of addresses. At least it is for now. When the branch office reaches the point at which six hosts are on the network, the address space in network 172.16.1.0/29 is exhausted. Another eight hosts can be added to the network if the subnet mask of all the hosts is changed form 172.16.1.0/29 to 172.16.1.0/28. The process of moving to a mask that permits more hosts per network is known as an *address upgrade.* The host IP addresses of the workstation need not change. This mask gives the branch office room for 14 hosts before the address space is exhausted and the network mask has to be changed once more, to 172.16.1.0/27 (which supports 30 hosts). If, sometime in the future, it is determined that the amount of growth was overestimated, the space that was set aside for the growth of that one branch office can be freed up for other allocations.

.0/24	.128/25	.192/26	.224/27	.240/28	.248/29	.252/30
0	0	0	0	0	Site A 0	0
1	1	1	1	1	A-1 1	1
2	2	2	2	2	A-2 2	2
3	3	3	3	3	3	3
4	4	4	4	4	4	4
5	5	5	5	5	A-3 5	5
6	6	6	6	6	A-4 6	6
7	7	7	7	7	7	7
8	8	8	8	8	Site B 8	8
9	9	9	9	9	B-1 9	9
10	10	10	10	10	B-2 10	10
11	11	11	11	11	11	11
12	12	12	12	12	B-3 12	12
13	13	13	13	13	B-4 13	13
14	14	14	14	14	14	14
15	15	15	15	15	15	15
16	16	16	16	16	Site C 16	16
17	17	17	17	17	17	17
18	18	18	18	18	C-1 18	18
19	19	19	19	19	C-2 19	19
20	20	20	20	20	C-3 20	20
21	21	21	21	21	C-4 21	21
22	22	22	22	22	22	22
23	23	23	23	23	23	23
24	24	24	24	24	24	24
25	25	25	25	25	25	25
26	26	26	26	26	26	26
27	27	27	27	27	27	27
28	28	28	28	28	28	28
29	29	29	29	29	29	29
30	30	30	30	30	30	30
31	31	31	31	31	31	31

Illustration 10-1 Portion of IP Address Worksheet

.0/24	.128/25	.192/26	.224/27	.240/28	.248/29	.252/30
0	0	0	0	0	Site B 0	0
1	1	1	1	1	B-1 1	1
2	2	2	2	2	B-2 2	2
3	3	3	3	3	3	3
4	4	4	4	4	B-3 4	4
5	5	5	5	5	B-4 5	5
6	6	6	6	6	6	6
7	7	7	7	7	7	7
8	8	8	8	8	8	8
9	9	9	9	9	9	9
10	10	10	10	10	10	10
11	11	11	11	11	11	11
12	12	12	12	12	12	12
13	13	13	13	13	13	13
14	14	14	14	14	14	14
15	15	15	15	15	15	15
16	16	16	16	16	16	16
17	17	17	17	17	17	17
18	18	18	18	18	18	18
19	19	19	19	19	19	19
20	20	20	20	20	20	20
21	21	21	21	21	21	21
22	22	22	22	22	22	22
23	23	23	23	23	23	23
24	24	24	24	24	24	24
25	25	25	25	25	25	25
26	26	26	26	26	26	26
27	27	27	27	27	27	27
28	28	28	28	28	28	28
29	29	29	29	29	29	29
30	30	30	30	30	30	30
31	31	31	31	31	31	31

Illustration 10-2 Address Upgrade

You may be wondering why, if growth was anticipated, I did not start off by allocating the larger of the three networks. In some regards it is a matter of choice and circumstance. If address space is at a premium, perhaps because of the use of globally unique addresses, it is easier to think of entire unused networks as available room for the entire intranet. Unused address space within a network is thought of primarily as room to grow within that single IP network. If address space were plentiful, I might preallocate all address space according to my corporation's five-year growth plan.

Attrition is the opposite of growth. When a site is shrinking, the IP addresses should be kept to the top or the bottom of the address space. See Illustration 10-3. At this moment the site requires address space from 172.16.1.0/28, which allows for up to 14 hosts. When one more workstation is "turned off," the network 172.16.1.0/29 will suffice for all six hosts on the network. This process is known as an *address downgrade.* This occurs whenever the network mask is changed to permit fewer hosts per network. The benefit of an address downgrade is that an IP network is freed up for use elsewhere. In Illustration 10-3, network 172.16.1.8/29 has been made available.

.0/24	.128/25	.192/26	.224/27	.240/28	.248/29	.252/30
0	0	0	0	0	0	0
1	1	1	1	RTR 1 1	1	1
2	2	2	2	WS 1 2	2	2
3	3	3	3	WS 2 3	3	3
4	4	4	4	WS 3 4	4	4
5	5	5	5	WS 4 5	5	5
6	6	6	6	WS 5 6	6	6
7	7	7	7	WS 6 7	7	7
8	8	8	8	8	8	8
9	9	9	9	9	9	9
10	10	10	10	10	10	10
11	11	11	11	11	11	11
12	12	12	12	12	12	12
13	13	13	13	13	13	13
14	14	14	14	14	14	14
15	15	15	15	15	15	15
16	16	16	16	16	16	16
17	17	17	17	17	17	17
18	18	18	18	18	18	18
19	19	19	19	19	19	19
20	20	20	20	20	20	20
21	21	21	21	21	21	21
22	22	22	22	22	22	22
23	23	23	23	23	23	23
24	24	24	24	24	24	24
25	25	25	25	25	25	25
26	26	26	26	26	26	26
27	27	27	27	27	27	27
28	28	28	28	28	28	28
29	29	29	29	29	29	29
30	30	30	30	30	30	30
31	31	31	31	31	31	31

Illustration 10-3 Address Downgrade

Unanticipated Change

There are always changes after an addressing scheme is implemented. An addressing plan should have *flex points* to permit changes without having to redesign completely. Flex points are essentially reservations of address space that might be used for specific purposes at some future date. In Illustration 10-2, space was reserved in case the branch office grew as anticipated. If at some point the corporate management decided that another Ethernet was justified to support a new application, the network 172.16.1.16/28 could be used. In other words, the space originally intended to permit growth can ultimately be used to accommodate unplanned change.

Small changes such as this one can often be absorbed into an addressing plan without too much difficulty. Large changes can be a different story. Companies are bought and subsidiaries sold. These are classic examples of large-scale unanticipated changes.

If the change is significant within the Internet, it is likely that the best approach to handling unanticipated change is to reevaluate the effectiveness of the addressing plan to achieve a desired criterion. As mentioned once before, renumbering is sometimes the only choice. Of course, this job is much easier if its possibility was planned for. BOOTP and, even more so, DHCP are capable of reducing the amount of effort required to execute the renumbering of a network. These protocols were discussed in Chapter 9.

Summary

Growth and change can be accommodated to some degree by leaving "holes" in the network addressing plan. These holes represent the reservation of space for some future need, anticipated or otherwise. Naturally, the more holes that are left in the address plan, the more inefficient the plan becomes.

When addressing with the private network allocation, such as the Class A network 10.0.0.0/8, it is possible to have much more address space than ever could be conceived as possible to exhaust. Even with this overabundance of address resources, it is possible to leave flex points that are ineffective and thus completely wasteful. The flex points that are placed in an address plan should be considered carefully to maximize their benefits.

There comes a time when a network addressing plan falls apart and no longer produces the benefit it was once designed to provide. For instance, the introduction of a new wide area network mechanism leaves the old wide area network that you have designed your IP network around obsolete. In some cases, it might be better to adapt the addressing scheme of the old WAN to that of the new WAN. In other cases, the addressing scheme may not be so flexible. It could be "patched" with obscure IP network addressing and the once-coveted route aggregation might suffer, or the entire IP address scheme could be redesigned and rejuvenated. BOOTP and DHCP can make the job much easier—if not this time, perhaps the next.

Practice Question

1. You have a /27 allocation and need to be able to accommodate two branch offices' IP addressing. You are reasonably sure that one of the branch offices is going to grow but you don't know which one or by how much. Each branch office currently has six hosts. Use Illustration 10-4 to sketch out an addressing plan that accommodates these growth requirements.

.0/24	.128/25	.192/26	.224/27	.240/28	.248/29	.252/30
0	0	0	0	0	0	0
1	1	1	1	1	1	1
2	2	2	2	2	2	2
3	3	3	3	3	3	3
4	4	4	4	4	4	4
5	5	5	5	5	5	5
6	6	6	6	6	6	6
7	7	7	7	7	7	7
8	8	8	8	8	8	8
9	9	9	9	9	9	9
10	10	10	10	10	10	10
11	11	11	11	11	11	11
12	12	12	12	12	12	12
13	13	13	13	13	13	13
14	14	14	14	14	14	14
15	15	15	15	15	15	15
16	16	16	16	16	16	16
17	17	17	17	17	17	17
18	18	18	18	18	18	18
19	19	19	19	19	19	19
20	20	20	20	20	20	20
21	21	21	21	21	21	21
22	22	22	22	22	22	22
23	23	23	23	23	23	23
24	24	24	24	24	24	24
25	25	25	25	25	25	25
26	26	26	26	26	26	26
27	27	27	27	27	27	27
28	28	28	28	28	28	28
29	29	29	29	29	29	29
30	30	30	30	30	30	30
31	31	31	31	31	31	31

Illustration 10-4 Practice Worksheet

Advanced Addressing Issues

section

At this point in the book, the bulk of what I had to say about anything related to IP addressing has been said. What remains are three topics that will imminently impact IP addressing.

Chapter 11 discusses multicast addressing with some details of its operation, including forwarding algorithms and multicast routing protocols. The MBONE, the multicast backbone in use on the Internet, is also presented.

Chapter 12 discusses mobility and nomadicity. The discussion on mobility for IPv4 (Mobile IP) covers how it allows for hosts to retain an IP address without regard to where the host actually attaches to the IP network. This capability facilitates a mobile host offering services independent of location.

Chapter 13 introduces IP version 6, also known as IP next generation (IPng), the long-term solution to depletion of unique networks. In addition to general IPv6 header changes, including the increased addressing capacity, this chapter covers the header extensions, neighbor discovery, stateless address autoconfiguration, and Mobile IPv6.

IP Multicast

chapter 11

IP multicast communications continues to gain acceptance. A majority of the work on IP multicast began in the late 1980s and early 1990s, although it is still seemingly a long way from widespread implementation. Only a few of the largest ISPs offer IP multicast support as of this writing. IP multicast, referred to throughout this chapter as simply "multicast" unless otherwise specified, was first introduced in this text during the discussion of IP addresses. Any IP address that has the four high-order bits set to "1110" is reserved for multicast usage. This would indicate that multicast addresses fall in the range from 224.0.0.0 to 239.255.255.255, inclusive.

Simply put, multicast permits packets to be sent from one station — the multicast originator — to zero, one, or many stations — the multicast recipients. Although the main thrust of this book is to present IP addressing and ways to optimize it, IP multicast is an emerging technology that affects and is affected by addressing, specifically Class D addresses.

Multicast is a way to communicate with more than one host simultaneously, although there may be zero members or one member of the group of multicast recipients. If communications were needed to only one other host, I would likely be better served by using unicasts, which permit communications between exactly two hosts. If communications were needed to all hosts, albeit rarely, I might be better served by using the more common IP broadcast capability, provided it services the domain to which I wish to broadcast. Indeed, multicast is best used to permit communications among more than one host and fewer than all hosts. Multicast itself is best used for two purposes: resource discovery and conferencing.

Resource Discovery

Multicast allows a device with no knowledge of the IP addresses of other systems on the network to ferret out all devices that have some commonality. The devices that are being searched for must be configured to listen for multicast datagrams destined for a specific Class D address. As an example, some well-known multicast addresses can be found in the Assigned Numbers RFC (currently RFC 1700), an excerpt from which is shown in Table 11-1.

Assigned No.	Description
224.0.0.0	BaseAddress(Reserved)
224.0.0.1	AllSystemsonthisSubnet
224.0.0.2	AllRoutersonthisSubnet
224.0.0.3	Unassigned
224.0.0.4	DVMRP Routers
224.0.0.5	OSPFIGP OSPFIGPAllRouters
224.0.0.6	OSPFIGP OSPFIGPDesignatedRouters

Assigned No.	Description
224.0.0.7	STRouters
224.0.0.8	STHosts
224.0.0.9	RIP2Routers
224.0.0.10	IGRPRouters
224.0.0.11	Mobile-Agents
224.0.0.12–224.0.0.255	Unassigned

Table 11-1 Excerpt of Assigned Numbers RFC for Well-Known Multicast Addresses

Note that the address 224.0.0.1 is used for "all systems on this subnet." You should be aware that multicast capability is not widely implemented throughout the Internet or in commercial TCP/IP stacks, although there are a few. It would naturally follow, therefore, that it is better to consider the address of 224.0.0.1 to mean "all [multicast-capable] systems on this subnet." It would not be good to assume that if you were to send a packet to 224.0.0.1, all hosts on the subnet would receive it. Further, you should note that the use of a subnet in this case is not consistent with the previous discussions in this text. This usage is intended to mean the physical network that the interface transmitting the multicast is participating in. The same discussion and caveats apply to the address 224.0.0.2.

Also note the addresses 224.0.0.5 and 224.0.0.6, which are used for OSPF routing (Interior Gateway Protocol, IGP). If a packet were to be distributed to all OSPF-designated routers within an autonomous system, this could easily be facilitated by sending the packet to 224.0.0.6. A problem is inherent to this transport, however. Sending a packet to a multicast address with the intent that it will reach only destinations on the local network is simple. Sending a packet to the same multicast address and expecting it to permeate the networks of the autonomous system is more difficult. The latter case requires the use of *multicast routers,* devices that can control the "flooding" of the multicast to all networks that have multicast recipients. Multicast routing capability is not inherent in all IP version 4 routers, and as such the transport of the multicast packet might be limited to the local network by necessity.

Conferencing

Another common use for multicast is the distribution of information to many hosts simultaneously. To distribute the information to hosts more distant than the local networks to which the multicast originator is connected requires multicast routers. Assuming for a moment that the backbone of the Internet and individual autonomous systems were capable of routing multicast packets, any host device would be able to receive multicasts. The uses of this are many, including audio and multimedia conferences or multicasts. Note that the term *broadcast* was not used, although a correlation can be drawn between a multicast conference and traditional broadcast media. If the conference were facilitated by broadcasts, the scope of the conference could be the entire Internet domain. Multicasting permits that transmission of packets to only those nodes having "registered" or "joined" the multicast group.

The addresses shown in Table 11-2 are some of the well-known multicast addresses used for conferencing purposes. The list is an excerpt from the Assigned Numbers RFC.

Assigned No.	Description
224.0.1.7	AUDIONEWS — AudioNewsMulticast
224.0.1.10	IETF-1 — LOW-AUDIO
224.0.1.11	IETF-1 — AUDIO
224.0.1.12	IETF-1 — VIDEO
224.0.1.13	IETF-2 — LOW-AUDIO
224.0.1.14	IETF-2 — AUDIO
224.0.1.15	IETF-2 — VIDEO
224.0.1.16	MUSIC — SERVICE
224.0.1.17	SEANET — TELEMETRY
224.0.1.18	SEANET — IMAGE

Table 11-2 Excerpt of Assigned Numbers RFC for Multicast Conferencing Addresses

In the recent past, there have been several demonstrations of the multicast conferencing capability in conjunction with the Internet Engineering Task Force (IETF) meetings. The multicast addresses of 224.0.1.10 through 224.0.1.15 are used to transport the audio or video to remote participants in the IETF meetings. Illustration 11-1 is an example of the programming offered over these services during the March 2000 IETF meeting. To participate, a user would require a TCP/IP stack that supports multicasts and a service provider that is participating in the *Mbone,* the experimental multicast backbone. This explanation is somewhat simplified. If you are interested in participating, please refer to the Mbone FAQ (Frequently Asked Questions) file on the IETF FTP servers.

MONDAY 0930-1130 1300-1500 1530-1730 1930-2200
(UTC) 1330-1530 1700-1900 1930-2130 2330-0200

CHAN 1	issll	ion	mmusic	ipngwg
CHAN 2	rps	mboned	applmib	rsvp

TUESDAY 0900-1130 1300-1500 1530-1730
(UTC) 1330-1530 1700-1900 1930-2130

CHAN 1	ipngwg	ion	ion
CHAN 2	rps	avt	avt

WEDNESDAY 0900-1130 1300-1500 1530-1730 1930-2200
(UTC) 1330-1530 1700-1900 1930-2130 2330-0200

CHAN 1	ipngwg	mobileip	intserv	iab
CHAN 2	mmusic	rsvp	idmr	applmib

THURSDAY 0900-1130 1300-1500 1530-1630 1630-1830
(UTC) 1330-1530 1700-1900 1930-2130 2330-0200

CHAN 1	otsv	mobileip	tech. ple-nary	open plenary
CHAN 2	nmarea	idmr	"	"

Illustration 11-1 Multicast Conference Programming for the March 2000 IETF Meeting

The Mbone

The Mbone experimental multicast backbone is an overlay on the Internet. This is due partly to the fact that the Mbone is an experiment, and many of the commercial routers being used on the Internet do not support multicast routing. You could argue, however, that the Mbone is becoming less of an experiment and more production oriented with each passing IETF meeting. The Mbone started in much the same way that the Internet was started — as an experiment involving a handful of participants — but now has more than 4200 multicast routers. With the momentum that it is gaining, the Mbone will soon be too large to considered an experiment.

The Mbone uses the Internet for transport to each of the multicast domains. This is accomplished through the use of high-bandwidth tunnels that connect multicast routers. Currently, multicast routers are commonly implemented in UNIX workstations running *mrouted,* the daemon software that implements the multicast routing functions. With continued acceptance and growth of the Mbone and multicasting in general, it is likely that the multicast routing capability will eventually be integrated into the Internet backbone routers. This would permit multicast conference participation by anyone interested, not just by the few who are "well connected." In some ways, this would cause the demise of the Mbone since it would no longer be required for multicast support in the Internet.

Internet Group Management Protocol (IGMP)

The *Internet Group Management Protocol* (IGMP) is the protocol that enables a host to join a multicast group or conference. The current version of IGMP is version 1 and is specified in RFC 1112, "Host Extensions for IP Multicasting." A host, using IGMP, notifies its local multicast routers of any IP multicast groups that it wishes to be a member of. The format of an IGMP message is shown in Illustration 11-2.

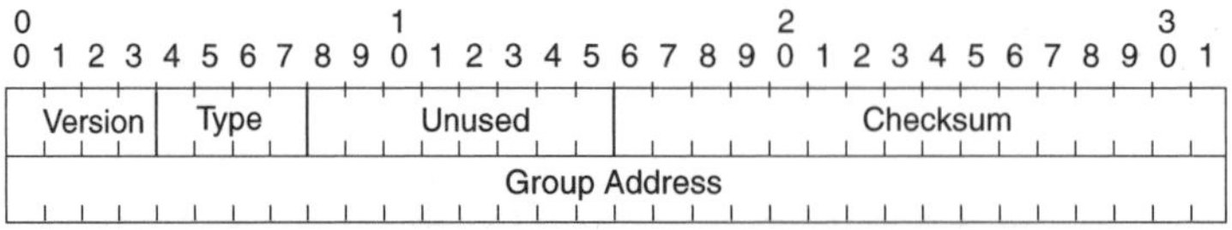

```
0                   1                   2                   3
0 1 2 3 4 5 6 7 8 9 0 1 2 3 4 5 6 7 8 9 0 1 2 3 4 5 6 7 8 9 0 1
+-------+-------+---------------+-------------------------------+
|Version| Type  |    Unused     |           Checksum            |
+-------+-------+---------------+-------------------------------+
|                         Group Address                         |
+---------------------------------------------------------------+
```

Illustration 11-2 IGMP Message Format

IGMP is a fairly simple protocol. Multicast routers are cognizant of all current multicast conferences, as well as the common, well-known multicast groups. For each multicast group that the router is aware of, it will send out a Host Membership Query. This is an IGMP message with Type = 1. It is sent to the destination of 224.0.0.1, which is the multicast address used to denote all multicast hosts on the local networks serviced by the multicast router. Each multicast host that has an interest in receiving the multicast transmission denoted by the Group Address field will respond with a Host Membership Report. This is an IGMP message with Type = 2. If at least one host on the local network is interested in receiving the multicast conversation, the router will forward the multicast packets that have an IP destination address equal to the multicast group required by the hosts on the network. Those multicast groups that are not "requested" by at least one host on a network are not propagated onto that network.

The multicast routers will occasionally send a new IGMP Host Membership Query to determine whether the last host interested in a multicast conversation has "discontinued its membership," in which case the router ceases to propagate the multicast packets for that particular group on that network. The periodic Host Membership Query will also indicate whether any hosts have reported a new interest in a multicast group that was heretofore not being propagated.

Multicast Routing Overview

One of the most difficult challenges of creating a usable multicast-capable Internet is creating a routing mechanism for dissemination of the multicast packets to each subscriber. Multicast packets have only one destination IP address, the Class D multicast group address. There can be as few as zero or as many as (theoretically) the entire Internet community participating in a multicast conference. The routing mechanism should forward the packets to all participants without wasting bandwidth. Ideally, if the multicast group has a membership of zero, the packet should not be sent beyond the first multicast router. The packets should be distributed in a timely manner. The very nature of some of the uses for multicasting (audio and video conferencing) suggests that it is essential that delays be kept to a minimum and that any delay be deterministic.

Certainly some, if not all, of the functionality offered through multicasting is also available with less difficulty through unicast transmission. It is really just a matter of how many more resources are consumed by a unicast approach weighed against the multicast difficulty. Consider Illustration 11-3. For the originator station to communicate with each of the recipient stations simultaneously using unicasts, four associations would be required. Associations were defined in Chapter 1 as

> {protocol, source IP address, source port, destination IP address, destination port}

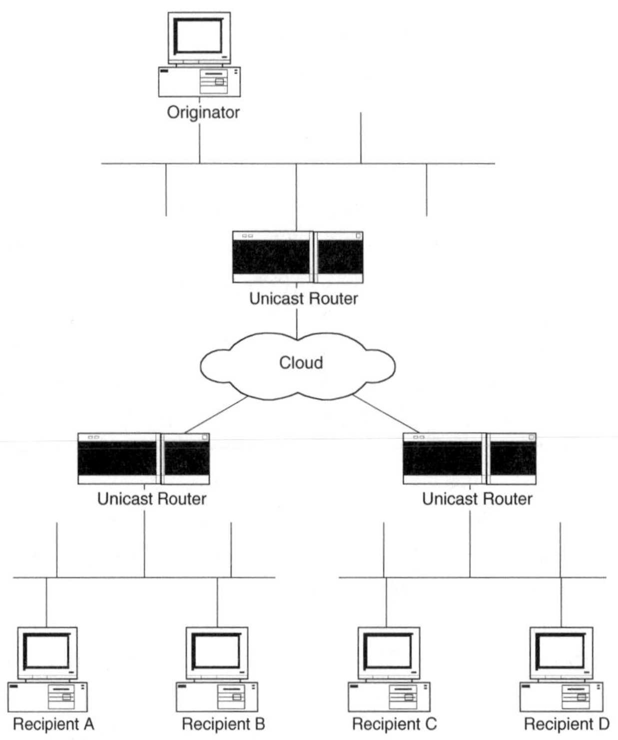

Illustration 11-3 One Originator to *n* Recipients Using Unicasting

In other words, there would have to be a TCP or a UDP connection between the originator and each recipient. Each packet that comprises the communication would have to be sent from the originator to each recipient. The Ethernet that the originator is on would see four times more traffic than in a similar situation using multicasting. Further, under the unicast configuration, if recipient A wished to assume the role of originator, perhaps to give an opinion on a topic, it would have to either set up an association with each of the other stations or have that communication relayed by the originator in Illustration 11-3. To permit every station to have both originator and recipient capabilities, the number of associations would be $[n \times (n-1)]/2$. This, in essence, creates a full-mesh network. It is true that broadcasts could provide the functionality; however, in cases in which the participants of the conference are a minority subset of the network community, broadcasts would likely not be appreciated.

As just mentioned, the same scenario using multicasting would be much more efficient. The originator would send a multicast packet to the multicast router on its Ethernet. The multicast router would forward the multicast packet to each multicast router that needs to get the packet. The routers would, in turn, send a link layer multicast onto each of their respective Ethernets, where it would be received by the recipients. Ideally, the multicast packet would only traverse any network one time.

Any recipient station that wished to assume the role of originator would do so by sending a multicast packet to the multicast group address being used for the conference. Naturally, this is a simplification of the process from the perspective that a conference is often chaired and mediated to ensure that order is maintained.

Up to this point, I have only briefly covered how packets are distributed in a multicast environment, through some form of distribution and routing mechanisms. Now let's look at these mechanisms in more detail, beginning with the distribution mechanisms that might be used for multicasting.

Multicast Packet Distribution

Several mechanisms can be used to distribute multicast packets within an Internet. Each has its own pros and cons. This section briefly discusses each method. For a more detailed perspective, refer to the now out of date Internet Draft document, "Introduction to IP Multicast Routing," <draft-rfced-info-semeria-00.txt>.

Flooding

Flooding in a multicast environment works very much as in the OSPF routing protocol. Whenever a multicast packet arrives at a multicast router, the router checks to see whether the packet has been previously seen. If the packet has not been seen by that router, the multicast router forwards the packet out all of its interfaces except the one that the packet was received on. If the multicast router has seen the packet before, it will quietly discard the packet and take no further action with regard to the packet.

Pros	Cons
Easy to implement	Requires table of previous packets
Robust	Inefficient use of network bandwidth
Fast distribution	

Spanning Tree (ST)

One of the problems with flooding the multicast packets to all of the multicast routers is that the packets are sent on all links within the multicast backbone to forward the packet. A more optimal solution is to build a single *spanning tree* (ST) that includes all multicast routers but includes only enough links to permit complete connectivity. Spanning trees are loopless and have exactly one path from any multicast router in the network to any other multicast router. A host that wishes to originate a multicast packet need only forward the packet to a single multicast router. That multicast router will use the spanning tree to forward the multicast packet to all other multicast routers.

Pros	Cons
Experience with implementation	Traffic concentration on links of ST
Robust	No alternate paths in ST
	ST may not use optimal links

Reverse Path Broadcast (RPB)

Reverse path broadcast (RPB) improves on the basic spanning tree forwarding by creating a spanning tree for each source in a multicast group. The fundamental algorithm permits a multicast router to forward multicast packets arriving from a specific source only if the packet arrived on the interface that is considered to be the preferred interface through which that router can reach the source. See Illustration 11-4.

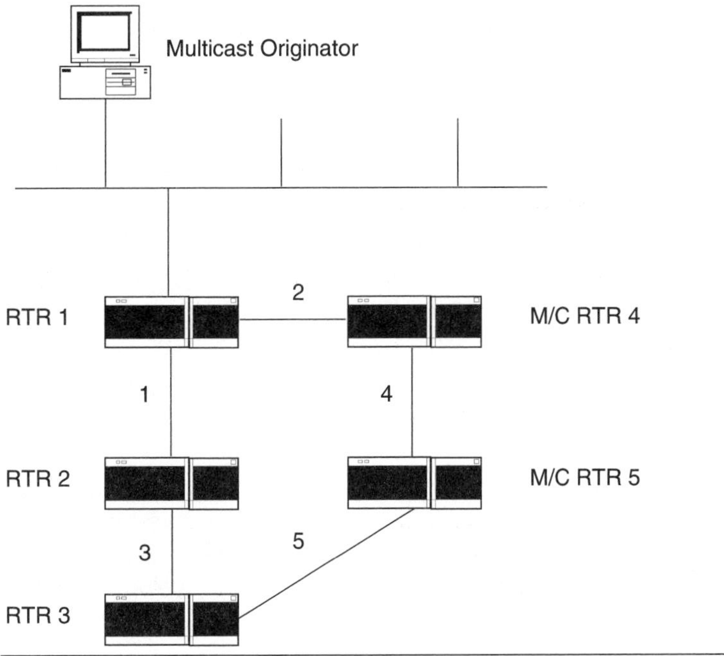

Illustration 11-4 Multicast Originator/Router Sample

Assume that the metrics for all of the numbered links in the illustration are equal. A multicast packet arrives at Multicast Router 3 with a source IP address for the host system, or Multicast

Originator. If the multicast packet arrives on the interface for link 3, that packet will be forwarded to Multicast Router 5 via link 5. However, if the multicast packet arrives at Multicast Router 3 via link 5, it will be quietly discarded, because Multicast Router 3 prefers link 3 over link 5 for routing of traffic destined to the Multicast Originator.

Using this basic algorithm, Multicast Router 3 will forward all traffic from the Multicast Originator received via link 3 to Multicast Router 5 via link 5. It is clear, however, that using this algorithm, Multicast Router 5 will discard that same packet just forwarded to it from Multicast Router 3, since link 3 is not the preferred path from Multicast Router 5 to the Multicast Originator. It is a natural extension to this forwarding algorithm that if a router can determine that the link it should forward a multicast packet onto is not the preferred link back to the source, it should not send the packet at all. In this case, Multicast Router 3 should not forward the multicast packet to Multicast Router 5 and vice versa.

Making this determination is not as difficult as it might seem at first glance. If the routing protocol being used for the unicast packets is a link-state protocol, such as OSPF, each router in the area has an identical topology database. Multicast Router 3 could compute the route entry to the Multicast Originator that Multicast Router 5 would have in its route table. If Multicast Router 3 determines from the computation that it would not be the next hop for a packet sent from Multicast Router 5 to the Multicast Originator, it will not forward the multicast packet to Multicast Router 5.

Distance-vector routing protocols do not require each router to have an identical topology database. They must rely on a different mechanism. In fact, in a distance-vector routing protocol the routers periodically send out updates representing their entire route tables. Adjacent routers can easily determine from these updates the information required to determine whether the multicast packet should be forwarded.

Pros	Cons
Efficiently uses network bandwidth	Requires route tables in decisions
Does not concentrate all M/C on single links	Does not consider group memberships
Fast	

Truncated Reverse Path Broadcasting (TRPB)

Truncated reverse path broadcasting (TRPB) is a slight modification of RPB. Through the use of a group membership protocol, such as IGMP, the router can determine which of the leaf networks it interfaces with have hosts that are members of the multicast group in the packet's destination address. The TRPB forwarding algorithm will not permit a multicast packet to be forwarded onto a leaf network where there are no group members. RPB dictates that multicast packets are forwarded to leaf networks. All other forwarding decisions in TRPB are the same as in RPB.

Pros	Cons
Efficiently uses network bandwidth	Requires route tables in decisions
Does not concentrate all M/C on single links	Spanning tree includes all M/C routers
Fast	
Considers group membership	

Reverse Path Multicasting (RPM)

Reverse path multicasting (RPM) is a refinement to TRPB, addressing one of the faults of TRPB: that all multicast routers within the multicast backbone are members of the spanning tree. With RPM, the spanning tree includes only as many routers as are necessary to provide reachability to all members of the multicast group. The process starts with the spanning tree that is computed by TRPB. This spanning tree includes all multicast routers but is computed to be optimal for a specific multicast source. From each router on the periphery of the multicast backbone, the ST determines whether there are any leaf networks that have members of the multicast group. If there are members, it forwards the multicast packet onto the leaf network. If there are no members, it quietly discards the packet and sends a "prune" message back toward the multicast source with a time-to-live (TTL) value of 1 in the IP header. The TTL value will limit the scope of the IP datagram to only one hop. Any multicast router receiving the prune message must not forward multicasts to that router in the future. This process continues, working its way back toward the source of the multicast. Eventually, the spanning tree includes only the multicast routers necessary to deliver the packets to the multicast group membership. Occasionally the pruned branches of the spanning tree are reinstated to pick up any hosts that had joined the multicast group since the tree was last pruned.

Pros	**Cons**
Efficiently uses network bandwidth	Requires route tables in decisions
Does not concentrate all M/C on single links	Requires occasional ST reinitialization
Fast	New members may have to wait
Considers group membership	
ST includes only necessary routers	

Core-Based Trees (CBT)

The philosophy behind the implementation of forwarding using *core-based trees* (CBT) differs from the other methods discussed previously. With CBT, each router that can service leaf networks must be configured with a unicast address of a multicast router that will act as the core for the multicast group. Whenever a host system wishes to join a multicast group, the multicast router on the leaf network will be notified via IGMP. If the router is already a member of the forwarding tree for the multicast group, it does nothing. If it is not a member, it forwards a unicast *CBT-join* request toward the statically configured core router(s). Each router that receives this packet takes note of the multicast group and the interface that the packet was received on and forwards the packet toward the core router. If the CBT-join message reaches either the core router or any multicast router that is already on the CBT, the packet is stopped, and an acknowledgment is sent back to the source of the unicast CBT-join packet. At this point, the CBT includes all multicast routers necessary to communicate to all multicast group members. There is a similar procedure for pruning unnecessary branches of the CBT when members leave the multicast group. RFCs 2201 and 2189 deliver more detailed information on the use of CBT with IP.

Pros	**Cons**
Efficiently uses network bandwidth	Requires route tables in decisions
Efficient joining of groups	Traffic concentration on links of CBT
Fast	
Considers group membership	
Includes only necessary routers	

Multicast Routing Protocols

Distance-Vector Multicast Routing Protocols (DVMRP)

The familiar interior routing protocol RIP was the basis for the initial design of the *Distance-Vector Multicast Routing Protocol* (DVMRP). Unlike RIP, which is a unicast routing protocol, the route table that the DVMRP maintains is oriented to provide next-hop information based on the source address in the multicast datagram. Due to the differences between the route tables used to forward unicast and multicast datagrams, a router that is capable of forwarding both types of traffic would require distinctly separate tables for each. The Mbone is mostly constructed using DVMRP routing.

The forwarding algorithm that DVMRP uses is reverse path multicasting, as described earlier. Multicast packets are initially sent to all multicast routers but then begin the process of pruning the subset of routers back to only what is required to reach all of the multicast group membership.

Similar growth problems dealt with in the earlier days of the Internet are now arising on the Mbone. A version of DVMRP is being developed that will address scalability issues. Essentially, as with the unicast Internet, the multicast backbone will be divided into small multicast autonomous systems, or domains. An exterior multicast routing protocol will handle routing multicast packets between domains. DVMRP was originally documented in RFC 1075, "Distance Vector Multicast Routing Protocol."

Multicast Extensions to OSPF (MOSPF)

Just as DVMRP used RIP as the basis for its development, *Multicast Extensions to OSPF* (MOSPF) is an extension to the OSPF interior routing protocol discussed earlier in this book and defined in RFC 1583. These extensions are defined in RFC 1584, "Multicast Extensions to OSPF."

OSPF is an excellent choice to extend to support multicasting. Because it is a link-state routing protocol, the router maintains a topology database identical to other routers within the same area. MOSPF adds a link-state advertisement (LSA) to the traditional ones supported by OSPF. This LSA is referred to as a *group membership LSA.*

IGMP is used between the host that wishes to participate in a multicast conference and a multicast router. In conjunction with the group membership LSA, the MOSPF routers are capable of computing a spanning tree that includes only the necessary routers to provide full connectivity. This computation is done on the fly with the receipt of multicast packets that describe a new multicast group. The spanning tree is cached for use by future multicast packets using the same group as the destination address.

Protocol Independent Multicast (PIM)

Protocol independent multicast (PIM), as the name implies, is independent of a unicast routing protocol. PIM comes in two flavors: dense and sparse. In PIM dense mode, like other multicast protocols, packets are flooded out all interfaces until the spanning tree is pruned and truncated. It is assumed that the downstream networks want to receive and will probably use the multicast packets that are forwarded to them. The downside of using dense mode is its default flooding behavior. In PIM sparse mode, the receivers are far apart. Packets are sent only if they are explicitly requested. In contrast to dense mode, with sparse mode the assumption is that downstream networks will likely not need the packets that are sent to them. The downside of using sparse mode is its need to keep state information and refresh that information regularly.

PIM sparse mode is defined in RFC 2362, "Protocol Independent Multicast–Sparse Mode (PIM-SM): Protocol Specification," dated June 1998. A more recent Internet Draft exists by the same name. PIM dense mode, as far as I can tell, does not have an RFC but has had several Internet Drafts named "Protocol Independent Multicast version 2 Dense Mode Specification." There was no current draft of the PIM dense mode specification on the IETF FTP servers at the time of this writing.

Summary

Certain applications could be better served by multicast architecture than by a unicast architecture with multiple associations. The applications include resource discovery and conferencing.

Resource discovery can be easier if all the resources that have similar attributes were assigned permanent multicast group addresses. A device that needed to locate those resources can send a multicast packet to the destination that specified the fixed multicast group that included those resources. The devices that received the packets and recognized that they belong to the group would respond accordingly.

Unlike resource discovery, which uses fixed multicast groups that are related to the functionality of the device, conferencing uses common, well-known multicast addresses or transient multicast addresses. The membership can vary. A host could elect to participate and then, after determining the content of the conference, discontinue membership, essentially in the same way as you might "channel surf" television programming.

Currently, an experimental multicast backbone called the Mbone is overlaid on top of the Internet. This backbone is used to test applications and routing mechanisms for potential future widespread deployment. There have been several tests of conferencing over the Mbone since 1992. The IETF meetings are now regularly multicast over the Mbone in audio and video media.

Multicast routing is a subject of ongoing research. The goal of the research is to find a way to distribute multicast packets to all members of a multicast group, using the minimum amount of resources, and to allow for rapid convergence in the event of network outages. The protocol used between a host that wishes to participate in a multicast group and the local multicast router is known as IGMP, Internet Group Management Protocol. Forwarding algorithms used to distribute packets to all other members of the group may or may not use the IGMP information to improve their effectiveness. Examples of forwarding algorithms include:

- Flooding
- Spanning tree
- Reverse path broadcast
- Truncated reverse path broadcast
- Reverse path multicasting
- Core-based trees

Multicast routing protocols use similar algorithms to those used by their unicast counterparts. Distance-Vector Multicast Routing Protocol (DVMRP) is based on RIP, and Multicast Extensions to OSPF (MOSPF) is truly an extension of the OSPF protocol version 2,which enables routing of multicast packets in addition to routing unicast packets. Protocol independent multicast (PIM) is independent of the unicast routing protocol and has two variations, sparse mode and dense mode.

Practice Questions

1. How many multicast addresses are there in the IPv4 address space?
2. What IP multicast group is used by RIPv2 routers?
3. What IP multicast group is used by SIP?
4. Who has reserved multicast groups 224.0.19.0–224.0.19.63?
5. What multicast routing protocol relies on extensions to OSPF for multicast support?
6. Which IGMP message has Type = 2?

chapter

12

Mobile IP

Mobility

Recent advances in wireless communications have brought about dramatic changes in the way we do business. The essence of the change is captured in the simple statement that "work is something that you do, not someplace that you go." We are, at the time of this writing, just starting to see mobile wireless data services being introduced throughout the world. The connections are fairly low speed at this time, with speeds typically falling into the range from 9.6 kbps to 19.2 kbps. Within the next several years, we will see this improve to the point that mobile data will rival typical 56k modem speeds. Shortly after that, we will see as much as 384 kbps to a mobile terminal at typical automobile highway speeds and as much as 2 Mbps to a stationary but wireless terminal. For me, the capabilities that are enabled by high-data-rate mobile terminals are very exciting. One of the best uses I have heard of is for relaying instructional video as you need it. Take golf for example. I could find myself in the rough on number 17 with a cross hill lie, feet above the ball into a stiff headwind. How in the world should I play this shot? Or when the nasty weather sets in, I can watch the Doppler radar loop to see how long before the storm passes over and we can resume play. See the value?

This chapter is being offered to introduce a few concepts that relate to IP addressing in a mobile environment and that specifically allow us to be reached by data services in the same way that we can be reached with current mobile telephony. Before I get into these technologies, there are two terms that I want to clarify. Both terms are easier for me to explain by example than by a dictionary definition. The first is the term *nomadicity.* Nomadicity is being able to take your portable computer to a location such as your home, office, or hotel room; plug your modem into a phone jack; dial into a remote access concentrator at an ISP or enterprise; and conduct business as normal. The second term is *mobility.* Mobility is being able to take your mobile phone, get in your automobile, and start driving. All the time you are driving, you are able to place calls, receive calls, and carry on a conversation without regard to your physical location. I apologize for not giving a good dictionary definition for these two terms; the main difference is that nomadicity requires users to discontinue communications as they move from place to place and mobility does not. For instance, a residential cordless phone allows a user to make calls and move about freely within a building but only within a given distance from the base station. This is really more of an example of untethered nomadicity than it is of mobility since the user cannot really change locations without unplugging the base station and taking it along to the new location.

True mobility is achieved when a person can use and provide services independent of their location. Ideally, this is transparent to the user as well. The average person is still technologically far from this for a number of reasons. One is that there is currently no single global infrastructure in place that enables this level of mobility. You can argue that those low-earth-orbit satellite systems provide this mobility but they have proven to be unacceptable as yet to the average consumer due to the pricing of the service offering and the bulk of the terminal (phone). Terrestrial wireless telephone systems come close to providing this level of mobility but only on a continental basis and even then with "holes" in the coverage areas. For instance, in North America, mobile phone service is predominately provided by Time Division Multiple Access (TDMA) technology, although other technologies such as Global System for Mobile (GSM) and Code Division Multiple Access (CDMA) can be found. In Europe, the predominant technology is GSM. Moreover, because of the difference in frequencies allocated to the mobile phone service in North America and Europe, a typical GSM phone cannot be taken from the United States to Europe and used. These types of problems are being solved with the use of multimode and multiband mobile phones, among other things. It is possible to buy dual-band and tri-band GSM phones that work in North America and Europe and dual-mode phones that work in North American GSM and TDMA coverage areas. As far as I know, there is no single phone that provides coverage in all of North America, Europe, and Japan except via satellite-based systems.

IP-based data services pose a different set of issues. It is difficult, as a nomadic user, for me to offer a service such as FTP to other users because the IP address assigned to my portable computer changes every time I change my point of attachment to the network. The users of my FTP service would not know what the IP address of my computer is so they could connect to it! One solution would be to have the users call to ask me what my temporary IP address is. (That won't happen.) Another is to have the user's reference my FTP server by domain name. This might be possible if I am only going to dial into a corporate-owned remote access server, but if I am dialing into an Internet service provider—or worse yet, multiple Internet service providers—it is not a viable solution.

It is much more desirable for me to be able to be allocated a permanent IP address that will always be used by my computer no matter where I am dialed into. This presents some significant challenges. Packets being routed through the Internet are forwarded based on IP network prefixes in route tables of the routers that make up the Internet. It would be necessary for me to install a host route for my computer's IP address into those route tables to force my packets to be routed toward my current attachment point and not to the network being advertised by my home autonomous system (AS). This is clearly absurd since we are having so many problems as it is with the Internet's route table explosion.

I used FTP as an example of a service that I might want to offer. FTP might have been a poor choice because there is no value gained by the server being mobile; only problems are gained. We are, however, on the verge of converging all sorts of real-time and non-real-time services on IP-based infrastructure. What if your voice telephony to your mobile phone was offered over an IP infrastructure? Don't think that this is a crazy idea; 3G wireless technology, which uses voice-over-IP-over-wireless for transport, is only a few years away! Millions of host routes injected into the Internet route tables would absolutely cripple the routing mechanism. This is not even considering the impact on domain name services in such a scenario!

Lucky for us, a group of folks in the IETF have been working on this problem for several years. Their solution is embodied in a series of recommendations called *Mobile IP.* The primary document produced by this group is RFC 2002, "IP Mobility Support," dated October 1996. The following section will introduce Mobile IP. For greater depth, please refer to the RFC and to the very good books devoted to Mobile IP.

Mobile IP

Before I get into the details of Mobile IP, I feel it is necessary to establish the terminology. Illustration 12-1 is a very simple diagram that I will use to explain the fundamentals of Mobile IP. For now, let's consider that Host A is a *mobile node.* Host A is connected to its *home network.* Host A's home network is an Ethernet identified by the IP subnet 192.168.1.0/29. Host B and Host C are *nonmobile nodes.* When Host B or Host C communicate with Host A, they are called *correspondent nodes.* If Host A were to unplug from the Ethernet on the left side of the illustration and plug into the Ethernet on the right side of the illustration, Host A would be connected to a *foreign network.* The foreign network in the Illustration is identified by the subnet 172.16.1.0/24. Router A, which has Mobile IP functionality, is called a *home agent.* The home agent, as will be explained later, provides mobility support to Host A. Router B also supports Mobile IP and is called a *foreign agent.*

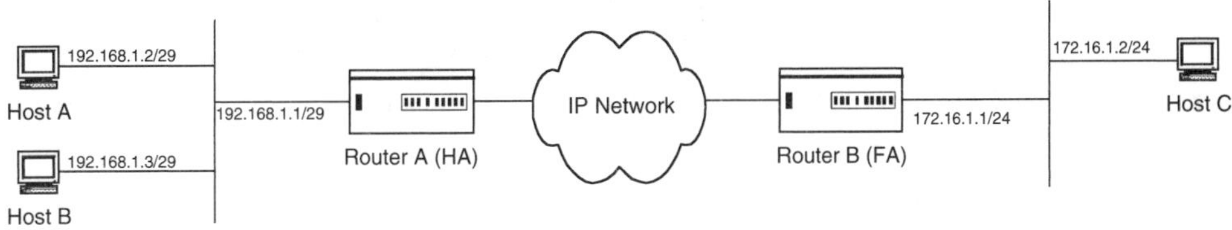

Illustration 12-1 Fundamental Mobile IP Network

When Host A is on its home network, it communicates with correspondent nodes as it would in normal IP. If Host C sends a packet to Host A's IP address, it is forwarded to Router B, which forwards it through the IP network to Router A. Router A resolves the IP address to a MAC address using ARP and forwards the packet to Host A. If Host B sends a packet to Host A, Host B would ARP for Host A's MAC address and forward the packet directly to Host A.

If Host A were to disconnect from its home network, packets sent to Host A's IP address from Host C would traverse Router B and the IP network but when it arrived at Router A, Router A would not be able to resolve Host A's MAC address and the packet would be undeliverable.

Now let's consider what would happen if Host A were to connect to the foreign network without Mobile IP support as shown in Illustration 12-2. When Host C tries to send a packet to Host A, the packet is forwarded to Router A but because Host A is not on its home network, the packet is undeliverable just as in the case where Host A is completely unattached.

Now, let's get into the Mobile IP protocol. Host A is typically configured to know that Router A is its home agent. The foreign agent (Router B) continuously advertises that it can function as a Mobile IP foreign agent. These agent advertisements contain the foreign agent's IP address. Host A receives this advertisement and sends a registration request to the Host A's home agent using the foreign agent as a next hop. The foreign agent learns the MAC address of Host A via this registration request so the foreign agent now knows that it can directly communicate with Host A at the link layer even though Host A is not a member of the 172.16.1.0/24 subnet.

Because the registration request being sent by Host A to its home agent is routed based on the normal destination IP address mechanism, the registration request has no problem finding the home agent. When the home agent parses the contents of the registration request, it finds that Host A included the IP address of the foreign agent as the *care-of address.* The home agent now builds a *binding,* which associates Host A's IP address with the address of the foreign agent. Now when the home agent needs to communicate with Host A, it does so by sending the packet to the foreign agent, who forwards the packet to Host A's MAC address. The home agent is able to do this by logically building a tunnel between itself and the foreign agent. Although there are several supported tunneling methods, it is mandatory that the Mobile IP agents support IP-within-IP tunnels. When the home agent needs to send a packet to Host A, it looks up Host A's binding, determines the foreign agent's IP address, wraps the packet in a new IP header using the destination address of the foreign agent, and forwards the resulting IP-within-IP packet to the foreign agent using normal routing mechanisms. When the foreign agent receives the packet, it sees that the Protocol field of the IP header contains a "4," meaning that IP is the next higher protocol. The tunnel header is stripped away and the resulting IP packet is forwarded to Host A.

At this point in the explanation, the home agent and the foreign agent know how to communicate with Host A when it is on the foreign network. How does Host B communicate with Host A? The home agent must somehow cause the packets that would be sent to Host A to be sent to the home agent instead. It can do this with Gratuitous ARP, Proxy ARP, and/or normal routing. In this case, when Host A registers with its home agent, the home agent will send out an ARP message on the Ethernet using its own MAC address and Host A's IP address. This Gratuitous ARP will cause Host B to flush out the old ARP cache for 192.168.1.2 and install a new ARP entry for 192.168.1.2 with the home agent's MAC address. Host B should now know that if it needs to send a packet to Host A, it should send it to the hardware address for the home agent as if it were delivering the packet directly to Host A. If Host B were to flush its ARP cache or if Host B were rebooted, it would not have an ARP entry in its cache to use to forward the packet. Instead, when Host B needs to send a packet to Host A, it needs to ARP for the MAC address of 192.168.1.2 (Host A). The home agent sees this ARP request and because Host A is currently registered with the home agent, the home agent will respond to the ARP request using its own MAC address. This is called Proxy ARP. Proxy ARP is defined in RFC 1027, "Using ARP to Implement Transparent Subnet Gateways."

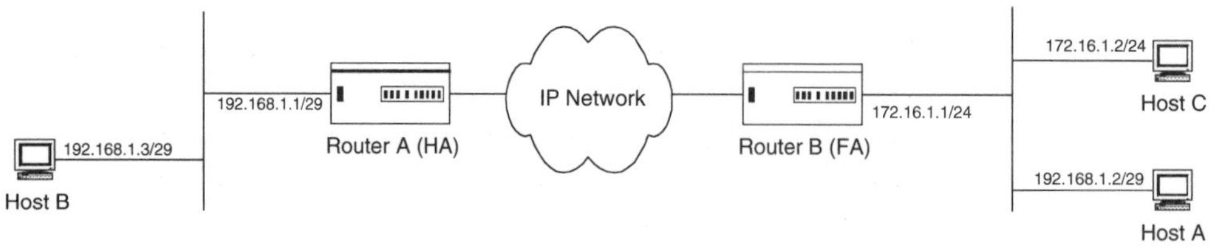

Illustration 12-2 Host A Connected to the Foreign Network

If Host C in Illustration 12-2 needs to send a packet to Host A, it does so by sending the packet to Router B. Router B forwards the packet to Router A, which knows that it does not send the packet onto its local Ethernet (Host A's home network) but instead puts the packet into the IP-within-IP tunnel to the foreign agent. The foreign agent strips away the tunnel IP header and forwards the packet to the hardware address for Host A. This illustrates the case where simply the normal routing mechanisms attracted the packet to the home agent for forwarding. It also illustrates one of the downsides of Mobile IP. Packets from Host C to Host A had to go through Router A. This is called *triangle routing.* Ideally, Host C would know Host A's care-of address and thus communicate directly to Host A or to Host A's foreign agent.

If Host A disconnects from the foreign network, packets to Host A will be forwarded using the Mobile IP tunnel that was setup, but the packets will be undeliverable. Let's assume that Host A returns to its home network. How does it know that it is back on its home network? Home agents send agent advertisements as well. Host A receives the agent advertisement and sees that the IP address for the agent has a prefix equal to Host A's network prefix. Note that there may be multiple home agents on the home network so Host A does not need to see an advertisement with its own home agent's IP address explicitly in it. Obviously, since Host A is back on its home network, it no longer needs the services of the home agent and sends a registration request to the home agent to deregister its binding. (A registration request with a "lifetime" of 0 is used to deregister the binding.) Host A should send a Gratuitous ARP at this time so that all the local hosts will flush the old home agent ARP entry out of their caches.

Since Mobile IP may not be fully deployed everywhere that a mobile node needs mobility support, there is a slightly different variation of Mobile IP that is used if the mobile node cannot find a foreign agent on the foreign network. This scenario is shown in Illustration 12-3. Host A attaches to the foreign network (172.16.1.0/24) and listens for a foreign agent advertisement. If Host A does not receive an advertisement, it has another option. Host A has the ability to send a DHCP request asking for an IP address lease. If a DHCP server exists and it has an IP address to provide to Host A, it provides an address and a default router address. Host A, using this IP address as its care-of address, now has the ability to be its own foreign agent and decapsulate the IP-within-IP tunnel. This is called a *collocated care-of address.* Host A now has two IP addresses associated with it, one for each of the two IP headers that it must use.

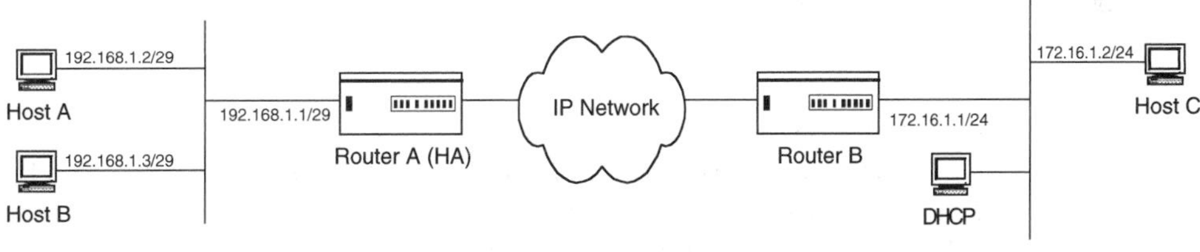

Illustration 12-3 Mobile IP Example 1

DHCP is not the only way in which Host A can get a collocated care-of address. In Illustration 12-4, Host A is connecting to the foreign network with a remote access server. The remote access server will provide an IP address to Host A by means of the IP Control Protocol (IPCP) of PPP.

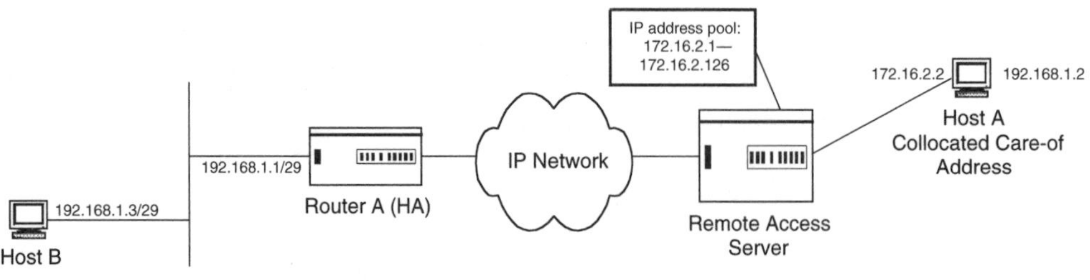

Illustration 12-4 Mobile IP Collocated Care-of Address Example 2

Now that I have discussed the two types of care-of addresses, I will primarily use only the foreign agent care-of address in the following discussions and illustrations.

Let's consider a slightly more complicated network illustration showing a mobile node that visits two foreign networks. In Illustration 12-5, Host A's home network is identified by the subnet 192.168.1.0/29. There are two potential foreign networks for Host A: 172.16.1.0/28 (served by Router C) and 10.0.1.0/28 (served by Router D). When Host A visits the 172.16.1.0/28 foreign network, it receives the agent advertisement from Router C and registers with the home agent. I won't go into detail here since the process is described in fair detail above. What is interesting though is the data path taken by packets as Host A on foreign network 172.16.1.0/28 communicates with Host D. Packets sent from Host A to Host D will go to Router C, then to Router D (by the shared link between the two routers), and then to Host D. Packets from Host D to Host A must go to Router D, which forwards the packets through the IP cloud to Router B. Router B, whether by Gratuitous ARP or by Proxy ARP, sends the packets for Host A to Router A, which tunnels the packets to Router C. Router C forwards the packets directly to Host A.

When Host A disconnects from the foreign network 172.16.1.0/28, it goes over to the foreign network 10.0.1.0/28 and attaches. Router D sends agent advertisements and Host A registers with its home agent specifying Router D as its new care-of address. The home agent deletes the first binding and installs a new binding for Host A using 10.0.1.1 (Router D) as the new care-of address.

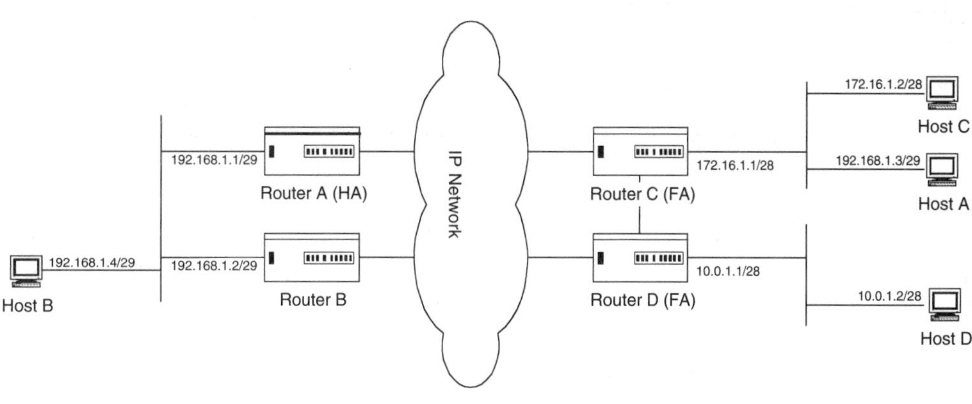

Illustration 12-5 Mobile IP Example 3

The above illustrations have all been geared toward an Ethernet-attached host that goes "into the field" and attaches to a wired foreign network. This, by our previous definition, is nomadicity. The use of Mobile IP has enabled the mobile node to seamlessly offer IP services to users no matter where the mobile node is attached but has not facilitated any kind of dynamic roaming. The following few examples show a wireless mobile node (true mobility) as it applies Mobile IP.

In Illustration 12-6, there are two mobile nodes in the coverage area for Radio A. Radio A is attached to Router A. Radio B and Radio C are serviced by Router B and Router C, respectively. Connecting the three routers is an IP network. Host C is a host within the IP network. This scenario is very similar to those presented in prior examples except that the mobile hosts are not connected into the network by physical wires (as they are with an Ethernet).

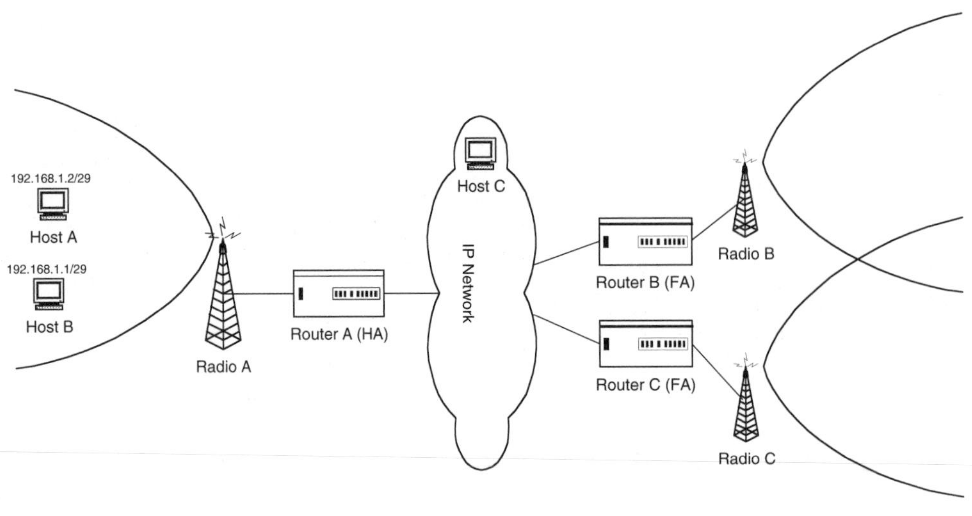

Illustration 12-6 Mobile IP with a Wireless Mobile Node Example 1

When Host A moves from the coverage area of Radio A into the coverage area of Radio B, as shown in Illustration 12-7, it first listens for agent advertisements. When it receives agent advertisements for Router B, Host A registers with its home agent. The home agent establishes the binding (builds the tunnel to Router B) and provides IP services to Host A as it roams. Again, this is pretty much the same as we have discussed previously.

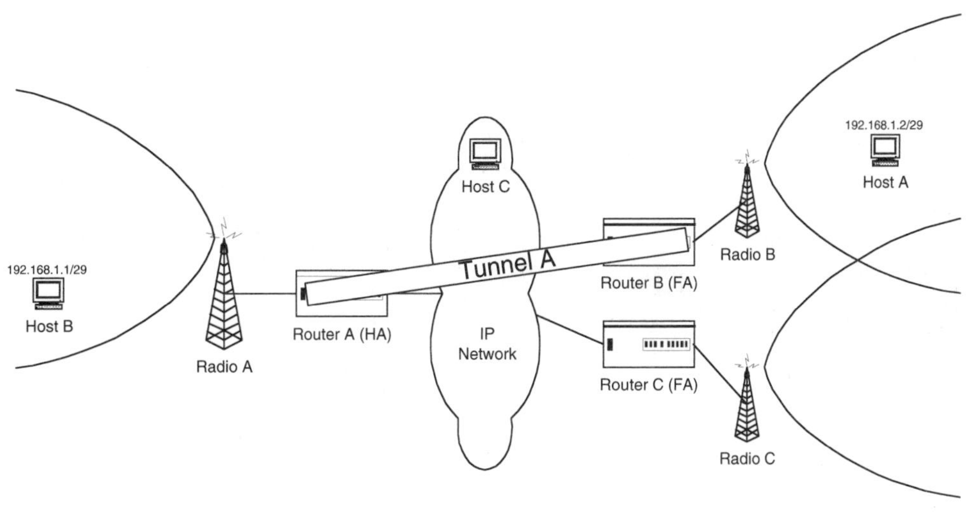

Illustration 12-7 Mobile IP with a Wireless Mobile Node Example 2

Since Host A is not plugged into an Ethernet and is using wireless communications to connect into the IP network, it is possible for the host to be in two coverage areas simultaneously, as shown in Illustration 12-8. Since it is not known whether Host A will go fully into Radio C's coverage area or return fully into Radio B's coverage area, it is necessary to have more than one binding in the home agent. Mobile IP allows Host A to have a binding using Router B as the care-of address and to add a second binding using Router C as the care-of address. There is a special bit, the S bit, used for this in the registration request. The S bit being set allows simultaneous bindings to exist. When the home agent has simultaneous bindings, it sends duplicate IP packets to each care-of address. The mobile node may receive duplicate copies of the same IP packets (after the tunnel IP header is removed).

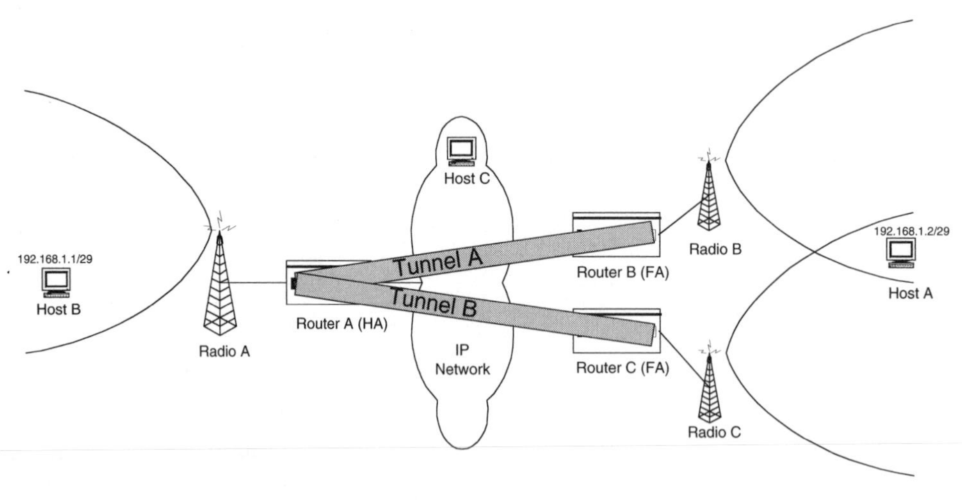

Illustration 12-8 Mobile IP with a Wireless Mobile Node Example 3

Mobile IP in an Enterprise

The following series of illustrations will show an example of how Mobile IP can be used in an enterprise to facilitate nomadicity. I'll start by setting up the example. The left side of Illustration 12-9 represents a fictional corporation's (Corp A) headquarters. In that headquarters, Router B connects to the Internet. There is a firewall that separates the internal offices and cubicles from the nonsecure public conference room. Mobile IP employs IPSec for secure traversal of firewalls. Router A functions as both a home agent for Hosts A, B, and C and as a foreign agent for any visiting hosts that have authorization to use the facilities. Corp A chooses to limit the access to the internal offices and cubicles to employees of Corp A only. For everybody else, Corp A has made Mobile IP services available to visitors in its public conference room. Router B has the ability to act as a foreign agent for conference room visitors and for Corp A employees. Corp A has also provided a DHCP server if the visitor would prefer to use Mobile IP with a collocated care-of address.

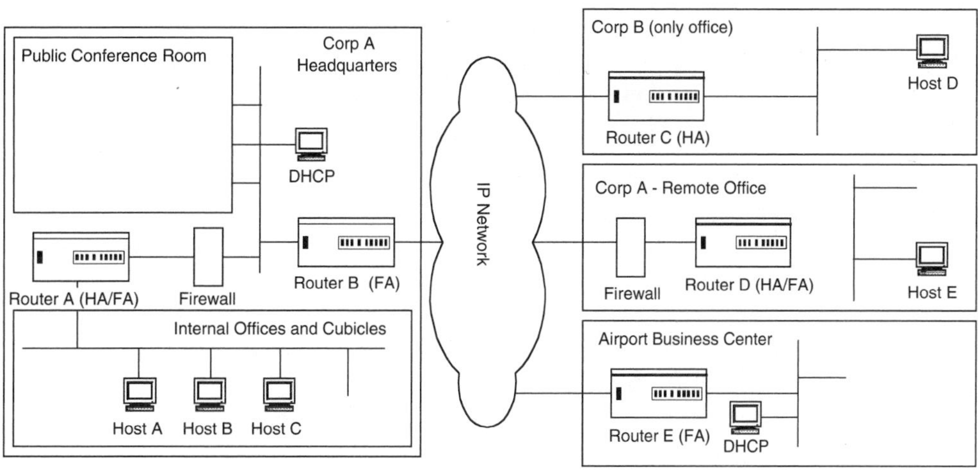

Illustration 12-9 Mobile IP in an Enterprise

On the right side of the illustration are three separate entities. The top entity is a representation of Corp B's sole office. Router C connects Corp B to the Internet but also provides home agent Mobile IP services to its nomadic employees. Corp B has chosen not to run a foreign agent on Router C since it has no satellite offices and prohibits visitors from attaching to its internal LAN.

The middle entity on the right depicts a remote office for Corp A. Router D, which sits behind a firewall, implements both a home agent for Host E and a foreign agent for corporate nomads that visit from the headquarters or from one of the other remote offices.

The bottom entity on the right depicts an airport business center — perhaps an airline courtesy club such as Delta Airline's

Crown Room or United's Red Carpet Club. Router E provides an Internet connection for the business center but also implements a Mobile IP foreign agent available to all nomadic travelers that are Mobile IP capable. The business center also offers a DHCP server for Mobile IP nodes that prefer to use collocated care-of addresses as well as non-Mobile-IP-aware nodes that simply want to use the Internet connection during their stay in the center.

The placement of the hosts in Illustration 12-9 shows the location of all the hosts in the example on their home networks. That is, the hosts are not currently roaming. Illustration 12-10 shows the hosts in one of many scenarios involving roaming. Here we see that Host A has moved from the secure cubicle area of Corp A headquarters up into the public conference room. Host A is joined in the conference room by Host D from Corp B and Host E from Corp A's remote office. Host C is en route to Corp A's remote office for a meeting but has stopped along the way at the airport business center. Host B has stayed on its home network.

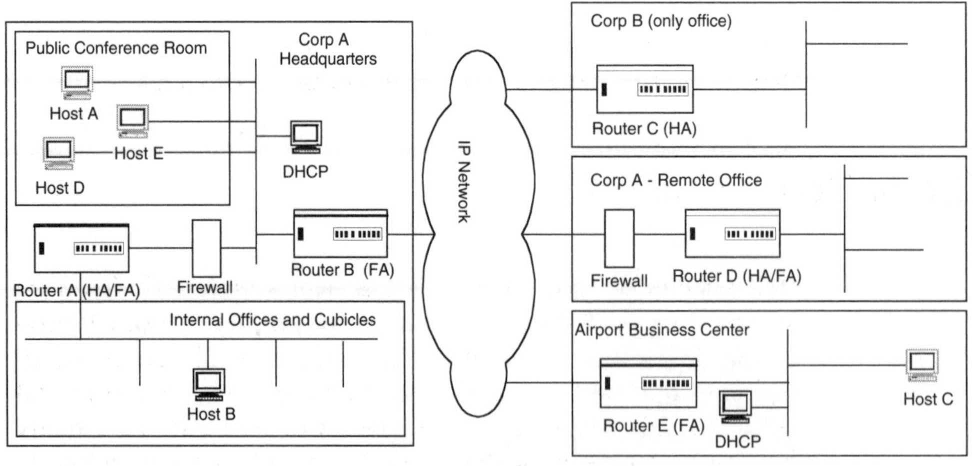

Illustration 12-10 Enterprise Mobile IP with Roaming Example 1

After the meeting that brought Hosts A, D, and E together in the conference room, Host D returns to Corp B and deregisters from the Mobile IP service. Host E moves into the secure office area of Corp A along with Host B. Host C is no longer in the airport business center but has moved into the secure office area of Corp A's remote office. This scenario is shown in Illustration 12-11.

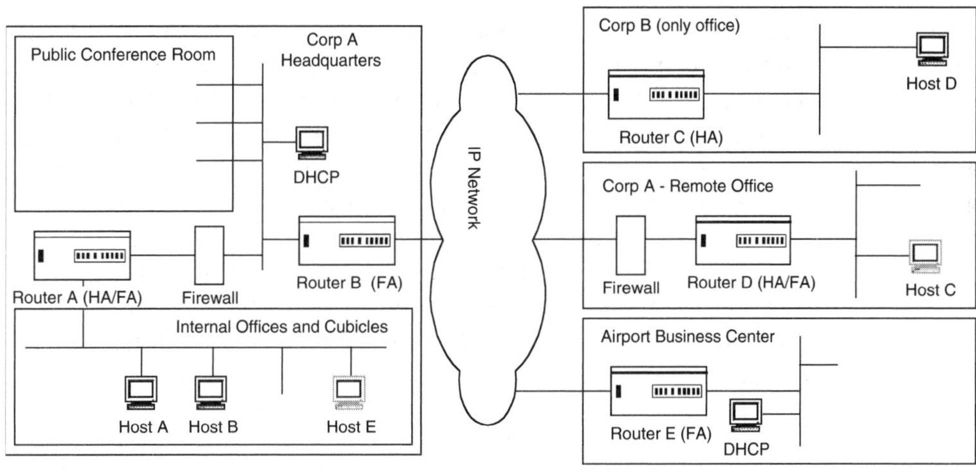

Illustration 12-11 Enterprise Mobile IP with Roaming Example 2

Virtual Home Network

One more point that I want to make regarding Mobile IP has to do with the possibility of a virtual home network. In Illustration 12-12, Host A is a mobile node. It has been allocated the IP address of 192.168.2.2/24 for its "lifetime." It is receiving and providing IP services via a radio network. As such, there really is no physical network that Host A can call its home network. You could say that Host A is typically in one location for 8 or 9 hours Monday through Friday and therefore that location should dictate the home network. You could also say that Host A is typically at another location when it is not in the first location and therefore that location should dictate the home network. Instead, the host might always be considered to be roaming and as such it is always on a foreign network. In a way, this simplifies things since it is a good assumption that if the host is not using a foreign agent, the host is not being used.

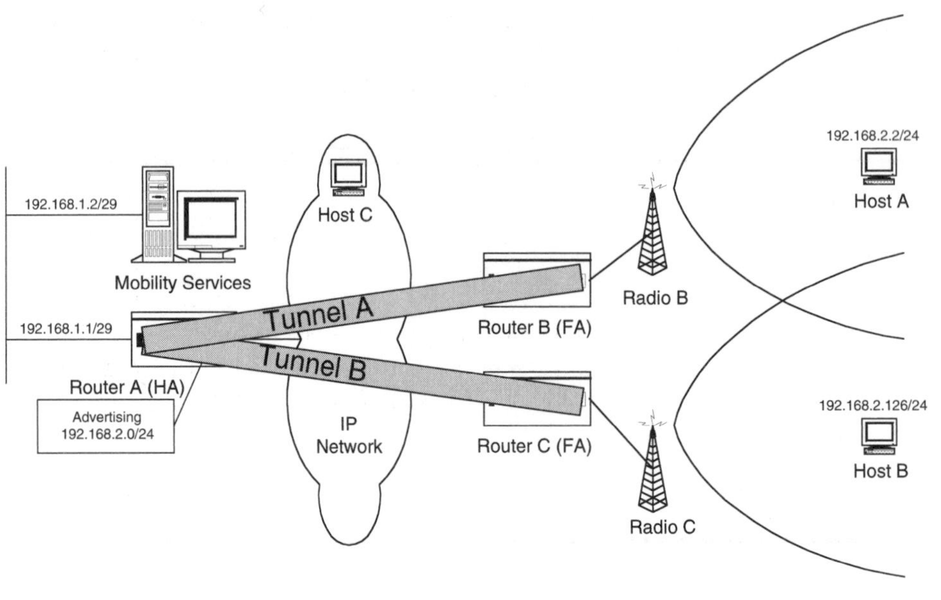

Illustration 12-12 A Virtual Home Network

Router A, on the left side of the illustration, is Host A's home agent. It also has an indirect connection to the Internet. It is advertising reachability to Host A's home IP network 192.168.2.0/24 via normal routing mechanisms. There is no physical network on Router A that is addressed using this IP network. In this sense, Host A only has a virtual home network. Hosts that wish to communicate with Host A can either be found in the IP network or in a radio coverage area. If Host C wanted to communicate with Host A, it would send a packet to 192.168.2.2, which would be routed through the IP network to Router A since it is advertising a route to 192.168.2.0/24. Router A would see the packet and redirect it over Tunnel A to the foreign agent Router B. Router B utilizes Radio B to send the IP data over the air interface of the radio access network.

If Host B needed to communicate to Host A, all packets would be sent through Router A for both parties. This is another illustration of the inefficiency of the data path.

It is interesting to note that while Router A maintains a virtual home network for Host A, it also has an Ethernet network on which there is a mobility server. This server will take over connection and service management functions from the Mobile IP home agent. This follows the trends we are seeing of late where control is being removed from devices such as switches. An example of this is the media gateway and media gateway controller functions used in the voice-over-IP MeGaCo architecture.

Summary

This chapter has introduced some key concepts in mobility. To this end, we defined (by example) the terms *nomadicity* and *mobility*. Nomadicity is where a node is required to detach from its servicing network to change locations. Mobility is where a node stays attached to its servicing network as it changes location.

Mobile IP is a way to make nomadicity and mobility transparent to the end user. Moreover, the end user is able to offer IP services to other network users without having to provide constant IP address updates to the subscribers of the service.

Mobile IP can be used in several scenarios. Of particular note is how Mobile IP might be deployed in an enterprise environment in order to facilitate nomadicity.

Practice Questions

1. Where are the tunnel end points found when a host uses a collocated care-of address in Mobile IP?
2. What types of tunneling is supported by Mobile IP?
3. How does a home agent intercept packets destined for a mobile node away from its home link?
4. What nodes in Mobile IP send Gratuitous ARP messages, and when are they sent?
5. Name two ways that a host can get a collocated care-of address in Mobile IP.

IP Version 6

chapter

13

Two problems noted in 1992 by the IETF prompted considerable action regarding the Internet Protocol. One was that the address space was being depleted at a much more rapid pace than expected. IPv6 addresses this problem by expanding the address space. The other problem was that the growing Internet backbone route tables were becoming unwieldy. IP version 6 has mechanisms built in, such as Aggregatable Global Unicast Address allocations, that in conjunction with an allocation strategy will curb the growth of the Internet route tables.

Chapter 1 discussed the construction of the TCP/IP layered architecture, including the network layer, the Internet Protocol (IP). The IP header was dissected to a level necessary to promote the overall topic of this text, IP addressing. Recall that the header takes a structure as shown in Illustration 13-1.

0		1		2	3
0 1 2 3	4 5 6 7	8 9 0 1 2 3 4 5	6 7 8	9 0 1 2 3 4 5 6 7 8 9	0 1
Version	IHL	Type of Service	Total Length		
Identification			Flags	Fragment Offset	
Time to Live		Protocol	Header Checksum		
Source Address					
Destination Address					
Options					
Data					

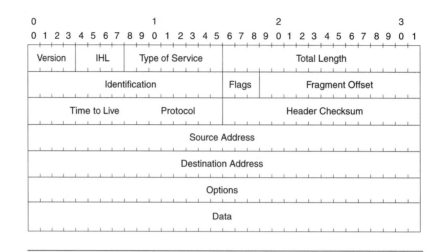

Illustration 13-1 IP Version 4 Header

In this chapter it is no longer sufficient to refer to this structure as the IP header. Instead, it is referred to as the IP version 4 (IPv4) header. This is required because of a new Internet Protocol version that has become necessary due to the depletion of IP address space. This new Internet Protocol is referred to as IP version 6, or simply IPv6, but might have been referred to in the past as IP next generation (IPng).

IPv6 is specified by RFC 2460, "Internet Protocol, Version 6 (IPv6) Specification," December 1998. RFC 2460 states that IPv6 was created to address the following five issues.

- *Expanded addressing capabilities:* Addresses in IP version 6 use a 128-bit field in the IP header. IP version 4 permitted addresses that had a length of only 32 bits. It is obvious that a 128-bit address field permits an increased number of hosts possible in the global address space. In fact, a 128-bit address will allow for

3.4×10^{38} unique IP addresses, whereas a 32-bit address field allowed for only 4.3×10^9 unique addresses.

- *Header format simplification:* Since the size of the header is going to increase as a result of the size of the IPv6 source and destination address, the header was simplified to try to reduce the overhead of the new IP header.
- *Improved support for extensions and options*
- *Flow labeling capability:* This adds the ability to assign handling characteristics for particular types of data traffic, or "flows."
- *Authentication and privacy capabilities:* Extensions are added to support authentication, integrity, and confidentiality of the data.

The last four issues, even combined, would likely not have merited a new version of IP. The clincher, as previously stated, was the need to counter the depletion of globally unique address space while at the same time providing an allocation strategy that combats the growth of the Internet route tables.

Even beyond the sheer increase in IP address space that IPv6 provides, the IPv6 protocol is significantly better than IPv4 in its ability to be processed more rapidly. IPv6 also adds some significant enhancements for the purpose of mobility; this will be discussed briefly at the end of this chapter.

The IP Version 6 Header

Illustration 13-2 shows the fields found in the basic IPv6 header as defined in RFC 2460. A description of each field follows.

0 1 2 3
0 1 2 3 4 5 6 7 8 9 0 1 2 3 4 5 6 7 8 9 0 1 2 3 4 5 6 7 8 9 0 1

Version	Traffic Class	Flow Label	
Payload Length		Next Header	Hop Limit
Source Address			
Destination Address			

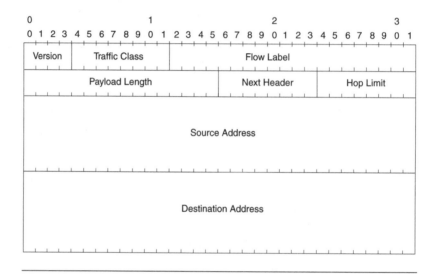

Illustration 13-2 IP Version 6 Header

- *Version:* Remember from Chapter 1 that the classic IPv4 uses a version of "4" in this field. IPv6 uses a "6" in this field, hence IPv4 and IPv6. To date, the Assigned Numbers RFC (RFC 1700) has assigned the versions shown in Table 13-1.

  You will no doubt note that version 6 is assigned to the Simple Internet Protocol (SIP). There were many contributors to the ideas that went into the final design of IPv6. Among the protocols advocated were

Decimal	Keyword	Version
0	—	Reserved
1–3	—	Unassigned
4	IP	Internet Protocol
5	ST	ST datagram mode
6	SIP	Simple Internet Protocol
7	TP/IX	TP/IX: The Next Internet
8	PIP	The P Internet Protocol
9	TUBA	TCP and UPP over Bigger Addresses
10–14	—	Unassigned
15	—	Reserved

Table 13-1 Assigned Internet Version Numbers (RFC 1700)

SIP, SIPP, TP/IX, PIP, and TUBA, some of which you see in Table 13-1. To some degree the final product, IPv6, was an amalgamation of the ideas proposed in these protocols.

- *Differentiated Services (Traffic Class):* An 8-bit field that is used to permit administration of classes and priorities of IPv6 packets in traffic passing through routers. While RFC 2460 (IPv6 specification) does not detail the format of this field (it actually calls this field the *Traffic Class*), RFC 2474, "Definition of the Differentiated Services Field (DS Field) in the IPv4 and IPv6 Headers," does define its intended usage. The DS field is allocated as shown in Illustration 13-3.

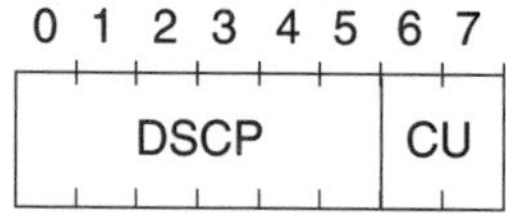

DSCP: differentiated services codepoint
CU: currently unused

Illustration 13-3 DS Field

Bits 0 through 5 comprise the differentiated services codepoint (DSCP). Each router along the forwarding path of the packet may examine the value of the DSCP to determine what kind of special treatments it needs to provide to the packet as it is being forwarded. The router may even alter the DSCP as necessary to provide a specific treatment. In that way, the router can provide differentiated service to all packets with the same DSCP value.

There are several DSCP values that are defined in advance and have "global" significance. One of these is a DSCP of binary 000000. This maps to the default per-hop behavior, which is basically best-effort routing without any preference.

Bits 6 and 7 of the DS field are not currently used.

- *Flow Label:* A 20-bit value used to uniquely identify traffic that should be handled using similar characteristics. This is still an experimental function. It is interesting to note that the length of the flow label is the same as the length of the label in the Multi-Protocol Label Switching (MPLS) header. This might suggest that an MPLS label edge router does not need to add the MPLS header to an IPv6 packet.

- *Payload Length:* A 16-bit value that represents the length in octets of the IP datagram less the length of the header.
- *Next Header:* An 8-bit value that defines the next-higher protocol found in the data portion of the IP datagram. The value expected in this field is the same as is used for the protocol field of an IPv4 header, with the exception of some values added specifically for IPv6 support. An example is ICMPv6, which has a next-header value of 58. See Table 13-2.

Decimal	Protocol
0	Hop-by-Hop Options
1	Internet Control Message
2	Internet Group Management
4	IPv4 in IP (encapsulation)
6	Transmission Control
17	User Datagram
41	IPv6 Header
43	IPv6 Routing Header
44	IPv6 Fragment Header
50	Encapsulating Security Payload Header
51	Authentication Header
55	IP Mobility
58	Internet Control Message Protocol for IPv6

continued

Decimal	Protocol
59	No Header (IPv6)
60	IPv6 Destination Options
101–254	Unassigned
255	Reserved

Table 13-2 Sample IPv6 Next-Header Values

- *Hop Limit:* A formalization of the fact that the IPv4 header field, Time-to-Live (TTL), was a misnomer. The TTL field was actually decremented by 1 by each router that forwarded the packet. Renaming the TTL as "Hop Limit" removes any ambiguity in its meaning. This field has the ability to limit the range that a packet is allowed to traverse before being discarded. This is known as *scope limiting.*
- *Source Address:* A 128-bit value used to define the node that originated the packet.
- *Destination Address:* A 128-bit value used to define the node that is the intended recipient of the packet.
- *Data:* The variable length payload of the IPv6 datagram.

IP Version 6 Address Representation

In IPv4 there were essentially two ways to represent an IP address: in hexadecimal notation, such as 0x0A019C5B, or in dotted decimal notation, such as 10.1.156.91. Even though it is easier to remember names like "Remote_Host" than addresses like those just listed, the addresses of IPv4 are far easier to deal with than the addresses in IPv6. Take the following IPv6 address as an example:

0x2A3F56E466EA210729FEAE67E65FF230

No doubt this is an extreme case, but it is a valid aggregatable global unicast address in IPv6.

To help make the addressing more palatable, there are other, easier-to-use notations. The preferred form is one in which the octets of the IPv6 address are grouped in pairs and are represented in hexadecimal format, separated by colons, as in x:x:x:x:x:x:x:x. The "x" would be replaced by the eight 4-tuple's hexadecimal equivalent. The above IPv6 address would be then represented as

2A3F:56E4:66EA:2107:29FE:AE67:E65F:F230

Although this representation is no shorter than the original, it is more readable. One nice feature about this representation is that leading zeros need not be included in each 4-tuple. Suppose we have the address

2A3F:0000:00EA:0000:0000:0000:005F:F230

That address can be reduced to

2A3F:0:EA:0:0:0:5F:F230

Further, any single run of all zeros in an IP address can be replaced by "::". Suppose, for example, we have the address

2A3F:0000:00EA:0000:0000:0000:005F:F230

That address can be represented instead as

2A3F:0:EA::5F:F230

There can be only one "::" in an IPv6 address. The number of zeros can be easily deduced, based on the number of digits required to represent the number when it has been expanded.

In the transition period while both IPv4 and IPv6 addresses must be used, a mechanism exists that permits reference to IPv4 addresses from within an IPv6 address. In this case, the last 32 bits can be referenced in dotted decimal notation, as was used in IPv4. IPv6 addresses with embedded IPv4 addresses are assigned out of the 0000:0000 format prefix space. The following addresses are all equivalent IPv6 addresses with an embedded IPv4 address:

0000:0000:0000:0000:0000:0000:0A01:9C5B

::A01:9C5B

::10.1.156.91

It is obvious that with 128 bits of address, any representation — no matter how efficiently it can be reduced — might be best represented by a human with a name via domain name services.

IP Version 6 Network Prefix Representation

IPv6 uses similar notation as was used with classless interdomain routing (CIDR) in IPv4. The format is

IPv6_Address/Prefix_length

or

IPv6_Network/Prefix_length

The IPv6_Address or IPv6_Network can be in any legal form of IPv6 address notation. The Prefix_length specifies how many bits of the IPv6_Address are significant as a prefix. For instance, 2A3F:0:EA::/48 might represent an enterprise's IP address allocation. This customer has 80 bits of address space available for host addresses and subnets.

IP Version 6 Addressing

The IP version 6 address is 16 octets, or 128 bits, long. Like the Class A through E addresses of IP version 4, a format prefix (FP) embedded in the address determines its usage. Table 13-3 lists the prefixes that had been defined at the time of this writing and the usage that the prefix denotes.

Allocation	Format Prefix (binary)	Fraction of Address Space
Reserved	0000 0000	1/256
Unassigned	0000 0001	1/256
Reserved for NSAP allocation	0000 001	1/128
Reserved for IPX allocation	0000 010	1/128
Unassigned	0000 011	1/128
Unassigned	0000 1	1/32
Unassigned	0001	1/16
Aggregatable Global Unicast Addresses	001	1/8
Unassigned	010	1/8
Unassigned	011	1/8
Unassigned	100	1/8

continued

Allocation	Format Prefix (binary)	Fraction of Address Space
Unassigned	101	1/8
Unassigned	110	1/8
Unassigned	1110	1/16
Unassigned	1111 0	1/32
Unassigned	1111 10	1/64
Unassigned	1111 110	1/128
Unassigned	1111 1110 0	1/512
Link-local use addresses	1111 1110 10	1/1024
Site-local use addresses	1111 1110 11	1/1024
Multicast addresses	1111 1111	1/256

Table 13-3 IP Version 6 Address Partitioning (RFC 1884)

Unicast Addresses

As you can see from Table 13-3, there are six allocations from the entire address pool that are used for some form of unicast addressing:

- *IPv6 addresses with embedded IPv4 addresses* (0000 0000 FP)
- *NSAP allocation:* OSI network service access point over IPv6 addresses
- *IPX allocation:* IPX over IPv6 addresses
- *Aggregatable Global Unicast Addresses:* The largest allocation pool comprised of one-eighth of the total IPv6 address space. This address pool is managed by an

overall hierarchy plan as dictated in RFC 2374, "An IPv6 Aggregatable Global Unicast Address Format."

- *Link-local use addresses:* Local use only (routers do not forward) addresses used on a single link (network). Its uses include auto-address configuration and neighbor discovery.
- *Site-local use addresses:* Addresses used at a single site that are not forwarded by a router onto a link that is not an IP subnet of the site-local network in use.

Site-local addresses are roughly analogous to the private internet network allocations set aside by RFC 1918, "Address Allocation for Private Internets." The difference in IPv6 is that routers did not inhibit the transmission of a packet outside of the site-local network in IPv4 except by filters.

The only two special unicast addresses defined in IPv6 are

- *Unspecified address:* 0:0:0:0:0:0:0:0 or ::
- *Loopback address:* 0:0:0:0:0:0:0:1 or ::1

The unspecified address is used in the same manner as the all-0s address in IPv4. It denotes "this host" and should be used only as the source address in an IPv6 datagram. The loopback address is used to permit a host to send an IPv6 datagram to itself. This is the same purpose that the loopback address, 127.x.x.x, was used for in IPv4. IPv6 packets containing the loopback address should never be sent outside the node's network interface.

Aggregatable Global Unicast Addresses

As mentioned before, RFC 2373 has allocated one-eighth of the IPv6 address space to Aggregatable Global Unicast Addresses. RFC 2374 specifies how that address space, with a format prefix of 001 (binary), should be managed. Illustration 13-4 depicts the way that RFC 2374 partitions the remaining 125 bits of the unicast addresses. Each field is described below.

3	13	8	24	16	64 bits
FP	TLA ID	RES	NLA ID	SLA ID	Interface ID

Illustration 13-4 Aggregatable Global Unicast Address Divisions

- *FP:* Format Prefix (defined in RFC 2373) as 001 for Aggregatable Global Unicast Address allocations.
- *TLA ID:* Top-Level Aggregation Identifier. Since there are 13 bits used for this field, it permits 8192 unique TLA Identifiers. Only the largest allocation authorities will be given TLA IDs and address space allocations.
- *RES:* Reserved. These eight bits have been reserved in case either the TLA ID field needs to be lengthened to support more than 8192 TLAs or the NLA ID needs to be lengthened to support more NLAs.
- *NLA ID:* Next-Level Aggregation Identifier. This field of 24 bits can be used by the TLA allocation authorities to subdivide their address space for next-tier service providers. If the space were allocated in a flat hierarchy, it could handle as many as 16,777,216 address space suballocations. Each suballocation could have as many as 65,536 IP subnets. Each subnet could theoretically have as many as 18,446,744,073,709,551,616

hosts! But that's getting ahead of myself. It is actually more likely that a TLA ID allocation authority will use a hierarchical allocation method when leasing addresses to next-level service providers. This will be much more efficient for the Internet route tables.

For instance, the NLA ID could be subdivided as shown in Illustration 13-5. The TLA could allocate five bits of the NLA ID field to a subordinate address authority, NLA1. NLA1 could allocate five bits of its 19 remaining NLA ID bits to a subordinate allocation authority, NLA2. Likewise with NLA3. NLA3 would have nine bits of address space to allocate IPv6 addresses to enterprises and other end users.

5	19 bits	16	64 bits
NLA1	Site ID	SLA ID	Interface ID

5	14	16	64 bits
NLA2	Site ID	SLA ID	Interface ID

5	9	16	64 bits
NLA3	Site ID	SLA ID	Interface ID

Illustration 13-5 Possible Subdivisions for the NLA ID Field

- *SLA-ID:* Site-Level Aggregation Identifier. This field has 16 bits and is available to the end users of the IPv6 address space. This field gives the end-user entity as many as 65,536 unique subnets, although it is likely that this field will be used in a hierarchy to reduce the complexity of the route table at the site. If the number of subnets is not adequate for the enterprise, it is possible for the enterprise to obtain more than one SLA-ID from their IP address allocation authority.

- *Interface ID:* Interface Identifier. These identifiers are used to identify a specific interface on a link. They must be unique on each link. Since 64 bits are being used for the Interface ID, it is possible to have as many as 18,446,744,073,709,551,616 hosts on a given link (although the likelihood of this happening is quite slim). The Interface ID used in IPv6 Aggregatable Global Unicast Addresses are required to be constructed using the IEEE's EUI-64 format. Details of this format can be found in the IEEE's "Guidelines for 64-bit Global Identifier (EUI-64) Registration Authority" on their *http://standards.ieee.org* Web site. With EUI-48 addresses (common MAC address format), there were 24 bits assigned to the company ID (the manufacturer of the interface card) and 24 bits assigned for each manufacturer to assign as unique serial numbers or identifiers that would guarantee the global uniqueness of the overall EUI-48 identifier. EUI-64 lengthens the number of bits available to each manufacturer from 24 to 40, which gives them greater management freedom as more devices worldwide become IP enabled. If a device is using an interface card that implements EUI-64 format identifiers, this identifier will be used as the Aggregatable Global Unicast Address Interface ID. If the device uses EUI-48 format identifiers for its interface cards, the EUI-48 ID will be adapted to EUI-64 format and used. Not all interfaces have EUI-48 or EUI-64 identifiers; such interfaces will be locally administered and assigned the Interface ID portion with the only stipulation being that it must be unique for the link that it is attached to.

Multicast Addresses

Table 13-3 indicates that any IPv6 address that has binary 1111 1111 in the high-order bits of the address is a multicast address. IP version 4 multicast addresses were discussed in Chapter 11. IP version 6 multicasts are slightly more structured than their IPv4 counterparts. The structure of an IPv6 multicast address is shown in Illustration 13-6.

8	4	4	112 bits
1111 1111	flgs	scop	group ID

Illustration 13-6 IP Version 6 Multicast Address Format

The three fields defined within an IPv6 multicast address are as follows.

- *flgs:* A set of four binary flags used to control the treatment of the multicast address. The flags are

  000T

  The three high-order flags are reserved. The fourth flag, the low-order flag, is used to discriminate between addresses that are well known and assigned by the IANA (T = 0) and those that are transient addresses, or not permanently assigned (T = 1).
- *scop:* A 4-bit field used to specify to the forwarding algorithm how the multicast packet should be "scope

limited." In IPv4, the only way to limit the scope of a multicast packet was to set the Time-to-Live (TTL) in the IP header to a low value. The Hop Limit field of IPv6 can still be used in this manner; however, the scope value imbedded in the multicast address has the ability to limit the scope of the multicast packet at a more abstract organizational level. The values for the field are defined as shown in Table 13-4.

Value	Field
0	Reserved
1	Node-local scope
2	Link-local scope
3	Unassigned
4	Unassigned
5	Site-local scope
6	Unassigned
7	Unassigned
8	Organization-local scope
9	Unassigned
A	Unassigned
B	Unassigned
C	Unassigned
D	Unassigned
E	Global scope
F	Reserved

Table 13-4 IP Version 6 Multicast Address Scope Values

- *group ID:* A 112-bit field within the multicast address that identifies the multicast group that is the destination for the multicast IPv6 packet.

The following well-known multicast addresses have been defined in the context of IP version 6 by RFC 2373, "IP Version 6 Addressing Architecture." (Note that the "s" indicates the scope-limiting field.)

• *Reserved multicast addresses:*	FF0s:0:0:0:0:0:0:0 (FF0s::)
• *Node-local all-nodes address:*	FF01:0:0:0:0:0:0:1 (FF01::1)
• Link-local all-nodes address:	FF02:0:0:0:0:0:0:1 (FF02::1)
• Node-local all-routers address:	FF01:0:0:0:0:0:0:2 (FF01::2)
• Link-local all-routers address:	FF02:0:0:0:0:0:0:2 (FF02::2)
• Site-local all-routers address:	FF05:0:0:0:0:0:0:2 (FF05::2)
• Solicited-node address:	FF02:0:0:0:0:1:FFXX:XXXX (FF02::1:FFXX:XXXX), where XX:XXXX represents the 24 low-order bits of a node's unicast address

IP version 6 does not define an address to be used for broadcasts. Instead, it uses a broad multicast to accomplish the same function that broadcasts were used for in IPv4.

Anycast Addresses

Anycast addressing, a new concept introduced in IP version 6, allows a device to send a packet to any of one or more network interfaces (usually the closest) that have been assigned to a single anycast address. Therefore, an anycast address is a special case of a unicast address. According to RFC 2460, if you assign the same unicast address to multiple interfaces, most likely on different devices, you will be defining an anycast address. RFC 2526 defines a set of reserved anycast addresses within each subnet prefix. It does this by setting aside the highest 128 interface identifiers in each subnet. A packet that is sent to an anycast address will be delivered to only one of the devices that has the IPv6 address specified in the datagram's destination IP address. Anycast addressing is still not very well understood but it could be a handy way of finding resources on a subnet. IPv6 anycast can be used in Mobile IP for a node to find its home agent.

IP Version 6 Address Allocation

IP version 6 is the long-term solution to address space depletion. Another problem that was recognized and addressed by classless interdomain routing (CIDR) is that of explosive route table growth in the Internet. IP version 6 does little to stave off this problem. However, some of the planning that went into the design of IPv6 will, along with a planned allocation methodology, help to reduce the route table explosion problem.

First and foremost, IP version 6 will be a fresh start. Haphazard allocations will not be made. Address allocation authority will be decentralized, and individual authorities will have to provide rigorous administration of their respective address allotments. Addresses will initially be allocated based on one scheme: the IPv6 Aggregatable Global Unicast Address scheme introduced in RFC 2373 and detailed in RFC 2374. That is, they will be allocated from the IPv6 addresses that begin with binary "001."

The addresses will be allocated in such a way that they will collapse into as small a route as possible for advertisement on the IPv6 Internet. If this sounds an awful lot like CIDR, there's a good reason; RFC 1887, "An Architecture for IPv6 Unicast Address Allocation," was edited by the same folks who edited RFC 1518, "An Architecture for IP Address Allocation with CIDR": Yakov Rekhter and Tony Li. A great many of the allocation and aggregation concepts presented in RFC 1518 made their way into RFC 1887. In fact, it is so similar that I will forgo a discussion on the topic here.

IP Version 6 Extension Headers

As mentioned in the early part of this chapter, IPv6 has a simplified header compared to the header found in IPv4. Only the most essential header elements are included in the base IPv6 header. To provide extended services in IPv6, the protocol uses extension headers to increase its capabilities. RFC 2460, the IPv6 specification, defines several of the common extension headers, which are described briefly in the following sections. Refer back to Table 13-2 for specific Next-Header values.

Hop-by-Hop Options Header (0)

Inclusion of a Hop-by-Hop Options header mandates that every node along a packet's route to the destination must examine and act on the option information. This is an efficient mechanism for distribution of control and signaling information since the Hop-by-Hop option can piggyback on other IP packets. A Hop-by-Hop Options header is shown in Illustration 13-7 and a description of each field follows.

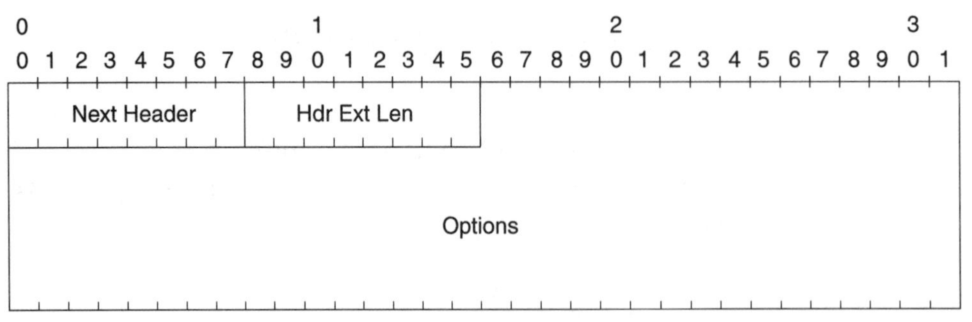

Illustration 13-7 Hop-by-hop Options Header

- *Next Header:* 8-bit value. Identifies the type of header immediately following the Hop-by-Hop Options header. Uses the values shown in Table 13-2.
- *Hdr Ext Len:* 8-bit unsigned integer. Length of the Hop-by-Hop Options header in 8-octet units, not including the first 8 octets.
- *Options:* Individual options are defined as shown here.

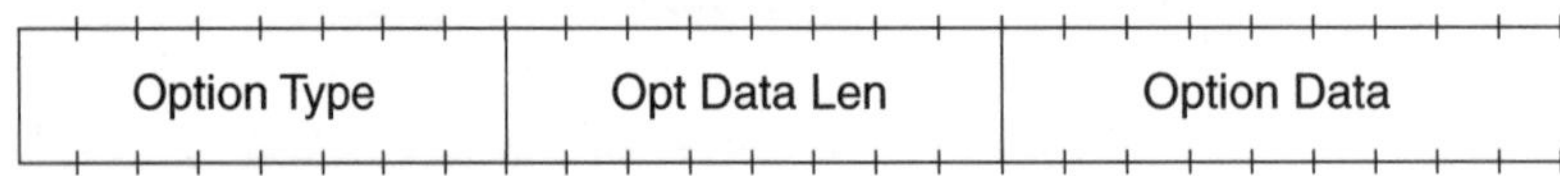

- *Option Type:* 8-bit identifier of the type of option.
- *Opt Data Len:* 8-bit unsigned integer. Length of the Option Data field of this option, in octets.
- *Option Data:* Variable-length field. Option-Type-specific data.

Destination Options Header (60)

Inclusion of the Destination Options header mandates that only the destination node for this IP packet should examine and act on the option information. Some notable option types are shown in Table 13-5.

Type	Name
0xC6	Binding Update option
0x07	Binding Acknowledgment option
0x08	Binding Request option
0xC9	Home Address option

Table 13-5 Destination Option Types

These Destination options are defined in the Internet Draft, "Mobility Support in IP," which defines Mobile IPv6. They will be discussed in the Mobility section later in this chapter. You probably noticed that the Binding Update and the Home Address options had a hexadecimal value of 0xC6 and 0xC9. The reason for this is that the high-order two bits of the Type field indicate how a node should react to the Destination option if the Type field is unknown. A node that receives an IPv6 packet with a Binding Update or Home Address option but does not know how to handle those types of options should discard the packet and send back an ICMP error message to the source of the packet. A node that doesn't know how to handle a Binding Acknowledgment or Binding Request option should skip the option and continue processing the IPv6 header.

The Destination Options header is shown in Illustration 13-8. Each field is described below.

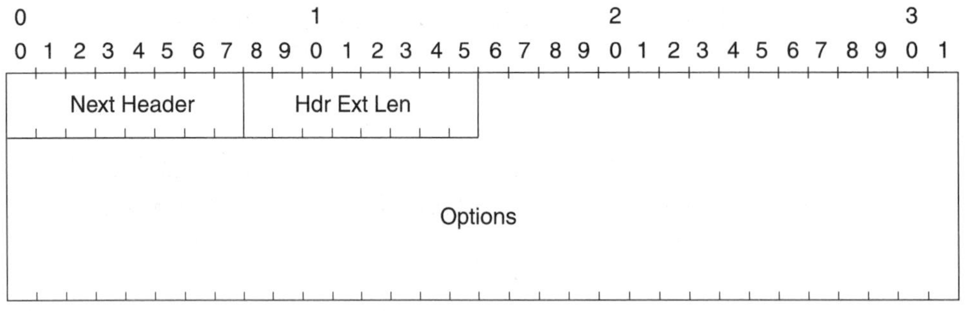

Illustration 13-8 Destination Options Header

- *Next Header:* 8-bit value. Identifies the type of header immediately following the Destination Options header. Uses the values in Table 13-2.
- *Hdr Ext Len:* 8-bit unsigned integer. Length of the Destination Options header in 8-octet units, not including the first 8 octets.
- *Options:* Variable-length field. The format for an individual option is the same as used by Hop-by-Hop options.

Routing Header (43)

The IPv6 Routing header allows a packet to be routed through specified intermediate nodes en route to its final destination. The function of the routing header is very similar to the Loose Source Routing option found in IPv4. The source of the packet determines which nodes should be visited and codes these addresses into the destination IP address field (for the first hop visited) and into the Type 0 routing header address fields (other intermediate destinations and the final destination) as required.

Mobile IPv6 makes use of the Routing header, as will be explained later. RFC 2460 defines the Routing header mechanics in detail. The format of the Routing header is shown in Illustration 13-9, and a description of each field follows.

0 1 2 3 4 5 6 7	8 9 0 1 2 3 4 5	6 7 8 9 0 1 2 3	4 5 6 7 8 9 0 1
Next Header	Hdr Ext Len	Routing Type =0	Segments Left
Reserved			
Address[1]			
Address[2]			
. . .			
Address[n]			

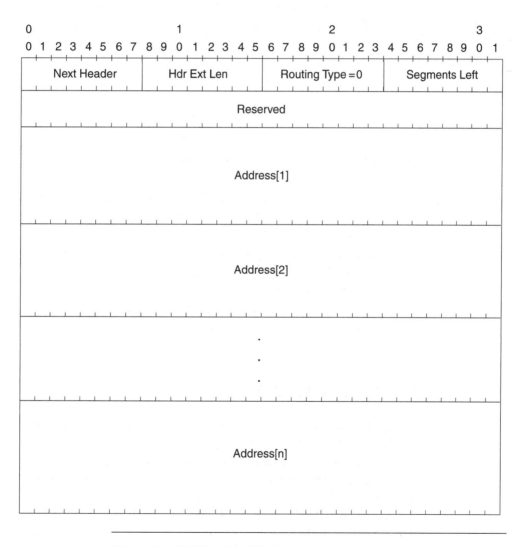

Illustration 13-9 Routing Header

- *Next Header:* 8-bit value. Identifies the type of header immediately following the Routing header.
- *Hdr Ext Len:* 8-bit unsigned integer. Length of the Routing header in 8-octet (64-bit) units.
- *Routing Type:* 8-bit identifier of a particular Routing header variant. Only Routing Type = 0 has been defined at the time of this writing.
- *Segments Left:* 8-bit unsigned integer. Number of route segments remaining.
- *Reserved:* 32-bit reserved field. Padded with zeros to preserve 64-bit alignment.
- *Address[1 . . . n]:* List of 128-bit addresses, numbered 1 to *n*.

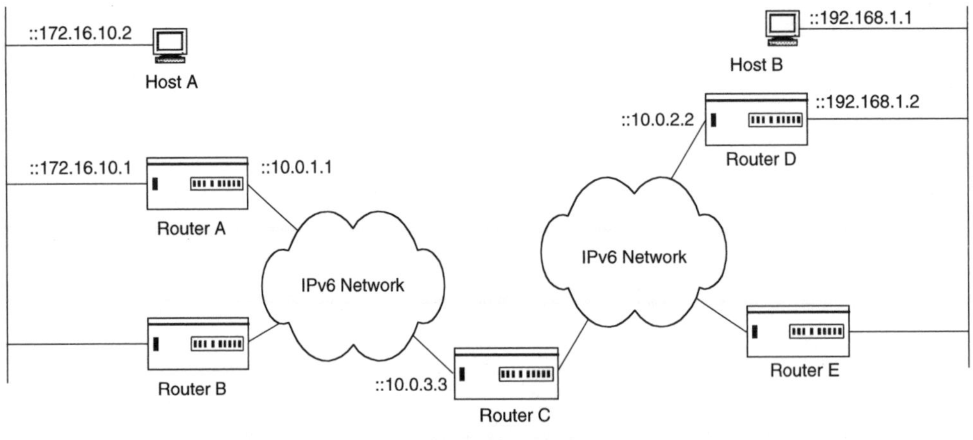

Illustration 13-10 Routing Header Example

As shown in Illustration 13-10, if Host A wished to send a packet to Host B via Router A, Router C, and Router D, Host A would need to send the following IP packet.

IPv6 Header

Version = 4

Next Header = 43

Source Address = ::172.16.10.2

Destination Address = ::172.16.10.1

Routing Header

Next Header = 6

Hdr Ext Len = 3

Type = 0

Segments Left = 3

Address[1] = ::10.0.3.3

Address[2] = ::10.0.2.2

Address[3] = ::192.168.1.1

TCP Header, etc.

Upon receipt of the packet, Router A sees that there is a routing header where the number of segments left is greater than 0. It swaps Address[1] with Destination Address in the IPv6 header, decrements the Segments Left counter, and sends the packet toward its new destination, ::10.0.3.3. Note that it could take several hops to get to the new Destination Address. This is why it is similar to Loose Source Routing and not Strict Source Routing. At this point, the packet received by Router C looks like the following.

IPv6 Header

Version = 4

Next Header = 43

Source Address = ::172.16.10.2

Destination Address = ::10.0.3.3

Routing Header

Next Header = 6

Hdr Ext Len = 3

Type = 0

Segments Left = 2

Address[1] = ::172.16.10.1

Address[2] = ::10.0.2.2

Address[3] = ::192.168.1.1

TCP Header, etc.

Because there are two segments left and there are three addresses in the Routing header, Router C knows to swap the IPv6 Destination Address with Address[2] in the Routing header. Having done this, Router C decrements the Segments Left counter and transmits the packet toward 10.0.2.2. The packet received by Router D now looks like the following.

IPv6 Header

Version = 4

Next Header = 43

Source Address = ::172.16.10.2

Destination Address = ::10.0.2.2

Routing Header

Next Header = 6

Hdr Ext Len = 3

Type = 0

Segments Left = 1

Address[1] = ::172.16.10.1

Address[2] = ::10.0.3.3

Address[3] = ::192.168.1.1

TCP Header, etc.

Router D recognizes that the packet contains a Routing header and that the Segments Left counter is now at 1. So Router D swaps Address[3] with the Destination Address, decrements the Segments Left counter, and forwards the packet to its true final destination, 192.168.1.1. When Host B receives the packet, it now looks like the following.

IPv6 Header

Version = 4

Next Header = 43

Source Address = ::172.16.10.2

Destination Address = ::192.168.1.1

Routing Header

Next Header = 6

Hdr Ext Len = 3

Type = 0

Segments Left = 0

Address[1] = ::172.16.10.1

Address[2] = ::10.0.3.3

Address[3] = ::10.0.2.2

TCP Header, etc.

Host B sees that there is a Routing header but the Segments Left counter is at 0. This is a trigger for the IPv6 node to process the remainder of the packet which, in this case, is TCP.

Note that the return packet from Host B to Host A need not follow the same route back as was taken to get there in the first place. There is no option in Type 0 routing for the response to be forced to visit the same nodes during the return leg. If there were, it would be a trivial matter to shuffle the addresses in the received IP packet with Routing header and use the values for the response packets.

Fragment Header (44)

A Fragment header is used when a source IPv6 node wishes to send a packet that is larger than the Path MTU to the destination address. Packets may only be fragmented by the source node. Fragment headers are only processed by the destination node. Fragmentation is not relevant to the current discussion but out of fairness, Illustration 13-11 shows the format of a Fragment header, and a description of each field follows.

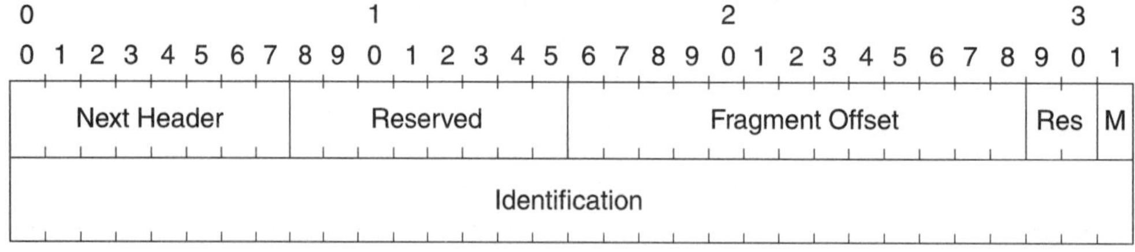

Illustration 13-11 Fragment Header

- *Next Header:* 8-bit value. Identifies the initial header type of the Fragmentable Part of the original packet.
- *Reserved:* 8-bit reserved field. Initialized to zero.
- *Fragment Offset:* 13-bit unsigned integer. The offset, in 8-octet units, of the data following this header,

relative to the start of the Fragmentable Part of the original packet.

- *Res:* 2-bit reserved field. Initialized to zero.
- *M flag:* 1 = more fragments; 0 = last fragment.
- *Identification:* 32 bits. Unique ID of the fragmented packet.

Authentication Header (51)

The IP Authentication header (AH) is used to provide connectionless integrity and data origin authentication for IP datagrams, and to provide protection against replays. The Authentication header is defined in RFC 2402, "IP Authentication Header," and is not relevant to the current discussion. For completeness, Illustration 13-12 shows the Authentication header format. Each field is described below.

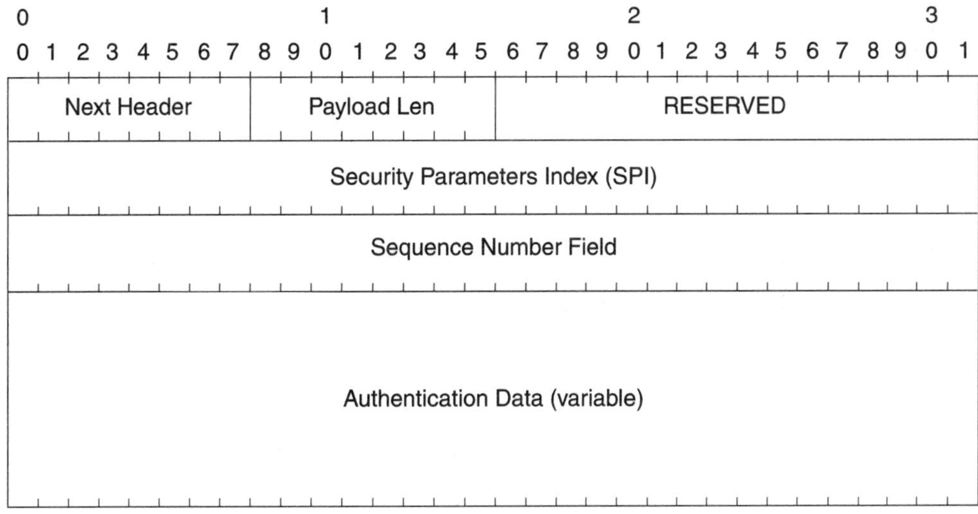

Illustration 13-12 Authentication Header

- *Next Header:* 8-bit value. Identifies the type of the next payload after the Authentication Header
- *Payload Len:* 8-bit field. Specifies the length of AH in 32-bit words (4-byte units), minus "2."
- *RESERVED:* 16-bit reserved field. Initialized to zero.
- *Security Parameters Index (SPI):* An arbitrary 32-bit value that, in combination with the destination IP address and security protocol (AH), uniquely identifies the Security Association for this datagram.
- *Sequence Number Field:* Unsigned 32-bit field. Contains a counter that increases with each packet transmitted. Used to prevent "replay attacks."
- *Authentication Data:* A variable-length field that contains the Integrity Check Value (ICV) for this packet.

Encapsulating Security Payload Header (50)

The Encapsulating Security Payload (ESP) header is used to provide confidentiality, data origin authentication, connectionless integrity, an antireplay service (a form of partial sequence integrity), and limited traffic flow confidentiality. ESP may be applied alone, in combination with the IP Authentication header, or in tunnel mode. The ESP header, like the AH header, is beyond the scope of the discussion. For more details, please refer to RFC 2406, "IP Encapsulating Security Payload (ESP)." The ESP header format is shown in Illustration 13-13, and a description of each field follows.

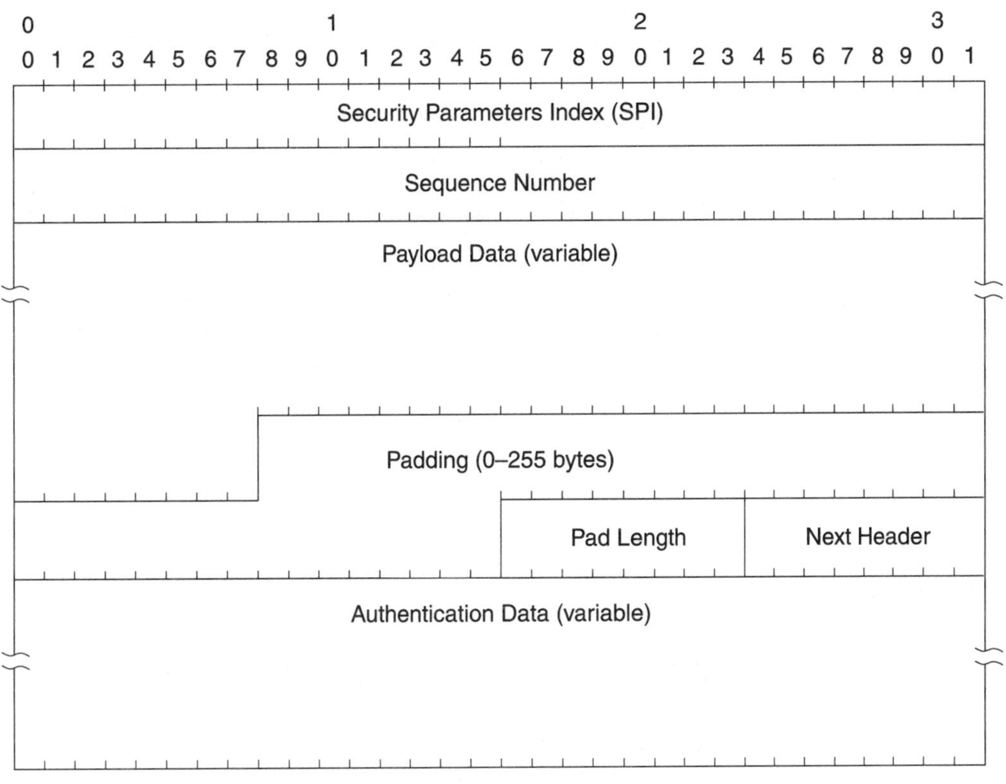

Illustration 13-13 Encapsulating Security Payload Header

- *Security Parameters Index (SPI):* An arbitrary 32-bit value that, in combination with the destination IP address and security protocol (AH), uniquely identifies the Security Association for this datagram.
- *Sequence Number:* Unsigned 32-bit field. Contains a counter that increases with each packet transmitted. Used to prevent "replay attacks."

- *Payload Data:* A variable-length field containing data described by the Next-Header field.
- *Padding:* Required by encryption. 0 to 255 bytes.
- *Pad Length:* Unsigned 8-bit field. Indicates the number of pad bytes immediately preceding it.
- *Next Header:* 8-bit value. Identifies the type of the next payload after the ESP Header.
- *Payload Len:* 8-bit field. Specifies the length of AH in 32-bit words (4-byte units), minus "2."
- *RESERVED:* 16-bit reserved field. Initialized to zero.
- *Authentication Data:* A variable-length field that contains the Integrity Check Value (ICV) computed over the ESP packet minus the Authentication Data.

IPv6 Header (41)

RFC 2473, "Generic Packet Tunneling in IPv6 Specification," defines how it is possible to create an IPv6-within-IPv6 tunnel by using a Next-Header value equal to 41. This value indicates that the next header is another IPv6 header with new source and destination IP addresses. These addresses identify the tunnel end points. Since this chapter began with a discussion of the format of the IPv6 header, it is unnecessary to repeat it here. Besides, doing so would cause a dangerous recursive loop.

ICMPv6 Header (58)

RFC 2463, "Internet Control Message Protocol (ICMPv6) for the Internet Protocol Version 6 (IPv6) Specification," defines the framework for the ICMPv6 protocol. Though ICMPv6 is not actually considered a header extension to IPv6, it does still operate within layer 3. RFC 2463 defines the header format as shown in Illustration 13-14. A description of each field follows.

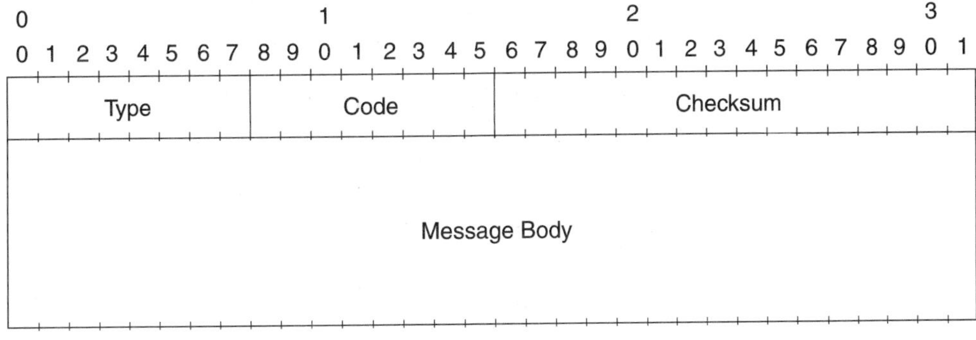

Illustration 13-14 ICMPv6 Header

- *Type:* Indicates the type of the message. Its value determines the format of the remaining data. If the high-order bit of the Type field is set to 0, it denotes an error message. If the high-order bit is set to 1, it is an informational message. Examples of ICMPv6 types are shown in Table 13-6.

Type	Message
1	Destination Unreachable
2	Packet Too Big
3	Time Exceeded
4	Parameter Problem
128	Echo Request
129	Echo Reply

continued

Type	Message
133	Router Solicitation
134	Router Advertisement
135	Neighbor Solicitation
136	Neighbor Advertisement
137	Redirect

Table 13-6 ICMPv6 Message Types

- *Code:* Depends on the message type and is used to create an additional level of message granularity. For instance, the ICMPv6 Destination Unreachable error message has several codes that are used to further define the nature of the error, as shown in Table 13-7.

Code	Message
0	No Route to Destination
1	Communication with Destination Administratively Prohibited
3	Address Unreachable
4	Port Unreachable

Table 13-7 ICMPv6 Destination Unreachable Codes

- *Checksum:* Used to detect data corruption in the ICMPv6 message and an IPv6 pseudoheader. For more information, you should definitely take a look at RFC 2460.

One thing is worth noting about the development of the ICMPv6 functions. RFC 2463 may have laid out the framework for ICMPv6 by defining the header format, but by itself, as defined in that RFC, ICMPv6 is not fully developed. RFC 2461, "Neighbor Discovery for IP Version 6 (IPv6)," defined five ICMP message types that gave ICMPv6 the functions of both ARP and ICMP for IPv4 in a single IPv6 protocol. These are message types 133 through 137 listed in Table 13-6, and are discussed in more detail in the Neighbor Discovery section in this chapter. The Type 134 Router Advertisement message format was modified in the "Mobility Support in IPv6" Internet Draft to include Home Agent Advertisement support. This is discussed in the Mobile IPv6 section in this chapter.

Upper-Layer Protocol Header (e.g., 6 = TCP, 17 = UDP)

At this point, we have actually gotten out of layer 3 and begun to work in layer 4. There is no TCPv6 or UDPv6. IPv6 was designed to be compatible with TCP and UDP at the IP interface. TCP and UDP, as well as applications that run on top of them, cannot discern whether IPv4 or IPv6 is operating at the network layer.

No Header (59)

The Next-Header value of 59 indicates that the current header is the last header; there are no more headers. Hop-by-Hop and Destination options can be used to "piggyback" information or requests on a TCP or UDP data packet, but it is possible for that same information or request to be sent if no data packet were available to piggyback onto. Such a packet would look like the following.

IPv6 Header

Version = 4

Next Header = 60

Source Address = ::172.16.10.2

Destination Address = ::192.168.1.1

Destination Options

Next Header = 59 (no header)

Hdr Ext Len = 3

Type = 0xC9 (home address)

Extension Header Ordering

The IP Version 6 specification says that an IPv6 node must accept and attempt to process the IPv6 extension headers in any order that they are placed in an IPv6 packet. However, the specification makes a strong recommendation that these headers should appear in a specific order. The order that RFC 2460 recommends is shown in Table 13-8.

Header
IPv6 Header
Hop-by-Hop Options Header
Destination Options Header (for options to be processed by the first destination that appears in the current IPv6 header's destination address plus subsequent destinations listed in the Routing header)
Routing Header
Fragment Header

Authentication Header

Encapsulation Security Payload Header

Destination Options Header (for options to be processed only by the final destination for the current IPv6 header. Because generic packet tunneling permits more than one IPv6 header per packet, it is not correct to say that the Destination Options header is to be processed by the final destination of the packet.)

IPv6 Header or Upper-Layer Protocol Header or No Header

Table 13-8 Order of Headers Recommended by RFC

The IPv6 specification RFC also recommends that each header appear only once per IPv6 header except for the Destination Options header, which can appear as many as two times. The Destination Options header can appear once before the Routing header and once before the Upper-Layer Protocol header, as previously stated in the Upper-Layer Protocol Header section. RFC 2473, "Generic Packet Tunneling in IPv6 Specification," allows for more than one IPv6 header per packet to facilitate IPv6-within-IPv6 tunneling. Where there is more than one IPv6 header per packet, each IPv6 header can have its own set of extension headers.

Neighbor Discovery for IP Version 6

As previously mentioned, although RFC 2463 defines ICMPv6, RFC 2461 defines five ICMPv6 message types that give the protocol ARP, ICMP router discovery, and ICMP redirect capabilities. Specifically, these messages enable router discovery, prefix discovery, parameter discovery, address autoconfiguration, address resolution, next-hop determination, neighbor unreachability detection, duplicate address detection, and redirect. These added message types are shown in Table 13-9.

Type	Message
133	Router Solicitation
134	Router Advertisement
135	Neighbor Solicitation
136	Neighbor Advertisement
137	Redirect

Table 13-9 Additional Message Types Defined by RFC 2461

Because the high-order bit of the message type is set, we know that these are informative ICMP message types as opposed to ICMP error messages. I will provide only a brief introduction to these message types. For more information, please take a look at RFC 2461, "Neighbor Discovery for IP Version 6 (IPv6)."

Router Advertisement (134)

Periodically, or in response to a solicitation, routers on a link must send an ICMP Router Advertisement. The format of this advertisement is shown in Illustration 13-15.

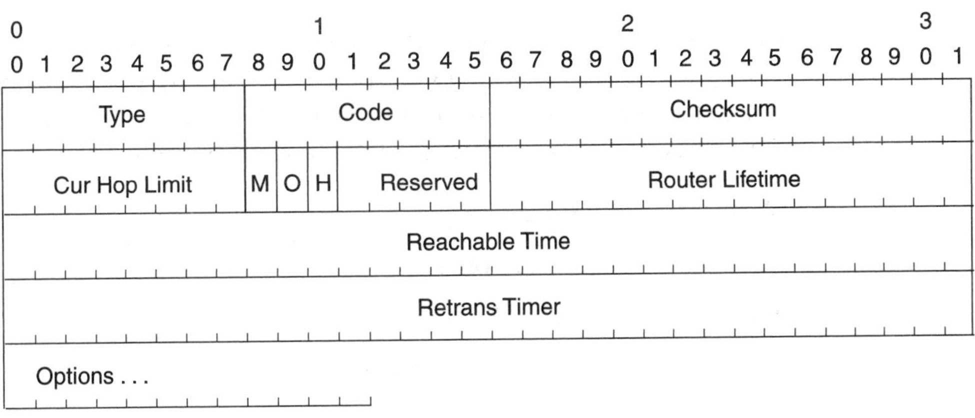

Illustration 13-15 ICMP Router Advertisement

It is worth noting that when a router sends an ICMP Router Advertisement, it does this with a source IP address equal to the link-local IP address for the interface from which the Router Advertisement is sent. The destination IP address could be the link-local all-nodes multicast address of FF02::1 or, if in response to a solicitation, the source address of the node soliciting for a Router Advertisement update. Of course, the IPv6 Next-Header value is ultimately set to 58 to indicate an ICMP message.

The Router Advertisement fields are described in the list below.

- *Type:* 134
- *Code:* 0
- *Checksum:* The ICMP checksum.
- *Cur Hop Limit:* 8-bit unsigned integer. The default value that should be placed in the Hop Count field of the IP header for outgoing IP packets.

- *M:* 1-bit Managed Address Configuration flag. When set, hosts use the administered (stateful) protocol for address autoconfiguration in addition to any addresses autoconfigured using stateless address autoconfiguration.
- *O:* 1-bit Other Stateful Configuration flag. When set, hosts use the administered (stateful) protocol for autoconfiguration of other (nonaddress) information.
- *H:* 1-bit Home Agent flag. Set to indicate that the router sending the advertisement has the ability to act as a Mobile IPv6 home agent.
- *Reserved:* A 5-bit reserved field. Initialized to zeros.
- *Router Lifetime:* 16-bit unsigned integer. The lifetime associated with the default router in units of seconds. The maximum value corresponds to 18.2 hours. A Router Lifetime of 0 indicates that the router is not a default router and *should not* appear on the default router list.
- *Reachable Time:* 32-bit unsigned integer. The time, in milliseconds, that a node assumes a neighbor is reachable after having received a reachability confirmation. Used by the Neighbor Unreachability Detection algorithm.
- *Retrans Timer:* 32-bit unsigned integer. The time, in milliseconds, between retransmitted Neighbor Solicitation messages. Used by address resolution and the Neighbor Unreachability Detection algorithm.

The next list shows the options available for the options field.

- *Source link layer address:* The link layer address of the interface from which the Router Advertisement is sent.
- *MTU:* Should be sent on links that have a variable MTU.

- *Prefix Information:* Specify all the prefixes that are onlink and/or are used for address autoconfiguration (which will be discussed later in this chapter).

Router Solicitation (133)

When a host first comes up on an IPv6 network, it may need to discover which routers can act as its default gateway. The host can either wait until the routers send their next Router Advertisement message or they can solicit for a Router Advertisement. If the host solicits for the advertisement, the advertisement will be sent back to the requesting host via unicast routing. Illustration 13-16 shows what a Router Solicitation message looks like.

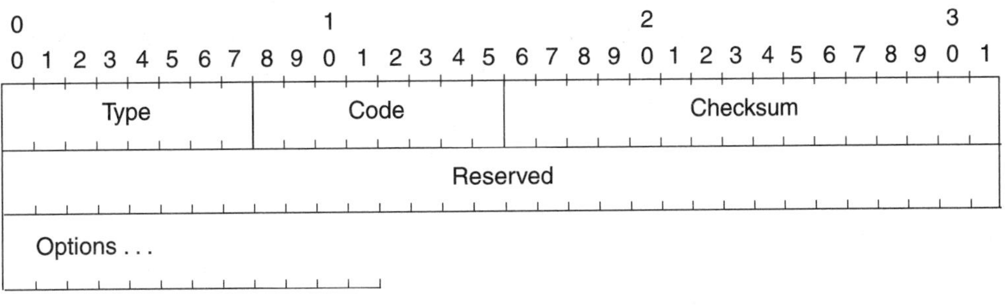

Illustration 13-16 ICMP Router Solicitation

In the IP header, the source address will be the IP address that was bound to the sending interface. It could also be the unspecified address (::) if the sending interface had no IP address assigned to it. The Router Solicitation fields are listed here.

- *Type:* 133
- *Code:* 0

- *Checksum:* The ICMP checksum.
- *Reserved:* Reserved. Initialize to zeros.

There is only one valid option for the Options field:

- *Source link layer address:* The link layer address of the sender, if known.

Neighbor Advertisement (136)

Periodically, or in response to a solicitation, nodes on a link must send an ICMP Neighbor Advertisement. This Neighbor Advertisement serves essentially the same purpose as ARP did in IPv4: It advertises the link layer address associated with an IP layer address. The format of this advertisement is shown in Illustration 13-17.

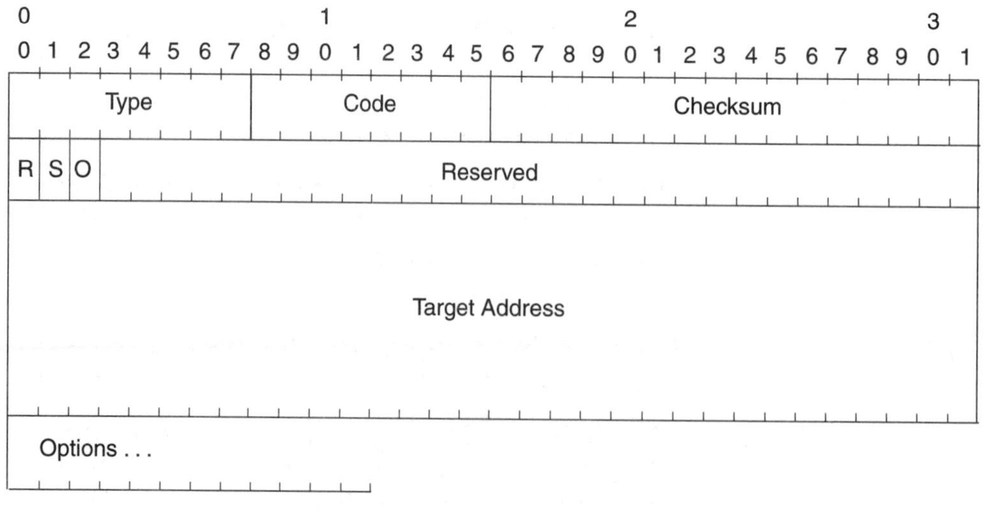

Illustration 13-17 ICMP Neighbor Advertisement

The source IP address will be set to the address assigned to the interface that the advertisement is sent out of. The destination address could be the unicast source address from the Neighbor Solicitation message that this advertisement is responding to. The destination address could also be link-local all-nodes multicast address if either the source address in the solicitation message were the unspecified address or if the advertisement were unsolicited. The Neighbor Advertisement fields are listed here.

- *Type:* 136
- *Code:* 0
- *Checksum:* The ICMP checksum.
- *R:* 1-bit Router flag. When set, the R bit indicates that the sender is a router. The R bit is used by Neighbor Unreachability Detection to detect a router that changes to a host.
- *S:* 1-bit Solicited flag. When set, the S bit indicates that the advertisement was sent in response to a Neighbor Solicitation from the destination address. The S bit is used as a reachability confirmation for Neighbor Unreachability Detection.
- *O:* 1-bit Override flag. When set, the O bit indicates that the advertisement should override an existing cache entry and update the cached link layer address.
- *Reserved:* 29-bit unused field. It *must* be initialized to 0 by the sender and *must* be ignored by the receiver.
- *Target Address:* For a solicited advertisement, the Target Address field in the Neighbor Solicitation message that prompted this advertisement. For an unsolicited advertisement, the address whose link layer address has changed.

The only possible option for the Options field is

- *Target link layer address:* The link layer address for the target, i.e., the sender of the advertisement. This option *must* be included on link layers that have addresses when responding to multicast solicitations. When responding to a unicast Neighbor Solicitation, this option *should* be included.

Neighbor Solicitation (135)

Whenever a host has an IP packet that it needs to send to another host in the same IP subnet, it needs to send out a solicitation to all nodes to see what link-layer address the packet should be delivered to. Neighbor Solicitation does this function. Illustration 13-18 shows the format for the Neighbor Solicitation message.

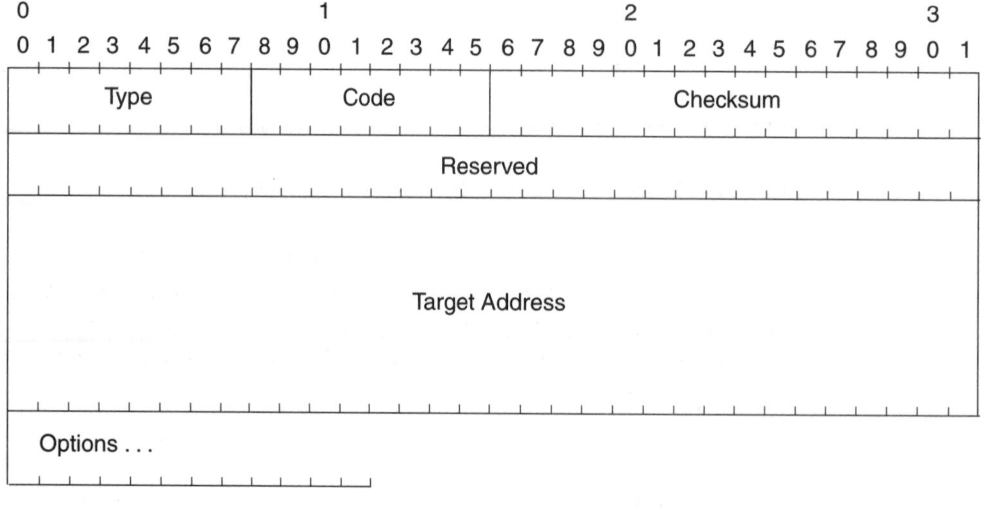

Illustration 13-18 ICMP Neighbor Solicitation

The source IP address could either be the address assigned to the interface that the advertisement is sent out of, or it could be the unspecified address. The destination IP address could either be the link-local all-nodes multicast address, or it could be the IP address of the node whose link layer address is being requested. The Neighbor Solicitation fields are shown here.

- *Type:* 135
- *Code:* 0
- *Checksum:* The ICMP checksum.
- *Reserved:* Reserved. Initialize to zeros.
- *Target Address:* The IP address of the target of the solicitation. The target is the host whose link layer address is being requested.

The only possible options for the Options field is

- *Source link layer address:* The link layer address for the sender.

Redirect (137)

In Chapter 4, ICMP Redirect was discussed as a way for IPv4 routers to inform hosts that there is a more optimal route using a different next hop. The ICMPv6 Redirect message works to do this but also lets a host know that another host in a different IP subnet is sharing the same data link and can be sent packets directly instead of through a router. The format for the Redirect message is shown in Illustration 13-19.

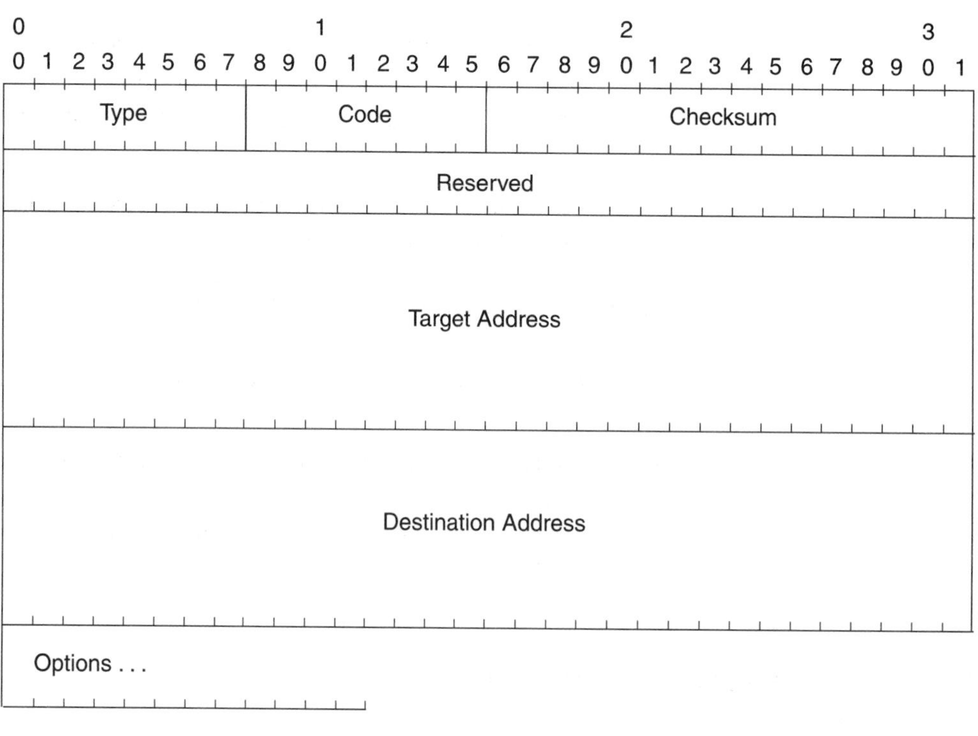

Illustration 13-19 ICMP Redirect

The source IP address will be set to the address assigned to the interface that the advertisement is sent out of. The destination IP address will be the source address of the packet that caused the redirect packet to be sent. The Redirect fields are listed here.

- *Type:* 137
- *Code:* 0
- *Checksum:* The ICMP checksum.
- *Reserved:* Reserved. Initialize to zeros.
- *Target Address:* An IP address that is a better first hop to use for the ICMP destination address. The Target

Address field should equal the Destination Address field (below) for redirects that indicate that the destination address is a neighbor of the sender and packets can be sent directly to its link layer address.

- *Destination Address:* The IP address of the destination, which is redirected to the target.

Possible options for the Options field are listed next.

- *Target link layer address:* The link layer address for the target.
- *Redirected header:* As much as possible of the IP packet that triggered the sending of the Redirect without making the Redirect packet exceed 1280 octets.

Address Autoconfiguration

Whenever an IPv6 host brings up an interface, the interface must go through some address autoconfiguration steps to be able to communicate with other nodes on the same network or on different networks. This configuration can be obtained by the host using stateless mechanisms as defined in RFC 2462, "IPv6 Stateless Address Autoconfiguration" or by stateful mechanisms such as Dynamic Host Configuration Protocol for IPv6 (DHCPv6). The stateless approach will ensure that an IP address is unique and routable but will not ensure that a host will get a specific IP address if tight controls are required. The stateful approach will ensure that a specific IP address or configuration information is provided to a specific host, but it requires DHCP servers to accomplish the assignments. It is possible, though arguably unmanageable, for hosts to be manually configured for specific IP parameters. At best, such a scenario could only work for nonmobile hosts.

Assuming that address autoconfiguration is desirable, the first thing an interface must do when attaching to a network is to create and verify the uniqueness of a link-local IP address. Earlier in the chapter, and especially in the Aggregatable Global Unicast Addresses section, we discussed the Interface ID portion of an IPv6 address. This 64-bit IEEE identifier can either be assigned to the hardware interface at the time of manufacture or it can be an adaptation of the 48-bit IEEE identifier (such as the 48-bit Ethernet MAC address). The link-local IP address for the host is an IP address that has the host's Interface ID as the low-order 64 bits of the address, the "link-local" address prefix (1111 1110 10) as the high-order 10 bits of the address, and as "0" the other 54 bits. This would look like: FE80::interface_id.

This derived link-local IP address needs to be verified as unique on the local link. This is easily done: The node sends a link-local all-nodes multicast Neighbor Solicitation using the IP address of which the node is verifying as the target address. Any node on the link that is currently using the intended IP address must answer up with a Neighbor Advertisement. If no Neighbor Advertisement is received, the IP address is considered unique and can be used to communicate with other IPv6 nodes on that local link. If the host wishes to communicate with other nodes that are not on the local link, the host must obtain an address that is unique for the domain that the host wishes to participate in (site-local or globally unique).

The host must create a Router Solicitation message to get information about the routers that are available and the IPv6 prefixes that are defined on the local link. The host sends a Router Solicitation to the link-local all-routers multicast address, requesting that Router Advertisements be sent. It uses the previously derived link-local IP address as the source IP address in the solicitation.

If no Router Advertisements are generated in response to the solicitation, it is assumed that no routers exist on the local link. If no router exists on the link, the host must use stateful address autoconfiguration if possible. If the link does not have routers or access to stateful address autoconfiguration services, the host has no way to create a site-local or global unicast address. Since there is no router on the link, the link-local address will be sufficient for the host's use until a router advertises its presence.

If a router is present on the link, it should respond to the Router Solicitation by sending out a Router Advertisement as a unicast to the host. When the host receives such a Router Advertisement, it can use the information to determine whether it should use stateful or stateless mechanisms to obtain an IP address or other parameters (M and O bits of the Router Advertisement). It can also use the information to determine whether the router can serve as a default gateway (Router Lifetime field) or as a home agent in Mobile IPv6 (H bit). The host can also see a list of IP prefixes on the local link for each router responding with an advertisement.

As mentioned above, if the M bit is set to one in the Router Advertisement, the host must use stateful address autoconfiguration to obtain an IP address (and possibly some other parameters if the O bit is also set). If the M bit is zero, the router must use stateless address autoconfiguration to obtain its address. It can still use stateful mechanisms to obtain other parameters if the O bit is set. The following sections discuss stateful and stateless address autoconfiguration.

Stateless Address Autoconfiguration

A complete definition of *stateless address autoconfiguration* includes all the steps mentioned above to get a link-local IP address, issue a Router Solicitation message, and obtain the Router Advertisement messages in response, plus the creation of one site-local or Aggregatable Global Unicast Address for each Prefix-Information option in the advertisements. Thus, the host will have an IP address for every prefix reported by the routers on that local link.

Stateful Address Autoconfiguration

If the M bit is set in the Router Advertisement flag or there is no router on the link, the host must use *stateful address autoconfiguration* to get a site-local or global IP address. The stateful address autoconfiguration method available in the IPv6 protocol suite is Dynamic Host Configuration Protocol for IPv6 (DHPCv6). The framework of the DHCPv6 protocol is defined in the Internet Draft, "Dynamic Host Configuration Protocol for IPv6 (DHCPv6)." In addition to the general procedures of the DHCP client–server protocol, this draft document defines two new multicast address types that can be used for DHCP resource discovery. In their link-local and site-local forms, they are

- *Link-Local all DHCP Agents address:* FF02:0:0:0:0:0:1:2 (FF02::1:2)
- *Site-Local all DHCP Agents address:* FF05:0:0:0:0:0:1:2 (FF05::1:2)
- *Link-Local all DHCP Servers address:* FF02:0:0:0:0:0:1:3 (FF02::1:3)
- *Site-Local all DHCP Servers address:* FF05:0:0:0:0:0:1:3 (FF05::1:3)

The draft also defines the following eight DHCP message formats dictated by the first field of the header, the Type field.

- *Solicit* (01): Used by DHCP clients to locate DHCP servers. Also permits a host to obtain a list of prefixes valid for the client's local link.
- *Advertise* (02): Sent by DHCP servers in response to DHCP solicitations. The Advertise message contains the DHCP server's site-local IP address as well as the list of IP prefixes on the local link, if requested in the Solicit message.

At the completion of DHCP server discovery, the DHCP client knows the IP address of the DHCP server, if available, and possibly the IP address of a DHCP relay agent if the DHCP server is not reachable due to IP address scope restrictions (link-local versus site-local).

- *Request* (03): Sent by the DHCP client to request information or configuration parameters for its operation from a DHCP server. This message format uses *extensions* to request specific information. The Internet Draft, "Extensions for the Dynamic Host Configuration Protocol for IPv6," defines several extensions supported by DHCP for use with the Request and Reply messages. The most relevant and arguably the most important to this book is the IP Address Extension, which allows a client to request an IP address for the duration of an agreed-upon period of time called a *lease.* See the subsection below on the format of the IP Address Extension. Other extensions, such as Domain Name servers and Network Time Protocol servers, can be also used to request network information.
- *Reply* (04): Sent by the DHCP server to respond to configuration requests made by a DHCP client. See the above discussion on the Request message for more information on the types of configuration parameters that DHCPv6 can currently provide.
- *Release* (05): Sent by a DHCP client to a DHCP server to request the release of a releasable configuration parameter such as an IP address.
- *Reconfigure* (06): Sent by a DHCP server to one of its managed DHCP clients to inform the client of a configuration parameter that has changed.
- *Reconfigure-reply* (07): Sent by a DHCP client to a DHCP server to acknowledge receipt of a previous Reconfigure message.

- *Reconfigure-init* (08): Sent by a DHCP server to a client to request the client to initiate a Request and Reply for a specified configuration parameter.

The IP Address Extension

The IP Address Extension is used in a DHCP Request to obtain a new IP address lease or to renew an existing IP address lease. It is used in a DHCP Reply to provide the new IP address lease or to affirm the renewal of a current lease. The format for the Extension is shown in Illustration 13-20. A description of each field follows.

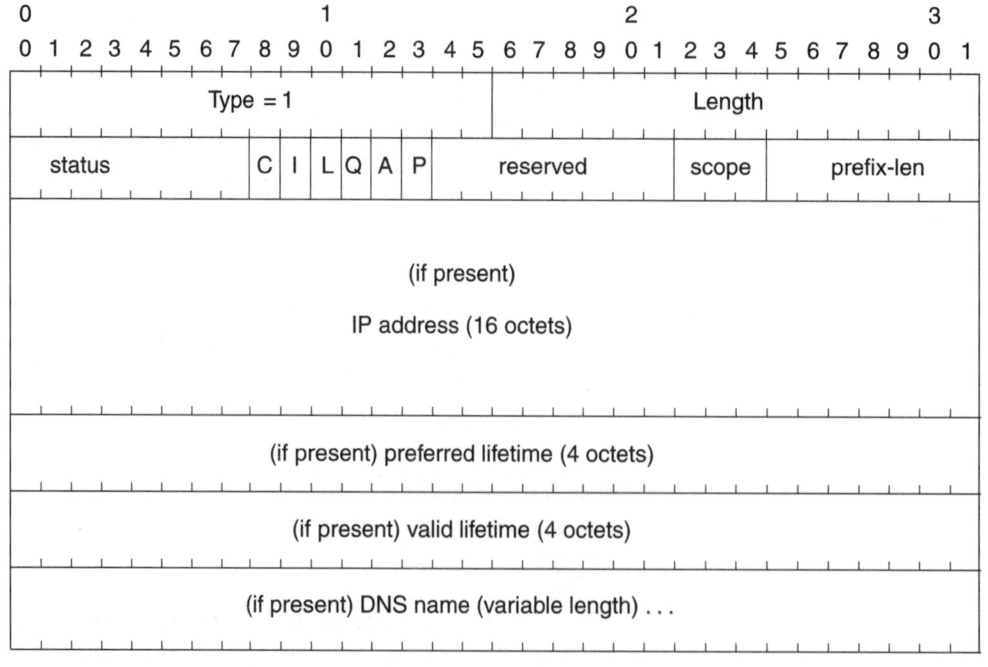

Illustration 13-20 DHCPv6 IP Address Extension

- *Type:* 1
- *Length:* The length of the extension in octets.
- *status:* The receiver's result of its attempt to honor the sender's request.
- *C:* If the C bit is set, the field containing the IP address is present in the extension.
- *I:* If the I bit is set, the client is informing the server that the IP address listed *was not* received from DHCP.
- *L:* If the L bit is set, the preferred and valid lifetimes are present in the extension.
- *Q:* If the Q bit is set, the fields included by the client are required.
- *A:* If the A bit is set, the client requests that the server updates DNS with a new AAAA/A6 record, as specified by the client's FQDN.
- *P:* If the P bit is set, the client requests that the server updates DNS with a new PTR record, as specified by the client's FQDN.
- *reserved: must* be zero.
- *scope:* 3-bit field used by the client to request an IP address of a certain scope. The three bits form a number (0–7) that can have the following settings:

  0 Don't Care

  1 Globally scoped address

  2 Site-local-scoped address

  3–7 Reserved
- *prefix-len:* If the IP address field is present (the C bit is set), a nonzero prefix-len is the number of leftmost bits of the IP address that make up the subnet prefix. If the C bit is not set, prefix-len *must* be zero.

- *IP address:* The IP address to be conveyed to the receiver from the sender. If the client is requesting an IP address be allocated by the server, the DHCP IP Address Extension Reply will use this field to provide the client with an IP address.
- *preferred lifetime:* The preferred lifetime of the IP address in seconds (the duration of the lease).
- *valid lifetime:* The valid lifetime of the IP address in seconds.
- *DNS name:* The DNS name associated with the IP address.

Be aware that the DHCPv6 and Extensions to DHCPv6 documents may still just be Internet Drafts. For more current information, please refer to the latest version of the Internet Drafts or the RFCs when they move along in the standards process.

Mobility in IP Version 6

The previous chapter dealt with mobility in IP version 4, specifically Mobile IP. I will assume that you have read Chapter 12 or are familiar with the nomenclature and operation of Mobile IP. Mobile IPv6 works very much like Mobile IP in IPv4 works, but there are some important differences:

- There are no foreign agents in Mobile IPv6. Mobile IPv6 uses a model that more closely resembles a col-located care-of address in IPv4. The Mobile IPv6 mobile node can have multiple IP addresses and gets or creates addresses for each link that it attaches to.
- Packets don't have to always be sent through the home agent in Mobile IPv6. Mobile IPv6 allows other

IPv6 nodes to receive binding updates from a mobile node so that they will know how to deliver packets directly to the mobile node.

- Not all packets are tunneled in Mobile IPv6. In Mobile IPv4, packets sent from the home agent to the mobile node were tunneled in IP-within-IP tunnels. In Mobile IPv6, IPv6-within-IPv6 tunnels are sometimes used, source routing is sometimes used, and other times, the mobile node can use the care-of address as its source address and access network resources directly without using Mobile IPv6 functions.

Let's see how Mobile IPv6 works by looking at an example. Illustration 13-21 shows the network that we will use. Host A is a mobile node with a network interface that has an IPv6 address of 2001::hosta/64. Note that "hosta" is used only in this text as shorthand for the 64-bit Interface ID used in the address. The format prefix of "001" is used by the Aggregatable Global Unicast Addresses. Since Host A is a host on the 2001::/64 network, this network is Host A's home link. Hosts B and C are non-mobile nodes. Router A is Host A's home agent. If Host A were to unplug from its home link (on the left side of the illustration) and connect to the Ethernet (on the right side of the illustration), Host A would be connected to a foreign link. The foreign link in the illustration is identified by the subnetwork 2002::/64. Router B is a normal IPv6 router.

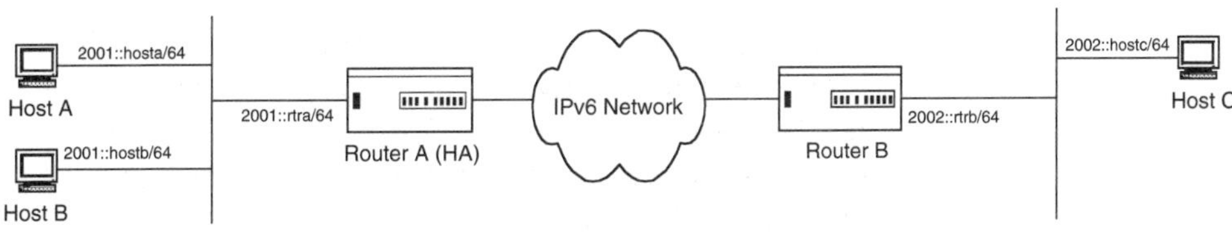

Illustration 13-21 Example Mobile IPv6 Network 1

When Host A is on its home link, it communicates with correspondent nodes as it would in normal IPv6. If Host C sends a packet to Host A's IP address, it is forwarded to Router B, which forwards it through the IP network to Router A. Router A resolves the IP address to a MAC address using neighbor discovery and forwards the packet to Host A. If Host B sends a packet to Host A, Host B would do neighbor discovery for Host A's MAC address and forward the packet directly to Host A.

If Host A were to disconnect from its home network, a packet sent to Host A's IP address from Host C would traverse Router B and the IP Network. But when the packet arrived at Router A, Router A would not be able to resolve Host A's MAC address and the packet would be undeliverable.

Now let's consider what would happen if Host A were to connect to the foreign network without Mobile IP support, as shown in Illustration 13-22. When Host C tries to send a packet to Host A, the packet is forwarded to Router A but because Host A is not on its home network, the packet is undeliverable just as if Host A were completely unattached.

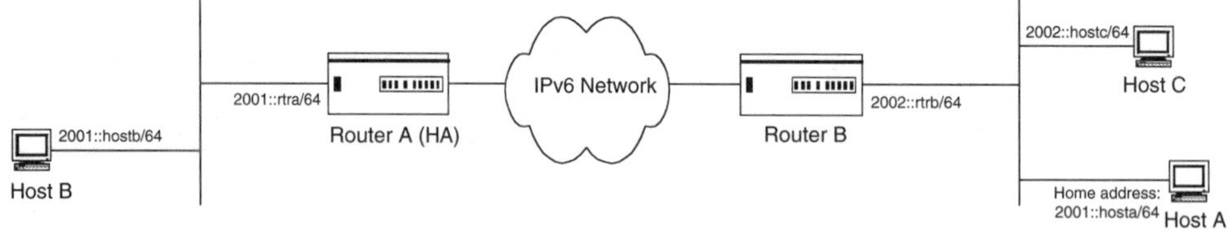

Illustration 13-22 Host A Connected to a Foreign Network Without Mobile IP Support

Now, let's get into the Mobile IPv6 protocol. Host A is typically configured to know that Router A is its home agent. As soon as Host A plugs into the foreign link, it goes through the steps of address autoconfiguration discussed earlier in the chapter. In summary, it creates a link-local address for its IP interface and verifies that it is unique. It sends out an ICMP Router Solicitation using its link-local IP address as the source and the all-routers multicast address as the destination. Router B responds to the solicitation with an ICMP Router Advertisement. From the information in the Router Advertisement, Host A will know whether it can use stateless address autoconfiguration or must use DHCP to construct global or site-local IP addresses for its interfaces. The information needed for stateless address autoconfiguration will also be in the contents of the Router Advertisement.

Once Host A constructs a site-local or global IP address, it registers this address by sending an IP packet, which includes a Binding Update destination option header, to its home agent (Router A). This packet will have a source IP address equal to the care-of address it is registering. The packet must have a Home Address option, which gives the node's home address for the binding. This destination option — as well as the Binding Acknowledge, Binding Request, and Home Address destination options — are defined in the Internet Draft, "Mobility Support in IPv6." The Binding Update as well as the Binding Acknowledge messages must be protected by the authentication header, ESP header, or both. Because of this authentication support, the home agent can confidently update its bindings to reflect the current care-of address. A home agent's binding table will cross-reference the mobile node's home address with its current care-of address. The home agent must then acknowledge the binding update by sending a Binding Acknowledge message back to the mobile node. Then, until the binding expires or it is removed by the mobile node, Router A as the home agent will intercept IP packets on the home link by sending Gratuitous and Proxy ICMP Neighbor Advertisements. Packets that are intercepted by the home agent are tunneled to the care-of address using IPv6-within-IPv6 tunneling as defined in RFC 2473, "Generic Packet Tunneling in IPv6 Specification."

Dynamic Home Agent Address Discovery is a mechanism defined in Mobile IPv6 that allows a mobile node to discover an alternate home agent in the event that its own home agent stops providing mobility services. It does this by sending an ICMP Home Agents Address Discovery Request to the Mobile IPv6 Home Agents anycast address.

Router B continuously sends ICMP Router Advertisements that can be used by the mobile node to determine whether the mobile node has changed links. In the event that it detects a link change, the mobile node must again go through address autoconfiguration and registration with the home agent for the new link.

Now, take a look at Illustration 13-23. Let's say that Host D wants to communicate with Host A. It sends its IP packet to Host A at 2001::hosta. Host A is not on its home link and therefore can't receive the packet directly. But because Host A has registered with Router A, its home agent, using a care-of address of 2002::hosta, Router A intercepts the packet and tunnels it to Host A. Host A strips off the tunnel header and sees that the destination IP address of the packet is the same as Host A's home address. Host A processes the packet and prepares a response for Host D. The response packet includes a Binding Update destination option header that tells Host D that it should, for the near future, send any packets to 2002::hosta that it would normally send to 2001::hosta. This information is cached and must be deleted when the entry's lifetime expires. Until then, Host D will communicate with Host A directly using Host A's care-of address instead of its home address.

If the mobile node sends packets that use its home address as the source address of the packet, the node must insert a Home Address option. Such a packet is constructed as normal using the home address as the source IP address in the IPv6 header, with the Home Address option added to the header using the node's home address in the Home Address field. The node's care-of address is placed in the IPv6 Source Address field. Whenever a node receives a packet with a Home Address option, the receiving node must immediately (before any further processing) replace the contents of the Source Address Field with the IP address contained in the Home Address field of the Home Address option. This feature permits a mobile node to communicate through a firewall that is implementing ingress filters that disallow IP packets that have source addresses allocated from the "inside" of the network to arrive into the firewall from an "outside" interface.

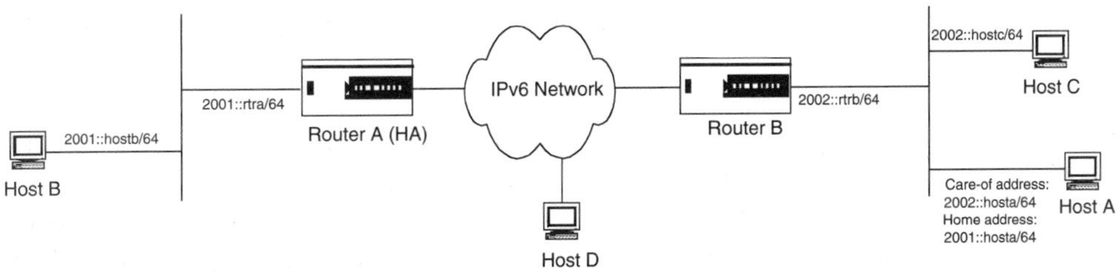

Illustration 13-23 Example Mobile IPv6 Network 2

When a mobile node returns to its home link, it must detect that it is back on its home link by its move detection mechanisms. This might include ICMP Router Discovery as well as some link layer mechanisms. Once it has detected that it is back on its home link, the mobile node must deregister with its home agent. It does this by sending a packet with a Binding Update option where the lifetime field is set to zero. After that, the mobile node operates normally on its home link without using mobility services.

Summary

IP version 6 was created with the primary purpose of creating an address space architecture that could handle significant growth of the Internet and globally unique addresses well into the future. There were, however, four other items that were accomplished during the renovation:

- Header format simplification
- Improved support for extensions and options
- Flow labeling capability
- Authentication and privacy capabilities

This chapter focused mostly on the implications of the new, larger, 128-bit addresses in IPv6. IPv6 defines three types of addresses. Unicast addresses are used for one-to-one node communications. Multicast addresses are used for one-to-many node communications. Anycast addresses are used for one-to-any node communications. Anycast addresses are new in IPv6. Broadcasts have been made obsolete in IPv6 since multicasts of a "broadcast" scope can be sent.

In the simplified header of IPv6, only the most essential header elements are included. Then, to increase its capabilities and services, IPv6 uses the following extension headers.

- Hop-by-Hop Options
- Destination Options
- Routing
- Fragment
- Authentication
- Encapsulating Security Payload

- IPv6
- ICMPv6
- Upper-Layer Protocol

Five ICMPv6 message types allow neighbor discovery in IPv6. These are Router Solicitation, Router Advertisement, Neighbor Solicitation, Neighbor Advertisement, and Redirect.

Address autoconfiguration is used when an IPv6 host brings up an interface. The interface must go through specific steps so that the host may communicate with other nodes on either the same or a different network. Either stateless or stateful address autoconfiguration may be used, depending on the content of the Router Advertisement.

Mobile IPv6 is much like Mobile IPv4 using a colocated care-of address, with three major differences occurring in Mobile IPv6:

- There are no foreign agents.
- Packets do not always have to be sent through the home agent.
- Not all packets are tunneled.

Practice Questions

1. Approximately how many unique addresses are theoretically possible with a 128-bit IP address?
2. How many unique subnets can be defined using the NLA ID in Aggregatable Global Unicast Addresses?
3. What is the Next-Header value that indicates that the next header is another IPv6 header?
4. What does the Next-Header value of 59 indicate?
5. What does the Next-Header value of 0 indicate?

6. State the type of IPv6 address for each of the following.
   a. 2001::1
   b. ::
   c. ::192.168.1.5
   d. FE80::1
   e. ::1
   f. FF02::2
7. What IPv6 node can do packet fragmentation?
8. What protocol is used for stateful address auto-configuration?

IP Network Number Request Template for ISPs

This document can be found at:

http://www.arin.net/regserv/templates/isptemplate.txt

02/99 ARIN ISP Address Request Template

******** PLEASE DO NOT REMOVE Version Number ********

ISP Network Version Number: 3.0

******** Please see attached detailed instructions ********

Internet Connections

0a. Directly connecting to peering points? Please list

0b. Connectivity via service providers? Please list

0c. Other

Reassignment Information

1a. Block ....:

1b. Assigned..........................:

1c. Reserved..........................:

1d. Available..........................:

1e. Reassignment option...............:

Technical POC

2a. ARIN-handle (if known)............:

2b. Name (Last, First)..................:

2c. Title ....:

2d. Postal address ....:

2e. Phone Number ....:

2f. E-Mailbox..........................:

3. Network name.....................:

4a. Name of Organization..............:

4b. Postal address of Organization ......:

4c. Maintainer ID (if known) ....:

5. CIDR Block requested...............:

6. Portable (P) Non-portable (N).......:

Host Information

7a. 3 month projection for dial
up customers ....:

7b. 3 month projection for leased
line customers ....:

7c. Additional information.............:

Primary Name Server

8a. Primary Server Hostname ....:

8b. Primary Server Netaddress ....:

Secondary Name Server(s)

9a. Secondary Server Hostname ....:

9b. Secondary Server Netaddress ....:

———————— CUT HERE ————————

Instructions for Completing the Internet Service Provider (ISP) Network Number Request Template

In order to ensure prompt and accurate processing of your ISP Network Number template, please precisely follow the instructions below. Any errors found may result in the template being returned to the submitting ISP for correction.

Internet Service Providers (ISPs) submit the ISP Network Template as part of the application process for obtaining a CIDR block of Internet Protocol (IP) Network Numbers. Please complete the template and submit via electronic mail, to hostmaster@arin.net.

Enter "ISP CIDR REQUEST" in the Subject field of the E-mail message address.

Please do not modify the form in any way. Please do not remove the version number.

Prior to requesting any initial allocation of addresses, please refer to:

a. the Internet Protocol (IP) Allocation Guidelines for Internet Service Providers (ISPs) found at: http://www.arin.net/ip-allocation.html

b. Initial Internet Protocol (IP) Address Space Requests by Internet Service Providers (ISPs) at: http://www.arin.net/initial-isp.html

c. RFC 2050.

The action of requesting of addresses from ARIN indicates you have read and agree to abide by the guidelines.

ARIN Registration Services will acknowledge receipt of your completed application via E-mail.

Section 0. Internet Connection

Please supply detailed information describing your organization's connection to the Internet. One of the three following options should be completed. Please provide the information requested in this section

0a. Directly connecting to peering points? Please list:

0b. Connectivity via service providers? Please list:

0c. Other:

Required fields are Technical POC: Network Name; Name of Organization, Postal Address, Provider/maintainer ID (if known); and Portable or Non-portable.

Section 1. Reassignment information

ARIN will review previously allocated blocks for efficient utilization prior to allocating additional addresses. Please follow the example below when listing information about previously allocated blocks.

1a. block: 204.123.0.0/16

1b. assigned: 192 (192 /24s worth of address space)

1c. reserved: 40 (40 /24s worth of address space)

1d. available: 24 (Network numbers available for customer use.)

NOTE: TERMINOLOGY

Assigned means issued to customers. Utilization of assigned address space will be verified via SWIP or your RWHOIS server. See Item 1e below.

Reserved refers to IP address space used for your internal network, terminal servers, virtual domains, etc. These reserved networks need to be identified and briefly described.

1e. Reassignment option.

Please submit reassignment information using one of two options:
SWIP or RWHOIS.

You will find the SWIP template at:

ftp://ftp.arin.net/pub/swip/swiptemplate.txt

Detailed instructions for the SWIP template can be found at:

ftp://ftp.arin.net/pub/swip/swipinstruction.txt

Information on establishing a Referral WHOIS (RWHOIS) server is provided at:

http://rwhois.internic.net/

When using RWHOIS, please include host and port number, such as:

rwhois.provider.net 4321

To place your RWHOIS server in the RWHOIS tree, send a referral template to rwhoisreg

ftp://rs.internic.net/templates/rwhois-template.txt.

All reassignment information must be submitted to ARIN using SWIP or RWHOIS within seven (7) days of the assignment of IP address space. Reassignment information must be up to date in order for additional address space to be allocated.

Section 2. Technical Point of Contact (POC)

The Technical POC is the person responsible for the technical aspects of maintaining the allocated CIDR blocks. The POC should be able to answer any utilization questions that ARIN may have.

2a. ARIN- handle.

Each POC in the ARIN database is assigned a user handle <ARIN- handle>, a unique tag consisting of the person's initials and a number. This tag is used on records in the database to indicate a POC for a network, domain, or other entity.

If you are unsure of the user handle or whether one is assigned, perform a "last name, first name" search in the WHOIS database.

If the technical POC's user handle is unknown, please leave item 2a blank.

2b. Name.

Place the last name and the first name of the POC on the same line, separated by a comma as shown: Last name, First name.

EXAMPLES:

Smith, Mary

Netman, John

2c. List the POC's title, if known.

2d. Postal Address.

This is the physical address of the POC at the organization requesting IP address space. Place the city, state, and zip code together on the same line directly below the Street Address or Post Office box. Use a comma to separate the city and state. Do not insert a period following the state abbreviation.

In the country field, please use the two-letter country code found at:

ftp://rs.arin.net/netinfo/iso3166-countrycodes

EXAMPLES:

111 Scenic Overlook Drive
Herndon, VA 22070
US

125 North Place
Montreal, QC H2S 2C8
CA

2e. Phone Number.

You must the list the complete telephone number of the POC, including area code and/or international telephone codes.

2f. E-mailbox

You must provide the E-mail address of the POC at the organization requesting IP address space.

Section 3. Network Name.

The Network Name is used as an identifier in Internet name and address tables. Supply a short name consisting of a combination of up to 12 numbers and/or letters for the network. You may use a dash (-) as part of the Network Name, but no other special characters. Please do not use periods or underscores.

NOTE: Use of syntax ending in .com, .net, .org (e.g., XXXX.com or XXXX.net), is not a valid network naming convention, and should be used only when applying for a domain.

Preferably, all future network names should be a continuation of the original name.

EXAMPLES: Network Name, Network Name Continuations

Internet-blk-1, Internet-blk-2, Internet-blk-3 . . .

Section 4. ISP, Organization Name; Location; Provider/maintainer ID.

4a. Name of Organization.

Identify the name and geographic location of the Internet Service Provider requesting the Classless Inter-Domain Routing (CIDR) block.

4b. Postal Address.

This is the physical address of the organization. Refer to 2d for directions.

4c. Provider/maintainer ID.

ARIN assigns a provider/maintainer ID to each ISP that is allocated Internet Protocol (IP) address space. The provider/maintainer ID is an Alphanumeric identifier that uniquely designates each ISP.

The provider/maintainer ID is used by ISPs when they submit IP address space reassignment information to ARIN via SWIP.

If you know your provider/maintainer ID, please list it here. If this is your first request, leave 4c blank. ARIN will assign a provider/maintainer ID to your organization.

Section 5. Size of CIDR Block Requested.

If your immediate-to-three-month requirement is less than /20, you are encouraged to contact your upstream ISP for address space. This will aid in the efficient deployment of CIDR.

Please be advised that allocations are made based on a slow-start model. The initial allocations will be relatively small. Subsequent allocated blocks may be increased based on utilization verification supplied to ARIN.

If you have not previously received address space from ARIN, please refer to the following address for Prepayment and Registration Information:

www.arin.net

Section 6. Portable/Non-Portable Address Space.

(P) Portable. If you allow your customers to take their assigned IP numbers with them when they change providers, please check (P) for Portable. ARIN does not encourage ISPs to break up their CIDR blocks.

(N) If you require the IP addresses assigned from your CIDR block to be returned, please check (N) for non-portable.

Section 7. Justification.

7a. Three-month projections for dialup customers. Indicate the number of /24s.

7b. Three-month projections for leased line customers.

Please list your three-month projections for dial-up customers and leased line customers. It is preferred that ISPs issue classless assignments whenever possible to help preserve the remaining address space.

7c. Additional information.

Please include any additional level of detail that will help explain your requirement.

Sections 8 and 9. New IN-ADDR (Inverse Mapping) Registration on the CIDR Block Requested.

To register the inverse mapping on the CIDR block you are requesting, complete this section of the template. Neither the name nor the number of a registered name server will be changed as a result of a new IN-ADDR.

Any modification to the inverse mapping must be sent via E-mail to ARIN at hostmaster@arin.net using the IN-ADDR template found at:

ftp://rs.arin.net/templates/inaddrtemplate.txt

Networks must provide at least two independent servers for translating address to name mapping for hosts in the domain. The servers should be in physically separate locations and on different networks if possible.

Sections 8a/8b. Primary Name Server Hostname/Netaddress.

8a. Primary Name Server Hostname.

Please provide the fully qualified name of the machine that will be the name server.

EXAMPLE:

machine.domainname.com

8b. Primary Name Server Netaddress.

Please provide the IP address of the name server.

It is suggested that the fourth octet of the IP address of a server should be neither 0 nor 255.

Sections 9a/9b. Secondary Name Server(s) Hostname/Netaddress.

The same procedures for specifying primary servers apply to secondary servers. If several secondary servers are required, copy Section 9 multiple times.

NOTE: Do not renumber or change the copied section. A maximum of six name servers may be added to a network record.

9a. Please provide the fully qualified name of the machine that will be the name server.

9b. Primary Name Server Netaddress.

Please provide the IP address of the name server. It is suggested that the fourth octet of the IP address of a server should be neither 0 nor 255.

For further information contact ARIN Registration Services:

Via electronic mail:

hostmaster@arin.net

Via fax: (703) 227-0676

IP Network Number Request Template for End Users

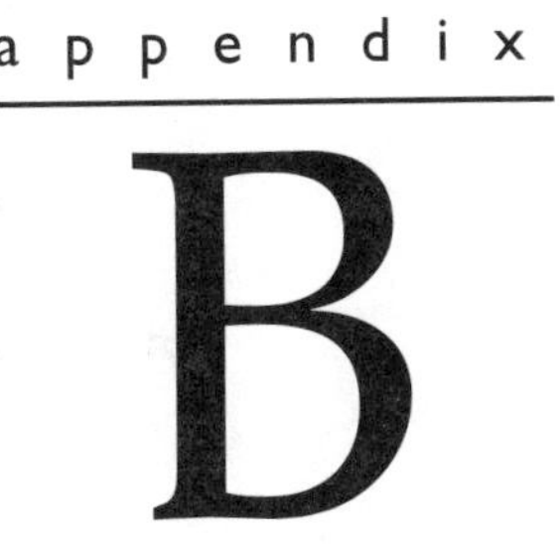

This document can be found at

http://www.arin.net/regserv/templates/networktemplate.txt

02/99 ARIN End User IP Request Template

******** PLEASE DO NOT REMOVE Version Number ********

Network Version Number: 2.0

******** Please see attached detailed instructions ********

1a. Approximate date of Internet connection ....:

1b. Name of Internet access provider (if known)........................:

Technical POC

2a. ARIN-handle (if known)............:

2b. Name (Last, First)..................:

2c. Title ....:

2d. Postal address ....:

2e. Phone Number ....:

2f E-Mailbox ....:

3. Network name......................:

4a. Name of Organization..............:

4b. Postal address of Organization ......:

5. Previously assigned addresses ......:

Explain how addresses have been utilized, to include:

5a. Number of hosts ....:

5b. Number of subnets.................:

5c. Subnet mask.......................:

Justification

Host Information

6a. Initially ....:

6b. Within 1 year ....:

Subnet Information

6c. Initially ....:

6d. Within one year....................:

7a. Number of addresses requested . . . . . :

7b. Additional supporting justification. . . . . :

If requesting 16 C's or more, you are required to submit the network topology plan in the format of the example below:

Subnet#	Subnet Mask	Max	Now	1yr	Description
1.0	255.255.255.224	30	8	16	Network Group (use 0!)
1.1	255.255.255.224	30	17	22	Engineering
1.2	255.255.255.224	30	12	12	Manufacturing
1.3	255.255.255.224	30	5	9	Management
1.4	255.255.255.224	30	10	15	Sales
1.5	255.255.255.224	30	7	8	Finance
1.6	255.255.255.224	30	0	0	(spare)
	Totals	210	59	82	

If requesting a Class B or 256 C's (/16 prefix), a network diagram should also be included with your request.

8. Type of network . . . . :

INSTRUCTIONS FOR REQUESTING
INTERNET PROTOCOL (IP) NUMBERS

Completion of the Network Version Number: 2.0 template above is required to obtain Internet Protocol (IP) Network Numbers.

Each line in the blank template must be copied EXACTLY AS IT APPEARS. Take care not to alter the established field names or spacing when you fill in the information. Any change to the template may cause an error that inhibits the processing of your template and delays the input of your request.

In the Subject field of the E-mail message, use the words: IP REQUEST.

Please submit the template via E-mail to ARIN at: hostmaster@ arin.net. When ARIN registration Services receives your complete template you will be notified via E-mail. If E-mail is not available to you, please fax hardcopy to ARIN, and indicate a return fax number for the Point of Contact at your organization.

Contact ARIN via fax at:

(703) 227-0676

For more information, see:

http://www.arin.net

Networks that will be connected/located within the European geographic regions maintained by RIPE (Reseaux IP Europeens) should use the European template located at:

ftp://ftp.ripe.net/ripe/forms/netnum-appl.txt

Please follow the instructions that RIPE provides for submission of that template.

Networks that will be connected/located within the geographic region maintained by the Asian-Pacific Network Information Center (APNIC) should use the APNIC template located at:

ftp://ftp.apnic.net/apnic/docs/isp-address-request

Please follow the instructions that APNIC provides for submission of that template.

***PLEASE READ THE FOLLOWING INFORMATION PRIOR TO REQUESTING AN IP NUMBER FROM ARIN:

Most end users receive IP address space from their upstream Internet Service Providers, not directly from ARIN. Provider-independent (portable) addresses obtained directly from ARIN are not guaranteed to be globally routable. The minimum block of IP address space assigned by ARIN is a /20. All individuals/entities that do not meet the requirements for a /20 will be referred to their upstream service provider. If allocations smaller than /20 are needed, organizations should request address space from their upstream provider.

If you have not selected an ISP, but plan to connect in the future or if your network will never be connected to the Internet, you are encouraged to use IP numbers reserved for non-connected networks (as set forth in RFC 1918) until you can utilize address space from the ISP of your choice.

NOTE: Your organization will be assigned address space for only for an immediate to one (1) year requirement.

Section 1. Internet Connection.

1a. Approximate date of Internet connection.

Please supply information on the approximate date of your connection to the Internet.

1b. Name of Internet access provider (if known).

Please provide the name of your Internet access provider, if known. If you have an Internet Service Provider (ISP), you should request IP address space from them.

Section 2. Technical Point of Contact (POC).

The technical POC is the person responsible for the technical aspects of maintaining an organization's IP address space. This person should be able to answer any utilization questions ARIN may have.

2a. ARIN- handle (if known).

Each POC entered in the ARIN database is assigned a user handle, a unique tag consisting of the person's initials and a number. This tag is used in database records to indicate a POC for a network, domain, or other entity.

If you are unsure of the user handle or whether one is assigned, perform a "Last name, First name" search in the WHOIS database. If the POC's user handle is unknown, leave 2a blank.

If item 2a is completed, leave items 2b through 2f blank.

2b. Name.

Place the last name and the first name of the POC on the same line, separated by a comma as shown: Last name, First name

EXAMPLES:

Smith, Mary

Netman, John

2c. Title.

List the POC's title, if known.

2d. Postal Address.

Provide the physical address of the POC at the organization requesting IP address space.

When completing question 2d, place the city, state, and zip code on separate lines. Use a comma to separate the city and state. Do not insert a period following the state abbreviation. In the country field, please use the two-letter country code found at:

ftp://rs.arin.net/netinfo/iso3166-countrycodes

EXAMPLES:

111 Main Street
Town Center, VA 22070
US

125 North Place
Montreal, QC H2S 2C8
CA

2e. Phone Number.

You must the list the complete telephone number of the POC, including area code and/or international telephone codes.

2f. E-mailbox.

You must provide the E-mail address of the POC at the organization requesting IP address space.

Section 3. Network Name.

The Network Name is used as an identifier in Internet name and address tables. Supply a short name consisting of a combination of up to 12 numbers and letters for the network. You may use a dash (-) as part of the Network Name, but no other special characters. Please do not use periods or underscores.

EXAMPLES: Network Name, Network Name Continuations

Internet-blk-1, Internet-blk-2, Internet-blk-3...

NOTE Use of syntax ending in .com, .net, .org, e.g., XXX.com or XXX.net), is not a valid network naming convention, and should be used only when applying for a domain.

Section 4. Organization Name and Postal Address.

Provide the name and physical address of the organization that will be utilizing the IP address space.

4a. Name of Organization.

4b. Postal Address.

Refer to item 2d above.

Section 5. Previously Assigned Addresses.

Please list all IP addresses previously assigned to your entire organization. Please repond to items 5a through 5c with a specific description regarding the utilization of those addresses.

5a. Number of hosts.

5b. Number of subnets.

5c. Subnet mask.

Section 6. Justification.

6a./6b.Host Information.

6a. Initially.

Please include here your estimates for the initial size of the network.

6b. Within 1 year.

Please include here your estimates for the size the network is projected to be one year from now. A "host" is defined as any node or any device, e.g, PC or printer, that will be assigned an address from the host portion of the network number.

6c./6d.Subnet Information.

6c. Initially.

Include the number of subnets that will be supported by the network initially.

6d. Within 1 year.

Include the number of subnets projected to be supported by the network one year from now.

Section 7. Number of Addresses Requested and Additional Supporting Documentation.

7a. Number of Addresses Requested.

Please state exactly how many addresses you are requesting.

7b. Additional justification.

Please state exactly how many addresses you are requesting along with any additional justification necessary. As stated on the template, if you are requesting 16 C's or more, you will need to complete the network topology plan in the format shown on the template.

Note: All requesters must submit the network topology plan.

If you are requesting 256 C's or a Class B (/16 prefix) or more, please include a copy of your network diagram.

Your organization is strongly encouraged to subnet where feasible.

Address space is issued based on the utilization of VLSM per RFC 2050.

If requesting 16 C's or more, you are required to submit the network topology plan in the format of the example below:

Subnet#	Subnet Mask	Max	Now	1yr	Description
1.0	255.255.255.128	128	102	116	Operations
1.1	255.255.255.192	64	44	48	Engineering
1.2	255.255.255.240	16	12	13	Management
1.3	255.255.255.240	16	11	14	Sales
1.4	255.255.255.240	16	10	15	Support
1.5	255.255.255.240	16	0	0	Spare
	Totals	256	179	206	

NOTE: This represents one /24 (Class C) using Variable Length Subnet Masking (VLSM).

Section 8. Type of Network.

Networks are characterized as being one of four types: Research, Educational, Government-Non Defense, or Commercial. Which type is this network?

For further information, contact ARIN Registration Services via E-mail at:

hostmaster@arin.net

or via Fax at

(703) 227-0676

appendix

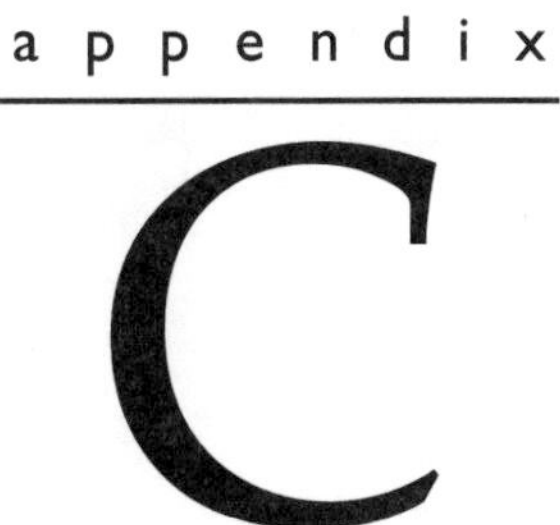

IP Addressing Worksheet

The following four pages constitute a worksheet that can be used to assist with subnetting a Class C or equivalent network. The usage is detailed in the section II introduction of this text.

I encourage you to photocopy these sheets and cut and paste the four pages together. I think that you will find this to be a valuable tool.

.0/24	.128/25	.192/26	.224/27	.240/28	.248/29	.252/30
0	0	0	0	0	0	0
1	1	1	1	1	1	1
2	2	2	2	2	2	2
3	3	3	3	3	3	3
4	4	4	4	4	4	4
5	5	5	5	5	5	5
6	6	6	6	6	6	6
7	7	7	7	7	7	7
8	8	8	8	8	8	8
9	9	9	9	9	9	9
10	10	10	10	10	10	10
11	11	11	11	11	11	11
12	12	12	12	12	12	12
13	13	13	13	13	13	13
14	14	14	14	14	14	14
15	15	15	15	15	15	15
16	16	16	16	16	16	16
17	17	17	17	17	17	17
18	18	18	18	18	18	18
19	19	19	19	19	19	19
20	20	20	20	20	20	20
21	21	21	21	21	21	21
22	22	22	22	22	22	22
23	23	23	23	23	23	23
24	24	24	24	24	24	24
25	25	25	25	25	25	25
26	26	26	26	26	26	26
27	27	27	27	27	27	27
28	28	28	28	28	28	28
29	29	29	29	29	29	29
30	30	30	30	30	30	30
31	31	31	31	31	31	31
32	32	32	32	32	32	32
33	33	33	33	33	33	33
34	34	34	34	34	34	34
35	35	35	35	35	35	35
36	36	36	36	36	36	36
37	37	37	37	37	37	37
38	38	38	38	38	38	38
39	39	39	39	39	39	39
40	40	40	40	40	40	40
41	41	41	41	41	41	41
42	42	42	42	42	42	42
43	43	43	43	43	43	43
44	44	44	44	44	44	44
45	45	45	45	45	45	45
46	46	46	46	46	46	46
47	47	47	47	47	47	47
48	48	48	48	48	48	48
49	49	49	49	49	49	49
50	50	50	50	50	50	50
51	51	51	51	51	51	51
52	52	52	52	52	52	52
53	53	53	53	53	53	53
54	54	54	54	54	54	54
55	55	55	55	55	55	55
56	56	56	56	56	56	56
57	57	57	57	57	57	57
58	58	58	58	58	58	58
59	59	59	59	59	59	59
60	60	60	60	60	60	60
61	61	61	61	61	61	61
62	62	62	62	62	62	62
63	63	63	63	63	63	63

.0/24	.128/25	.192/26	.224/27	.240/28	.248/29	.252/30
64	64	64	64	64	64	64
65	65	65	65	65	65	65
66	66	66	66	66	66	66
67	67	67	67	67	67	67
68	68	68	68	68	68	68
69	69	69	69	69	69	69
70	70	70	70	70	70	70
71	71	71	71	71	71	71
72	72	72	72	72	72	72
73	73	73	73	73	73	73
74	74	74	74	74	74	74
75	75	75	75	75	75	75
76	76	76	76	76	76	76
77	77	77	77	77	77	77
78	78	78	78	78	78	78
79	79	79	79	79	79	79
80	80	80	80	80	80	80
81	81	81	81	81	81	81
82	82	82	82	82	82	82
83	83	83	83	83	83	83
84	84	84	84	84	84	84
85	85	85	85	85	85	85
86	86	86	86	86	86	86
87	87	87	87	87	87	87
88	88	88	88	88	88	88
89	89	89	89	89	89	89
90	90	90	90	90	90	90
91	91	91	91	91	91	91
92	92	92	92	92	92	92
93	93	93	93	93	93	93
94	94	94	94	94	94	94
95	95	95	95	95	95	95
96	96	96	96	96	96	96
97	97	97	97	97	97	97
98	98	98	98	98	98	98
99	99	99	99	99	99	99
100	100	100	100	100	100	100
101	101	101	101	101	101	101
102	102	102	102	102	102	102
103	103	103	103	103	103	103
104	104	104	104	104	104	104
105	105	105	105	105	105	105
106	106	106	106	106	106	106
107	107	107	107	107	107	107
108	108	108	108	108	108	108
109	109	109	109	109	109	109
110	110	110	110	110	110	110
111	111	111	111	111	111	111
112	112	112	112	112	112	112
113	113	113	113	113	113	113
114	114	114	114	114	114	114
115	115	115	115	115	115	115
116	116	116	116	116	116	116
117	117	117	117	117	117	117
118	118	118	118	118	118	118
119	119	119	119	119	119	119
120	120	120	120	120	120	120
121	121	121	121	121	121	121
122	122	122	122	122	122	122
123	123	123	123	123	123	123
124	124	124	124	124	124	124
125	125	125	125	125	125	125
126	126	126	126	126	126	126
127	127	127	127	127	127	127

.0/24	.128/25	.192/26	.224/27	.240/28	.248/29	.252/30
128	128	128	128	128	128	128
129	129	129	129	129	129	129
130	130	130	130	130	130	130
131	131	131	131	131	131	131
132	132	132	132	132	132	132
133	133	133	133	133	133	133
134	134	134	134	134	134	134
135	135	135	135	135	135	135
136	136	136	136	136	136	136
137	137	137	137	137	137	137
138	138	138	138	138	138	138
139	139	139	139	139	139	139
140	140	140	140	140	140	140
141	141	141	141	141	141	141
142	142	142	142	142	142	142
143	143	143	143	143	143	143
144	144	144	144	144	144	144
145	145	145	145	145	145	145
146	146	146	146	146	146	146
147	147	147	147	147	147	147
148	148	148	148	148	148	148
149	149	149	149	149	149	149
150	150	150	150	150	150	150
151	151	151	151	151	151	151
152	152	152	152	152	152	152
153	153	153	153	153	153	153
154	154	154	154	154	154	154
155	155	155	155	155	155	155
156	156	156	156	156	156	156
157	157	157	157	157	157	157
158	158	158	158	158	158	158
159	159	159	159	159	159	159
160	160	160	160	160	160	160
161	161	161	161	161	161	161
162	162	162	162	162	162	162
163	163	163	163	163	163	163
164	164	164	164	164	164	164
165	165	165	165	165	165	165
166	166	166	166	166	166	166
167	167	167	167	167	167	167
168	168	168	168	168	168	168
169	169	169	169	169	169	169
170	170	170	170	170	170	170
171	171	171	171	171	171	171
172	172	172	172	172	172	172
173	173	173	173	173	173	173
174	174	174	174	174	174	174
175	175	175	175	175	175	175
176	176	176	176	176	176	176
177	177	177	177	177	177	177
178	178	178	178	178	178	178
179	179	179	179	179	179	179
180	180	180	180	180	180	180
181	181	181	181	181	181	181
182	182	182	182	182	182	182
183	183	183	183	183	183	183
184	184	184	184	184	184	184
185	185	185	185	185	185	185
186	186	186	186	186	186	186
187	187	187	187	187	187	187
188	188	188	188	188	188	188
189	189	189	189	189	189	189
190	190	190	190	190	190	190
191	191	191	191	191	191	191

.0/24	.128/25	.192/26	.224/27	.240/28	.248/29	.252/30
192	192	192	192	192	192	192
193	193	193	193	193	193	193
194	194	194	194	194	194	194
195	195	195	195	195	195	195
196	196	196	196	196	196	196
197	197	197	197	197	197	197
198	198	198	198	198	198	198
199	199	199	199	199	199	199
200	200	200	200	200	200	200
201	201	201	201	201	201	201
202	202	202	202	202	202	202
203	203	203	203	203	203	203
204	204	204	204	204	204	204
205	205	205	205	205	205	205
206	206	206	206	206	206	206
207	207	207	207	207	207	207
208	208	208	208	208	208	208
209	209	209	209	209	209	209
210	210	210	210	210	210	210
211	211	211	211	211	211	211
212	212	212	212	212	212	212
213	213	213	213	213	213	213
214	214	214	214	214	214	214
215	215	215	215	215	215	215
216	216	216	216	216	216	216
217	217	217	217	217	217	217
218	218	218	218	218	218	218
219	219	219	219	219	219	219
220	220	220	220	220	220	220
221	221	221	221	221	221	221
222	222	222	222	222	222	222
223	223	223	223	223	223	223
224	224	224	224	224	224	224
225	225	225	225	225	225	225
226	226	226	226	226	226	226
227	227	227	227	227	227	227
228	228	228	228	228	228	228
229	229	229	229	229	229	229
230	230	230	230	230	230	230
231	231	231	231	231	231	231
232	232	232	232	232	232	232
233	233	233	233	233	233	233
234	234	234	234	234	234	234
235	235	235	235	235	235	235
236	236	236	236	236	236	236
237	237	237	237	237	237	237
238	238	238	238	238	238	238
239	239	239	239	239	239	239
240	240	240	240	240	240	240
241	241	241	241	241	241	241
242	242	242	242	242	242	242
243	243	243	243	243	243	243
244	244	244	244	244	244	244
245	245	245	245	245	245	245
246	246	246	246	246	246	246
247	247	247	247	247	247	247
248	248	248	248	248	248	248
249	249	249	249	249	249	249
250	250	250	250	250	250	250
251	251	251	251	251	251	251
252	252	252	252	252	252	252
253	253	253	253	253	253	253
254	254	254	254	254	254	254
255	255	255	255	255	255	255

References

Request for Comments (RFC)

In order according to RFC number.

Postel, J., "Internet Protocol," STD 5, RFC 791, USC/Information Sciences Institute, September 1981.

Postel, J., "Internet Control Message Protocol," STD 5, RFC 792, USC/Information Sciences Institute, September 1981.

Plummer, D., "An Ethernet Address Resolution Protocol," STD 37, RFC 826, MIT, November 1982.

Hornig, C., "Standard for the Transmission of IP Datagrams over Ethernet Networks," RFC 894, Symbolics, April 1984.

Finlayson, R., T. Mann, J. Mogul, and M. Theimer, "A Reverse Address Resolution Protocol," RFC 903, Stanford, June 1984.

Mogul, J. and J. Postel, "Internet Standard Subnetting Procedure," STD 5, RFC 950, Stanford, USC/Information Sciences Institute, August 1985.

Croft, B. and J. Gilmore, "Bootstrap Protocol (BOOTP)," RFC 951, Stanford University, Sun Microsystems, September 1985.

Carl-Mitchell, S. and J. S. Quarterman, "Using ARP to Implement Transparent Subnet Gateways," RFC 1027, October 1987.

Hedrick, C., "Routing Information Protocol," RFC 1058, Rutgers University, June 1988.

Deering, S., "Host Extensions for IP Multicasting," STD 5, RFC 1112, Stanford University, August 1989.

Internet Engineering Task Force (R. Braden, Editor), "Requirements for Internet Hosts — Communication Layers," STD 3, RFC 1122, USC/Information Sciences Institute, October 1989.

Internet Engineering Task Force (R. Braden, Editor), "Requirements for Internet Hosts — Application and Support," STD 3, RFC 1123, USC/Information Sciences Institute, October 1989.

Bradley, T. and C. Brown, "Inverse Address Resolution Protocol," RFC 1293, Wellfleet Communications, Inc., January 1992.

McGregor, G., "The PPP Internet Protocol Control Protocol (IPCP)," RFC 1332, May 1992.

Malkin, G., "RIP Version 2 Carrying Additional Information," RFC 1388, January 1993.

Reynolds, J., "BOOTP Vendor Information Extensions," RFC 1395, January 1993.

Gerich, E., "Guidelines for Management of the IP Address Space," RFC 1466, May 1993.

Rekhter, Y. and T. Li, "An Architecture for IP Address Allocation with CIDR," RFC 1518, T. J. Watson Research Center, IBM Corp., cisco Systems, September 1993.

Wimer, W., "Clarifications and Extensions for the Bootstrap Protocol," RFC 1542, October 1993.

Moy, J., "OSPF Version 2," RFC 1583, Proteon, March 1994.

Moy, J., "Multicast Extensions to OSPF," RFC 1584, Proteon, Inc., March 1994.

Rekhter, Y., B. Moskowitz, D. Karrenberg, and G. de Groot, "Address Allocation for Private Internets," RFC 1597, T. J. Watson Research Center, IBM Corp., Chrysler Corp., RIPE NCC, March 1994.

Lear, E., E. Fair, D. Crocker, and T. Kessler, "Network 10 Considered Harmful (Some Practices Shouldn't be Codified)," RFC 1627, July 1994.

Reynolds, J. and J. Postel, "Assigned Numbers," STD 2, RFC 1700, USC/Information Sciences Institute, October 1994. (This document is periodically updated and reissued with a new number.)

Huitema, C., "The *H* Ratio for Address Assignment Efficiency," RFC 1715, INRIA, November 1994.

Heinanen, J. and R. Govindan, "NBMA Address Resolution Protocol (NARP)," RFC 1735, Telecom Finland, ISI, December 1994.

Baker, F., "Requirements for IP Version 4 Routers," STD 1, RFC 1812, cisco Systems, June 1995.

Deering, S. and R. Hinden (Editors), "Internet Protocol, Version 6 (IPv6) Specification," RFC 1883, Xerox PARC, Ipsilon Networks, December 1995.

Hinden, R. and S. Deering (Editors), "IP Version 6 Addressing Architecture," RFC 1884, Ipsilon Networks, Xerox PARC, December 1995.

Rekhter, Y. and T. Li, "An Architecture for IPv6 Unicast Address Allocation," RFC 1887, cisco Systems, December 1995.

Rekter, Y., B. Moskowitz, D. Karrenberg, G. J. de Groot, and E. Lear, "Address Allocation for Private Internets," RFC 1918, February 1996.

Cole, R., D. Shur, and C. Villamizar, "IP over ATM: A Framework Document," RFC 1932, April 1996.

Perkins, C., "IP Mobility Support," RFC 2002, October 1996.

Hubbard, K., M. Kosters, D. Conrad, D. Karrenberg, and J. Postel, "Internet Registry IP Allocation Guidelines," RFC 2050, November 1996.

Droms, R., "Dynamic Host Configuration Protocol," RFC 2131, March 1997.

Alexander, S. and R. Droms, "DHCP Options and BOOTP Vendor Extensions," RFC 2132, March 1997.

Fenner, W., "Internet Group Management Protocol, Version 2," RFC 2236, November 1997.

Moy, J., "OSPF Version 2," RFC 2328, April 1998.

Estrin, D., D. Farinacci, A. Helmy, D. Thaler, S. Deering, M. Handley, V. Jacobson, C. Liu, P. Sharma, and L. Wei, "Protocol Independent Multicast-Sparse Mode (PIM-SM): Protocol Specification," RFC 2362, June 1998.

Hinden, R. and S. Deering, "IP Version 6 Addressing Architecture," RFC 2373, July 1998.

Hinden, R., M. O'Dell, and S. Deering, "An IPv6 Aggregatable Global Unicast Address Format," RFC 2374, July 1998.

Bradley, T., C. Brown, and A. Malis, "Inverse Address Resolution Protocol," RFC 2390, August 1998.

Malkin, G., "RIP Version 2," RFC 2453, November 1998.

Deering, S. and R. Hinden, "Internet Protocol, Version 6 (IPv6) Specification," RFC 2460, December 1998.

Narten, T., E. Nordmark, and W. Simpson, "Neighbor Discovery for IP Version 6 (IPv6)," RFC 2461, December 1998.

Thomson, S. and T. Narten, "IPv6 Stateless Address Autoconfiguration," RFC 2462, December 1998.

Conta, A. and S. Deering, "Internet Control Message Protocol (ICMPv6) for the Internet Protocol Version 6 (IPv6) Specification," RFC 2463, December 1998.

Conta, A. and S. Deering, "Generic Packet Tunneling in IPv6 Specification," RFC 2473, December 1998.

Nichols, K., S. Blake, F. Baker, and D. Black, "Definition of the Differentiated Services Field (DS Field) in the IPv4 and IPv6 Headers," RFC 2474, December 1998.

Johnson, D. and S. Deering, "Reserved IPv6 Subnet Anycast Addresses," RFC 2526, March 1999.

Senie, D., "Changing the Default for Directed Broadcasts in Routers," RFC 2644, August 1999.

IETF Internet Draft Documents

In order according to the document identifier.

Perkins, C., J. Bound, and M. Carney, "Dynamic Host Configuration Protocol for IPv6 (DHCPv6)," <draft-ietf-dhc-dhcpv6-15.txt>, May 2000.

Perkins, C., J. Bound, and M. Carney, "Extensions for the Dynamic Host Configuration Protocol for IPv6," <draft-ietf-dhc-dhcpv6exts-12.txt>, May 2000.

Ballardie, A. J., "Core Based Trees (CBT) Multicast: Architectural Overview," <draft-ietf-idmr-cbt-arch-03.txt>, University College London, February 1996.

Ballardie, A. J., S. Reeve, S. and N. Jain, "Core Based Trees (CBT) Multicast: Protocol Specification," <draft-ietf-idmr-cbt-spec-05.txt>, University College London, Bay Networks Inc., April 1996.

Fenner, W., "Internet Group Management Protocol, Version 2," <draft-ietf-idmr-igmp-v2-03.txt>, June 1996.

Perkins, C. and D. Johnson, "Mobility Support in IPv6," <draft-ietf-mobileip-ipv6-12.txt>, April 2000.

Borella, M., J. Lo, D. Grabelsky, and G. Montenegro, "Realm Specific IP: Framework," <draft-ietf-nat-rsip-framework-04.txt>, March 2000.

Borella, M., D. Grabelsky, J. Lo, and K. Tuniguchi, "Realm Specific IP: Protocol Specification," <draft-ietf-nat-rsip-protocol-06.txt>, March 2000.

Manning, B., "Why Consider Renumbering Now," <draft-ietf-pier-consider-00.txt>, Cisco Systems, June 1996.

Ferguson, P., "Network Renumbering Overview: Why Would I Want It and What Is It Anyway?" <draft-ietf-pier-renum-ovrvw-00.txt>, Cisco Systems, June 1996.

Berkowitz, H., "Router Renumbering Guide," <draft-ietf-pier-rr-01.txt>, PSC International, June 1996.

Semeria, C. and T. Maufer, "Introduction to IP Multicast Routing," <draft-rfced-info-semeria-00.txt>, 3Comy Corporation, March 1996.

Textbooks

Comer, Douglas E., *Internetworking with TCP/IP. Volume 1: Principles, Protocols, and Architecture,* Second Edition, Prentice-Hall, Englewood Cliffs, NJ, 1991.

Huitema, Christian, *Routing in the Internet,* Prentice-Hall, Englewood Cliffs, NJ, 1995.

Huitema, Christian, *IPv6, The New Internet Protocol,* Prentice-Hall, Upper Saddle River, NJ, 1996.

Nemeth, Evi, Garth Snyder, Scott Seebass, and Trent R. Hein, *UNIX System Administration Handbook,* Second Edition, Prentice-Hall, Englewood Cliffs, NJ, 1995.

Perlman, Radia, *Interconnections: Bridges and Routers,* Addison-Wesley, Reading MA, 1992.

Soloman, James D., *Mobile IP: The Internet Unplugged,* Prentice-Hall, Upper Saddle River, NJ, 1998.

Stevens, W. Richard, *TCP/IP Illustrated. Volume 1: The Protocols,* Addison-Wesley, Reading MA, 1994.

Other

Shoch, John, "Internetwork Naming Addressing and Routing," *Proceedings of COMPCON*, 1978.

Index

A

F

G

H

I

L

M

N

Q

R

U

V

W

X